Arduino Music and Audio Projects

■ ■ ■

Mike Cook

Foreword by Massimo Banzi and David Cuartielles,
Founders of the Arduino Project

Apress®

Arduino Music and Audio Projects

ISBN-13 (pbk): 978-1-4842-1720-7

ISBN-13 (electronic): 978-1-4842-1721-4

Managing Director: Welmoed Spahr
Lead Editor: Michelle Lowman
Editorial Board: Steve Anglin, Pramila Balan, Louise Corrigan, Jonathan Gennick, Robert Hutchinson, Celestin Suresh John, Michelle Lowman, James Markham, Susan McDermott, Matthew Moodie, Jeffrey Pepper, Douglas Pundick, Ben Renow-Clarke, Gwenan Spearing
Coordinating Editor: Mark Powers
Copy Editor: Kezia Endsley
Compositor: SPi Global
Indexer: SPi Global
Artist: SPi Global

Distributed to the book trade worldwide by Springer Science+Business Media New York, 233 Spring Street, 6th Floor, New York, NY 10013. Phone 1-800-SPRINGER, fax (201) 348-4505, e-mail orders-ny@springer-sbm.com, or visit www.springeronline.com. Apress Media, LLC is a California LLC and the sole member (owner) is Springer Science + Business Media Finance Inc (SSBM Finance Inc). SSBM Finance Inc is a Delaware corporation.

For information on translations, please e-mail rights@apress.com, or visit www.apress.com.

Apress and friends of ED books may be purchased in bulk for academic, corporate, or promotional use. eBook versions and licenses are also available for most titles. For more information, reference our Special Bulk Sales–eBook Licensing web page at www.apress.com/bulk-sales.

Any source code or other supplementary materials referenced by the author in this text is available to readers at www.apress.com/9781484217207. For detailed information about how to locate your book's source code, go to www.apress.com/source-code/. Readers can also access source code at SpringerLink in the Supplementary Material section for each chapter.

This book is dedicated to my lifelong friend Arthur Broughton. When you are at school you might expect to make friends that last a lifetime but you seldom expect that friend to be the father of a friend. He introduced me to the delights of good beer, good music and a wonderful sense of humor. He is what you would call an old fashioned gentleman. Now in his nineties he remains active of mind and very much like he was when I first met him.

Contents at a Glance

Contents

About the Author

Mike Cook has been making electronic things since he was at school in the 60s. He would have been a chemist except his school had no chemistry lab so he turned his attention to physics. He left school at the age of 16 to get a job in electronics. Day release part time study earned him the qualifications required to take a BSc (Hons) in Physical Electronics. Subsequently he did post graduate researched into a novel form of digital sound compression in the mid 70s. This was before the advent of microcomputers, when everything had to be made using logic gates. Then an academic career followed reaching the level of Senior Lecturer (a post known as Professor in the USA) in Physics, at Manchester Metropolitan University. During his time at the University he wrote more than three hundred computing and electronics articles in the pages of UK computer magazines starting in the 1980s for 20 years. Mainly for The Micro User and Acorn Computing, these were magazines devoted to the computers produced by Acorn Ltd, the inventers of the RISC processor.

Leaving the University after 21 years, when the Physics department closed down, he got a series of proper jobs where he designed digital TV set top boxes and access control systems. Now retired and freelancing, he spends his days surrounded by wires, exhibiting at Maker Fairs, and patrolling the Arduino forum as Grumpy Mike.

He is the co-author of three books about the Raspberry Pi, all published by Wiley: *Raspberry Pi for Dummies, First and Second editions* (with Sean McManus); *Raspberry Pi Projects* (with Andrew Robison); and *Raspberry Pi Projects for Dummies* (with Jonathan Evans & Brock Craft). He also has a monthly column in *The MagPi*, an online and print magazine published by the Raspberry Pi foundation. Which is not bad for a dyslexic or, as it was known when he was at school, thick.

Acknowledgments

I would like to thank my editor Mark Powers for his help and encouragement and also Michelle Lowman for believing in, and commissioning this book. I would also like to thank Kezia Endsley for her accurate and sympathetic copy editing, along with all the other professionals at Apress who had a part in the production of this book.

I would also like to thank the team who created the amazing Arduino project, Massimo Banzi, David Cuartielles, Tom Igoe and David Mellis without whose inspiration the modern maker movement would not be what it is today.

Foreword

We first met "Grumpy Mike" Cook at the Arduino forum, where we spent long hours giving support to people from all over the world. We created special categories for our users depending on the amount of answers they would write to the questions popping up in the forum. For awhile, you would be listed as "God" if you had answered over 500 posts in the forum and someone, already in 2010, defined the "Grumpy Mike" level, since he had over 9,000 posts answered.

We began adding new levels using names of scientists and technologists, and Grumpy Mike quickly reached the highest level—Brattain—the one reserved for those having answered over 15,000 posts.

Besides his amazing capability to help people, Grumpy Mike builds his own projects. We happened to meet him in person for the first time at Maker Faire Rome 2013, where he displayed his RFID music sequencer. As researchers in Interactive Interfaces, we have to say that it is pretty complex to handle big antenna arrays with multiple RFID readers, but Grumpy Mike solved it without problems.

Not only is he good technically, and at solving complex questions in the forum…he happens not to be grumpy at all! Grumpy Mike is one of the least grumpy people we've ever met in the geek world.

We hope you will enjoy reading his book as much as I enjoy looking through his projects.

—David Cuartielles and Massimo Banzi
Co-Founders, The Arduino Project

Introduction

The Arduino series of controller boards has revolutionized the way that inventors and creators can realize their imaginings. Originally a low cost platform delivering the same computing power as a early 1980 hobby computer with a form factor and price an insignificant fraction of its predecessors. It has grown, over the last ten years, into a range of controller boards with varying form factors and raw computing power. Unhindered by the burden of an operating system every ounce of computing power can be directed towards your own project. It has almost reached the stage that if you can imagine it then the odds are you can do it with one of the Arduinos on offer...

The Arduino has built up a community of dedicated enthusiasts who congregate around the company's official forum. Moderated entirely by unpaid volunteers, it aims to educate and inspire newcomers to the platform. It has developed a collective ethos about behavior and conduct on its pages with an organic consensus. Its overriding concern is that no question is considered too simple or stupid and yet no legal project is off limits. It aims to be beginner friendly and many beginners stop on to help others once they have developed. There is also a section of professional engineers that are ready to dispense wisdom from a long career in the subject. It is amazing what a collection of specialties the collective membership can muster.

One lesser considered aspect of applying Arduinos to projects is when it comes to audio, and it is this that this book aims to correct. Here, in one place, is a grounding in the theory and practice of most aspects of the subject. This book does not pretend to be definitive in all aspects of audio because it would take many volumes to do that, but it will provide a through grounding into most aspects of what you would want to do in a project. The book is split into three parts. Part one looks at high level audio control mainly concerned with the MIDI system and the associated message systems of Open Sound Control (OSC). The second part looks at the direct generation of audio signals from the Arduino. The final third part considers signal processing, that is reading in real time audio data, processing it and outputting it again. Thought the book not only the theory is explained but project examples using this theory are given. These projects range from a quick ten minute demonstration to full blown three month long projects. No matter what the length of the project they can all be freely adapted to put your own spin on them allowing you a stepping stone to creating something totally unique to you.

■ ■ ■

PART I

MIDI and OSC

The first part of the book looks at the MIDI system universally used for passing data between musical systems. MIDI is not concerned with the sounds themselves; rather it is a system of messages that tell other things to generate the sound. Rather like the difference between sheet music and a tape recorder. OSC (Open Sound Control) is a similar idea brought up to date for networked systems.

The data gathered from a keyboard, in a form that is capable of expressing all the subtitles of a performance, to computer generated notes, these can be expressed as MIDI data. On the receive side sound generators can turn this data into sounds of quality that are as deep as your pocket. As well as music, other things can be controlled by MIDI like lights or motors. This part of the book explores in depth the wide possibilities that are on offer with MIDI and other forms of messages.

CHAPTER 1

■ ■ ■

Basic Arduino

This chapter covers:

- Arduino models and capabilities—what to look for
- Understanding and reading a schematic
- Some basic prototype construction techniques
- Adding extra parts to an Arduino

About this Book

This book is about using the Arduino development platform for audio applications. It is not intended for absolute beginners but for those who have a little experience with the platform, those who have set up the system, have gone through some of the built-in examples, and are wondering what to do next. You should know the basics of the C language, like what a function is and what structures you can put in them (for loops and if statements). I am not expecting you to be a programming wizard. I know that different people will be coming to this book with different degrees of knowledge and so this first chapter is a sort of foundation level, catching-up chapter to ensure that we all start from the same level. You might already know the majority of what is here in this first chapter, but if you struggle with large parts of it then it is best to do more foundation work before diving into the rest of the book.

This book also contains projects—some are simple and can be completed in an hour or two; others are much longer, cover a whole chapter, and can take months to complete. When projects get to this level then rather than just trying to replicate what I did, it would be great if you put your own input into it by putting your unique twist on the project. There are suggestions to help you do this at the end of the big projects. So let's start by looking at the Arduino itself.

The Arduino

The Arduino project has a long and prestigious linage. Its roots can be traced back to the influential John Maeda who worked as a supervisor for Casey Rease. I first came across both these people's work in the classic book, *Creative Code,* by Thames and Hudson, 2004, and it didn't take a genius to spot their talent. Casey and Ben Fry worked on a project designed to make coding accessible to a non-technical artistic audience, as by then, computing has moved away from the home coder that was so much part of the 80s micro-computer revolution. The result was a programming language called *Processing*, perhaps one of the worst names for a computer language, despite quite steep competition. Then Casey and Massimo Banzi supervised a student named Hernando Barragan to develop a version of Processing that did the same sort of thing for hardware that Processing did for software; it was called *Wiring*. The last step was in 2005, when Massimo and David Cuartielles took the basic code from these two open source projects and forged it into their own Arduino project, which itself is open source both in software and hardware. It is a testament to the power of the open source concept, it shows how previous work can be built on and extended without the normal commercial constraints and secrecy. And also without the mega bucks development budget that starting from scratch on a project like this would entail.

The brief was simple, so the system had to be simple and accessible both in terms of hardware and software. The fact that all these years later, you are reading this book is testament to how well they achieved that goal. The continued success and evolution of the project speaks volumes about their dedication and insight. They started making the boards in a small factory close to Turin in northwest Italy, today there are manufacturing facilities in Europe, the Far East and the USA, selling under the brand of Arduino in the UAS and Genuino in the rest of the world. A schism in 2015 with the original manufacturer has resulted in a so far unresolved legal disputes over the Arduino name outside the USA.

Arduino Architecture

The number of models or types of Arduino continue to grow by the year and I assume you have at least one. So to enable you to evaluate the existing models and see where the new models fit into picture, I want to look at the architecture of an Arduino and describe how various models enhance one, or more, particular aspects of it.

The design philosophy has been to bring out a basic design concept and then add variations to it, building up families of Arduinos some with specialist functions. However, the current basic vanilla Arduino is the Uno, whose name was chosen not the least so that it could be pronounced by non-Italians. Earlier basic models went under the name of Duemilanove, Arduino NG (Nuova Generazione), and Diecimila. These are very close variants of the same basic board, but much harder to pronounce, for me at least. Figure 1-1 shows the basic anatomy of an Arduino. It consists of five major blocks:

- The processor
- Communications
- User I/O pins
- Power supply control
- Peripherals

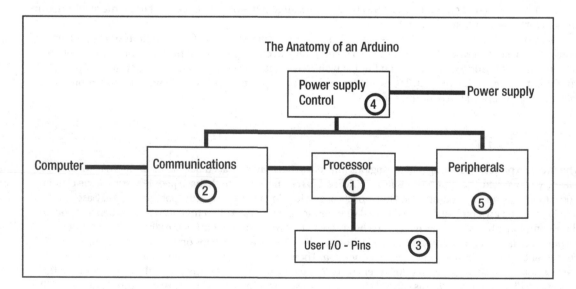

Figure 1-1. *The basic blocks of an Arduino*

Arduino models and variants play with, or alter, one or more of these blocks. So to understand the models, you have to understand, or at least appreciate, these basic blocks. Each block is numbered and discussed in the following sections.

The Processor Block

The heart of the Arduino is the processor, and in many ways it defines the capabilities of the whole board. It is based around processor families and the normal philosophy is to have as much of the processor's resource available to the user as possible. When a manufacturer makes a processor, they normally make a number of variants that have a basic core functionality but have a different amount of the different types of memory. For example, the basic vanilla Arduino always had an ATmega x8 processor; that isn't the part number but the generic base part number where x is substituted for a number representing the variant. The first Arduino used the ATmega 8 chip but soon moved onto the ATmega 168 and then onto the ATmega 328 used today. The main difference between these is the amount of memory they had for storing the program, known as Flash memory, and the amount of memory for storing data, known as SRAM (Static Random Access Memory). A third, less important, sort of memory is the EEPROM (Electrically Erasable Programmable Read Only Memory), and it provides a small provision for non-volatile storage of data. Non-volatile means that it persists even after the power has been removed.

The processor is normally in a DIL (Dual In Line) package, which means it is a plug and socket arrangement. This is great for user replacement when the inevitable accidents happen. However, manufacturing chip shortages have forced some variants to use surface mount processors, whereas the later models use processors that are only available in surface mount packages. This is true of the other processors used in Arduino boards—the ATmega 2560 used in the Arduino Mega boards is essentially the same core processor but with more internal peripherals like extra timers and four serial ports along with many more I/O (input/output) pins. The 32uX series of processors support USB, thus allowing them to look to the computer like other USB devices such as keyboards, mice, or MIDI devices. The Leonardo model uses the 32u4 processor with Arduino Micro being essentially the same but with a much smaller from factor. The other processor in the Arduino stable is the SAM3X8E ARM Cortex-M3 and is in the Arduino Due and the Arduino Zero. This is a huge step up in processor technology and is at least two orders of magnitude greater than the other processors used.

There is a new class of Arduino beginning to emerge—one that uses two or more processors. An example of this is the Arduino Yun. The proposed TRE has a traditional Atmel processor but also a much more powerful one running Linux, with the two processors communication over a "bridge".

The Communications Block

The communications block shown in Figure 1-1 is the other main differentiator in the Arduino zoo. This is usually a USB/Serial converter of some sort, but it can be other things. The very first Arduino used a simple serial interface but computers do not fit those any more, so some sort of conversion from USB is needed. For many models, this block was provided by a dedicated chip called the FTDI chip. Later this has been replaced with another programmable processor using the ATmega8U2. Some models do not have this block at all and rely on you providing that function separately. This is for boards you are building permanently into projects and therefore don't require communications with a computer in the final configuration.

The User I/O Pins

The user I/O pins are often considered very important especially by beginners. However, any basic Arduino is capable of being expanded to an almost unlimited number of pins. It is worth mentioning here that the use of the word "pin" to mean a single input/output line is unique to the Arduino and is sometimes confused with the physical pin on a chip. Traditionally processor I/O has been grouped into ports consisting of eight bits on each port. What the Arduino does is abstract those bits into individual pins. Mapping those pins from the port is controlled by the software, which takes into account the model you have chosen. In that way many programs can be run as-is on different models, making the system appear a lot more uniform than they actually are.

■ **Note** The use of the word "pin" to mean a single input/output line is unique to the Arduino and is sometimes confused with the physical pin on a chip.

The Power Supply Control Block

Perhaps the least glamorous is the power supply control. On the first Arduinos this was simply a movable link that controlled whether the power came from the USB socket or an external input power jack. People were always forgetting this and thinking their entire system had broken. On all modern Arduinos, there is a circuit that automatically detects if there is power being supplied through the external power jack and, if so, switches to it. Designs have changed slightly, but the function remains the same.

The Onboard Peripherals Block

There are two sorts of onboard peripherals—those inside the processor and those mounted on the Arduino board itself. At this stage, you might not understand all of them and their importance for audio work. When you need to use them in this book, I will fully explain them.

Peripherals Inside the Processor

The processor-based peripherals are things like the number of internal hardware counter/timers and number of serial ports, the pin interrupt capabilities (more about these in Chapter 3), and the A/D (Analogue to Digital) converter. They are best assessed by reading the data sheet of the processor involved and often result in changes to the pin functions.

For example, the hardware counter/timers are registers that work autonomously; that is, they do not need any program intervention. They can be set up to produce a fixed frequency PWM (Pulse Width Modulation) signal and each counter/timer can control two PWM outputs. The basic ATmega 328 processor has three counter/timers so any board using this processor can produce six PWM signals. On the other hand, the Arduino Mega has an ATmega 2560 processor with many more timers with different modes and offers 15 PWM signals.

Peripherals Mounted on the Board

The peripherals mounted on the board are easier to understand and most of the time they define the Arduino model. For example, the Arduino Ethernet has an Ethernet controller built-in, and the Arduino WiFi has a WiFi module built-in. No prizes for guessing what an Arduino Blue Tooth has built-in. These are built into the board as opposed to the other option of an add-on board, or "shield," as it is called. These are plug-in boards that add extra chunks of functionality and can be added to many different basic Arduino boards. They do not belong in this section and will be discussed later in this chapter. Other boards have more mundane peripherals built-in. For example, the Arduino Esplora, shown in Figure 1-2, has a microphone, slider, joystick, push buttons, speaker, light sensor, and LEDs all built on the board. These are arranged to look a bit like a games controller and although the microphone input would appear to be useful for sound, it is not because it is configured as an envelope detector and so only records the peak amplitude of sound.

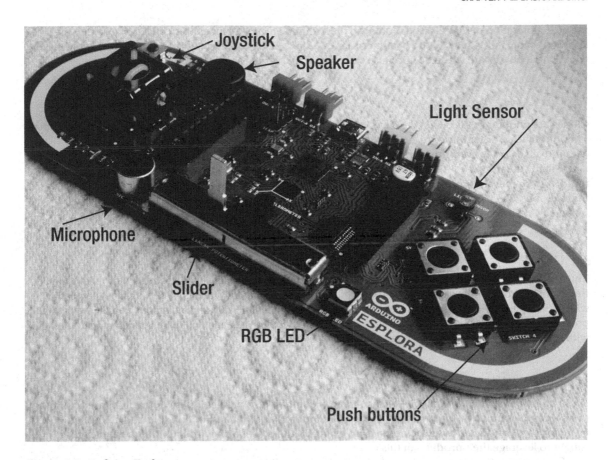

Figure 1-2. *Arduino Esplora*

Arduino Ripoffs, Clones, and Compatibles

The phenomenal success of the Arduino has spawned many copies. Being an open source project, all schematics and PCB (Printed Circuit Board) layout files are freely available—so what is the problem? Well, some people try to deceive you into thinking you are buying the "real thing," whereas others are quite up-front as to what you are buying. It is important to differentiate between the ripoffs, the clones, and the compatibles.

Ripoffs

Although it is perfectly acceptable to make and sell your own version of an Arduino, making it look exactly like the official ones, down to the names and logos, is illegal, and is known as "passing off". This allows the customs officials of your country to confiscate such a board, in theory. This does not happen very often but there are a few cases of this actually happening. Often this form of ripoffs use inferior components like low-quality PCBs, LEDs, and connectors, but the processors are all from the same source and so are likely to work just as well. However, what is more important than the quality of any ripoff model is the fact that the perpetrators of these boards are not adding anything to the project as a whole, but are just acting as parasites on the system. Moneys raised by the Arduino company go into educational projects, research for the next generation of models, and funding of the Arduino Forum, an incredible collection of some very knowledgeable individuals with a beginner-friendly ethos. Also, working conditions and wages in the places where most boards are made do not cause controversy like some Far East factories might.

Clones

Clones are another matter. They are clearly marked and labeled so that you know they are not official boards. They often bring other things to the party as well. For example, some have features not found on other Arduinos like power over Internet, built-in RGB LED matrix and many powering options. Others might have a physically different layout, or be sold as an unpopulated PCB. There are some with ruggedized protected input/output pins and some with different sorts of connectors to access the input/output pins. There are many clones. Since their only value lies in the lower cost to the end user and this is to the determent of income to the whole Arduino project, I do not encourage you to buy them.

Arduino Certified Boards

The Arduino Galileo is the first of the Arduino Certified boards. It is made by Intel with the cooperation of the Arduino project, so it can be said to be an official Arduino. Basically, this is a Pentium class processor with an Arduino style interface. This extends to both the physical hardware connections and the way you program it using an Arduino IDE look-alike. This is a single processor and will run a version of Linux as well, with all the joys and sorrows that entails.

Compatibles

Some boardsX use the "compatible" term to try to boost their own profiles. These normally consist of having the I/O on the same type of connectors in the same order as an Arduino. Some of these boards are produced by major semiconductor manufacturers. It is a tribute to the power of the Arduino Brand that they have sought to leverage their products in this way.

Some compatibles push the boundaries of what is possible in an Arduino environment. One example of this is the Teensey from PRJC, the latest model 3.2 being based on the MK20DX256VLH7 32-bit ARM Cortex-M4,. The physical footprint certainly lives up to its name, being 1.5" by 0.8" with earlier models using different processors being even smaller. However, this compatible is important in the context of this book because it offers the easiest way of implementing a system that looks like a USB MIDI device to a computer connecting to it. It does this in an easy-to-use way and it integrates nicely into the Arduino IDE (Integrated Development Environment or "the software") by adding just a few menu options. As you'll see in Chapter 3, it is possible to do this with some models of official Arduinos, but there are drawbacks.

Roll Your Own

When you make your own project and you want it to be permanent, you don't have to sacrifice an Arduino board to it. The major functions can easily be replicated and built on strip board. Then you can simply transfer just the processor from the Arduino and place it in the circuit, and then get just another processor to replace the one in your Arduino. The only thing you have to watch is that the replacement processor has built into it some code called a "boot loader". Many people sell processors like this, and if you get one without a boot loader, you can always program one in yourself if you have a hardware programmer. The great thing about the Arduino project is that you can make a hardware programmer using an Arduino itself, so it can program in the boot loader yourself quite easily. The alternative, and it is one that I favor, is that you can have a programing header built in to your project and use an Arduino or some USB to serial board to program and continue to develop your project. In effect, you're turning your project into an Arduino compatible with your own on-board peripherals.

Arduino for Audio

From the point of view of audio, the more powerful the processor the better. However, there is still a lot you can do with the less powerful processors. We will be exploring both ends of the spectrum in this book. The shortcomings in terms of peripherals can, in many cases, be accommodated for by adding additional input/output pins using external chips. Even the lack of memory of the Uno may be compensated for by adding extra memory chips. This memory, however, is not part of the general memory; that is, it can't be used to store variables or arrays. However, it can be used to store data in a byte-by-byte manner, in the same way as the built-in non-volatile EEPROM memory, as you'll see later Chapter 13. Figure 1-3 shows the Arduino Due.

Figure 1-3. Arduino Due

The Arduino Due

Currently the best Arduino to use for audio is the Due. At 96K of SRAM, it a decent amount of memory, although when it comes to audio you can hardly have too much memory. The A/D converter is capable of 12-bit resolution (4096 steps), as opposed to the normal 10-bit resolution (1024 steps) of the other Arduino boards. Unlike the other boards it also has two built-in D/A (digital to analogue converters) so that makes it ideal for generating sound using the techniques in the last two parts of this book. It also has lots of I/O, making it suitable for the sound controllers covered in the first part of the book.

The only downside to the Due is that fact that it works on a 3v3 (that is the way professionals refer to 3.3 volts) and the output capacity of the pins with regard to current is much lower than the other Arduinos. The smaller working voltage is a trend in the electronics industry and even lower voltages are being used to allow the cramming of more and more components onto a chip (called component density). You see, the lower the voltage the less heat the switching circuits generate and so the more circuits you can cram into any given space. Other voltages used are 2v3 and 1v8, but we have not seen these in Arduinos yet. So in short, while the Due is the best, it is a bit more delicate and can require extra components when you're interfacing other devices to it. The Arduino Zero is a recently introduced upgrade for this board.

The Arduino Uno

For the beginner, I recommend the Arduino Uno to start with, because it is a lot more forgiving of mistakes and can be expanded in terms of input/output. It lacks true grunt in its processing power, but it is still capable of generating some quite extraordinary sounds and is more than adequate when it comes to being used as a controller. It can even be made so that the computer sees it as a true MIDI device, as you'll see in Chapter 3. However, the downside to this is that when you make it perform like this, it becomes much more awkward to program. Using the Teensy can overcome this when you want a true MIDI device. Using the Teensy is optional, not being an "official" Arduino. As of November 2015 the 1.6.6 version of the IDE allows this feature to be used with the Arduino Leonardo and the Arduino Micro. This is done by using a library called MIDIUSB available from https://github.com/arduino-libraries/MIDIUSB. It makes the Arduino look like a USB HID MIDI device and so behaves just like a MIDI device connected through a MIDI interface. Some of the code examples on the book's web site include examples of its use. Note: when reprogramming such an Arduino, hold down the reset button until the "Downloading" message is seen, and then release it.

Figure 1-4 shows the comparative size of the Uno and the Teensy.

Figure 1-4. *Arduino Uno and the Teensy 3.0 from PJRC*

Schematics

If you want to build anything non-trivial in electronics, you need to learn how to read, and to a lesser important extent, draw a schematic. I used to think there were no rules for drawing schematics, but given some of the abominations you see online now I think there are definite rules. Despite what some beginners might think, the point of a schematic is to make a simple, clear, and uncluttered representation of an electronic circuit. Many years ago I visited Russia with my family and I bought an electronics construction set for my son. One of those types with a block containing a component with the symbol on the top Although we spoke and read no Russian, we could still use the set fully with the instruction book because the language of schematic diagrams is universal.

Many beginners think you need some sort of special software to draw schematics and indeed there are many packages out there that cater to this. However, a word of caution—most are designed as a front end for a printed circuit layout package and have little flexibility over things like the positioning of pins on an integrated circuit. This results in schematics that are a lot messier and harder to read than they should be. Packages that allow this flexibility are often expensive and very difficult to use. Another thing is that the process of symbol is sometimes tricky and you can spend hours looking for the symbol you need, only to find it does not exist. Some people then use symbols for other components, which makes the schematic absolutely useless. My advice is to ignore these packages and just use a generalized 2D drawing package to draw schematics.

What a Schematic Is and Isn't

A schematic shows which pins, or connections, of which components are connected. What it should not show is how these components and wires are physically arranged. The schematic should show only the topological connections, not any physical ones. This is because this normally makes the interconnections look a lot messier and hard to follow. The translation between the schematic and physical layout is a separate step and not one that needs to necessarily be documented. This is mainly because any such documentation tends to look like a mess and is impossible to follow, so there is little point in creating it.

If you make something from a physical layout and it does not work you really have nowhere to go. If, however, you use a schematic then you can follow the signal flow on the page and pick points on the circuit to check. Of course, the error might be in translation from schematic to physical and if so you will not see the signal you expect and you can check again just that one step in the wiring. You can't do this if all you have is a physical layout. In fact many people, when faced with trying to find a fault using only a physical layout, often resort to dismantling the whole thing and wiring it up again. This is a great waste of time and unfortunately there is a good chance of making the same mistake again.

Of course there are always exceptions to abstracting the physical component to a symbol or plain box. Personally I find having a modicum of physicality applied to components with odd configured connections like some plugs and sockets. MIDI connectors are a case in point; the numbering of the connectors does not follow any logical pattern I can see and this is perhaps the number one reason why beginner's MIDI projects fail. The schematics for the projects in Chapters 3 to 7 will be drawn that way.

Symbols

The key to reading a schematic is to know the symbols used to represent the components; however these symbols are not, as you might expect, universal but normally a mish-mash of several standards. This is made a bit more chaotic by the fact that new components are being invented all the time and official symbol standards take time to catch up. You might think that given this, you would not stand a chance of understanding a schematic, but it is not the case. Most of the time you can work out what a symbol stands for. Also next to the symbol will be a part number, which uniquely identifies the component.

Part Symbols

Typing a part number directly into Google is almost always successful in locating information about it and places to buy it. While the physical appearances of components can vary vastly, the symbol will remain the same. For example, a capacitor can be something the size smaller than a grain of rice and sometimes larger than a can of beer, yet the symbols are the same because they essentially do the same job. Having said that, there is a variation in symbols used throughout the world as various standards have been set by institutions. As usual, or so it seems, this mainly breaks down to what is used in the United States and what is used in the rest of the world. However, these variations are minor and you will see a mixture of them in the circuits you find. Figure 1-5 shows some component symbol variations you might come across.

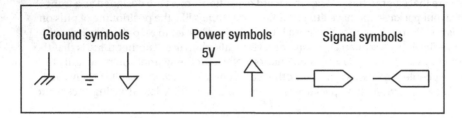

Figure 1-5. *Some schematic symbols*

Connection Point Symbols

The other trick of schematics is to use a symbol to denote common connection points (see Figure 1-6). The most common of these is a ground or earth signal. When you see this, you know that all wires connected to this symbol are connected electrically to the same point. This simplifies the diagram considerably by removing a lot of wires from the diagram. While this is normally reserved for power connections or ground, it can also be used for signals. But excessive use of this technique for signals results in a schematic that is impossible or at least very difficult to read. This technique is often used by equipment manufacturers that have the obligation to include a schematic, but want to obfuscate the design as much as they can. Signals symbols are most useful when a schematic covers more than one sheet, and the signal goes from one sheet to another.

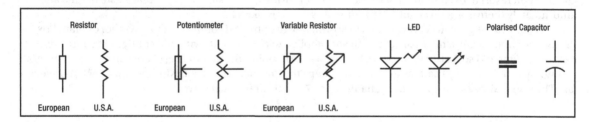

Figure 1-6. *Schematic symbols and wires*

Wire Crossings

There is also a convention used for wires joining and crossing over each other. These are shown in Figure 1-7. There are three ways of showing that a wire has crossed another wire and is not joined to it. I favor the technique shown as option B, as it shows clearly one wire goes under the other, and is easier to draw than C. However, you might still come across the A convention. When A is used, the symbol for a wire joint must include a dot at the joint and four wires should not all meet at the same point. For the other two methods, you should also avoid having four wires joining at the same point for clarity.

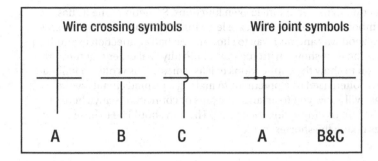

Figure 1-7. *Schematic conventions for wire joining and crossing*

Integrated Circuits

When it comes to ICs (Integrated Circuits), there are two ways to show them. The first is to show them as a simple rectangle with the part number in the rectangle; the second is to use a symbol that represents the individual parts of the circuit. For example, you might have an IC that has six logic inverters in it. These are best shown as individual inverters distributed throughout the diagram where they are needed and not all packaged in the same block. An example of this is shown in Figure 1-8.

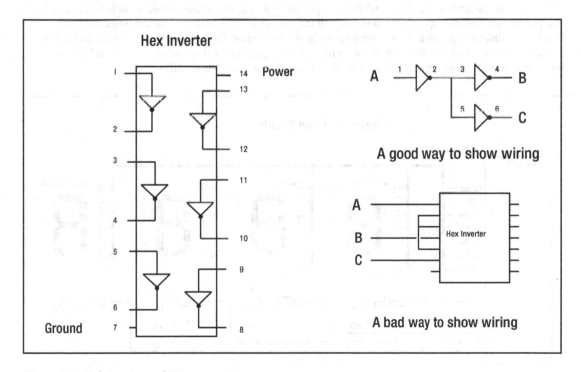

Figure 1-8. *Schematics and ICs*

Note that the device is called a hex inverter, not because it inverts hexes, but that it is a logic inverter and there are six of them in this one IC package. An inverter is a circuit that has a logic output that is the inverse of the input. In other words if you put a logic one in, you get a logic zero out.

This can only be applied to ICs that contain multiple well known functions. Sometimes the IC has a unique function for which there is no symbol. In these cases, you are left with no option other than to show it as a rectangular box, but here there is a good way and bad way to show it. The bad connection example in Figure 1-8 is compounded by the fact that the IC is shown with the pins in the physical order that they are on the chip. Again, this normally forces you to show the connections to it as a mess. This is often a hallmark of low-quality schematic capture software, often used as a precursor to making a printed circuit layout. Good-quality software, or hand drawings, will allow you to arrange the pins or connections anywhere on the rectangle representing the IC, with the aim of simplifying the wiring. The aim should be to have as few crossing points as possible with the wires taking the shortest route.

Layout

The overall layout of a schematic is important as well. Having positive connections at the top of a diagram and the negative or ground at the bottom simplifies the task of reading the schematic. You only realize how important this is when someone breaks the rule. Also as much as possible have signal flow from left to right. That means in general, inputs on the left and outputs on the right. This last point is not vital but it does help the viewers orientate themselves with what is happening.

Another technique that can aid clarity and simplify layout is to use bus wiring. Here, a line represents not just one wire but a whole bunch of them and is normally represented by a thicker line. We need to be able to identify the individual wires at the ends where the connection with components are made, but we don't need to see the path of individual wires all in parallel going under or over other wires because again it looks too messy. Bus wiring is often used when all the wires have the same overall use. For example, a popular way of displaying a number is with a seven-segment display. Each segment needs an individual wire to control it, but they all do essentially the same thing.—they control the display—so this would be a good candidate for using bus wiring on a schematic. Figure 1-9 shows an example of this.

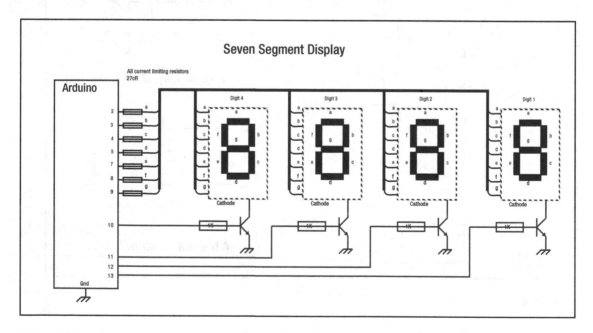

Figure 1-9. *Bus wiring*

The thick black line represents the bus or bundle of connections; each wire entering or leaving the bus is wired normally with a small radius rather than at right angles. So for example, the g segment is wired to all the other g segments on the display, plus a resistor whose other end is connected to pin 9 of the Arduino. If you consider the alternative of showing each segment as a wire, you would have a mess of wires crossing each other. This way is much cleaner and, when you can read it, so much easer to interpret.

Constructional Techniques

Given a schematic of a circuit you want, you will be faced with the problem of building it. In this section, we'll cover different board options, hand tools, soldering, and supply decoupling.

Boards

There are many prototyping techniques and prototyping is something you should always do prior to making a printed circuit board. Surface mount components—those with no wire leads but just tabs directly onto the component—can often be difficult to prototype but there are general-purpose adaptor PCBs that can help.

Solderless Bread Board

Many beginners choose solderless bread boards. These are available in many sizes and consist of rows of push connectors on a 0.1" spacing. A typical example is shown in Figure 1-10.

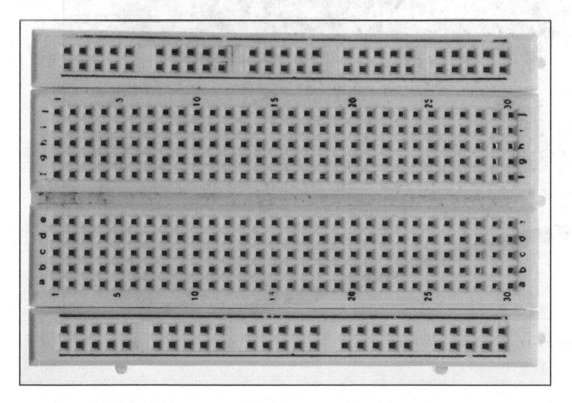

Figure 1-10. *Solderless bread board*

The idea is that you can simply slot component leads into them and use wire links to make the connections. The top and bottom two rows are connected horizontally and the upper and lower middle five rows are connected vertically. If used at all they should only be used for temporary experiments. They are mainly a bad idea. This is because the push contacts widen over time and stop making proper contact. Also some components have leads that are not the ideal diameter to make good connections. This leads to a fault-finding technique of waggling the components about in the hope that it is not working because of some improper connection. All too often this succeeds in only widening the connectors even further, making them even less reliable. On several occasions at exhibitions, I have seen exhibitors forlornly sitting over a bread board absolutely crammed with components rocking each component backward and forward in a desperate attempt to make the project work. I would not recommend them outside an introductory class on electronics that has to run on a unrealistically small budget.

Strip Board

What I do recommend is using strip board or prototyping board to make a permanent circuit. These consist of single-sided copper-clad boards with a matrix of holes on a 0.1" pitch and with strips of copper connecting rows of holes, as shown in Figure 1-11.

Figure 1-11. *Prototyping strip board*

Components can be mounted on the top side and tracks cut on the bottom side to make the interconnections work the way you want them to. The connections can be made with thin sleeved wires either on the underside or through the holes on the top side. This often results in a messy looking tangle of wires, but if you use a variety of different colors, the technique can result in something that is very easy to troubleshoot. Typical of the results is the board in Figure 1-12.

Figure 1-12. *A typical strip board project*

There are two basic ways you can break the strips. The simplest is that you can break the strips at the position of the holes. You can do this with a twist drill bit pushed into the holes by hand, or with a special tool designed for the job called a "spot face cutter". With either tool the idea is to make a small countersink hole and at the same time remove copper from both sides of the hole. This can leave very small strands of copper still making contact. I pointed this out to a student of mine on his board and he said, "yes but it is only very thin". To which I replied, how big do you think an electron is? The point was taken.

Nowadays, I prefer to use a scalpel. You place the scalpel point in the hole and give a small twist, resulting in a nick in the copper. Then turn the board around and repeat making a nick in the other direction. The small piece of copper on the edge of the hole should drop out. This is repeated on the other side of the hole. This leaves much more of the copper intact and ensures a clean break.

I have recently devised another way of breaking a track, this is to cut between the holes. This is useful if you are short of space and want to break the track but can't afford the 0.1" space to do it in. Here you take a metal rule and score one or often more tracks with a scalpel. Then, move the rule by as smaller distance as you can and make another score mark. Finally, take your blade and pry off the copper between the two score marks. It is easy to use surface mount resistors by bridging the cuts with the component.

Figure 1-13 shows the cut strips of the underside of the board with some surface mount resistors.

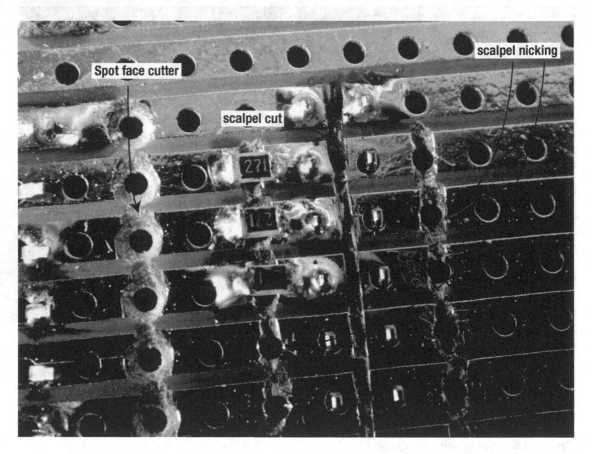

Figure 1-13. *Three ways to break a track*

The column of breaks on the left side were done with a spot face cutter; the next right and far right were done with a scalpel nicking each side of the hole; finally, the second from the right column were cut between the holes using two parallel scores. This last technique is especially useful for sockets based on a 0.1" pitch between the rows.

The numbers on the surface mount resistors give its value in ohms. The first two numbers are the first two numbers of the value and the last number is the number of zeroes to add to the end of the value. So these resistors are 270 Ohms or, as we say, 270R.

Strip Board Variations

As well as plain strips, there are patterns of strips that help in wiring ICs and there can be all sorts of finish on the board from plain copper to solder tinned. Another type of board consists of each individual hole surrounded by an area of copper. You make your own strips by wiring rows of thin plain copper wire between them or by using the component leads themselves to bend over and make a run of connections. Some of these boards are double-sided, allowing wiring to take place on both sides. Yet others have a continuous sheet of copper on one side with holes for the components. This overarching sheet of copper is used for what is known as a ground plane, which provides some shielding from electrical pick-up signals and reduces any radiation of interference that might be generated in the wiring. These are known as colander ground planes. One really unusual type of board I had was the single hole type, but each alternate row was offset by 0.05″. Figure 1-14 shows an example of how I used it.

Figure 1-14. *Unusual prototyping board with offset holes*

You might notice the thin wires I used here. These are from a system known as the Vero Wiring system. This can be a very useful system when there are a lot of interconnections on a board. The thin wire is dispensed with a wiring pencil, shown in Figure 1-15, where a small reel of wire is attached to a pencil-like dispenser. You normally wire from the underside of the board to the pins of the IC socket by pushing the wire between the hole and the IC pin and fixing it by wrapping the wire around several times. Then the wire is pulled out and guided through plastic combs to the destination where again it is wrapped around and snipped off. The wire is covered in a polyurethane varnish that melts when you apply the soldering iron to it. Figure 1-15 shows what the back of the board looks like. The front of the board has no wires showing and the whole thing looks very neat. Well, from the component side at least.

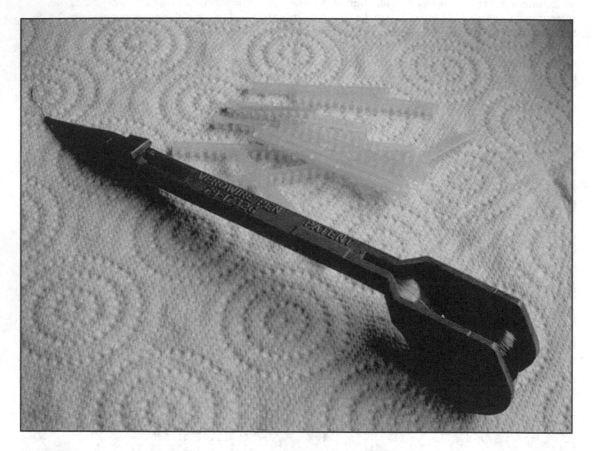

Figure 1-15. *The Vero wiring pen and combs*

I only use Vero wire for the signals. Anything carrying power I still use normal wire to give a low impedance to the supply and help with decoupling. See if you can spot the surface mount capacitors soldered between adjacent tracks. Unlike resistors, there are no markings on capacitors; they all look the same. Don't mix them up, as the only way to determine their value is to measure them.

If you want to learn more about the different types of *prototyping board,* just enter those words into Google.

Shield Prototyping Board

You cannot talk about Arduino prototyping without mentioning shields. A "shield" is basically a circuit board that fits over the Arduino board and plugs into all the header sockets. This allows beginners to add extra circuits without having to actually wire anything to the Arduino—it is just plug and play. If the design of the shield allows it, you can even stack shields on top each other because a shield can have extra sockets arranged like the Arduino that you can plug a shield into. There is a flaw with this idealized concept and it is that two shields might require the same pins in order to function. Some shields have a degree of flexibility, allowing pins to be changed by jumpers or soldered link wires, but this is not always possible. Some shields require processor resources that cannot be altered or shared. For example, a shield that controls lots of LEDs by using an IC called a TLC5940 also requires the use of one of the processor's internal timers. This will not be compatible with a shield that uses that timer to drive a PWM (pulse width modulated) signal that otherwise would also require that timer. So a single shield is often the best approach. You can get shield prototyping boards for all types of Arduinos. Figure 1-16 is a picture of one for an Arduino Mega board. This is a printed circuit board with holes for the connectors to allow shields to be stacked, places for an duplicate Reset button and LED, as well as an undedicated area of free holes for your own circuit.

Figure 1-16. The Vero wiring system with plastic guide combs

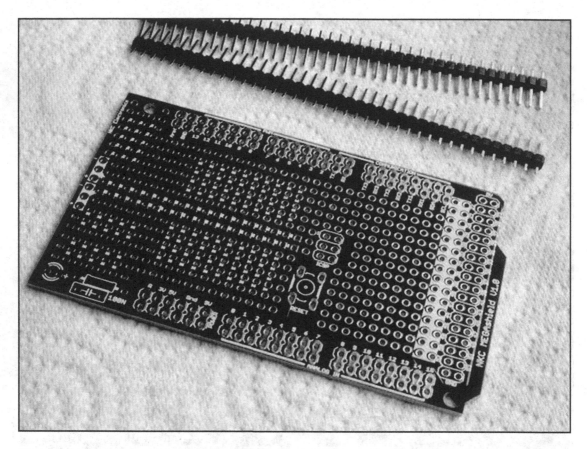

Figure 1-17. *Prototyping shield board for Mega or Uno*

You can also make your own shields, but there is a "got-ya" in that the spacing between two of the rows of connectors is not on a 0.1" pitch that strip board gives you but is shifted by half a hole pitch—that is 0.05". It was a mistake on the very first Arduino and has been perpetuated ever since so that existing shields would still fit. Some Arduino compatibles make a feature of having the spacing on a 0.1" pitch. There are various ways around this and you can search the Internet to find various techniques. One I have developed is at http://www.thebox.myzen.co.uk/Hardware/Arduino_Sheld.html, but there are many more techniques. This is what makes buying a shield prototyping board so attractive.

Printed Circuit Boards

Of course, the ultimate prototyping is a PCB (Printed Circuit Board), and these days you can get small quantities cheaply from the Far East. However, it is still the most expensive option and it is rare that you get a PCB right first time. That means either you have to modify it with a scalpel and wires, or you have to get it made again.

Then there is the layout software you have to use. There are some free layout packages, but they are rarely decent. Also there is a pretty steep learning curve associated with these packages and even then the layout of even a simple circuit can take days.

With a PCB there is little flexibility about what components you use. For example, capacitors come in a seemingly infinite variety of shapes and lead spacing. Once you lay out a printed circuit board, you are committed to using that specific capacitor for all the circuits. However, once you have made a board, it is easy to assemble and this can even be automated. Personally, I don't think there is much point in making a printed circuit board unless you plan to make at least 10 circuits.

Hand Tools

You need a few good tools when construction purposes. The minimum I recommend are:

- A pair of long-nosed pliers
- A pair of fine tweezers
- A pair of fine side cutters

I prefer the snipe-nosed pliers; they are bent at the end. A good pair are not cheap and in my opinion the top of the heap is the manufacturer Lindstrom. They are a solid investment and should last a lifetime. My pliers and side cutters are shown in Figure 1-18.

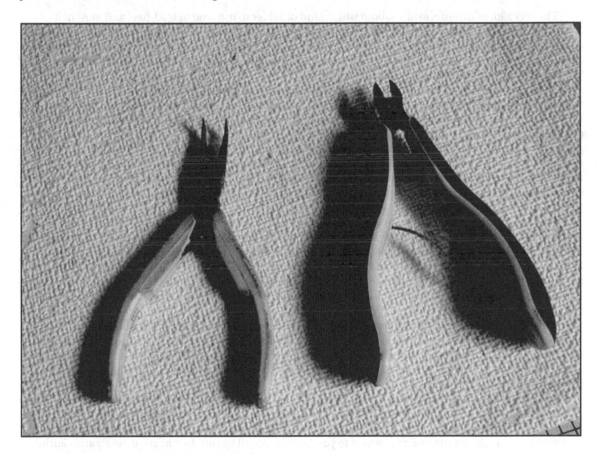

Figure 1-18. *Snipe-nosed pliers and side cutters*

The side cutters on the right might seem to have rather bulky handles. This is because they are actually conductive but with a high resistance. They are sold as static dispersive handles, designed to protect components but prevent electric shocks if you are careless enough to cut something live. However, the main reason I got them was that one place I worked had carpets that could build up static and give you a healthy shock. I carried them around with me and discharged myself painlessly on any metal object when I reached my destination.

Soldering

Now we come to the topic of soldering. The basic tools you will need include:

- Solder (I recommend 60/40 tin lead solder, 22 gauge or thinner, with a built-in solder flux core)
- Soldering iron with temperature control
- Stand for the soldering iron
- Damp sponge

There is a lot of misinformation about which kind of solder to use, lead or lead-free, and most of it is peddled by governments. I spent three years in a previous job ensuring that the products made by my company complied with the RoHS legislation. This involved me having to read lots of regulatory information as well as attending seminars on both European and worldwide legislation. It wasn't the most riveting work but I now know exactly what you need in any situation.

So to dispel one myth for a start—there is no need to use lead-free solder in your own projects. Not only is it not a legal requirement there is no known health implications either. The lead found in solder is not in a form that can be absorbed into the body and the only reason it was banned in commercial consumer electronic goods is the fear that when, at the end of its life, it ends up in landfill, there would be a risk of polluting water courses. The other effects of water courses going through landfill sites might pose a lot more cause for concern. However, the law is that if you want to sell anything in Europe, it has to conform with the RoHS (Reduction of Hazardous Substances pronounced "rossh") regulation, which includes lead-free construction. There are lots of exceptions to the presence of lead in the RoHS regulations, so to call it lead free is a misnomer.

Lead-free solder is more expensive, requires higher temperatures, produces an inferior joint, and reduces the lifetime of anything built with it. Ironically this causes more electronic equipment to end up in landfill. It also does not wet as well, which means the solder tends to clump rather than flow around a joint. I recommend a good 60/40 tin lead solder, 24 gauge or thinner, with a built-in solder flux core. You won't go far wrong with that. It is not for nothing that military equipment is exempt from RoHS regulations; it needs to be reliable. Other areas of the world have their own "standards," and most base them on the European model with individual twists, exceptions, and requirements.

A good soldering iron is also important, and one with a temperature control mechanism is essential. It will heat up rapidly, but it won't overheat. A stand and sponge are also essential. The iron should be wiped on a damp sponge to remove flux residue before returning the iron to the stand. If you don't do this, the flux will build up and form a glassy insulating layer on the tip, which will stop solder melting on the tip and heat being transferred to the joint.

When soldering, there are fumes from flux. You can get non-fuming fluxes but the results are not good; they just don't seem to adequately wet the joints. The ones I have tried are simply rubbish. Flux fumes should be avoided if at all possible; you will find that the stream of smoke from the soldering iron seems to have an almost magnetic attraction to you. This is caused by your face heating the air and causing a small rising current of air that guides the flux fumes to you. A fume extraction system of some sort is recommended, and this can be as simple as a fan sucking air away from the iron or as complex as a fully filtered control system. Ventilation should be good.

Supply Decoupling

The topic of supply decoupling is so important and yet is hardly mentioned at all. Because all professional engineers know it's important, it is taken as read and hardly mentioned. A good percentage of the problems on the Arduino forum can be traced back to a lack of proper supply decoupling. So what is it? Well, basically it is interference from the working chips of a system preventing the other chips from working correctly. This interference is transmitted from chip to chip along the power supply lines, both positive and ground. It is caused by the variation in current draw of the chips as the various components inside it switch on and off. This causes a small variation in the voltage and that voltage in turn adds to the interference generated by the next chip. See Figure 1-19. Be on the lookout for intermittent operation, especially when heavy currents are switched rapidly.

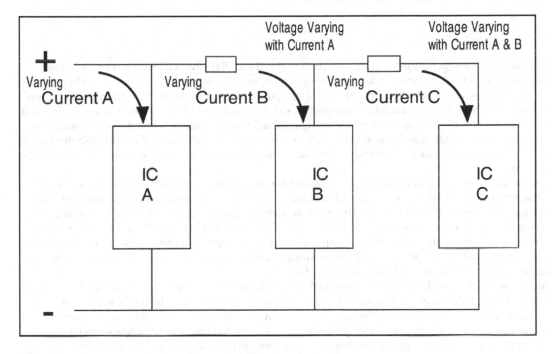

Figure 1-19. *Power supply disturbance caused by supply coupling*

The first line of defense is to put a ceramic capacitor of 100nF across the power supply of every chip, or every other chip. Sometimes you also need a few larger values like a 47uF capacitor. The small capacitors handle the high frequency interference and the large capacitors smooth out the low frequency large current demands. A very popular page on my website is the one on decoupling. You can find it at http://www.thebox.myzen.co.uk/Tutorial/De-coupling.html or just Google the term for other pages on this topic.

Adding Extra Parts to an Arduino

A lot of projects will require adding components to the Arduino, either in terms of extra I/O or extra functions like an A/D (analogue to digital) converter. There are basically two ways of doing this: through one of the bus systems built into the Arduino's processor, or through the individual existing I/O pins.

There are two major, and some what similar, bus systems available in the processors of the Arduino boards—these are the I2C and SPI buses. It's possible you will use one or both of these systems in the same project.

First let's look at the I2C bus.

The I2C Bus

I2C is pronounced "eye squared cee," and it is sometimes called IIC, which stands for Inter-Integrated Circuit Connection, the squared bit is a sort of geeky joke. As the name implies, it is designed for connecting circuits, originally in TV sets. It has since spread into almost all aspects of electronics. It is a bus, which means that many devices can share the same connections.

The Nature of a Bus

Ironically the thing most people associate a bus with today is the USB (Universal Serial Bus), which is not actually a bus at all. This is because its connection topology is strictly a one-to-one connection, whereas a true bus has its connections common among several components. Because these connections are common, there has to be a way of distinguishing between devices so you can control the one you want. Therefore, each I2C IC has its own address. It is up to the system designer, that's you, to make sure that these are unique on any one system. These addresses are seven bits long, so that leaves you with a total of 128 possible devices on one bus. Of course, most of the time you have absolutely nothing like that many devices—more than three or four is unusual.

Most devices also have a external pin or two so that the address can be altered a little and you can have at least two of the same device on a bus. Each device has two connections—clock and data—with the same two wires going to each device on the bus. This gives its alternate name, "the two wire bus," although in the Arduino world this is shortened to simple wire. This is a little unfortunate because there is another system known as the one wire bus and while it's not supported by the processor, it can be accessed through software and using a technique called "bit-banging". This is where individual signal lines, or bits, are set high and low, with the timing required to meet the specifications of the bus.

There is no need for such bit-banging with the I2C bus because all the protocol is built into the processor and most of it can be performed without any processor intervention. The bus is arranged as a master/slave setup, and the master is the only device allowed to initiate communications. The master sends a message that it wants to talk to a slave at a specific address, and the slave responds when it is ready. Then the master either requests the slave to send it some bytes or sends the slave some bytes. When the transaction is complete, the master indicates that the bus is free again, and all the slaves connected to the bus start listening for their address again. While we could go into the detail of exactly how this is accomplished, it doesn't buy us much for the effort, especially considering the uses we are going to put to this bus in this book. In essence, you just connect it and it all works like magic.

Signal Lines

We do need to consider the two signal lines. The clock goes from the master to all the slaves and synchronizes the data transfer. In that way it is considered a one-way, or unidirectional, signal. The data line can send data from the slave to the master or from the master to the slave. Data can flow in either direction, but of course not at the same time, so this line is known as a bidirectional line.

The nature of these lines is different from the normal digital lines in that they are what is known as open collector lines. That means that they can connect the line to ground or release it, that is, not connect it to ground. When a line is not connected to anything we say it is floating, something we normally do not want to happen. So in order to stop the line from floating it must be connected to the supply voltage rail through a resistor. This is called a pull-up resistor because it pulls the line up high when nothing is connecting it to ground. The Arduino enables the processor's internal pull up resistors to do this, but they are not strong enough for the job and so when using this bus you always need external pull-up resistors.

For a 5V system this should normally be a value of 4K7 and, for a 3V3 system this should be 2K7, although the values are not too critical. The clock and data pins location are fixed by the hardware inside the processor and cannot be changed. Unfortunately, these are not always the same pins on different processors. One recent improvement to the Arduino boards saw two extra connections being brought out that were just copies of whatever pins carried the I2C pins for that processor. This makes it easier for shields to work on a number of different Arduino boards. Figure 1-20 shows the general layout of an I2C bus.

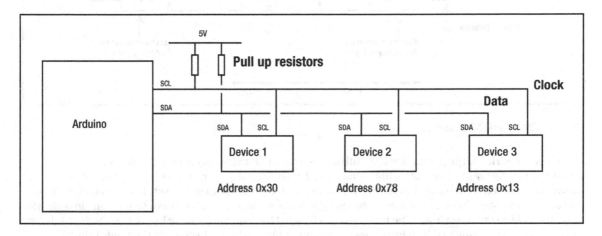

Figure 1-20. An I2C bus system

The speed of the I2C depends on the specific chip, but the Arduino's standard I2C library's clock speed is 100KHz. Since each byte transfer takes ten clock cycles, this gives a communication speed with the chip of about 10 kilobytes per second. This is not considered fast in the world of electronics, but it's not too slow either. Nowadays most chips can perform faster than this and there are I2C libraries that will allow you to alter the clock speed and have a faster transfer rate. The next "standard speed: is 400KHz and then onto 1MHz. Note that when changing the speed of the bus all chips on the bus must be capable of working at the faster speed. The maximum speed of the bus is also determined by its length; the longer the bus the slower it needs to go. The bus was only designed for lengths of about a foot and a half, but can be made to go further with special drivers and wiring with a low stray capacitance. That means that using twisted pairs is the last thing you want to do when wiring this bus.

The SPI Bus

The SPI bus is somewhat more variable than the I2C bus, and often has only one device attached to it. However, this bus is capable of having many devices. Chapter 5 has an example of two port expanders connected to this bus. Also, like the I2C bus it is a master/slave arrangement, with the Arduino being the master and calling all the shots. Whereas an I2C bus had a built-in address for every chip, an SPI chip generally speaking does not. In place of an address, an SPI device expects its chip-enabled pin to be driven low to tell it to pay attention to what is on the bus. Therefore, each device on the SPI bus requires its own output pin, and the Arduino software needs to activate this before initiating a transfer. In a very similar way to the I2C bus, data transfer is controlled by a data signal and a clock. However, the data signal is unidirectional, so to transfer data in both directions you need two signal wires. Figure 1-21 shows a typical data transfer from the master to a slave SPI device.

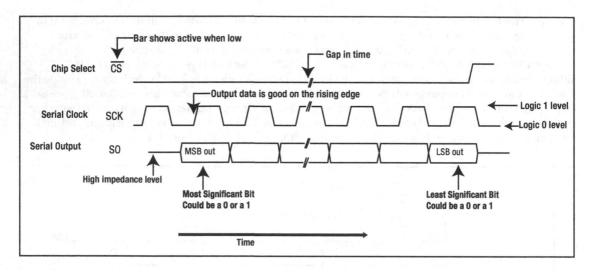

Figure 1-21. *Basic SPI transfer*

Only the serial output (or to give it its full name—Master Out Slave In) is shown here, as the converse signal MISO (Master In Slave Out) is not being used. This is what is known as a timing diagram because it shows the time sequence of operations of each bit in a system. A diagram of this sort has a few conventions that are worth noting here. Transitions between logic levels are normally shown as a sloping line in order for parameters like signal rise time to be indicated. Each signal has potentially three levels, logic high or 1, logic low or 0, and a disconnected high impedance state sometimes called a tri-state. This last state is in effect a switched-off state and allows many device's outputs to be connected to the same line without causing problems. If you look at the SO line, you will see that the logic level is both high and low. In real life it can't be in both states at the same time, so this means that it is either high or low, depending on the data being transferred. The sausage-like links show where the line can potentially transition between the two logic states.

An SPI transfer can be many bytes long, and so to shorten the diagram to manageable lengths, a gap is introduced into the diagram to show that this continues for a while in the same manor. Unlike the I2C bus there are a number of variants that can be applied to this bus standard. The first is the order in which the data is output or input; in Figure 1-20 the most significant bit of a byte comes out first but it could be the other way around. Likewise the diagram shows that the output is most stable, that is furthest from any transition, during the rising edge of the clock. Other devices can require this transfer on the other edge, the falling edge, of the clock signal. The Arduino SPI library has options for changing those two variable conditions.

This library also has options to change the speed of the clock, and in general SPI devices can work much faster than I2C devices. It is not uncommon to use clock speeds of 1MHz or even 5MHz. Because the bus device selection is done by a chip select pin, there is no requirement for all the devices on the bus to be able to work at the current speed of the bus. You can change the speed when talking to a fast device and lower it when talking to a slower device. Again, like the I2C bus, the pins involved with SPI transfer are fixed by the processor's internal hardware.

The Arduino's SPI library uses the SPI interface built into the processor chip, which is efficient because the transfer occurs without program intervention. However, this has a few restrictions, the main one being that it will only transfer eight bits at a time. This works fine for SPI devices requiring a transfer of a number of bytes but some devices require odd numbers of bits. When you get a device like this, you have no option but to bit-bang them, which means you can use any pins you like. It is much easier bit-banging an SPI than an I2C.

Roll Your Own

Finally, it is not always necessary to use a bus to interface other devices to the Arduino. You can use the normal I/O pins and bit-bang an interface. Popular ways of adding extra inputs and outputs is using external shift registers. You need a different shift register if you are going to make an input or an output, but you only need three Arduino I/O pins and you can have an unlimited number of input/outputs. This is because shift register can be connected, or chained together, almost without limit. The price you pay for this, however, is that the longer the chain, the more program resource and hence the longer it takes to read all the inputs or write to all the outputs. You cannot address individual bits; you have to read/write them all, even to access just one bit. Figure 1-22 shows how data gets put into a shift register one bit at a time.

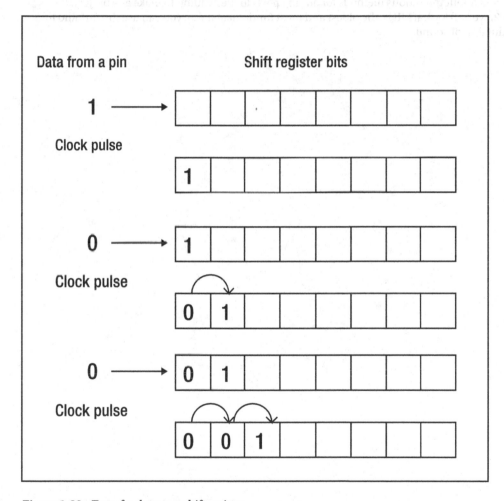

Figure 1-22. *Transfer data to a shift register*

What we see here is that each data bit is transferred on a clock pulse into a shift register. In fact, shift registers are inside I2C and SPI devices, and when data is transferred into one bit, all the other bits already in are shifted one place to the right. Data bits that fall out of the end can be fed into the input of another shift register to continue the chain.

Most other devices do not require the use of serial data. Those devices just need I/O pins connecting to their inputs and those bits driving high or low in the appropriate manner.

Summary

You have seen the different functional blocks of the various Arduinos and learned how to evaluate new and old models. For Audio, use the Uno and Due as the primary board versions. The compatible Teensy offers an interesting option for some projects. You looked at schematics and the various ways that good schematics can be drawn and had a quick introduction to the options available when making prototype hardware. Finally, you learned about the various methods for adding parts to the Arduino to make any project.

In Chapter 2, we will look at MIDI, the oldest and most fundamental way you can use the Arduino to control the production of sound.

CHAPTER 2

■ ■ ■

Basic MIDI

This chapter covers:

- Using the MIDI signal
- Understanding MIDI messages
- Hardware handling of MIDI signals
- Building a MIDI shield
- Sending and receiving MIDI messages

Using MIDI is perhaps the simplest way to get the Arduino to interact in a musical context. It is simple to send and receive, and its language is understood by a countless number of musical instruments and controllers. It has a simple electrical interface and is designed to be compatible with a wide variety of electronic systems. MIDI is totally ubiquitous in modern music and, despite its obituary having been written many times, it is still going strong. It is a useful first step when exploring sound on the Arduino.

In this chapter, I cover the fundamentals of a MIDI signal, including how it is composed of a series of bytes transported over an asynchronous data link, how those bytes are grouped together to form messages, and how two of those messages work in detail. Then, I discuss the hardware involved in transporting those messages into and out of the Arduino. Then I show you how to make a MIDI input/output shield for an Arduino and explain the code necessary to drive it.

What Is MIDI?

MIDI stands for Musical Instrument Digital Interface and has been around a long time. It was introduced in 1983 but was proposed two years earlier, and, as its name implies, it was designed for controlling musical instruments. It was created to standardize the different methods of control that each manufacturer of electronic synthesizers had developed. Things were getting to be like the tower of Babel, with many different and incompatible systems appearing. MIDI quickly brought order to this chaos, to the benefit of all. It is not restricted to controlling musical notes and can be used for any sort of control involving music or not. It can be used to control lighting effects, movement of automation and robots, and the more conventional applications involving music. Its great strengths are that it is simple to understand, easy to implement, and widely implemented. Not only does the MIDI standard define the protocol, it also defines the physical interface in terms of voltage, current, and connectors. So let's look at MIDI in more detail and see how this fits in with the Arduino. Remember that a lot of this detail is not vital to know in order to simply use MIDI, but it is important if you want to understand what you are doing.

The Electrical Signal

MIDI uses an asynchronous serial interface, which is standard in computers, but at a very non-standard speed or baud rate as it is called. It uses a speed of 31.250KHz, which at first seems odd. However, the chips that generate and receive asynchronous data, called UARTs—Universal Asynchronous Receive Transmitters, need a clock oscillator that is 16 times the required speed, and this speed is known as the baud rate. A 1MHz crystal is a cheap and easy thing to build into an oscillator and if you feed this first into a divide by two circuits and then into a UART you automatically get 31.250KHz. That was reason this speed was used— historically it was easy to implement. Conventional baud rates are based on multiples of old mechanical teleprinter machines, so you get speeds like 300 baud, 1,200 baud, 9,600 baud, and so on. While these look nice and simple, when you work out the actual frequency you have to feed a UART, you get a series of horrendous frequencies, very non-standard and with lots of numbers after the decimal point. This makes it more difficult, or at least expensive, to generate.

A UART chip has all the logic for sending and receiving an asynchronous data stream, and there is one built into all Arduino processors and most other micro-controllers as well. Processors like the ATmega2560 in the Arduino Mega have four UARTs and this makes development using this processor much easer. For example, you could connect one UART to your MIDI interface and use another for downloading sketches and getting a printout to debug your code. If you only have one UART like in the Uno then there is the option of using a software-emulated UART, known as software serial. However, this is not as good as using the hardware due to speed and latency limitations.

Asynchronous serial data is data that is sent one bit at a time. It is formatted in such a way that the receiving circuit synchronizes to the data once every byte. There are various variations but basically there is a start signal, followed by data signals, and ending with a stop signal. The signals are basically binary, that is two possible levels, but this can take on many physical forms. So when talking about serial data, you don't talk of logic levels high and low but of *mark* and *space*.

The nomenclature used in talking about this is derived for the early use of telegraph machines first demonstrated at the Mechanics Institute in New York in 1844. A mark level is the normal undriven state of the line, whereas a space is the driven state of the line. When nothing is being sent on a serial line, it sits in its mark state, then when a byte of data is sent, it starts by driving the line to the space state of a time that is determined by the baud rate. The term *baud* means "data bits per second" and was named after one of the early telegraph engineers Émile Baudot. However, it is still used in computer systems today. A simple system like this corresponds in a one-to-one fashion with the maximum number of transitions per second of the line. In more complex modulation systems, you can get baud rates that are faster than line transitions but there is no need to consider that in this book.

Data is sent by first sending a start bit, which is a space state for a baud time, followed by the data bits sent as either mark or space, depending on if they are logic zeros or logic ones (logic one corresponds to a mark). This data is followed by an optional parity bit and finishes off by a stop signal. This stop signal is a mark state for either one, one and a half, or two baud periods. After this, the next packet of data can follow immediately, or at any time after the end of the stop bit. The point is that the start of the next byte is not synchronized to the baud rate of the previous byte, and that is why the format is called asynchronous.

Figure 2-1 is a timing diagram where time runs from left to right. After the start bit the data bits follow, with the least significant bit coming first. Notice that there is nothing to signify where one bit ends and another starts apart from the time that has elapsed. If the following bit is at the same state then the line does not change. If the bit is at a different state then the state changes at the baud time. This time is referenced from the start of the start bit; that is, from the first falling edge, which is the synchronizing point. There is only one such point per byte, so this requires the transmitter and receiver to have good timing accuracy. Figure 2-2 shows three different byte values being sent.

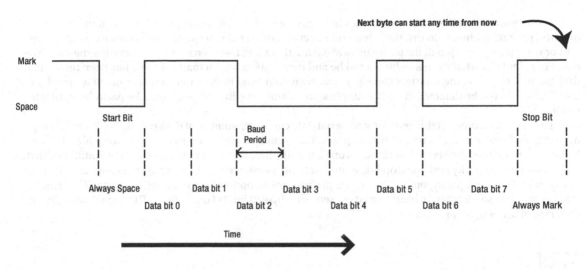

Figure 2-1. The timing diagram of serial data

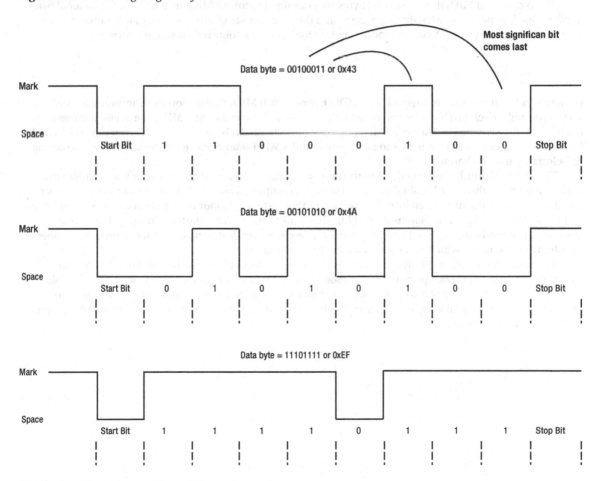

Figure 2-2. The pattern of three different data values

There is an optional extra bit that comes between the last data bit and the stop bit, called the "parity bit," and its state is chosen so that there is an odd or even number of mark states. You can have what is called odd or even parity. The job of the parity bit is to ensure that there has been no error in sending the data. The receiver calculates what the parity bit should be and then tests to see if it matches what has been received. If they are not the same, then the receiver signals an error. Mind you there could be two errors that cancel out and this would not be detected in such a simple system. However, in MIDI signaling the parity bit option is not used.

There are a number of different formats serial data can have, number of data bits, 5, 7 or 8, odd even or no parity and one, one and a half, or two stop bits. These choices are known as the data's word format. The MIDI system defines the serial data to use as one start bit (there is never anything else but it is still specified) eight data bits, no parity and one stop bit, sometimes abbreviated to 8-N-1. Other formats have an E for even parity or an O for odd parity, but as I have said, parity is not an option used in the MIDI format. If you add that up, you will see it takes 10 baud periods to send one byte (8 bits) of data. For a MIDI signal, that gives a data rate of 3,125 bytes per second.

MIDI Messages

In order to control a MIDI device, several bytes are combined to form a MIDI message. The number of bytes used varies depending on what the message is, and there are classes of MIDI messages to control various aspects of a music system. A good introduction is to look at how a "note on" message is formed.

Note On

Generally a MIDI message is targeted at a MIDI channel. Each MIDI connection can communicate with 16 MIDI channels. Each MIDI device can be set to be on one or several different MIDI channels, and there are normally some switches on the device that control which channel it is on. However, it is not unusual to find a MIDI receiving device that responds to all channels and a MIDI sending device that can only tag its message as belonging to one channel.

The channel number is embedded in the first byte of the MIDI message as the four least significant bits, and here is where there is a bit of a disconnect between computers and musicians. Humans like to think of the channels as being numbered from 1 to 16. In a binary system with four bits, there are indeed 16 different combinations, but there is a combination of bits that is all zeros, so in computer terms the channels are actually numbered from 0 to 15. This can lead to a little confusion. Just think of it as the computer number signifying the channel, which is one less than the channel number.

The note on message's first byte contains two pieces of information—the channel number and the sort of message it is. This last piece of information determines how many other bytes make up the whole message, and the first byte of a MIDI message is often called the "status byte". In the case of the note on message, there are two other bytes associated with this message. Figure 2-3 shows the anatomy of a note on message with three bytes.

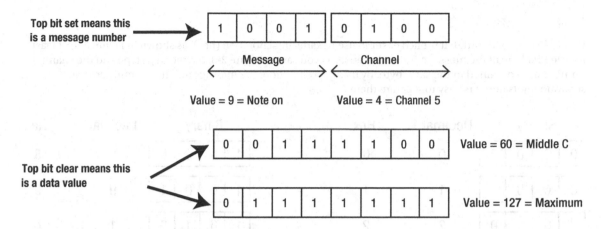

Figure 2-3. *The anatomy of a note on message*

The important point to take from this is that the first byte of a MIDI message has the most significant bit set, whereas all subsequent bytes in the message have this bit clear. The two other bytes in this message contain the note number and the on velocity, or how hard the note is struck. Because these two bytes must have the top bit clear, the numbers sent can only be from 0 to 127. Each subsequent note number is a semitone higher than the proceeding note and a range of 128 semitones covers all the audio spectrum. In fact, most MIDI sound generators do not produce sound for numbers in the two extremes of the range. The numbers corresponding to the velocity have no physical meaning other than the bigger it is, the harder it is struck, with 127 being as hard as it is possible. This is normally converted to the note's volume, although more expensive MIDI note generators also modify the note's timbre, as the sound color of a piano changes depending on how hard you hit the key, or a trumpet by how hard you blow it.

Note Off

The note on message is almost always accompanied by a matching note off message some time later. Here, the MIDI system allows two ways of turning a note off. The first is with its own note off message, with the data being the note number and the velocity being how quickly it was released. This is often ignored in many sound modules and some keyboards return a fixed value here, typically a 0. However, there are some uses for this parameter; for example, some sampling modules use it to trigger a final sample for the sound end. A typical use of this is a timpani roll, where the note off triggers the final hit and fade sample, and the velocity of the release can affect the pitch or velocity of the final hit. The note off velocity can also be used to control the release time of a note, but the use of note off velocity is not consistently implemented across devices.

The other way of turning a note off is to send a note on message, but have the note on velocity set to 0. Any system receiving MIDI should be capable of coping with both methods of turning a note off. If there is not a note off message that matches a previous note on message, a note can become stuck on. With percussive sounds, this is not normally an issue but with other types of MIDI voice, you can be left with a constant drone, which is annoying. Fortunately, there is a MIDI message to deal with that, an all notes off or reset message. Unfortunately, not all systems implement this correctly and musicians have been known to remove the power and then reconnected it while uttering the obligatory expletive.

Hexadecimal Notation

When dealing with MIDI, it is often easer to use hexadecimal notation (hex), as shown in Figure 2-4, at least for the first byte of the message. This is because, as you saw in Figure 2-3, the message type and the channel number are contained in the same byte. By using hex notation, the message and the channel are two separate digits and it is easy to separate them.

Binary				Decimal	Hex		Binary				Decimal	Hex
0	0	0	0	0	0		1	0	0	0	8	8
0	0	0	1	1	1		1	0	0	1	9	9
0	0	1	0	2	2		1	0	1	0	10	A
0	0	1	1	3	3		1	0	1	1	11	B
0	1	0	0	4	4		1	1	0	0	12	C
0	1	0	1	5	5		1	1	0	1	13	D
0	1	1	0	6	6		1	1	1	0	14	E
0	1	1	1	7	7		1	1	1	1	15	F

Figure 2-4. *Hex notation*

Hex numbers are often prefixed with 0x to show they are in hex format. So a note on message for channel 5 would be formed with 0x94 and a note on message for channel 9 would be 0x98. Remember the channel number bit pattern is one less than the real number to counter the perception that musicians can't cope with the concept of channel 0. With those two examples, it is easy to separate the command, the 9, from the channel's second digit if you use hex notation. Contrast that with expressing the same bit pattern in decimal. The first example, note on for channel 5, would be 148. The second example, note on for channel 9, would be 152. There is no easy way to separate command and channel, especially in your head, so the extra small effort of learning hex notation pays off handsomely.

The note on and velocity are not so complex and so these are often shown in decimal for convenience, although there is nothing wrong with using hex here. The only thing you need to be aware of is that the most significant bit of these two quantities must be 0. This means that the maximum number you can send is 127.

MIDI Connections

All MIDI connections use the same sort of cable; however, there are three sorts of MIDI sockets you can have on a device—IN, OUT, and THRU. The rule is that when connecting different devices, a MIDI OUT must be connected to a MIDI IN. The MIDI THRU is simply a copy of the signal on the MIDI IN and can be used to chain one MIDI OUT to several devices; see Figure 2-5. The THRU connection becomes in effect an OUT;. The signal from it is not modified in any way by the device; it is simply what is on the MIDI IN. That is, all the information is on the MIDI IN line; the device does not filter any data out. You can think of it as a simple splitter. This surprisingly simple arrangement allows complex configurations to be constructed and driven from one simple MIDI interface. In fact there are boxes you can buy that simply have one MIDI IN and several MIDI THRU outputs to cope with the fact that not all MIDI devices actually have a MIDI THRU socket.

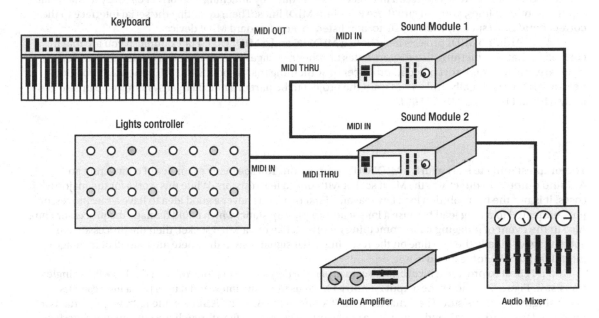

Figure 2-5. *Possible MIDI interconnections*

MIDI signals are connected physically using a 180 degree 5-pin DIN connector on pins 5 and 4. These are cheap and, by today's standards, rather clunky.

Despite there being five connections, only two or three of them are used and a MIDI cable consists simply of two wires. Sometimes these wires are screened, that is, surrounded by a wire mesh to try to cut down on electrical interference pickup. In fact, the MIDI standard says that all the cables should consist of a screened twisted pair with the screen attached to pin 2 at each end. However, the screen should be connected to a ground wire at the MIDI OUT end only. Connecting a ground to the MIDI IN can cause all sorts of problems known as ground loops. It can also generate hum in an audio system. Properly constructed, a MIDI cable can be used up to 50 feet (15 meters); however, in practice I have used short MIDI cables wired with unscreened twin core cable without any problems.

Unfortunately, the DIN socket's pins are not numbered as you would expect and there is further confusion caused by diagrams not stating if the socket is seen from the wiring side or the plug side. The upshot of this is that sometimes when you're making a MIDI system, pins 5 and 4 can be swapped, and this results in the system not working. To counter this issue, it is important to include some reverse protection on any MIDI input circuit.

Technically, the way of transmitting the data is known as a 5mA balanced current loop, and in order to isolate systems that might be at different potentials, a optical isolator (opto isolator) is used on the input. An opto isolator consists of two parts—an LED and a photo transistor. The input current lights up the LED and the light from that turns on a photo transistor. All this is sealed inside a chip so you don't see any light. The light couples the input and output circuits and so there is no need for a common electrical connection, or signal ground, as it is known. It is important that all MIDI input circuitry has an opto isolator to ensure there is no electrical connection between it and the system sending it data.

Arduino Implementation

Well, what does this all mean for the Arduino? The Arduino has a UART built into the processor chip, and it uses it to upload sketches and send and receive serial data. By attaching the correct circuitry to the serial input and output lines, you can turn these lines into MIDI lines. Then, by setting the serial interface to the correct baud rate (speed), you can talk to, and listen to, any standard MIDI device.

Not all Arduino MIDI projects need both a MIDI IN and a MIDI OUT. For example, if you are making a controller, that is something that triggers notes or other messages, you do not need a MIDI IN. Conversely, if you are making some sort of sound producer or something that responds to a MIDI message, you do not need a MIDI OUT. Finally, unless you want the project to be part of a much larger system, you can also get away with not having a MIDI THRU.

MIDI OUT

The simplest thing to start with is a MIDI OUT connection. You see many examples of connecting an Arduino output pin directly to the MIDI socket with only a few resistors. While this works for the majority of cases, it is not the best solution for a few reasons. First of all, it is never a good idea to have a raw processor pin connected to a long lead because a long lead can pick up static, which could damage the processor chip. Also in the event of plugging it into something incorrect, like not a MIDI socket, then the processor can get damaged. Finally the rise time on the resulting MIDI signal is such that there are a small percentage of modules that will not respond to it.

So it is best to provide a bit of buffering to provide a degree of isolation. You can do this with a single transistor. Figure 2-6 shows the output circuitry I have used many times, and it uses just a few resistors and a single PNP transistor. The signal from the TX line of the Arduino is already the right way up, that is a logic one (the mark state), and in that state you want no current to flow through the current loop interface. When the base of the transistor is high, then that transistor is off and no current flows through it. However, when the transistor's base is taken low, as it is when the start bit is produced, the transistor turns on and allows current to flow. If the MIDI OUT is connected to anything, that is. So the high/low voltage turns into a current/no current signal.

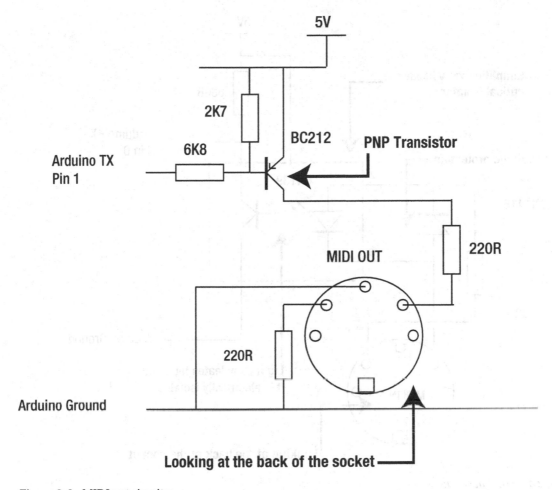

Figure 2-6. *MIDI out circuitry*

MIDI IN

On the MIDI receive side, this current is used to light up an LED inside an optical isolator. Figure 2-7 shows the receive circuit. Note here that the opto isolator is shown as a dotted box with a simplified view of the components visible inside. Sometimes this component is just shown as a simple block with pin numbers, but here, when meeting it for the first time, I thought it was useful to see inside the part, as it were.

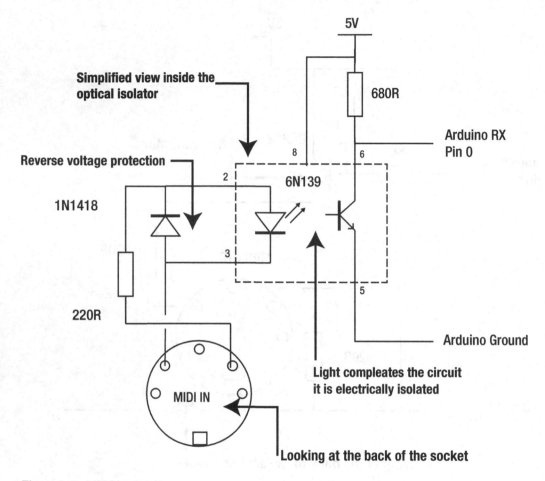

Figure 2-7. *MIDI in circuitry*

The signal comes from the MIDI socket and first passes through a resistor to limit any current, then it goes on to the LED. There is also a diode connected across the LED in the reverse direction. Normally, no current will flow through this diode because it is, as we say, reverse biased. However, if there were a wiring error and the input voltage were to be reversed, then this diode would conduct and protect the LED from the effects of a reverse voltage. We say this provides reverse polarity protection, so if everything is always connected correctly you would not need this, but like car seat belts, it is a very good idea to have one fitted. The output transistor of the opto isolator can be connected directly to the Arduino's serial input pin.

MIDI Shield

As I said, most projects only need one or the other of these two circuits. However, it is easy to combine these two circuits into one MIDI input/output interface. Many commercial shields are available ready-made, but making your own is often much more rewarding. The combined input/output circuit is shown in Figure 2-8. It is essentially the circuits of the last two figures combined.

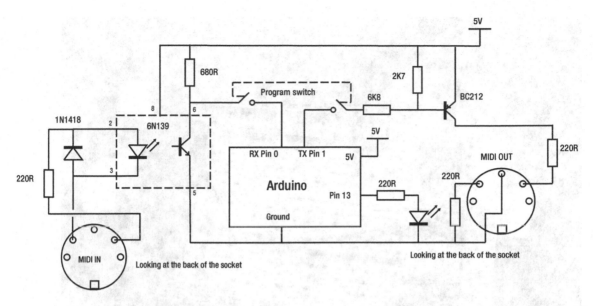

Figure 2-8. *Schematic of the MIDI shield*

There are two additions—an LED and a switch. The LED simply mirrors the LED on the board connected to pin 13. Note that you do need a series resistor unlike what a lot of books might like to tell you. The current limiting resistor is no longer built into the Arduino board and hasn't been since about 2008. It is useful to have this LED because the shield covers up the one on the board.

The other addition, that of a switch on the serial connections to the Arduino, is necessary because it uses its serial port to upload or program its sketches, and if you have anything connected to those pins during that upload process, two things can happen.

First, the messages from the Arduino back to the programmer saying it is ready for another block will also be sent out of the MIDI interface. This is going to be at a different speed from a normal MIDI message and it will just be random data, but it could be enough to make the MIDI device make a spurious response. Second, the RX or receive pin will be being driven by two outputs, one from the serial to USB converter and the other from the MIDI interface. Connecting two outputs directly together is a big no-no in electronics and the Arduino's circuitry includes a resistor to prevent any damage if this were to happen. Nevertheless, this means that the MIDI input circuit will hold the RX pin steady and no program information will make it into the Arduino.

This is why it is wise to include a switch so the MIDI circuit is disconnected during code upload. The two switches are shown connected by a dotted line, which means they are ganged together. That is, with one switch action you control two switches, and these are known as "double pole" switches.

Construction

The construction can take many forms, but one of the most popular ways is to build a circuit as a shield. You can get prototype shield boards for most Arduinos, as you read in Chapter 1, and using such a system makes a lot of sense. However, for the ultimate in economy, you can use a strip board shield. The snag with that is that you have to find some way of coping with the 0.15-inch gap between pins 7 and 8 on the Arduino.

Figure 2-9 is a photograph of a shield I made using this circuit. The point to note is that I used PCB mounting DIN sockets for the MIDI IN and OUT. On a shield, these are much more convenient than the cheaper panel mounting sockets, but it does save you the extra work of mounting a bracket on the shield for the sockets. I used a label maker to indicate which socket was the IN and which the OUT.

Figure 2-9. *The MIDI shield*

Software MIDI Output

Driving the MIDI shield is simple enough, and the code in Listing 2-1 shows you how this is done. It simply sends a series of random notes out of the MIDI socket. You can hear the notes if you connect it to a MIDI sound generator.

Listing 2-1. Generating MIDI output

```
/* MIDI note fire - Mike Cook
 *
 * send MIDI serial data, automatically for a test
 *
 */
#define midiChannel (byte)0  // Channel 1

void setup() {
 // Setup serial
   Serial.begin(31250);  // MIDI speed
}

void loop() {
  int val;
```

```
    val = random(20,100);
      noteSend(0x90, val, 127); // note on
      delay(200);
      noteSend(0x80, val, 127); // note off
    delay(800);
      } // end loop function

// plays a MIDI note
 void noteSend(char cmd, char data1, char data2) {
  cmd = cmd | char(midiChannel);  // merge channel number
  Serial.write(cmd);
  Serial.write(data1);
  Serial.write(data2);
}
```

The setup function simply sets the serial port to the MIDI speed, and the loop function generates a random note and sends a note on message for that note. Then, after a delay of 0.2 seconds, it sends a note off message for that note and delays for 0.8 seconds. This is repeated continuously. The noteSend function takes in three numbers—the command, note number, and velocity. Then the command is merged with the channel number by using an inclusive OR operation and, finally, all three bytes are transmitted out of the serial port.

There are a number of programs that you can run on your computer that are MIDI monitors. These are like simple terminal programs but display MIDI messages coming into your system in words rather than numbers. A Google search for "MIDI monitor" will show you several options for your particular machine and its operating system. Figure 2-10 shows the typical output of such programs running the code in Listing 2-1.

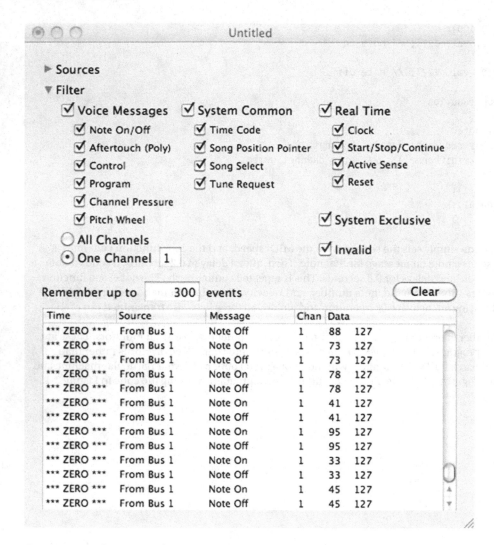

Figure 2-10. *The output of a MIDI monitor*

Software MIDI Input

Looking at MIDI input is a bit more complex than producing output. This is because there are many different MIDI messages, and so far you have only looked at two of them—note on and note off. Therefore, this example code only recognizes those two messages. You have to sort these messages from the mass of other messages that might be flowing through the system, which is known as "parsing" the message. This is not an uncommon requirement, because you don't want to have to put in all the code to recognize a message if you can't do anything with it. In the example shown in Listing 2-2, any note on message will simply turn on an LED on pin 13 of the Arduino, and any note off message will turn it off.

Listing 2-2. Parsing note on/off messages

```
/* Midi input - Mike Cook
 * -----------------
 * listen for MIDI serial data,
*/

//variables setup
  byte channel = 1;      // MIDI channel to respond to
                         // (in this case channel 2)

//setup: declaring inputs and outputs and begin serial
void setup() {

  pinMode(13,OUTPUT);        // LED to light up
  digitalWrite(13,LOW);      // Turn LED off
  Serial.begin(31250);       // start serial with MIDI baud rate

}

//loop: wait for serial data, and interpret the message
void loop () {
  checkIn(); // see if anything has arrived at the input
  }

void checkIn(){
  static int state=0;      // state machine variable 0 = command waiting
                           // 1 = note waiting : 2 = velocity waiting
  static char note = 60;
  static boolean noteDown = LOW;

  if (Serial.available() > 0) {
    // read the incoming byte:
    byte incomingByte = Serial.read();

   switch (state){
      case 0:
    // look for as status-byte, our channel, note on
        if (incomingByte== ( 0x90 | channel)){  // read only one channel
           noteDown = HIGH;
           state=1;
        }
    // look for as status-byte, our channel, note off
        if (incomingByte== (0x80 | channel)){   // read only one channel
           noteDown = LOW;
           state=1;
       }
```

```
        case 1:
        // get the note to play or stop
          if(incomingByte < 128) {
             note=incomingByte;
             state=2;
          }
          else {
             state = 0;  // reset state machine as this should be a note number
          }
        break;

        case 2:
        // get the velocity
          if(incomingByte < 128) {
              doNote(note, incomingByte, noteDown); // do something with the note on message
          }
          state = 0;  // reset state machine to start
      }
    }
}

void doNote(byte note, byte velocity, boolean down){
  // if velocity = 0 on a 'Note ON' command, treat it as a note off
  if ((down == HIGH) && (velocity == 0)){
     down = LOW;
  }
  // do something with the note message
  // this just toggles Pin 13 and ignores the note value and velocity
    digitalWrite(13, down);
}
```

The way this program works is by implementing a state machine. There is a variable called state that holds the key to what to do next. This is needed because the bytes that make up the MIDI message arrive one at a time, so when one arrives you have to know what to do with it. The checkIn function determines if there is at least one byte available in the serial buffer to read, and if there is, it reads it. It uses three variables that are declared as static variables; this means that the value of them persists between calls to the function. This is better programming practice than declaring them as global variables because they can't get inadvertently changed by other functions. Initially, the state variable is set to 0, which means it is waiting for a command message. Remember that a MIDI message always has its most significant bit set, but in this code you just look for the note on or note off message.

To check if it is a message for the channel you want to respond to, the message byte is ORed with the channel number to form what you would expect to receive. If there is a match, the state variable is changed to 1, which means that next time a byte is received you do the actions in case 1. If the byte is not one of these two messages, the state variable is not advanced and next time a byte is received you look again to see if it one you are interested in. By this method the MIDI stream can be synchronized and any missing bytes do not throw the whole thing permanently out. There is also a variable set called noteDown, which is used later in the code to cope with the note on message with zero velocity also being used as a note off message. At this stage you can't tell which is which, because the velocity byte has not arrived yet.

When the state variable equals 1, the byte received is stored in a variable called note if it is less than 128 and the state variable is advanced to a value of 2. However, if the byte is greater than 127 it means it is a message byte not a data byte. As this is not what was expected, the state machine variable is reset to 0, which causes the next byte to be examined to see if it is a message you are interested in. Finally, when the state variable is 2 and the byte is less than 128, all the bytes of the message are in, and now is the time to do something with the message. This is done by calling the function doNote, which in this simple example will turn the LED on pin 13 on or off. The noteDown variable is passed to this function and is called down. It is used along with the value of the velocity to determine the logic level to write out to the LED. The final line in the function sets the LED accordingly.

So in operation any note on message will turn the LED on and a note off up will turn it off. You can check this by connecting it to a keyboard set to send data on channel 2. Hold a key down and the LED will light until you release it. If you hold several keys down, the LED turns on and turns off again as soon as one is released.

As an exercise, try to modify the code so that the LED goes on with any key down but only turns off when all the keys are released. Hint: You need a variable that increases a count on with each note on message and decreases it with each note off message. Only when this count is 0 should the LED be off.

Summary

Now that you have an understanding of the fundamentals of a MIDI signal, know how a simple message is formed, and can get it into and out of your Arduino, you are all set to explore the possibilities of MIDI. In later chapters, you look at other sorts of MIDI messages and build instruments and controllers.

■ ■ ■

CHAPTER 3

More MIDI

This chapter covers

- More MIDI messages
- System MIDI messages
- Using helper applications to handle MIDI on your computer
- Making the Arduino look like a MIDI device

You have already seen in the last chapter the essence of a MIDI message by looking at the note on and note off MIDI messages. Now it is time to delve into more MIDI by looking at the wider range of messages that MIDI has to offer. You will see how to change the MIDI voice, or sound, and what MIDI control parameters are all about. Then you'll look at the real-time messages that affect the whole system. Next you will look at how to use helper applications on your laptop or PC to convert serial data from the Arduino into a MIDI stream. This means that you do not require MIDI standard hardware and converters. Finally, you will see ways of making the Arduino look like a native USB MIDI device.

More MIDI Messages

MIDI has a lot more going for it than the note on/note off message. While these two messages provide the essentials for playing notes, there are several other classes of MIDI message that can be very useful, so let's look at them and see what they can do for you. A MIDI controller is a device or message that controls something about the sound. This might be the volume, an effect like vibrato, or the position of the instrument on the stereo stage. There are basically two types of messages—a channel message aimed only at one playing channel, and a system message aimed at the whole system. We'll start with channel messages and then move on to system messages.

There are five types of channel voice messages:

- Note on/note off
- Controller change
- Program change
- Pitch bend
- Aftertouch

You have seen two of these already with note on/note off. The others are Controller Change; Program Change; Pitch Bend; and Aftertouch. For a full specification of all things MIDI, see the MIDI manufacturers association's web site at http://www.midi.org/techspecs/. This might be a little daunting to look at first, so let's take a brief overview of the messages that are available.

Controller Change (CC) MIDI Messages

In MIDI, the term CC stands for "controller change" and it is a method, as the name says, for providing control information. There can be up to 120 controllers on each MIDI channel to control anything you want. Each controller channel contains a value between 0 and 127 and the CC messages allow these values to be changed. Some control channels have a standard use, but that use is neither fixed nor compulsory. Just think of them as a whole bunch of variables your instrument can use, or your controller can manipulate.

A controller channel can be used as a simple on/off switch, in which case it will store 0 or 127. On the other hand, it can store a number between 0 and 127, and finally you can use two controller channels together to store numbers between 0 and 16,384. Here, one channel holds a coarse value and the other a fine value. Let's see how this pans out in practice.

Figure 3-1 shows the anatomy of a control change message. Note how similar this is to the note on message you looked at in the previous chapter. There, the value of the message nibble (the top four bits of the byte) was 11 in decimal or 0xB in hex. The lower nibble contains the channel number as usual. The next two bytes are the controller number and the new value you want it to contain. So one simple message can set the controller value to anything between 0 and 127. Note that, in the space for the controller number, there is room to put 127 controllers not the 120 mentioned earlier. These extra eight controllers are reserved for Channel Mode messages. These are like controllers but have a specific meaning in the MIDI specification. These are summarized in Table 3-1 and controller channel messages are often referred to by their number proceeded by CC.

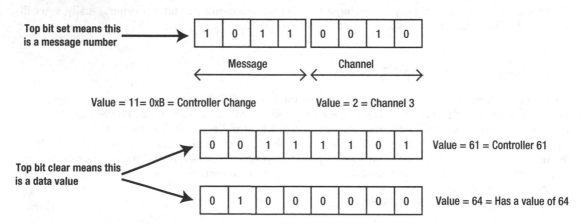

Figure 3-1. *The anatomy of a control message*

Table 3-1. *Controller Channel Message*

Controller	Value	Meaning
120	0	All sound off—turn all notes on this channel off.
121	0	Reset all controllers to their default value.
122	0	Local control off—respond only to MIDI messages.
122	127	Local control on—respond to local inputs like a keyboard.
123	0	All notes off.
124	0	Omni mode off.
125	0	Omni mode on.
126	M	Mono mode on (poly mode off) where M is the number of channels.
127	0	Poly mode on (mono mode off).
		Note the last four messages also cause all notes to be off.

Note that message CC120 (all sounds off) and CC123 (all notes off) look rather similar and it is true that they will do a similar job. The main difference is that CC123 will have no effect on a note sustained due to an unresolved CC64 (Sustain Peddle hold) or CC65 message (Portamento Pedal), whereas CC120 will.

While the controllers can be used as anything, there is a recommended standard that helps interconnectivity, as shown in Table 3-2. If you are going to implement any of these features then it is best that you do them with these controller numbers for maximum compatibility. The first thing you will notice is that there are some controller numbers missing; these are called "undefined" controllers and they can be used for anything. Did you notice that the first 64 controllers are mainly split into two parts—an MSB (most significant byte) and an LSB (least significant byte)? Strictly speaking, this is wrong as there are only seven bits of control in each, not the eight bits implied by the name byte. Note that the LSB of each controller follows exactly 32 controller numbers away from the MSB. In binary terms, this equates simply to a change in bit 6 of the controller number. These combine, as shown in Figure 3-2. This shows the two controllers, CC7 and CC39, that combine to form the main volume control for a channel.

Table 3-2. *Channel Controller Messages*

Controller Number	Function	Controller Number	Function
0	Bank Select MSB	32	Bank Select LSB
1	Modulation MSB	33	Modulation LSB
2	Breath Control MSB	34	Breath Control LSB
4	Foot Pedal MSB	36	Foot Pedal LSB
5	Portamento Time MSB	37	Portamento Time LSB
6	Data Entry MSB	38	Data Entry LSB
7	Channel Volume MSB	39	Channel Volume LSB
8	Balance MSB	40	Balance LSB
10	Pan MSB	42	Pan LSB
11	Expression MSB	43	Expression LSB
12	Effect-Type Selector #1	44	Undefined

(continued)

Table 3-2. (*continued*)

Controller Number	Function	Controller Number	Function
13	Effect-Type Selector #2	45	Undefined
16	General Purpose 1 MSB	48	General Purpose 1 LSB
17	General Purpose 2 MSB	49	General Purpose 2 LSB
18	General Purpose 3 MSB	50	General Purpose 3 LSB
19	General Purpose 4 MSB	51	General Purpose 4 LSB
64	Sustain Pedal (On/Off)	65	Portamento Pedal (On/Off)
66	Sostenuto Pedal (On/Off)	67	Soft Pedal (On/Off)
68	Legato Pedal (On/Off)	69	Hold 2 (On/Off)
70	Sound Control 1 (Sound Variation)	71	Sound Control 2 (Harmonic Content)
72	Sound Control 3 (Release Time)	73	Sound Control 4 (Attack Time)
74	Sound Control 5 (Brightness)	75 to 79	Sound Control 6 to 10 (Undefined)
80	General Purpose 5	81	General Purpose 6
82	General Purpose 7	83	General Purpose 8
84	Portamento Control	91	Reverb Depth
92	Tremolo Depth	93	Chorus Depth
94	Celeste Detune Depth	95	Phaser Depth
96	Data Increment	97	Data Decrement
98	NRPN LSB	99	NRPN MSB
100	RPN LSB	101	RPN MSB

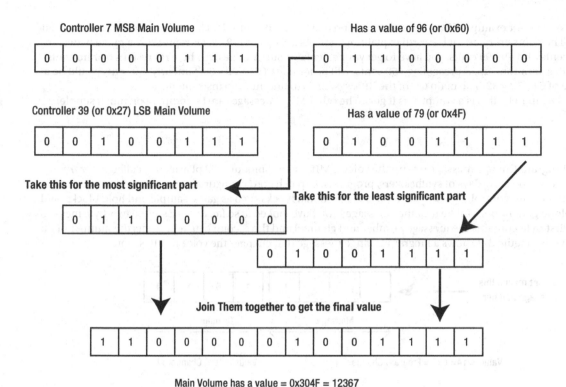

Figure 3-2. *The main volume controller*

Note how the most significant bit of the least significant byte is effectively removed because it will always be 0. This gives a 14-bit control value ranging from 0 to 16,383—fine enough control for anyone I think.

While there are a number of free controllers you can use for your own special-purpose control, there is also a back door into having a lot more controllers. This is known as "bank switching," and there are two banks you can use. These are called RPNs (registered parametric numbers) on CC100 and C101 and NRPNs (non-registered parametric numbers) on CC98 and CC99. Registered means that their function has been registered with the MIDI standards body and non-registered means you are free to do anything you like.

The way they work is that you first send the value of the extended parameter number you want to change to controller values CC100 and CC101, then you send the MSB of the data for this parameter to CC6 and the LSB data to CC38, and finally you shut the door on that parameter by setting CC100 and CC101 both to 127. This might sound complex, and it can be confusing, but the sequence of operations is quite straightforward. For example, RPN 0 sets the range of the pitch bend control, also sometimes called pitch bend sensitivity. Suppose you want to set this to a range of +/- 8 semitones and +50 cents (hundredths of a semitone). You would send the following set of controller change messages:

```
CC101 -> 0
CC100 -> 0
CC6 -> 7
CC38 -> 96
CC101 -> 127
CC100 ->127
```

Where, for example CC101 -> 0 means send a message to controller channel 101, setting it to the value of 0. The cents entry might be worth explaining here. As a range of 128 values represents a range between -100 cents and +99.99 cents, you have to get your calculator out. A value of 64 here represents 0 or no cents, so half a semitone up, representing +50 cents, will be a value of 64 + 32 = 96. Similarly -50 cents would be a value of 64 - 32 = 32. The main use of the RPN system is to fine-tune an instrument.

Fortunately, this is a complex as it gets. The other MIDI messages are by comparison much simpler.

Program Change MIDI Messages

The Program Change message sets up the voice a MIDI sound module will play in. It is called *program* because in the early days of synthesizers, programs, or patch cord configurations, were used to route oscillators and controlling voltages to various functional blocks such as gates, sample and hold blocks, and envelope generators. Unlike the other messages you have looked at so far, this is a simple two-byte message. The first byte contains the message number and channel and the second byte represents the number of the new voice. Figure 3-3 shows a Program Change message that changes the voice to a Bassoon.

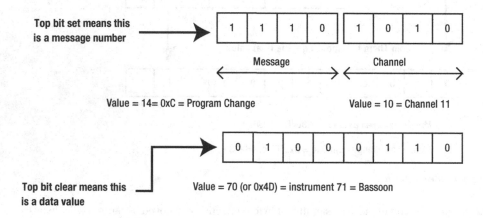

Figure 3-3. *The Program Change message*

Just like the channel numbers, instrument numbers run from 1 to 128, but the actual value you send is in the range 0 to 127. Therefore for instrument number 71 you send the value 70. Initially voices did not have numbers specifically allocated to them and that lead to quite a bit of non-standardization in early systems. Here, a Program Change of 8 could equally well mean a violin or a double base. To counter this, an addition to the MIDI standard was made to define the names of all 128 possible voices. This was known as "general MIDI" or GM for short. Basically, it defined voice number ranges into families of instruments, shown in Table 3-3, and then each family was split these into individual voice names. Note however that the specification did not say anything about the characteristics of the sound; they were only intended as a guide. The voices for the first group, Piano, are split over the first eight values and are shown in Table 3-4.

Table 3-3. *The Families of Instruments*

Range	Family Name	Range	Family Name
1-8	Piano	9-16	Chromatic Percussion
17-24	Organ	25-32	Guitar
33-40	Bass	41-48	Strings
49-56	Ensemble	57-64	Brass
65-72	Reed	73-80	Pipe
81-88	Synth Lead	89-96	Synth Pad
97-104	Synth Effects	105-112	Ethnic
113-120	Percussive	121-128	Sound Effects

Table 3-4. *The Piano Group of Instruments*

Range	Family Name
1	Acoustic Grand Piano
2	Bright Acoustic Piano
3	Electric Grand Piano
4	Honky-tonk Piano
5	Electric Piano 1
6	Electric Piano 2
7	Harpsichord
8	Clavi

Some manufacturers found restricting the voices to just 128 was a bit limiting and so further voices were made available through bank switching on controller channels CC0 for the most significant byte and CC32 for the least. This applied to each voice so, if required, there could be 16,384 versions of an acoustic grand piano. Potentially that gives a total number of voices of 16,384 X 128 = 2,097,152—enough for anyone. In practice I don't think this limit has been even approached. Some sound modules do offer in excess of 300 voices but only six or seven voices are selectable by bank switching on a few of the sounds.

As a further addition, GM specifies that channel 10 be for percussion. Here every note number in the range 35 to 81 corresponds not to the pitch of a note, but to a different drum or percussion sound. Indeed many manufacturers have note values outside this range corresponding to other sounds. Also by using the bank selector CC values, many different sorts of drum kits can be implemented, like a hard rock kit or a jazz kit. You need to check the documentation of your particular sound module or sound synthesizing software to see what it supports. Remember these sounds are only what can be implemented, and not what will be implemented. The full list of GM sounds can be found on the MIDI Manufacturers Association web site at http://www.midi.org/techspecs/gm1sound.php#instrument.

Further upgrades have been made to the GM standard, and they are all compatible with the previous versions. For a full list, see http://www.midi.org/techspecs/gm.php.

Pitch Bend MIDI Messages

Pitch Bend is a continuous controller that, as the name implies, will change the pitch of the note being played. It is often connected to a pitch wheel or a ribbon controller. This is a three-byte message but it is unusual in that the two data bytes that follow it form the 14-bit value to use. Figure 3-4 shows its make up.

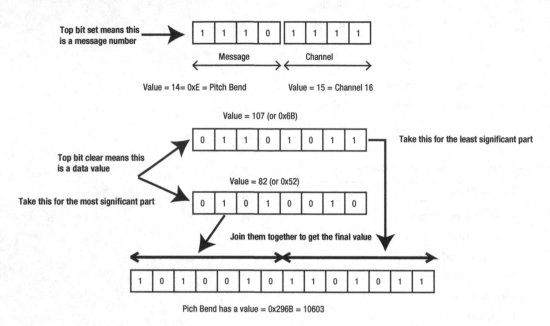

Figure 3-4. *The Pitch Bend message*

You can see that the data is sent with the least significant bits first; this is known as the "little endian" system or byte sex. The way you write numbers is in big endian. A number with six hundreds four tens and two units would be written 642. In a little endian system, this would be written as 246. Much bluster and fierce debate is conducted in computing circles as to which is the true way, and some microcomputer architectures even offer a choice of endianness. However, here you have no choice, as the Pitch Bend command is in little endian. The data in a Pitch Bend message is 0x2000 at the center for no change.

Pitch Bend perhaps more than any other sort of controller can generate a flood of messages. This is because you always have your hand on it and the slightest movement will generate a message. Other controllers tend to be adjusted and left, but a bend is something you are constantly changing. This can have the effect of clogging the MIDI system and making it harder/taking longer for the note on and off messages to get through. If you are recording the MIDI input from an instrument, you might want to edit or cut down on the Pitch Bend messages especially before a note is playing. This is because the messages are sent whenever the controller is touched and not only during a playing note. The reason why Pitch Bend is not implemented as a controller channel but is its own command is an attempt to cut down on the number of bytes sent down the system. A full Pitch Bend message takes three bytes, whereas to do it with two controller channels would take six bytes, twice as much data.

Aftertouch MIDI Messages

The last of the channel voice messages is the Aftertouch message, which is the least widely implemented feature of all the messages. Basically, Aftertouch represents how hard you press down on the keys. There are two types of Aftertouch—monophonic and polyphonic. With monophonic Aftertouch one reading is sent representing the total pressure on all the keys, and this is often implemented by a pressure-sensitive bar under the keys. This is the cheapest method to implement. Polyphonic Aftertouch has a sensor for each individual key. Not only is it more expensive, but it will also generate a lot more data.

Many sound modules only implement one, if any, form of Aftertouch. It is rare for both forms to be implemented. If your sound module does not implement Aftertouch, there is little point in generating it in the first place. Aftertouch is implemented as a two-byte message, as shown in Figure 3-5.

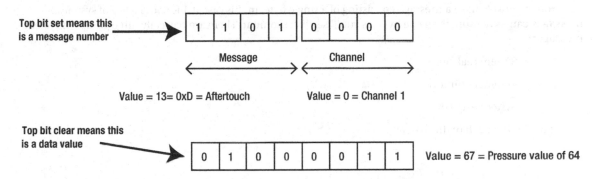

Figure 3-5. *The Aftertouch message*

The pressure values do not correspond to any absolute measure; they are just relative readings with 127 meaning pressing down as hard as you can and 0 indicating the lightest of touches. Note that if you change the pressure while holding down a note, a new Aftertouch message will be generated.

System MIDI Messages

The other class of MIDI messages is the system message. The point of these messages is that they are not targeted at any particular channel but to the MIDI system as a whole. Therefore, the structure of such messages is somewhat different than the previous channel messages. You saw in the channel message that the first byte was split into two halves; the first half was the message number and the second half was the channel number. With system messages there is no need to specify a channel; the message number is all ones or 0xF and the lower half of the byte that used to give the channel now represents the type of system message. Figure 3-6 shows this for a reset message.

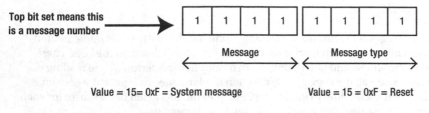

Figure 3-6. *The reset message*

You effectively have a message consisting of a single byte; in this case 0xFF. Some types of system messages can have more than one byte, as you'll see in a moment. There are basically three groups of system messages:

- System real-time
- System common
- System exclusive

We'll look at each of these now.

System Real-Time Messages

System real-time messages are used to synchronize the timing between several MIDI devices or between a device and a recording system. There are basically five types of messages:

- *System Reset (0xFF)*—This is perhaps a deeper reset than you might expect. It can cause devices to wipe their memory clean. Few systems actually respond to this.

- *MIDI Clock (0xF8)*—Sent 24 times per quarter of a note, it is a sort of metronome that forces the receiving device to keep the same time as the sending device.

- *Start (0xFA), Stop (0xFC), Continue (0XF9)*—Used for controlling sequencers.

- *Active Sensing (0xFE)*—This is optional but once it is sent the receiver will expect to see a message like this three times a second. If the receiver stops getting these messages, it assumes something is wrong and shuts down turning all notes off.

- *Reserved (0xF9)*—This message is reserved for future revisions; currently it has no use.

Using these messages is the simplest way of synchronizing devices. For example, to synchronize a drum machine with a sequencer, set the sequencer to send a MIDI clock and the drum machine to receive it.

System Common Messages

The purpose of System Common messages is to control and synchronize other devices. Some of these messages consist of two or three bytes after the initial byte. They are summarized as the following:

- *MIDI Time Code (0xF1 + one data)*—This is 100 pulses per second system used to synchronize MIDI with audio or video tape.

- *Song Pointer (0xF2 + two data)*—This is a 14-bit value that records how many MIDI beats there have been since the start of the song. One MIDI beat consists of six MIDI clocks.

- *Song Selector (0xF3 + one data)*—This specifies which sequence or song is to be played or in the case of a drum machine what chain of patterns.

- *Tune Request (0xF6)*—A message to ask analogue synthesizer to retune their oscillators.

- *Reserved (0xF4 & 0xF5)*—Two unused messages.

System Exclusive Messages

System Exclusive messages (SysEx) are perhaps the most complex messages on a MIDI system. For the purposes of this book, you need not delve too deeply into them. They are basically a catch-all way of extending the MIDI protocol for a specific manufacturer. Each manufacturer must register a unique number with the MIDI standards people, and that number is incorporated into the System Exclusive message. Typically they tell devices to load or save sound samples or other data. A device should only respond to its own manufacturers ID number; therefore, these messages are specific to certain devices.

These messages work rather differently from the others in that they start with the byte 0xF0 and end with the byte 0xF7. They can be any number of bytes long, but the data bytes between these start and stop bytes must have their most significant bits clear, like all the other data bytes in MIDI. This is shown in Figure 3-7.

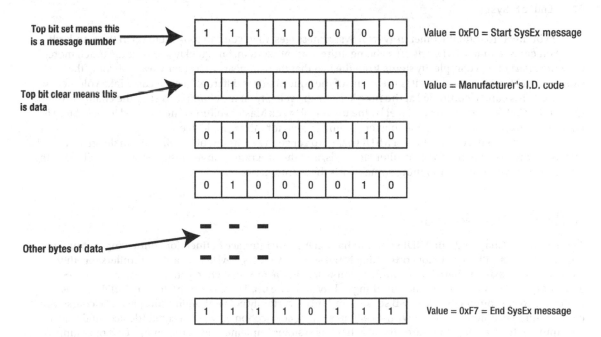

Figure 3-7. A System Exclusive message

In Figure 3-7, you see that there is an indeterminate number of bytes between the framing bytes of start SysEx and end SysEx. Note that real-time messages may be mixed into a SysEx message, as they are single byte and have their most significant bit set.

Universal System Exclusive Messages

There is a class of System Exclusive messages that are not in fact exclusive, but are known as Universal System Exclusive messages. These are shown in the following list:

- *Master Volume*—The global volume for the device

- *Master Pan*—The pan position for an entire devices output

- *Time Signature*—The current metronome rate

- *MIDI Machine Control*—To control other hardware such as tape recorders video and DAT

- *MIDI Show Control*—To control theater equipment like lights and pyrotechnics

- *General MIDI*—To switch on or off a devices voice mapping to General MIDI.

Let's look at this last one. This can be recognized by all General MIDI (GM) devices regardless of manufacturer and basically has two actions—turn GM on and turn GM off. To send this message, you have to send the following bytes:

```
F0 - Start SysEx message
7E - Universal ID number
7F - Device ID another reserved number
09 - Means this is a message about GM
01 - Means Turn on GM ( a value of 02 would be turn off)
F7 - End of SysEx
```

If you need to send the other universal SysEx messages, then you can look them up in the standards.

You can see that MIDI starts off as being quite a simple system, but quickly can become much more complex. Part of this complexity stems from the fact that there appears to be many ways of doing the same thing. However, normally it is the scope of the control that is different in each case. Take volume, for example. This can be controlled at the note level by the velocity, at the channel level by the channel volume CC7 and CC39, and at the device level by the universal SysEx Master volume. The channel level volume is good for track mixing, whereas the master volume is good for mixing in devices.

However, you don't have to be a MIDI wizard to get good results out of MIDI. You can do an awful lot by just using the note on/off, the controller channels, and the program change messages, as you will see in the next chapter, when you start putting some of this theory into practice.

MIDI Direct to USB

As you read in Chapter 2, the MIDI standard has a hardware interface defined for connecting instruments together. This is still relevant for connecting MIDI sound modules, keyboards, and controllers together. However, increasingly there is a computer somewhere in the mix and while you can get a MIDI-to-USB adaptor quite cheaply, it is yet another thing to buy and wire up. There is a trend to plug MIDI devices directly into computers through USB sockets and this is certainly convenient in some cases. Of course you can't chain instruments together with a USB; it is only a connection between a client (device) and a host (computer). Increasingly there are virtual MIDI bus systems implemented in the computer's operating system that allow virtual MIDI components to be interconnected.

The USB system consists of a number of classes of devices. MIDI devices are one device in the HID (Human Interface Device) class; others in this class include keyboards, both numeric and musical, mice, and joysticks. Basically, because a human is involved the data transfer rate, is comparatively slow. Note that a USB HID MIDI interface is not part of the official MIDI specification, but the specifications acknowledge its existence.

There are many ways you can go about getting MIDI into your computer without using the conventional MIDI transport hardware. Two of the most widely implemented ways are by means of a USB serial port emulator and directly emulating a USB HID MIDI device.

MIDI Through a Serial to USB Converter

The Arduino uses a dedicated chip to make the computer think it is communicating with a serial device, whereas in fact it is actually communicating with a USB device. It does this by having a dedicated USB bridge chip to convert USB into actual serial data. Earlier models of Arduino used a chip from FDI for this purpose, and later ones had a small micro-controller programed to act like a USB to serial device. So straight out of the box the Arduino could talk directly to a computer.

Unfortunately many of the applications that use MIDI can only talk to the computer's internal MIDI bus and not directly to a serial port, so there needs to be a helper application to present the serial data to MIDI software as if it were MIDI data. You can take two approaches with this—ready made or roll your own.

One of the first and most popular converters of this sort was the vanilla named "Serial MIDI converter" from Spikenzie Labs at http://www.spikenzielabs.com/SpikenzieLabs/Serial_MIDI.html. It is free and there are versions for Mac or Windows. It has some limitations in that it only handles three-byte MIDI messages and there is about a 26mS lag or latency between sending a note on message and the sound starting.

A new kid on the block is Hairless MIDI Serial at http://projectgus.github.io/hairless-midiserial/. Again this is free but is much easer to set up. There are Mac, Windows, and Linux versions and it's available as source code or ready to run. It really is very simple to use, and the sketch in the Arduino needs to be exactly the same as if you were using a proper MIDI hardware, with the exception that the baud rate is set to 115,200 baud instead of the normal MIDI speed of 31,250 baud.

In use it presents the single window shown in Figure 3-8. There is a drop-down menu on the left of the screen showing all the serial ports connected to your machine; you simply choose the one associated with your Arduino. On the right of the screen are two drop-down menus that allow you to pick what MIDI bus you want the MIDI out from the Arduino to go to, and another menus for where the MIDI in to your Arduino should come from. The choices of these MIDI buses may depend on what software you are running.

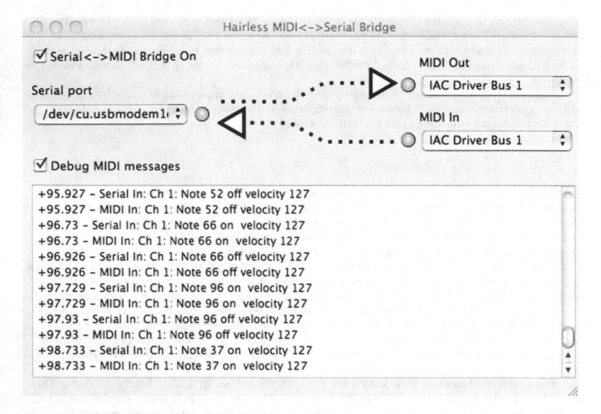

Figure 3-8. *The Hairless window*

Notice also that there is a Debug MIDI Messages dialog box. This is like a built-in MIDI monitor for the data traveling over the serial port. The messages are decoded; that is, they indicate whether there is a note on/note off, program change message, or whatever as well as showing the parametric data. The left side also shows a timestamp in seconds of when the message passed through the system. Turn these messages off once you have your system running to save computer bandwidth.

Along with Hairless is an optional MIDI library called Ardumidi, which provides simple calls to shorten the code you are writing and take you one step away from sending the raw bytes. I am not a great fan of many Arduino libraries as they tend to hide from you what is going on and they generally take up more space than optimal. This is because they offer features that you will never use but you still have to load them into the code.

While I am on the subject of MIDI libraries, a comprehensive one is the Arduino MIDI library; see http://playground.arduino.cc/Main/MIDILibrary. This is discussed in the next chapter.

If you want to roll your own application then the source code for both these applications is freely available and I suggest you start there and modify the code. However, Hairless in particular is simple and easy to set up, so making your own isn't really necessary.

MIDI Through a HID USB

While converter or bridge applications can work perfectly fine, for the ultimate in portability and ease of setup, you might want the Arduino to look like a MIDI interface to the USB port of the computer you plug it into. This means you don't have to be concerned about getting the helper application onto your computer, which is a great help if you are using other people's computers. People generally aren't, or should not be, happy to have applications loaded onto their computers by others.

Using the Arduino Uno and Mega

If you want to use the Arduino then there is the Hiduino project found at https://github.com/ddiakopoulos/hiduino. You can use this software to reprogram the ATmega 8u2 or 16u2 used as the serial-to-USB adaptor chip on the Arduino Uno rev 2 or 3. That in itself is not too difficult, although it does require the use of a hardware programmer to replace the existing code in the chip. However, the real pain is that once the software is in the 8U2/16u2 chip, you can no longer program the Arduino through the normal boot-loader process in the IDE. This means that during development you have to constantly swap between the HID software and the normal USB serial software. So the turn-around time for testing your code is a lot longer and more involved than it normally would be. This is quite a disadvantage and negates a lot of the Arduino's simplicity, which is such a selling point. It is because of this complexity that this method is not really recommended, although it could be useful for the software-orientated musicians out there.

Using the Teensy

Since the Arduino is not recommended for easily emulating a USB MIDI device, up to the plate steps the Teensy. This is very easy to use, but it's not a real Arduino. The Teensy 3 is a ARM-based Arduino look-alike board capable of running at a clock speed of up to 96MHz, which is six times faster than the normal Arduino. The fact that it is a 32-bit ARM chip also boosts execution speed. However, its USB connectivity is of interest here, over the fact that it runs faster.

You first need to download a loader application from http://www.pjrc.com/teensy/loader.html and make sure that it supports the version of the Arduino IDE you have. There are versions specific to each IDE release and there might be a small time lag between a new version of the IDE and a compatible loader. Follow the on-screen instructions and run the loader. It applies a patch to the Arduino IDE so that the next time it opens, you will find the supported Teensy board in the Tools ➤ Board menu list. You'll also see a few other items in the Tools menu, as shown in Figure 3-9.

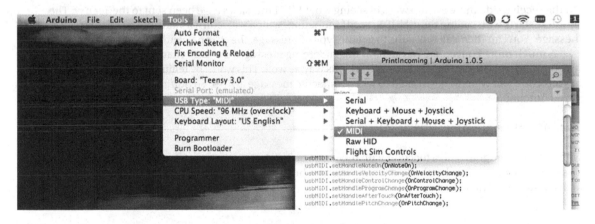

Figure 3-9. *The Tools menu after running the Teensy loader patch*

You can see that there are a couple of new items. The one of most interest to us is the USB Type option. In Figure 3-9, you can see that I have selected this to be MIDI. This means when your sketch is loaded and running, the board will appear to the computer as an HID MIDI device and not as the normal serial port emulator.

Sending MIDI Messages with the Teensy

The Teensy also contains some new functions that you can call to access the MIDI drivers. On the transmit side there are functions to send the MIDI message types, as shown in Listing 3-1.

Listing 3-1. MIDI Message Types from the Teensy

```
usbMIDI.sendNoteOn(note, velocity, channel)
usbMIDI.sendNoteOff(note, velocity, channel)
usbMIDI.sendPolyPressure(note, pressure, channel)
usbMIDI.sendControlChange(control, value, channel)
usbMIDI.sendProgramChange(program, channel)
usbMIDI.sendAfterTouch(pressure, channel)
usbMIDI.sendPitchBend(value, channel)
usbMIDI.sendSysEx(length, array)
```

When you call these functions, the messages are held for a brief time in a buffer to allow up to 16 messages to be sent at once. This is less than one millisecond, so if no other message is sent then there will be a very short delay between calling the function and sending the message. If, however, you want to send a message immediately, you can follow the message function call with this command:

```
usbMIDI.send_now()
```

As you might expect, this will send the messages immediately.

Receiving MIDI Messages with the Teensy

On the receive side there are two ways of seeing what MIDI messages have been sent to the Teensy. The simplest starts with calling the usbMIDI.read() function, which will return a value of True if there is a new message. You can then call functions to get the type of message, the channel, and the data.

A much more convenient way of handling incoming messages is to use what is known as a "callback function". Some Arduino MIDI libraries work this way as well. This works by telling the system what function in your code you want to have called to when a specific message arrives. So putting this line in the sketch's setup function

```
usbMIDI.setHandleNoteOn(OnNoteOn);
```

will make the program call a function with the name of OnNoteOn in your sketch. Of course, you have to write this function yourself and make it do what you want, but it takes away all the hassle of writing code that looks at each message and calls the required function.

Using the Arduino Leonardo & Micro

The Arduino Leonardo and the Micro use the ATmega 32u4 processor and handles the USB interface directly without needing a separate chip. As of IDE version 1.6.6 the PluggableUSB system allows you to use libraries that present a different class of device to the host USB. One of these that is especially relevant to the work in this book is the MIDIUSB library found at https://github.com/arduino-libraries/MIDIUSB. It offers by far the simplest way of making an Arduino present a MIDI interface. It uses a data structure called midiEventPacket_t which is simply a collection of bytes. Then a MidiUSB.sendMIDI function is called to transfer this structure into the output buffer. This data however is only sent when the buffer is full (which is not too helpful) or when you invoke the MidiUSB.flush method which sends everything in the buffer. This can be very useful for accumulating several MIDI messages and sending them out as close together as possible. As the Arduino no longer has a serial interface to reprogram it you must hold down the reset button until the IDE message says "Uploading" and then release it.

Summary

Armed with the knowledge of MIDI messages, you can now go on to the next three chapters, where you'll explore practical projects that you can do to enhance your MIDI music making. You can make things that intercept and modify a MIDI message to add echo, or chorus effects, to your music. You can make controllers that allow you to translate physical inputs into MIDI messages, like a bend sensor that generates pitch bend messages. You can make instruments that you can use to control a MIDI sound generator, like a MIDI Theremin, or make machines that play real instruments in response to MIDI messages. All these and more are waiting for you in the next three chapters.

■ ■ ■

CHAPTER 4

MIDI Manipulation

This chapter covers

- MIDI manipulation
- Double and triple tracking
- Automatic generation of triad chords
- A MIDI arpeggiator
- Delays and echoes
- A MIDI looper pedal

In the last chapter, you saw the wide range of MIDI messages available. Now it is time to do some magic and manipulate MIDI to achieve some funky tricks. The projects you will do in this chapter all have the same overall structure: they look at the MIDI messages coming in and then do something to them. This involves basically modifying the message and then outputting the modifications. By simply adding or subtracting a number to a note message as it flies past, you can transpose the note, or you can hold on to the message and send it later or even repeatedly send a MIDI message. There are a wide variety musical effects that can be obtained in this way, and no doubt you can come up with new ideas of your own to implement.

The MIDI Setup

The projects in this chapter intercept MIDI data from a keyboard or other MIDI instrument and basically muck about with it before passing it on. So what you need is an Arduino system with a MIDI input and output. The MIDI shield you saw in Chapter 2 is ideal for that sort of thing. The basic arrangement is shown in Figure 4-1.

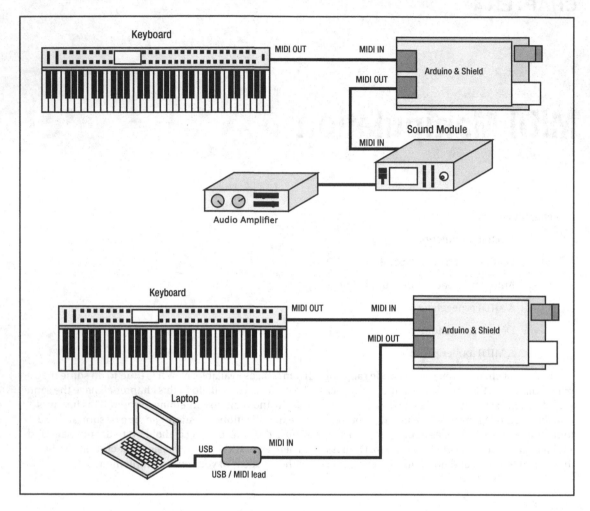

Figure 4-1. *Two basic MIDI setups*

Figure 4-1 shows two possible setups. Both have a MIDI keyboard outputting standard MIDI to the MIDI shield. In the top arrangement, the MIDI shield is connected to a sound module and therefore to an audio amplifier and speaker. This is great for live performances and is completely independent of any computer. The bottom arrangement shows the output of the MIDI shield being connected to a computer or laptop via a USB/MIDI lead or interface. Both those arrangements require a keyboard with a conventional MIDI output.

Many of the cheaper keyboards nowadays have only a USB output; with one of these you will need a different arrangement. As we saw in Chapter 2, the Arduino or Teensy can be made to act as a USB HID MIDI device, so if you do not know too much about USB you might be forgiven for thinking you could simply connect your keyboard to one of these devices. Unfortunately, there are two types of USB device, host and client. A host device is basically what your computer or laptop act as; it's the device that controls and gathers information from USB client devices. Client devices are sometimes called slave devices. Their job is to behave like a USB device and respond to requests sent by the host. So while it is comparatively easy to make a system that behaves like a client, behaving like a host is a lot more complex.

The upshot of this is that you can't plug in a keyboard to an Arduino or Teensy because they cannot very easily be made to be a host. So to get around this problem you need to use another type of setup, one that first connects your keyboard via USB to your computer and then routes it out to either a USB/MIDI interface or a USB HID MIDI-enabled Arduino or Teensy. That also includes the case of a normal Arduino along with running a helper program like Hairless on your computer. These two arrangements are shown in Figure 4-2.

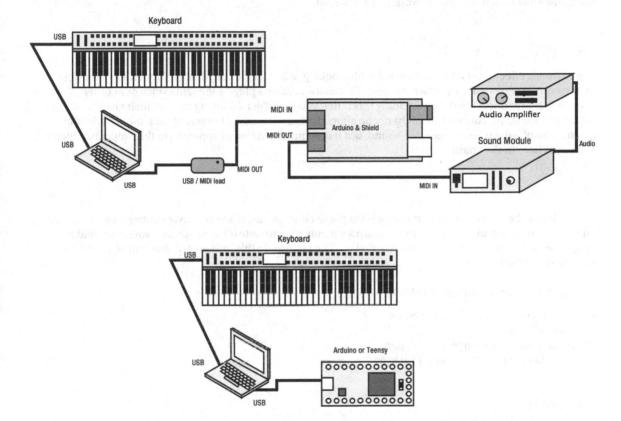

Figure 4-2. *Two USB keyboard setups*

Again the top one is great for live work despite having to drag your laptop to the gig. The bottom one is best for recording or interfacing with other programs like Ableton Live. The only snag with these arrangements is that you have to route your keyboard through to the MIDI/USB converter or the MIDI USB HID device. How you do this will depend on the MIDI software you have on your computer, but it will be just the same as any other MIDI routing you do in your system. For example, using the Hairless application, you route your keyboard into the MIDI IN of the Arduino, and you route the MIDI OUT from Hairless into your sound module or DAW (Digital Audio Workstation).

I tried this arrangement with GarageBand, but you will run into all sorts of difficulty if you try that. This is because GarageBand does not handle MIDI very well. I ended up getting infinite loops with output notes triggering input notes in a sort of MIDI howl around. Routing through to a language like PD was much easier.

However, easiest of all is to use the application MIDI patch bay from http://notahat.com/midi_patchbay/. This allows you to easily set up what MIDI IN or OUT goes to what device. If you are on a Mac running OSX 10.8 or later when you double-click you will get a message saying that this is from an unrecognized developer and will not run it. Fortunately, there is an easy way around this. You click on the icon and select Open, and then you get a dialog box where you can bypass the running restriction.

While it is not possible to get the Arduino to act as a USB host to directly connect to a USB keyboard, it is possible to get another processor to act as a host and connect that to the Arduino. To that end there are a number of so-called USB host shields that you can use between the keyboard and Arduino and replace the laptop shown in Figure 4-2. One popular shield is made by Circuits@home (http://www.circuitsathome.com). They have two versions: a full size 5V system and a miniature 3V3 one. While there are no MIDI examples as such, the Xbox USB interface will work as a MIDI host.

Double Tracking

The simplest effect you can get is that of double tracking, which occurs anytime an input note on or note off message is repeated on another channel. This channel can be playing the same voice or another complementary one. One danger of doing this is that you might get a flanging effect, which gives an overall unnatural sound (of course, this might not be altogether unwelcome). One way of overcoming this effect is to add a bit of a delay to the repeated sound, but that requires a different approach to the program, which I will cover later in the chapter.

Basic Double Tracking

The Arduino sketch to do double tracking is simple in concept. Just read every byte coming in and repeat it on the output. Then monitor the input stream for a note on and note off message, and when you find one simply send that note out on the next channel up. The code to do this with an Arduino and MIDI shield is shown in Listing 4-1.

Listing 4-1. Double Tracking for Shield

```
/* MIDI Double Track - Mike Cook
 * -----------------
 * listen for MIDI note on/off data,
 * and plays it on the next track up
 */

//variables setup
  boolean noteDown = LOW;
  byte channel = 0;  // MIDI channel to respond to (in this case channel 1)
                     //change this to change the channel number
                     // MIDI channel = the value in 'channel' + 1

//setup: declaring inputs and outputs and begin serial
void setup() {
  Serial.begin(31250); //start serial with MIDI baud rate
}

//loop: wait for serial data, and interpret the message
void loop () {
  checkIn(); // see if anything has arrived at the input
 }

void checkIn(){                          #A
  static byte note = 60;
  static byte state=0; // state machine variable 0 = command waiting
                       //: 1 = note waiting : 2 = velocity waiting
```

```
if (Serial.available() > 0) {
  // read the incoming byte:
 byte incomingByte = Serial.read();
 Serial.write(incomingByte); // act as a MIDI THRU

 switch (state){
    case 0:                                            #B
  // look for as status-byte, our channel, note on
     if (incomingByte == ( 0x90 | channel)){  // read only one channel
        noteDown = HIGH;
        state=1;
     }
  // look for as status-byte, our channel, note off
     if (incomingByte == (0x80 | channel)){   // read only one channel
        noteDown = LOW;
        state=1;
    }
     // look for any after touch, or program message
     if ((incomingByte & 0xE0) == 0xC0){
        state=4;  // just wait for the data
     }
     // look for any control or polyphonic after touch
     if ((incomingByte & 0xE0) == 0xA0){
        state=3;  // just wait for two bytes of data
     }
     // look for any pitch wheel or Channel Mode data
     if ((incomingByte & 0xF0) == 0xA0 || (incomingByte & 0xF0) == 0xB0){
        state=3;  // just wait for two bytes of data
     }
     break;
    case 1:                                            #C
   // get the note to play or stop
     if(incomingByte < 128) {
        note=incomingByte;
        state=2;
     }
     else {
       state = 0;  // reset state machine as this should be a note number
     }
     break;
    case 2:                                            #D
   // get the velocity
     if(incomingByte < 128) {
         doNote(note, incomingByte, noteDown);
     }
     state = 0;  // reset state machine to start
     break;
    case 3: // first of two bytes to discard         #E
    state = 4; // next byte to discard
     break;
```

```
       case 4: // data to discard                                    #E
       state = 0; // reset state machine
    }
  }
}

void doNote(byte note, byte velocity, int down){
  // if velocity = 0 on a 'Note ON' command, treat it as a note off
  if ((down == HIGH) && (velocity == 0)){
     down = LOW;
  }
  // send out this note message
  if(down == LOW) noteSend(0x80,note,velocity); // note off
  else  noteSend(0x90,note,velocity); // note on

}
 void noteSend(byte cmd, byte data1, byte data2) {
  cmd = cmd | byte((channel +1) & 0xf);   // next channel number up
  Serial.write(cmd);
  Serial.write(data1);
  Serial.write(data2);
}
```

#A The state machine for reading in a MIDI message over several bytes
#B This is the first byte so look and see what sort of message it might be
#C The second byte in a note message will be the note number
#D The third byte is the velocity - now we have all the note message
#E A multi byte message that we are not interested in so we just let the data pass

The bulk of the code is in the checkIn() function this reads each byte in turn and latches onto the note on and off messages for our channel. When it finds one it is a simple matter to output the note on the next channel up. Rather than simply add one to the channel, the code in the function adds one and then ANDs the result with 0xf. This ensures correct wrap round of the channel. That is, if the channel you have set the system to respond to is the highest one, channel 15 (MIDI channel 16), adding one to that would give a number that is five bytes long and would interfere with the message half of the byte. The AND function simply wipes all but the lower four bits from the channel number.

Analogue Double Tracking

There is an analogue studio effect known as ADT (analogue double tracking), and it takes a sound that would normally be panned close to the center of the stereo stage and doubles it by sending one note to the left and the other to the right. It is easy to change this code to do this; all you need to do is to replace the setup function and add another function, called controlSend, as shown in Listing 4-2.

Listing 4-2. Modifications to Listing 4-1 for the ADT Effect

```
void setup() {
  Serial.begin(31250); //start serial with MIDI baud rate
// set pan for the two channels
  controlSend(10, 0, channel); // MSB                                #A
  controlSend(42, 0, channel); // LSB                                #A
```

```
    controlSend(10, 127, (channel+1) & 0xf); // MSB                    #A
    controlSend(42, 127, (channel+1) & 0xf); // LSB                    #A
}

void controlSend(byte CCnumber, byte CCdata, byte CCchannel) {    #B
    CCchannel |= 0xB0; // convert to Controller message
     Serial.write(CCchannel);
     Serial.write(CCnumber);
     Serial.write(CCdata);
}
#A Set up the stereo position of each channel
#B Function to send out a controller change message to the specific channel
```

What you see here is that the setup function generates a controller message to set the pan positions hard left and right for the two channels. The extra controlSend function is rather like the noteSend function, but instead of passing in the command number and merging it with the channel, here the channel is passed in and merged with the command number for the Controller Change message.

Triple Tracking

Well, if two notes are good, then three might be even better. This is called triple tracking. You can make a variation of this effect where you send three notes, one to the left, one to the right, and the third to the middle of the channel. Just to make things sound fatter, the center note can be an octave lower and not as loud. The changes you have to make are shown in Listing 4-3. (Note that these are changes to the original Listing 4-1.)

Listing 4-3. Modifications to Listing 4-1 for the Triple Tracking Effect

```
void setup() {
    Serial.begin(31250); //start serial with MIDI baud rate
// set pan for the three channels
    controlSend(10, 0, channel); // MSB                                #A
    controlSend(42, 0, channel); // LSB
    controlSend(10, 127, (channel+1) & 0xf); // MSB                    #A
    controlSend(42, 127, (channel+1) & 0xf); // LSB
    controlSend(10, 64, (channel+2) & 0xf);  // MSB                    #A
    controlSend(42, 0, (channel+2) & 0xf);   // LSB
}
void doNote(byte note, byte velocity, int down){
    // if velocity = 0 on a 'Note ON' command, treat it as a note off
    if ((down == HIGH) && (velocity == 0)){
        down = LOW;
    }
    // send out this note message
    if(down == LOW){ // note off
     noteSend(0x80,note,velocity, 0x1);
     noteSend(0x80,note-12,velocity, 0x2);                            #B
    }
```

```
  else { // note on
    noteSend(0x90,note,velocity, 0x1);
    float v = (float)velocity * 0.75;                    #C
    noteSend(0x90,note-12,(byte)v, 0x2); // send third note
  }
}
 void noteSend(byte cmd, byte data1, byte data2, byte offset) {
  cmd = cmd | byte((channel + offset) & 0xf);  // next channel number up
  Serial.write(cmd);
  Serial.write(data1);
  Serial.write(data2);
}

void controlSend(byte CCnumber, byte CCdata, byte CCchannel) {
  CCchannel |= 0xB0; // convert to Controller message
   Serial.write(CCchannel);
  Serial.write(CCnumber);
  Serial.write(CCdata);
}
#A Set up the stereo position of each channel
#B Note an octave or 12 semitones lower
#C Reduce the volume by 75%
```

You can see that the controlSend function is just the same as the ADT effect and the setup function has an extra channel in it. However, the main change is to replace the doNote function with the one in the listing and change the noteSend function so that it accepts a channel offset parameter. Of particular interest are these lines:

```
float v = (float)velocity * 0.75;
noteSend(0x90,note-12,(byte)v, 0x2); // send third note
```

This does two things. First, it modifies the note by moving it down an octave. This is simply done by subtracting 12 from the note number. As each interval between note numbers is a semitone, then subtracting 12 shifts it down 12 semitones or an octave. Second, it reduces the velocity and hence the loudness of the note by 75%. This is achieved by multiplying the velocity value by 0.75. As the velocity value is a byte normally multiplying it by a fractional number would make it equal to zero, we first create a new variable of the type float to hold the result of the multiplication and then the velocity variable v is cast as a float. Cast is a C term meaning temporally treat this variable as one of another type. Note that we also have to cast the result back into a byte for the noteSend function. You have to watch the polyphony of your sound module, because for every key you press you are sending three and the total number of notes sounding at any time can quickly mount up.

Bonus: Doubling a Note with Triple Tracking

Finally, for a bit of fun, try modifying the program so that a note is repeated or doubled on channel 9. This, in General MIDI, is the default track for percussion and each note is a different percussion instrument. This makes the output a hilarious seemingly random collection of thumps, whistles, and hoots. I am not sure how artistic it is, but it is certainly a laugh.

All this applies to the Arduino and MIDI shield, if you want to use the Teensy in a USB-only setup then this can be done with Listing 4-4. This shows the triple tracking version of the code.

Listing 4-4. Triple Tracking for the Teensy

```
/* MIDI Double Track 3 - Mike Cook
 * for the Teensy board
 * -----------------
 * listen for MIDI note on/off data,
 * and play it on the next track up
 * pan this channel hard left and the other hard right
 * send a third note panned in the middle
 */

//variables setup
  const int led = 13;
  long time;
  boolean noteDown = LOW;
  const byte ourChannel = 1;  // MIDI channel to respond to (in this case channel 1)

//setup: declaring inputs and outputs
void setup() {
  pinMode(led, LOW);
  time = millis() + 2000;
// set up call back channels                                          #A
 usbMIDI.setHandleNoteOff(doNoteOff);
 usbMIDI.setHandleNoteOn(doNoteOn);
 usbMIDI.setHandleVelocityChange(doVelocityChange);
 usbMIDI.setHandleControlChange(doControlChange);
 usbMIDI.setHandleProgramChange(doProgramChange);
 usbMIDI.setHandleAfterTouch(doAfterTouch);
 usbMIDI.setHandlePitchChange(doPitchChange);
// set pan for the three channels                                     #B
 usbMIDI.sendControlChange(10, 0, ourChannel); // MSB
 usbMIDI.sendControlChange(42, 0, ourChannel); // LSB
 usbMIDI.sendControlChange(10, 127, (ourChannel+1) & 0xf); // MSB
 usbMIDI.sendControlChange(42, 127, (ourChannel+1) & 0xf); // LSB
 usbMIDI.sendControlChange(10, 64, (ourChannel+2) & 0xf);  // MSB
 usbMIDI.sendControlChange(42, 0, (ourChannel+2) & 0xf);   // LSB
}

//loop: wait for serial data, and interpret the message
void loop () {
  usbMIDI.read();                                                     #C
 }

  // call back functions basically echo most stuff
  void doVelocityChange(byte channel, byte note, byte velocity){      #D
    usbMIDI.sendPolyPressure(note, velocity, channel);
  }

  void doControlChange(byte channel, byte control, byte value){       #D
    usbMIDI.sendControlChange(control, value, channel);
  }
```

```
  void doProgramChange(byte channel, byte program){               #D
    usbMIDI.sendProgramChange(program, channel);
  }


  void doAfterTouch(byte channel, byte pressure){                 #D
    usbMIDI.sendAfterTouch(pressure, channel);
  }

  void doPitchChange(byte channel, int pitch){                    #D
    usbMIDI.sendPitchBend(pitch, channel);
  }

  void doNoteOn(byte channel, byte note, byte velocity){          #E
    digitalWrite(led, HIGH);
    usbMIDI.sendNoteOn(note, velocity, channel);
    if( channel == ourChannel){ // pick out the note we are looking for
      doNote(note, velocity, true);
    }
  }
  void doNoteOff(byte channel, byte note, byte velocity){         #E
    digitalWrite(led, LOW);
    usbMIDI.sendNoteOn(note, velocity, channel);
     if( channel == ourChannel){ // pick out the note we are looking for
      doNote(note, velocity, false);
    }
  }

void doNote(byte note, byte velocity, int down){
  // if velocity = 0 on a 'Note ON' command, treat it as a note off
  if ((down == HIGH) && (velocity == 0)){
      down = LOW;
  }
  // send out this note message
  if(down == LOW){ // note off
    usbMIDI.sendNoteOff(note, velocity, (ourChannel + 1) & 0xf);
    usbMIDI.sendNoteOff(note, velocity, (ourChannel + 2) & 0xf);
  }
  else { // note on
    usbMIDI.sendNoteOn(note, velocity, (ourChannel + 1) & 0xf);
    float v = (float)velocity * 0.75;
    usbMIDI.sendNoteOff(note -12,(byte)v, (ourChannel + 2) & 0xf);
  }
}
```

#A Tell the built in MIDI library what function to call when each MIDI event happens
#B Send stereo position information to your sound module
#C Checks for any MIDI message and calls the previously declared function if one has arrived
#D We don't want to do anything about these messages just pass them through
#E This is a message we want to do something with

Here you see the code is made very much shorter by the use of the MIDI library functions. Most of the code involves setting up the callback function and writing functions that just act as a MIDI THRU. Then when the note on and off messages are detected, the execution is directed to the doNote function, which is not too dissimilar from the normal Arduino function. By studying this program, you should be able to see how to modify the other sketches in this chapter for the Teensy.

The One Finger Wonder

Imagine if you had limited keyboard skills but could pick out a note with one finger and that produced a whole glorious chord. This is what the One Finger Wonder program can do for you. This is similar to the double tracking program, only here the Arduino is used to generate a triad chord from any input note. What is more, the type of the chord can be changed by external switches and the whole effect can be turned on and off from a foot switch, to make a much more configurable effect. This requires a few hardware switches to be added to the Arduino, but that is all. First though, let's examine the anatomy of a triad.

Triad Chord Basics

As the name implies, a triad is three notes—a root note is played at the same time as two other notes spaced one third and one fifth away from the root. In fact, there are four types of triad: major, minor, diminished, and augmented. The differences are made by slight changes in the two notes above the root. Table 4-1 shows the four different types and the notes that make it up.

Table 4-1. *The Four Types of Triad Chord*

Type	Third	Fifth
Major	+4 from root	+7 from root
Minor	+3 from root	+7 from root
Diminished	+3 from root	+6 from root
Augmented	+4 from root	+8 from root

From a musical perspective, the triad chord is shown in Figure 4-3.

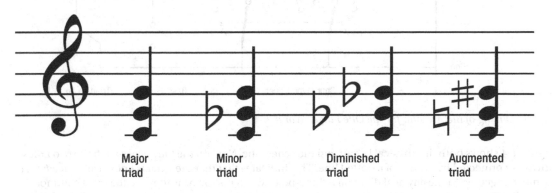

Figure 4-3. *The four types of triad chord on a stave*

Creating a Triad Chord with Arduino

The best way of controlling the type of triad is with a four-way rotary switch wired up to give a two-bit binary count. To do this, you need a four-way two-pole switch; however, what you will find at component suppliers is a four-way three-pole switch. This is fine; just ignore the other pole.

The wiring of the switches is shown in Figure 4-4. Note that no pull-up resistor is required because the internal pull-up resistors will be enabled in the software.

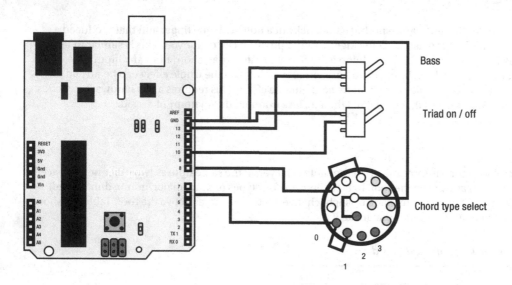

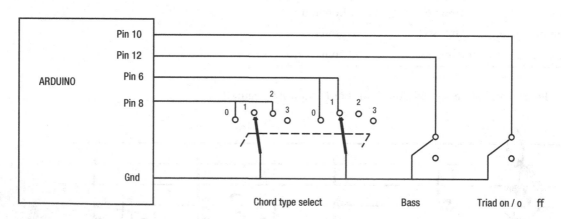

Figure 4-4. *Wiring of the Arduino for the One Finger Wonder*

Figure 4-4 shows both the physical layout and the schematic. Note on the four-way switch the two poles are shown as connected by the use of a dotted line. This indicates that they are what is known as *ganged*; that is, they move together. In the physical diagram a three-pole switch is shown, as they are the most common type you will find, and one of the poles is unused. It might be difficult to locate exactly what contact is what. Use a continuity meter if there is any doubt to check. The switch positions are labeled 0 to 3 and these correspond to the chord types shown in Table 4-1. The Triad on/off switch might be best if it is implemented as a foot switch, because it allows the performer to easily turn the effect on or off. Once you have wired the switches, you need to enter the code shown in Listing 4-5 for an Arduino.

Listing 4-5. The One Finger Wonder

```
/* Midi One Finger Wonder - Mike Cook
 * -----------------
 * Generates triads,
 */

//variables setup
  boolean noteDown = LOW;
  byte channel = 0;  // MIDI channel to respond to
                     // MIDI channel = the value in 'channel' + 1
  boolean bass = true, enableTriad = true;
  byte triad = 0;
  const int bassPin = 12, triadPin = 10;
  const int triadPin1 = 8, triadPin2 = 6;
  // Major, minor, diminished, augmented
  byte thirds [] = {4, 3, 3, 4};
  byte fifths [] = {7, 7, 6, 8};

//setup: declaring inputs and outputs and begin serial
void setup() {
  pinMode(bassPin, INPUT_PULLUP);                    #A
  pinMode(triadPin, INPUT_PULLUP);                   #A
  pinMode(triadPin1, INPUT_PULLUP);                  #A
  pinMode(triadPin2, INPUT_PULLUP);                  #A
  Serial.begin(31250); //start serial with MIDI baud rate
}

//loop: wait for serial data, and interpret the message
void loop () {
  checkIn(); // see if anything has arrived at the input
  getControls(); // get switch values
  }

void getControls(){                                #B
  bass = digitalRead(bassPin);
  triad = (digitalRead(triadPin1) & 0x1) | ((digitalRead(triadPin2) & 0x1) << 1);
  enableTriad = digitalRead(triadPin);
}

void doNote(byte note, byte velocity, int down){
  // if velocity = 0 on a 'Note ON' command, treat it as a note off
  if ((down == HIGH) && (velocity == 0)){
     down = LOW;
  }
```

```
 // send the other notes of the triad
 if(down == LOW) { // note off
  if(enableTriad){                                              #C
     noteSend(0x80,note+thirds[triad],velocity);
     noteSend(0x80,note+fifths[triad],velocity);
     if(bass) noteSend(0x80,note-12,velocity);
    }
   }
  else{ // note on
   if(enableTriad){                                             #C
      noteSend(0x90,note+thirds[triad],velocity);
      noteSend(0x90,note+fifths[triad],velocity);
      if(bass) noteSend(0x90,note-12,velocity);
    }
  }
}

 void noteSend(char cmd, char data1, char data2) {
  cmd = cmd | char(channel);  // next channel number up
  Serial.write(cmd);
  Serial.write(data1);
  Serial.write(data2);
}

void checkIn(){
  static byte note = 60;
  static byte state=0; // state machine variable
  if (Serial.available() > 0) {
    // read the incoming byte:
   byte incomingByte = Serial.read();
   Serial.write(incomingByte);

   switch (state){                                              #D
      case 0:
    // look for as status-byte, our channel, note on
        if (incomingByte == ( 0x90 | channel)){  // read only one channel
           noteDown = HIGH;
           state=1;
        }
    // look for as status-byte, our channel, note off
        if (incomingByte == (0x80 | channel)){   // read only one channel
           noteDown = LOW;
           state=1;
           }
       break;
      case 1:
      // get the note to play or stop
        if(incomingByte < 128) {
           note=incomingByte;
           state=2;
        }
```

```
        else {
           state = 0;  // reset state machine as this should be a note number
           }
        break;
     case 2:
     // get the velocity
        if(incomingByte < 128) {
            doNote(note, incomingByte, noteDown); // do something with the note on message
            }
        state = 0;  // reset state machine to start
     }
   }
}
#A Tell the Arduino to enable the internal pull up resistors so the inputs don't float
#B Look at the state of the switches incase they have changed
#C Send three notes all relative to the original note
#D We have seen this before in the other listings - tease the MIDI message from the input
   stream
```

Some of the functions are very much like those you have seen in the other code listings. The checkIn function is a bit simpler as it only has to fish out note on and note off messages. However, there are other functions needed to handle the switch inputs. The four physical pins you need to use are set up in the code as the data type const int, this means you can't change them in the code without generating a compile error. If you want to assign the switch inputs to other pins, here is where you change the assignments. There are two arrays declared called thirds and fifths. These hold the number of semitones offset from the root of the note. The setup function sets these pins to be inputs and enables the internal pull-up resistor. This means that with nothing connected to the pins, they will read as a logic 1. Likewise, when a pin is connected to ground, it will read a logic 0.

The loop function does two jobs—it calls the checkIn function like before and calls the getControls function to read the switches. Setting the enableTriad and the bass variables is just a matter of reading the appropriate pin; however, when it comes to the triad variable this is made from the four-way switch and puts the value read from the triadPin1 pin in the least significant bit of the byte. The value read from triadPin2 input is placed in the next bit up. Thus a two-bit number is formed that can range from 0 to 3, and it's used as an index for the look-up table or array.

The doNote function is called when there is a note to send, and if the Triad on/off switch is set to on, the two notes forming the third and fifth interval are generated by looking the note offset to use. This offset is then added to the note number of the root note to calculate the note numbers to use. Then, if the bass note is enabled, a third note is generated an octave down from the note played.

The result sounds rather good. Fat dramatic chords replace thin notes and you feel that a beginner has just moved up to the next level.

The Arpeggiator

The arpeggiator plays at regular intervals any note that is held down. So hold down a single note and you will get a constant stream of the same note. Hold down two notes and these two will play alternately and continuously. The same applies when many notes are held down. This brings up a concept you have not seen before. In previously programs in this chapter the Arduino only generated a note or notes when other notes were received, but now there has to be a note generated in the absence of any keyboard input. This requires two new techniques. First of all, the note, and the time it must be played, must be held in an area of the processor's memory, or as we say, a *buffer*. Second, when it comes time to send that note you have to be careful that it is not produced in the middle of another MIDI message being received or passed on, as this would garble both messages. This is done by looking at the state variable, and only generating a MIDI message when the state variable indicates it is waiting for the start of a message and only when it is time to output the message. If a MIDI message starts in the middle of sending a new note message, this is no problem because it will be held in the serial buffer of the Arduino until it has time to read it all. This sounds like it could delay things, but in practice it all runs so very fast that any extra delays introduced are simply not perceivable.

Building a Simple Arpeggiator

In the simple version of the arpeggiator you only need to implement one external control—that is a potentiometer, or *pot*, which controls the delay between the notes. Figure 4-5 shows both the physical and schematic wiring.

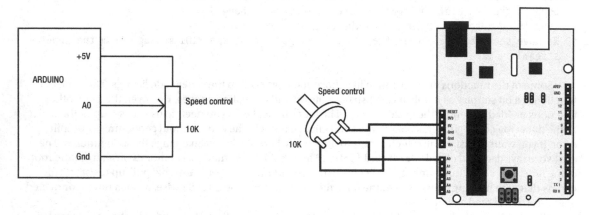

Figure 4-5. *The Arpeggiator speed control*

Note that it is the center connection on the pot that is the wiper you need to connect to the analogue input. The best value of pot to use is 10K, although you can use up to 50K (any larger and the readings tend to be prone to interference and you will not get a steady value read from the pot).

Having wired it up, you can then enter the code shown in Listing 4-6.

Listing 4-6. A Simple Arpeggiator

```
/* Midi arpeggiator - Mike Cook
 * ------------------
 * Repeats all notes held down note
 * interval controlled by pot on A0
 */

#define bufferLength 40
  //variables setup
    boolean noteDown = LOW;
    const int led = 13;
    byte channel = 0;      // MIDI channel = the value in 'channel' + 1
    byte state=0;          // state machine variable 0 = command waiting :
                           // 1 = note waiting : 2 = velocity waiting
```

```
// buffer for delayed notes
  byte storeNote[bufferLength];
  byte storeVel[bufferLength];
  unsigned long aDelay = 300;
  unsigned long time = 0;

//setup: declaring inputs and outputs and begin serial
void setup() {
  pinMode(led,OUTPUT);       // LED to light up
  digitalWrite(led,LOW);     // Turn LED off
  Serial.begin(31250);       //start serial with MIDI baud rate
  time = millis() +aDelay;
 }

//loop: wait for serial data, and interpret the message
void loop () {
  checkIn(); // see if anything has arrived at the input
  if(state == 0) checkOut(); // see if we need to send anything out    #A
  aDelay = analogRead(0);    // read delay value
  }

void checkIn(){                                                        #B
  static byte note = 60;

  if (Serial.available() > 0) {
    // read the incoming byte:
    byte incomingByte = Serial.read();
    Serial.write(incomingByte); // make thru everything received

   switch (state){
      case 0:
      // look for a status-byte, our channel, note on
         if (incomingByte == ( 0x90 | channel)){  // read only one channel
            noteDown = HIGH;
            state=1;
         }
      // look for a status-byte, our channel, note off
         if (incomingByte == (0x80 | channel)){   // read only one channel
            noteDown = LOW;
            state=1;
         }
      // look for as after touch, our channel
         if (incomingByte == (0xD0 | channel)){   // read only one channel
            state=3;
         }
        break;
       case 1:
       // get the note to play or stop
         if(incomingByte < 128) {
            note=incomingByte;
            state=2;
         }
```

```
            else {
               state = 0;  // reset state machine as this should be a note number
            }
          break;

        case 2:
        // get the velocity
           if(incomingByte < 128) {
               doNote(note, incomingByte, noteDown); // do something with the note on message
           }
           state = 0;  // reset state machine to start
        break;

        case 3: // aftertouch data
        state = 0; // reset state machine
      }
   }
}

void doNote(byte note, byte velocity, int down){
  // if velocity = 0 on a 'Note ON' command, treat it as a note off
  if ((down == HIGH) && (velocity == 0)){
     down = LOW;
  }
  // do something with the note message

  if(down == LOW) { // remove the note from the buffer
     bufferRemove(note,velocity);
     digitalWrite(led, LOW);     // Turn LED off
  }
  else{ // save the note on in a buffer
    bufferSave(note,velocity);
    digitalWrite(led, HIGH);      // Turn LED on
  }
}
void noteSend(byte cmd, byte data1, byte data2) {
  cmd = cmd | channel;  // add channel
  Serial.write(cmd);
  Serial.write(data1);
  Serial.write(data2);
}

void bufferSave(byte note, byte vel){                      #C
  // search for a free space
  int place = 0;
  while( storeNote[place] !=(byte)0 && place < bufferLength) place++;
  if(place < bufferLength){ // found one
    storeNote[place] = note;
    storeVel[place] = vel;
    time = millis() + aDelay; // reset arpeggiator timing
  }
}
```

84

```
void bufferRemove(byte note, byte vel){                              #D
  // search for the note
  int place = 0;
  while( storeNote[place] != note && place < bufferLength) place++;
  if(place < bufferLength){ // found it
    noteSend(0x80, storeNote[place], 0); // stop note from sounding
    storeNote[place] = 0;
  }
}

void checkOut(){ // see if we need to send anything from the buffer
 static int place =0;
 int count = 0;
 if(millis() > time){                                                #E
   place++;
   if(place >= bufferLength) place = 0;
   time = millis() + aDelay;
    while(storeNote[place] == 0 && count < bufferLength){
      place++;
      if(place >= bufferLength) place = 0;
      count++;
    }
 if(count < bufferLength) { // found next note to output
     noteSend(0x80, storeNote[place], 0); // turn previous note off
     noteSend(0x90, storeNote[place], storeVel[place]); // trigger note again
  }
 }
}
```
#A Only look to send out a MIDI message when we are waiting for a message to start otherwise
    the message being sent out at the time will be screwed up
#B Just as we have seen before only the state variable is global so other routines can see
    it and not send something out mid message
#C Store the note and velocity so we can play it back later
#D That note key has now been released so there is no need to keep on playing it
#E See if it is time to play a note, if it is take a copy out of the buffer and play it

Again this code owes a lot to the previous projects. The main change to the checkIn function is that now the state variable is not local to the function but is global. This means it can be read anywhere in the code. This has its dangers in that it could be changed anywhere in the code and thus mess up the state machine. You just have to be careful not to do this.

The memory buffer to hold the information about the currently held down notes consists of two arrays: storeNote and storeVel. Each one has the same size. This is controlled by the bufferLength hash definition. The idea is that when a note on message is received, that note and its velocity are stored in the buffer by the bufferSave function. When a note off message is received, that note is removed from the buffer by the bufferRemove function. Removal simply consists of setting the note number to zero.

Notes could be going on and off in any order, and this results in a buffer that can be full of holes. That is, there can be entries that are being used anywhere in the buffer. Therefore, when it comes time to play a note from the buffer, the program must search through the buffer until it finds a non-zero note value. It should then play that note and remember where it found the note so that it starts looking from the next entry the next time it comes to play a note.

The speed of outputting the buffer is controlled by the pot connected to the analogue input. This gives a reading between 0 and 1023, and the value can be used directly as a delay value in milliseconds. This program uses the millisecond system clock that returns the number of milliseconds that has elapsed since the Arduino was powered up. The current time plus the reading from the pot allows you to generate the time variable, which is the value that must be reached by the system clock before the next note is output. The checkOut function will test to see if it is time to produce the next note and, if it is, it will search the buffer for it. When it finds the note it then sends a note off message to stop the note from last time and then send a note on message to play it again.

Building an Enhanced Arpeggiator

While this simple arpeggiator is useful and fun, with the addition of a few switches and LEDs, you can make it much more interesting and even enable it to generate rhythms on its own. Figure 4-6 shows the schematic wiring of the enhanced arpeggiator. When it gets to this many components, a physical view of the wiring is just not helpful. It looks a mess of tangled wires. With the schematic the diagram is as simple as it can be, and in this case it is very easy to follow.

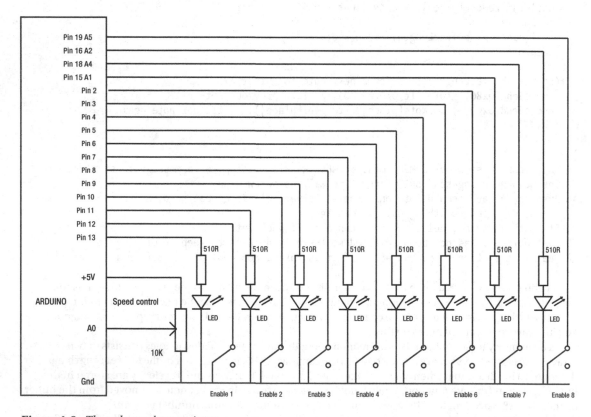

Figure 4-6. *The enhanced arpeggiator*

The idea is that each switch controls whether a note will be sent from the buffer or not, whereas the LED next to the switch will light when a note is played. I used a 510R resistor for LED current limiting. This will not light them up fully, but they will be bright enough to look at directly. If you are using this in a low light level environment, you might even consider making these resistors larger; a value of 1K or 2K2 is not out of the question. Also note that I have used some of the analogue inputs as digital inputs or outputs: the input A0 is referred to as pin 14, A1 as pin 15, and so on. The code that drives this is basically the same as the simple arpeggiator with a few minor changes. These changes are shown in Listing 4-7.

Listing 4-7. Changes to the Simple Arpeggiator Listing 4-6

```
byte inPins[] = {12, 10, 8, 6, 4, 2, 15, 16};                          #A
byte outPins[] = {13, 11, 9, 7, 5, 3, 18, 19};
byte sequenceLength = 8;

void setup() {
  for(int i=0; i<8;i++){
    pinMode(inPins[i], INPUT_PULLUP);
    pinMode(outPins[i], OUTPUT);
  }
  Serial.begin(31250); //start serial with MIDI baud rate
  time = millis() +aDelay;
}

void checkOut(){ // see if we need to send anything from the buffer
 static int place =0;
 static int lastStep = 0, arpStep = 0;
 int count = 0;
 if(millis() > time){
   place++;
   if(place >= bufferLength) place = 0;
   time = millis() + aDelay;
     while(storeNote[place] == 0 && count < bufferLength){
       place++;
       if(place >= bufferLength) place = 0;
       count++;
     }
  if(count < bufferLength) { // found next note to output
     arpStep++;
     if(arpStep >= sequenceLength) arpStep = 0;
     digitalWrite(outPins[lastStep],LOW); // turn last LED off
     if(digitalRead(inPins[arpStep])){                                 #B
       noteSend(0x80, storeNote[place], 0); // turn previous note off
       noteSend(0x90, storeNote[place], storeVel[place]); // trigger note again
       digitalWrite(outPins[arpStep],HIGH);
     }
         lastStep = arpStep;
   }
 }
}
#A Define the pins to use for input and output
#B Only play a note and light an LED if that playing position is enabled with a switch
```

The first two lines defining the pins used for the input and output should be placed at the start of the code, outside of any function, whereas the setup and checkOut functions should replace the function code in Listing 4-6. So now, hold down a single key and watch the lights run along as each note is produced. Clicking the switches will put gaps in that output and give the arpeggiated notes a rhythm. As there are eight steps in a sequence before repeat, it is ideally suited to music in the 4:4 time signature. If you want something better suited to other time signatures, you can change the variable sequenceLength to other values like 6 or 5, in fact anything less than 8. There is even a free input left on the Arduino, pin 17 or A3. You could add a switch to that and choose two different sequence lengths.

Echo and Delays

Going back to the double or triple tracking project, remember when I said that one way to avoid flanging was to have a small delay between the note from the keyboard and the repeated note? Well, that sort of thing is known as an *echo*. As in previous projects, there are two versions of this effect—a simple single echo and a configurable multi-echo system. Let's start with the simpler one first.

The Single Echo

You will need to add a speed control pot to your Arduino like you did on the Simple Arpeggiator project shown in Figure 4-5. This controls the amount of delay on the echo. In a way this is a combination of the arpeggiator and the double tracking. Whenever a note on or off message is detected, that note is placed into a buffer, only with this project, the time when the note has to be played is also stored in another array. This time is made up from the time now, when the note was played as given by the system clock, plus the delay time given by the pot reading. When it comes to outputting the note, the playing function must search all the entries in the time array to find one that is not zero and whose time value has passed the current system time. If it finds one, then that note message is sent and the buffer entry is cleared by setting the time array entry to zero. Let's look at the code to do this, shown in Listing 4-8.

Listing 4-8. Single Echo

```
/* Midi Echo 1 - Mike Cook
 * -----------------
 * Echoes a note on the same channel after a delay
 */

#define bufferLength 20

//variables setup                                                    #A
  boolean noteDown = LOW;
  byte channel = 0; // MIDI channel = the value in 'channel' + 1
  static int state=0; // state machine variable 0 = command waiting
 // buffer for delayed notes
 unsigned long time [bufferLength];
 byte storeAction[bufferLength];
 byte storeNote[bufferLength];
 byte storeVel[bufferLength];
 unsigned long eDelay = 800;

//setup: declaring inputs and outputs and begin serial
void setup() {
  Serial.begin(31250); //start serial with MIDI baud rate
}
```

```
//loop: wait for serial data, and interpret the message
void loop () {
  checkIn(); // see if anything has arrived at the input
  if(state == 0) checkOut(); // see if we need to send anything out
  eDelay = analogRead(0); // read delay value
  }

void checkIn(){                                          #B
  static byte note = 60;
  if (Serial.available() > 0) {
    // read the incoming byte:
    byte incomingByte = Serial.read();
    Serial.write(incomingByte);

  switch (state){
      case 0:
      // look for as status-byte, our channel, note on
          if (incomingByte == ( 0x90 | channel)){  // read only one channel
            noteDown = HIGH;
            state=1;
          }
      // look for as status-byte, our channel, note off
          if (incomingByte == (0x80 | channel)){   // read only one channel
            noteDown = LOW;
            state=1;
        }
          // look for any after touch, or program message
          if ((incomingByte & 0xE0) == 0xC0){
            state=4;  // just wait for the data
          }
          // look for any control or polyphonic after touch
          if ((incomingByte & 0xE0) == 0xA0){
            state=3;  // just wait for two bytes of data
          }
          // look for any pitch wheel or Channel Mode data
          if ((incomingByte & 0xF0) == 0xA0 || (incomingByte & 0xF0) == 0xB0){
            state=3;  // just wait for two bytes of data
          }
          break;
        case 1:
        // get the note to play or stop
          if(incomingByte < 128) {
            note=incomingByte;
            state=2;
          }
          else {
            state = 0;  // reset state machine as this should be a note number
          }
          break;
```

```
        case 2:
        // get the velocity
          if(incomingByte < 128) {
              doNote(note, incomingByte, noteDown); // do something withh the note on message
          }
          state = 0;   // reset state machine to start
        break;
        case 3: // first of two bytes to discard
        state = 4; // next byte to discard
          break;
        case 4: // data to discard
        state = 0; // reset state machine
      }
    }
}

void doNote(byte note, byte velocity, int down){
  // if velocity = 0 on a 'Note ON' command, treat it as a note off
  if ((down == HIGH) && (velocity == 0)){
      down = LOW;
  }
  // do something with the note message

  if(down == LOW) { // save the note off in a buffer
      bufferSave(0x80,note,velocity);
  }
  else{ // save the note on in a buffer
      bufferSave(0x90,note,velocity);
  }
}
void noteSend(byte cmd, byte data1, byte data2) {
  cmd = cmd | ((channel+1) & 0xf);   // next channel number up
  Serial.write(cmd);
  Serial.write(data1);
  Serial.write(data2);
}

void bufferSave(byte action, byte note, byte vel){
  // search for a free space
  int place = 0;
  while( time[place] !=0 && place < bufferLength) place++;
  if(place < bufferLength){ // found one
    time[place] = millis() + eDelay;
    storeAction[place] = action;                        #C
    storeNote[place] = note;
    storeVel[place] = vel;
  }
}
```

```
void checkOut(){ // see if we need to send anything from the buffer
  for( int place=0; place < bufferLength; place++){
    if(time[place] !=0 && millis() > time[place]){ // time to send something out
      noteSend(storeAction[place], storeNote[place], storeVel[place]);
      time[place] = 0; // wipe buffer entry
    }
  }
}
#A These are the global variables used to control and store the notes
#B You should be getting used to this function by now
#C We store the sort of message here, not on or note off
```

In contrast to previous programs, this one has four arrays making up the buffer. The extra two are time for storing the system time when the MIDI message must be replayed and storeAction for storing the sort of message—note on or note off. Most of the code is as before, so let's focus on what's new and different. As it stands, you get a maximum delay of just over a second from the values read from the pot. An easy way to double or halve this range is to apply a simple shift to the line that reads in the code like this:

```
eDelay = analogRead(0) << 1; // give a 2 second maximum delay
eDelay = analogRead(0) >> 1; // give a 0.5 second maximum delay
```

If you want to change the delay range of the pot, then one of those lines should replace the original line in the function. With a single echo set to a longish time, you can play small phrases and have it automatically repeated, while setting the delay to a very short time will give a fuller sound to the single note. You can also experiment here by reducing the on velocity of the echoed note just like you did with the triple tracking program. This is because echoes normally fade away, but you can make them get louder if you want.

The Multi-Echo

Well, if one echo is good, then what about more? If you are prepared to add a bit of extra hardware, you can control the number of echoes and the timing between them. This gives multiple effects depending on the delay value you set. For example, if you enable the maximum number of echoes, which is four (plus the original note makes five notes), and you set a very short time between them, using a guitar type sound you get a very good multiple "plectrum plucking" effect that is used on lots of indie guitar songs.

So to get control for this effect you need to add four pots to set the delays, four switches to enable each echo, and two switches to set the delay mode. This is shown in the schematic of Figure 4-7.

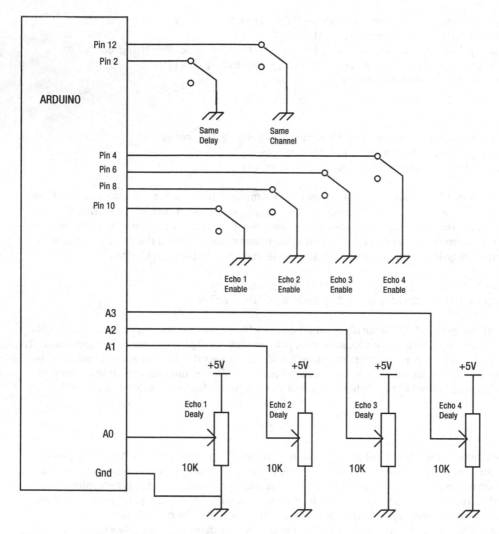

Figure 4-7. *Enhanced echo schematic*

Again I have included the schematic because with this many components the physical layout diagram looks more daunting than it really is. Note the use of the ground symbol to show points that are connected together and to the ground without having a lot of wires crossing each other. The same goes for the 5V on the analogue pots.

The Echo Enable switches control if an echo is produced at each of the four possible delay times. These switches govern if the note is entered into the memory buffer. The Same Delay switch governs if the delay between all the echoes is the same. If it is, they are all controlled by the first pot, called Echo Delay 1. If not, each pot controls the delay to the next echo note. This includes situations where the delay is inhibited, as the inhibited delay time still contributes to the delay for the next note. How this comes together in the software is shown in Listing 4-9. This time I have included the whole code because there are sufficient changes from the simple echo code to make this the simplest option.

Listing 4-9. Enhanced echo code

```
/* Midi Echo 2 - Mike Cook
 * -----------------
 * Echoes a note on the same channel after a delay
 * Up to four echoes with individual time control
 * and mode control for the timing.
 */

#define bufferLength 80                                    #A

//variables setup
  boolean noteDown = LOW;
  const int led = 13;
  byte channel = 0;  // MIDI channel = the value in 'channel' + 1
  static int state=0; // state machine variable 0 = command waiting
  // buffer for delayed notes
  unsigned long time [bufferLength];
  byte storeAction[bufferLength];
  byte storeNote[bufferLength];
  byte storeVel[bufferLength];
  unsigned long eDelay1 = 800, eDelay2 = 800, eDelay3 = 800, eDelay4 = 800;
  boolean echoChan = false, delay1 = false, delay2 = false,  delay3 = false;
  boolean delay4 = false, sameDelay = false;
  const byte echoChanPin = 12;                             #B
  const byte delay1Pin = 10;                               #B
  const byte delay2Pin = 8;                                #B
  const byte delay3Pin = 6;                                #B
  const byte delay4Pin = 4;                                #B
  const byte sameDelayPin = 2; // gives all echos same delay from one pot

//setup: declaring inputs and outputs and begin serial
void setup() {
  pinMode(led,OUTPUT);         // LED to light up
  pinMode(echoChanPin, INPUT_PULLUP);
  pinMode(delay1Pin, INPUT_PULLUP);
  pinMode(delay2Pin, INPUT_PULLUP);
  pinMode(delay3Pin, INPUT_PULLUP);
  pinMode(delay4Pin, INPUT_PULLUP);
  pinMode(sameDelayPin, INPUT_PULLUP);
  digitalWrite(led,LOW);       // Turn LED off
  Serial.begin(31250); //start serial with MIDI baud rate
}

//loop: wait for serial data, and interpret the message
void loop () {
  checkIn(); // see if anything has arrived at the input
  if(state == 0)digitalWrite(led,LOW); else digitalWrite(led,HIGH);
    if(state == 0) checkOut(); // see if we need to send anything out
    else {
      getControls();
    }
  }
```

```
void getControls(){
  // get analogue delays
    eDelay1 = analogRead(0)<< 1;                                    #C
    eDelay2 = analogRead(1)<< 1;
    eDelay3 = analogRead(2)<< 1;
    eDelay4 = analogRead(3)<< 1;
 // get digital controls
   echoChan = digitalRead(echoChanPin);
   delay1 = digitalRead(delay1Pin);
   delay2 = digitalRead(delay2Pin);
   delay3 = digitalRead(delay3Pin);
   delay4 = digitalRead(delay4Pin);
   sameDelay = digitalRead(sameDelayPin);
}

void checkIn(){
  static byte note = 60;
  if (Serial.available() > 0) {
    // read the incoming byte:
    byte incomingByte = Serial.read();
    Serial.write(incomingByte);

  switch (state){
      case 0:
    // look for as status-byte, our channel, note on
        if (incomingByte == ( 0x90 | channel)){  // read only one channel
          noteDown = HIGH;
          state=1;
        }
    // look for as status-byte, our channel, note off
        if (incomingByte == (0x80 | channel)){   // read only one channel
          noteDown = LOW;
          state=1;
      }
        // look for any after touch, or program message
        if ((incomingByte & 0xE0) == 0xC0){
          state=4;  // just wait for the data
        }
        // look for any control or polyphonic after touch
        if ((incomingByte & 0xE0) == 0xA0){
          state=3;  // just wait for two bytes of data
        }
        // look for any pitch wheel or Channel Mode data
        if ((incomingByte & 0xF0) == 0xA0 || (incomingByte & 0xF0) == 0xB0){
          state=3;  // just wait for two bytes of data
        }
        break;
```

```
        case 1:
        // get the note to play or stop
          if(incomingByte < 128) {
              note=incomingByte;
              state=2;
          }
          else {
            state = 0;   // reset state machine as this should be a note number
          }
        break;
        case 2:
        // get the velocity
          if(incomingByte < 128) {
              doNote(note, incomingByte, noteDown); // do something with the note on message
          }
          state = 0;   // reset state machine to start
          break;
        case 3: // first of two bytes to discard
        state = 4; // next byte to discard
          break;
        case 4: // data to discard
        state = 0; // reset state machine
      }
    }
}

void doNote(byte note, byte velocity, int down){
  // if velocity = 0 on a 'Note ON' command, treat it as a note off
  if ((down == HIGH) && (velocity == 0)){
     down = LOW;
  }
  // do something with the note message
  byte action = 0x90;
  if(down == LOW) { // save the note off in a buffer
  action = 0x80;
  }
  if (sameDelay){// use one pot for all delays                    #D
    if(delay1) bufferSave(action,note,velocity,eDelay1);
    if(delay2) bufferSave(action,note,velocity,eDelay1*2);
    if(delay3) bufferSave(action,note,velocity,eDelay1*3);
    if(delay4) bufferSave(action,note,velocity,eDelay1*4);

  }
  else { // use a separate pot for each delay                    #E
    if(delay1) bufferSave(action,note,velocity,eDelay1);
    if(delay2) bufferSave(action,note,velocity,eDelay1+eDelay2);
    if(delay3) bufferSave(action,note,velocity,eDelay1+eDelay2+eDelay3);
    if(delay4) bufferSave(action,note,velocity,eDelay1+eDelay2+eDelay3+eDelay4);
  }
}
```

```
void noteSend(byte cmd, byte data1, byte data2) {
  if(echoChan) {
  cmd = cmd | channel;
  }
  else{
  // cmd = cmd | 9; // send on drum channel
  cmd = cmd | ((channel+1) & 0xf);  // next channel number up
  }
  Serial.write(cmd);
  Serial.write(data1);
  Serial.write(data2);
}

void bufferSave(byte action, byte note, byte vel, long int echo){
  // search for a free space
  int place = 0;
  while( time[place] !=0 && place < bufferLength) place++;
  if(place < bufferLength){ // found one
    time[place] = millis() + echo;
    storeAction[place] = action;
    storeNote[place] = note;
    storeVel[place] = vel;
  }
}

void checkOut(){ // see if we need to send anything from the buffer    #F
  for( int place=0; place < bufferLength; place++){
    if(time[place] !=0 && millis() > time[place]){ // time to send something out
      noteSend(storeAction[place], storeNote[place], storeVel[place]);
      time[place] = 0; // wipe buffer entry
    }
  }
}
```
#A This sets the size of the buffer to use Arduinos don't have too much free memory so don't
   go mad here
#B Setting up the pins to use for the echo inhibit switches
#C The shift one place to the left is a quick way of saying multiply by two
#D All delays equally spaced in time
#E Delay is determined by the pot value plus all the previous delays
#F With all the delays in the pipe line the buffer will be fuller than in previous programs

While many of the functions are the same, there are quite a few new ones. At the start there are a number of lines defining the pins and the logic variables for the controls. Then the setup function has to initialize these pins to be inputs with the pull-up pins enabled. Also there is the getControls function, which reads in the switches and the pots. Note here the pot values are shifted to the left or multiplied by two to give a maximum time of just over two seconds per pot. As before that could be changed if you like.

The doNote function is a bit more complex. The down variable is used to make the action variable a note on or note off message. Then the sameDelay variable is used to prime the buffer with different delays. This is an increasing delay derive from the one pot reading, or the summation of all the delay values up to the delay required.

MIDI Looper

The final project in this chapter is a cross of some functions you have seen before with a new twist—a MIDI looper pedal. Here, notes are recorded as they are played while a record button or pedal is held down. When it is released, these notes are played back in a continuous loop until a new recording is made or a stop button is pressed. This is like a sample pedal but for MIDI data.

There are a few switches and LEDs required for control and feedback that have to be assembled first. This is shown in Figure 4-8.

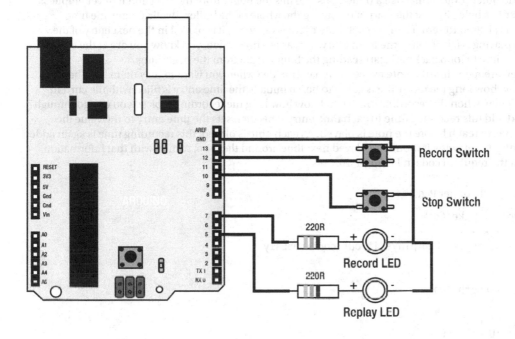

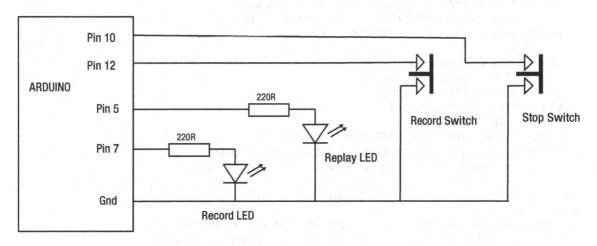

Figure 4-8. *MIDI sample pedal schematic*

Figure 4-8 shows a very simple circuit, so both the schematic and physical layout are shown. In all the previous projects in this chapter I have used toggle switches. These switches, however, are of the push type—push to make, to be precise. Note these have a different sort of schematic symbol—a bar that can be pushed to connect together two terminals. For this project it is best if both these are foot-operated switches. The LEDs could be different colors for an even clearer indication. Note the physical diagram shows a flat on the cathode of the LED. Occasionally, you will find an LED that has the flat on the anode, but these are rare. Normally the anode is indicated by the longer of the two leads, but again I have known rare exceptions. In the event of the LED not lighting up, try reversing the LEDs.

Unlike the other projects that use a buffer, this one fills the buffer from the start and it never empties; that is, it never has holes in it. At the start of recording the whole of the buffer—well actually the time component—is cleared to zero. Then, as each note event is detected, it is placed in the next entry of the buffer. When playing back, if you come to an entry with a zero time value, you know you are at the end of the buffer and it is time to loop back and start reading the buffer again from the beginning.

When you are recording the note events, you have no idea when you want to play them back because you don't know how long the recording is going to be, so initially the time entry is filled with the current system time. Then, when the recording ends, you know how long the recording took so you can go through the buffer and add this recording time to each time entry. This then sets the time entry to the value the system clock has to reach before the note is played. As each note is played, this recording time is again added to the time entry to set when it should be played next time around the loop. Armed with that information, have a look at the required code in Listing 4-10.

Listing 4-10. MIDI Looper Pedal

```
/* MIDI Looper - Mike Cook
 * -----------------
 * records MIDI input then plays it out continuously
 */

#define bufferLength 100

//variables setup
  boolean noteDown = LOW;
  const int recordLed = 7, replayLed =5; // onboard LED
  byte channel = 0;  // MIDI channel = the value in 'channel' + 1
  int state=0;        // state machine variable
  int place;
 // buffer for delayed notes
  unsigned long time [bufferLength];
  byte storeAction[bufferLength];
  byte storeNote[bufferLength];
  byte storeVel[bufferLength];
  unsigned long startTime=0, endTime=0, bufferTime=0;
  boolean recording = false, playback = false, empty = false;
  const byte recordPin = 12, stopPin = 10;

//setup: declaring inputs and outputs and begin serial
void setup() {
  pinMode(recordLed,OUTPUT);        // LED to light up when recording
  pinMode(replayLed,OUTPUT);        // LED to light up when replaying
  digitalWrite(recordLed,LOW);      // Turn LED off
  digitalWrite(replayLed,LOW);      // Turn LED off
  pinMode(recordPin, INPUT_PULLUP);
```

```
  pinMode(stopPin, INPUT_PULLUP);
  Serial.begin(31250); //start serial with MIDI baud rate
}

//loop: wait for serial data, and interpret the message
void loop () {
  checkIn(); // see if anything has arrived at the input
  if(state == 0) checkOut(); // see if we need to send anything out
  getControls(); // read switches
  }

void getControls(){
  static long debounce = 0;
  static long debounceTime = 25;                              #A
  boolean rec = !digitalRead(recordPin);
  if(!recording && rec && digitalRead(stopPin) && millis() > debounce){
    recording = true;
    debounce = millis() + debounceTime;
    if(playback){
        playback = false;
        wipeBuffer();
    }
    startTime = millis();
    digitalWrite(recordLed, HIGH);
  }
  if(recording && !rec && millis() > debounce){ //debounce
     recording = false;
     playback = true;
    debounce = millis() + debounceTime;
    time[place] = 0; // mark buffer end
    bufferTime = millis() - startTime;
    digitalWrite(recordLed, LOW);
    prepBuffer();
  }
   if(!digitalRead(stopPin)){
      recording = false;
      playback = false;
      wipeBuffer();
   }
}

void wipeBuffer(){                                          #B
  for(int i =0; i<bufferLength; i++){
    time[i] = 0L;
  }
  place = 0;
}

void prepBuffer(){ // set buffer for next time it should play   #C
  int i=0;
  while(time[i] != 0){
    time[i] += bufferTime;
```

```
        i++;
    }
    place = 0;
}

void checkIn(){
    static byte note = 60;
    if (Serial.available() > 0) {
        // read the incoming byte:
        byte incomingByte = Serial.read();
        Serial.write(incomingByte);

    switch (state){
        case 0:
        // look for as status-byte, our channel, note on
            if (incomingByte == ( 0x90 | channel)){  // read only one channel
                noteDown = HIGH;
                state=1;
            }
        // look for as status-byte, our channel, note off
            if (incomingByte == (0x80 | channel)){   // read only one channel
                noteDown = LOW;
                state=1;
        }
            // look for any after touch, or program message
            if ((incomingByte & 0xE0) == 0xC0){
                state=4;  // just wait for the data
            }
            // look for any control or polyphonic after touch
            if ((incomingByte & 0xE0) == 0xA0){
                state=3;  // just wait for two bytes of data
            }
            // look for any pitch wheel or Channel Mode data
            if ((incomingByte & 0xF0) == 0xA0 || (incomingByte & 0xF0) == 0xB0){
                state=3;  // just wait for two bytes of data
            }
            break;
        case 1:
        // get the note to play or stop
            if(incomingByte < 128) {
                note=incomingByte;
                state=2;
            }
            else {
                state = 0;  // reset state machine as this should be a note number
            }
            break;
        case 2:
        // get the velocity
            if(incomingByte < 128) {
                doNote(note, incomingByte, noteDown); // do something with the note on message
            }
```

```
        state = 0;  // reset state machine to start
        break;
      case 3: // first of two bytes to discard
      state = 4; // next byte to discard
        break;
      case 4: // data to discard
      state = 0; // reset state machine
     }
  }
}

void doNote(byte note, byte velocity, int down){
  // if velocity = 0 on a 'Note ON' command, treat it as a note off
  if ((down == HIGH) && (velocity == 0)){
     down = LOW;
  }
  // do something with the note message

  if(down == LOW) { // record the note off in the buffer
    bufferSave(0x80,note,velocity);
  }
  else {
    bufferSave(0x90,note,velocity);
  }
}

void noteSend(byte cmd, byte data1, byte data2) {
  cmd = cmd | channel;
  Serial.write(cmd);
  Serial.write(data1);
  Serial.write(data2);
}

void bufferSave(byte action, byte note, byte vel){
  // place note in next position in buffer                    #D
  if(recording){
     time[place] = millis();
     storeAction[place] = action;
     storeNote[place] = note;
     storeVel[place] = vel;
     place++; // for next time
       if(place >= bufferLength) { // come to the end of the buffer
       // make it start recording again because record key is still held
       recording = false;
       playback = true;
       }
  }
}

void checkOut(){ // see if we need to send anything from the buffer
  if(playback && time[0] != 0L) {
    digitalWrite(replayLed,HIGH);
```

101

```
    if(millis() > time[place]){
      noteSend(storeAction[place], storeNote[place], storeVel[place]);
      time[place] += bufferTime; // set buffer entry for next play            #E
      place++; // point at next play
      if(time[place] ==0) place = 0; // wrap pointer around
    }
    digitalWrite(replayLed,LOW);
  }
}
#A Time in milli seconds to allow the switch to settle after making a transition
#B Wipe the time element of the buffer only because whit a time as zero that entry is
   considered to be empty
#C Now we know how long the recording lasts we can add the length to the time of that event
to get a tine when to play it again
#D No need to search for a free entry, the buffer is filled up when each note event occurs
#E Now we have played it set the time to play it again by adding the total recording time
```

Again, the overall look of the code by now should look familiar, but there are some new elements here. The getControls function actually controls the function switching between recording and playback. When I was developing this I had some problems with contact bounce, so there is a variable called debounceTime that controls how quickly you can change modes. When the mode changes, this time is added onto the system time and a mode change cannot occur again until this time has elapsed, even if the switches seem to be in the right condition.

The checkOut function turns the Replay LED on and off as each buffer entry is examined. Since the program spends most of its time determining whether it is the time to play the next entry, the LED is only off for a very short time. The result is that it looks like it is on continuously, but as soon as the buffer stops being read, it goes out. In the bufferSave function there is a line that checks for the limit of the buffer being reached. The buffer length is 100 messages and you're not likely to exceed it. If you do, the code will wrap round and start overwriting the notes at the beginning. You might want to add an overrun LED to the system and turn it on here, turning it off in the wipeBuffer function, but I found this unnecessary.

Summary

So there you have it—just some of the tricks you can perform by intercepting and manipulating MIDI messages. After all, a MIDI message tells the sound system what to do, and as you have seen, manipulation is easy. It only involves adding or subtracting some number to some parameter or storing the message and sending it later.

There are many more tricks you could implement using the same techniques as you have seen in this chapter. What about a system that periodically sends Controller Change pan messages so that the instrument automatically sweeps back and forth through the stereo field, or have a certain note trigger a rapid sweep or position change? How about having a MIDI looper pedal, but this time have two or more buffers to write into and output at the same time, allowing you to layer loops? What about a system where you can continue to play in the key of C, but this is transposed to any key you want? Once you have these basic skills, imagination is your only limit.

All this has been restricted to modifying MIDI messages. In the next chapter, you will learn how to make MIDI controllers or instruments that will turn some physical action into MIDI signals. This opens up a whole new world of possibilities.

CHAPTER 5

■ ■ ■

MIDI Instruments

This chapter covers

- Expanding the Arduino's input/outputs

- Using sensors

- Making a Spoon-o-Phone

- MIDI Theremin

- MIDI air drums

- Light show controlled by MIDI

Up to now, the chapters have looked at the MIDI message, including how to get it into and out of your Arduino and how to mess about with it to make effects like delays, automatic chords, and echoes. In this chapter, you will see how to generate MIDI messages from switches and sensors to make instruments and controllers. I will explain techniques you can use to interface even more stuff into the limited number of pins an Arduino Uno has, and also how to use some sophisticated sensors in a number of MIDI instruments. Finally, I will go on to discuss things you can do with MIDI messages other than use them to generate sounds as we explore a MIDI-controlled lighting system.

Sensors and I/O

The basic Arduino Uno has 20 input/output (I/O) pins and for many projects this is enough but there is always that project that demands a few or even a lot more. You are then faced with the choice of switching to an Arduino with more I/O like the Mega or tailoring your own solution by adding extra port expanders. I prefer the latter solution as this means not only is it more economic, but also that I can also get a close match to the actual I/O requirements of my project.

Sensors basically take some form of physical phenomena and turn it into an electrical signal, then we can use that signal to monitor the phenomena or use it to control something else. As far as we are concerned in this book, that something is normally a MIDI message. So we can take something as simple as the turn of a knob and get a reading out of it. You have already seen an example of that in the last chapter, where a knob was used to control a time delay. You might want a whole pile of knobs to control your DAW by converting the knob turning into MDI CC (Controller Change) messages.

While useful, a knob is not a very exciting form of sensor. It is rather conventional. How about an X-Y pad to control two parameters, or a light sensor, or even turning how hard you press on a pad into musical information, either in the form of note on/off messages or CC messages? I will show you how to connect these and more up to your Arduino in this chapter.

Port Expander

The standard response to more I/O on an Arduino is to use a shift register, as they are relatively easy to understand. However, the major disadvantage is that you need a different type of shift register for input or outputs. Also, there is no support for interrupts with a shift register and there is no way of knowing if an input has changed other than clocking in the whole of the shift register chain and examining the individual input bits. In my opinion, a much better way of handling extra I/O is to use port expander chips. These come in various forms, but perhaps the best one is the MCP32S17. This is connected by an SPI connection and contains two full 8-bit I/O ports identified as ports A and B. What is more, up to eight of these can easily be connected to the Arduino at any one time, giving a total of 128 I/O lines. With some slight complication, an almost unlimited number can be accommodated. So let's have a look at how to use this component. The hardware wiring is quite simple and is shown in Figure 5-1.

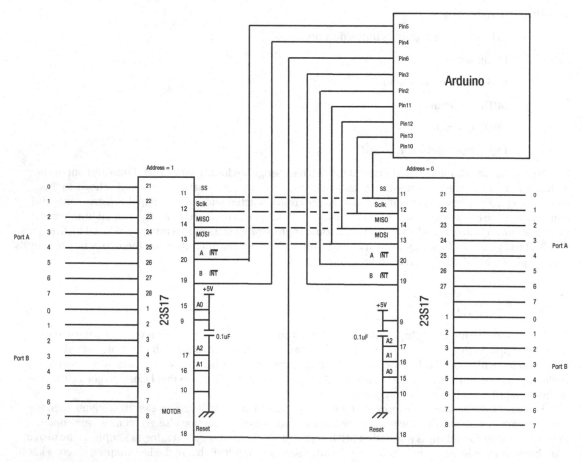

Figure 5-1. *Connecting two MCP32S17 chips to the Arduino*

They are both attached to the same four pins on the Arduino. Each chip gets its unique address from the logic level on each of the three address lines. Each chip must have different logic levels here, which means that the total number of chips connected together can be eight because three lines can have eight different ways of connecting them high or low. To determine the combination for any number of lines, simply take 2 raised to the power of the number of lines.

From the software side of things, each chip looks like a number of registers or addresses. If you download and look at the data sheet you will see the full details; however, some people find data sheets daunting because they contain almost too much data. It is further complicated with this chip because the data sheet contains information on two versions of the chip. The MCP32017 is the I2C version and the MCP32S17 is the SPI version (and the one we are using here).

You communicate with this chip through its 22 control registers. These can be configured as two separate banks, one for port A and the other for port B. They also can be configured as interleaved banks, where each port A register has its port B equivalent register next to it. It powers up in the interleaved mode so it is simplest to use it in this mode. Each register has a name and an address associated with it. The chip will only understand the address but for us programming it a name is easiest to remember; therefore, it is simple to set up an association between the name and the address in the software. The code in Listing 5-1 shows how this is done.

Listing 5-1. MCP23x17 Address Name/Number Association

```
// MCP23S17 addresses in IOCON.BANK = 0
#define IODIRA (byte) 0x00
#define IODIRB (byte) 0x01
#define IPOLA (byte) 0x02
#define IPOLB (byte) 0x03
#define GPINTENA (byte) 0x04
#define GPINTENB (byte) 0x05
#define DEFVALA (byte) 0x06
#define DEFVALB (byte) 0x07
#define INTCONA (byte) 0x08
#define INTCONB (byte) 0x09
#define IOCON (byte) 0x0A
#define GPPUBA (byte) 0x0C
#define GPPUBB (byte) 0x0d
#define INTFA (byte) 0x0E
#define INTFB (byte) 0x0F
#define INTCAPA (byte) 0x10
#define INTCAPB (byte) 0x11
#define GPIOA (byte) 0x12
#define GPIOB (byte) 0x13
#define OLATA (byte) 0x14
#define OLATB (byte) 0x15
// Bits in the IOCON register
#define BANK (byte) 0x80
#define MIRROR (byte) 0x40
#define SEQOP (byte) 0x20
#define DISSLW (byte) 0x10
#define HAEN (byte) 0x08
#define ODR (byte) 0x04
#define INTPOL (byte) 0x02
```

Note how I refer to the chip as MCP23x17. The x in the middle means that there is more than one variant and the information covers all variants. This is a standard piece of shorthand in the component industry. I normally include this code in a separate tab on the Arduino sketch. This is easy to do but is often neglected by beginners. At the top-right corner of the sketch window is a magnifying glass icon, and under that is a downward-pointing icon. Click that and select New Tab from the drop-down menu. Then you enter a name for the tab and it appears at the top. Just click it to access the code it contains. This is great for hiding away things like this. Store the code in Listing 5-1 in a new tab like this whenever you want to use this device.

One of the great features of a chip like this is the interrupt output. Despite the name you don't have to use it to trigger an interrupt, but it can be used to indicate that one or more inputs in a group of inputs you define has changed. This saves the computer's time reading in all the inputs just to see if something has changed. There are two outputs per chip, one for each port. They can be wired together in what is known as a wired OR configuration or wired to separate pins for finer grained monitoring. This is shown in Figure 5-1, where these outputs are wired to pins 2 to 5 of the Arduino. There is also a reset pin on this chip, which can be all connected together and controlled by one output pin.

Analogue Multiplexer

Well, that is how you get more digital input outputs, but what about analogue inputs? This requires a different sort of circuit one called an analogue multiplexer. A multiplexer is another name for a multiway switch and the analogue bit means that basically the voltage you put in is the voltage you get out. What is more this is a two-way process inputs and outputs can be interchanged, just like the mechanical version. Multiplexers come in a number of different configurations, but the 4051 is perhaps the most useful. It has one channel that can be distributed to any one of eight others. This is known as an eight-channel analogue multiplexer/demultiplexer. The general arrangement is shown in Figure 5-2. Note that you can also get a dual four-channel analogue multiplexer/demultiplexer (4052) and a triple two-channel analogue multiplexer/demultiplexer (4053). The big daddy of them all is the 4067; it provides 16 channels to select from.

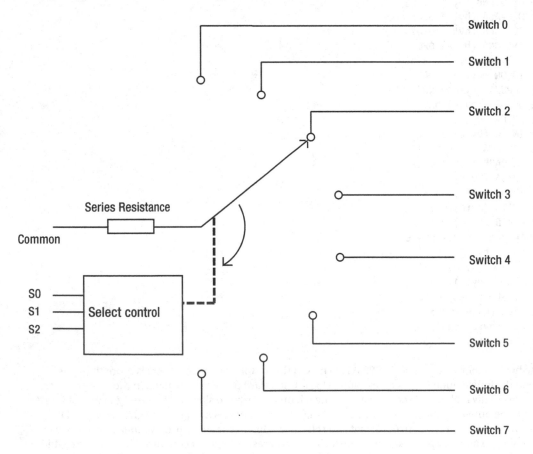

Figure 5-2. *An analogue multiplexer*

While in theory the common connector is routed through to the switch connectors, in practice there is a small series resistance. The value of this depends on which manufacturer's 4051 you get. There will be a prefix or post-fix identification that shows the manufacturer and the appropriate data sheet will list the resistance value. The parameter is marked in the data sheets as R_{on} and the MC14051B has a typical value of 250R, although this can change with temperature and supply voltage. In practice this does not matter too much because this resistance is normally small compared to what you are switching. Another point to note is that there is a limit on the amount of current you can switch at about 25mA. Despite what you might see in some online tutorials on the Arduino site, it is not a good idea to use a multiplexer like this for generating more output pins. This is because when the multiplexer is not switched through the output is not connected to anything.

There are logic level inputs. The select or control pins that determine what switch in/out is connected to the common line are normally driven by the Arduino. If your Arduino model has six analogue inputs, you can put a 4051 on each of these inputs to have 48 analogue inputs. Hang a pot off each one of those and you have the potential to make a large MIDI controller. If that is not enough for you, then using the 4067 will double this, to 96 analogue inputs. However, for an almost unlimited number of inputs, you can cascade the multiplexers, so the signal passes through two multiplexers on its way to the Arduino's analogue input. By the way, the Arduino processor itself has an analogue multiplexer in front of its single A/D converter, which is why you can select one of six channels to read. Figure 5-3 shows these two arrangements.

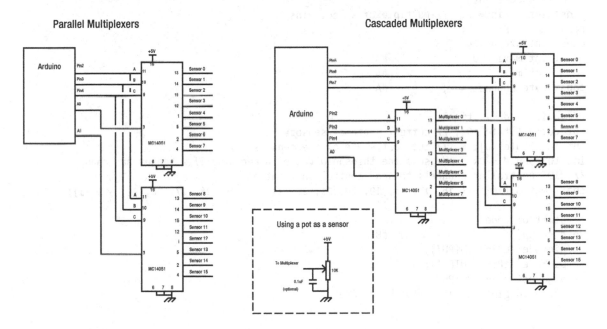

Figure 5-3. *Parallel and cascaded multiplexer circuits*

Figure 5-3 shows only two multiplexers connected in the cascaded circuit for simplicity but up to eight multiplexers can be included in this second bank. This would give 64 analogue inputs. You could go for a third bank of multiplexers to give you 512 inputs, but I can't think of anything practical you would make that contains that many analogue inputs.

In the parallel circuit, each multiplexer is fed into a separate analogue input, whereas with the cascaded type, only one analogue input on the Arduino is used. The cascaded system does have the disadvantage of doubling the effective value of R_{on}, because a signal passes through two multiplexers before getting to the analogue input.

   In both circuits, you have the problem of addressing the output you need by putting the appropriate binary number corresponding to the input you want to read onto the pins connected to the multiplexer's select lines. This is where beginners tend to get themselves into all sorts of code messes. They have a three-digital write instruction for each different analogue input they want to read, which produces some turgid code. The proper way to do it is by using bit manipulation and separating each binary digit in the number to set the multiplexer input select pin. The code in Listing 5-2 shows you how to do this, in the three lines after the "select multiplexer channel" comment. Finally, there is a small block in the schematic that shows you how to wire up a pot as an input to the multiplexers. Note there is an optional capacitor from the wiper to the ground; use this only if you get too much jitter on the readings. This jitter will be caused by interference picked up for either a noisy environment or from poor physical layout of your circuit.

Listing 5-2. Controller Change Message Generator from Multiplexed Inputs

```
/* Multiplexed analogue inputs - Mike Cook
* For two 4051 multiplexers parallel wiring
* 16 inputs with threshold control
*/

// Define constants
const int s0Pin = 2;   // multiplexer select pins
const int s1Pin = 3;
const int s2Pin = 4;
const int mux1 = 0;              #A
const int mux2 = 1;              #A
const byte channel = 0;         #A

// Variable definitions
int currentState[16]; // current state of sensors
int lastState[16];    // the last state of the sensors
int threshold = 0x4;  // sets the threshold value in deciding if a sensor has changed
// MIDI controller channels to send control data out on
char control[16] = { 16, 17, 18, 19, 20, 21, 22, 23, 24, 25, 26, 27, 28, 29, 30, 31};

// Start of code
void setup() {                  #B
   pinMode(s0Pin, OUTPUT);
   pinMode(s1Pin, OUTPUT);
   pinMode(s2Pin, OUTPUT);
   Serial.begin(31250); //MIDI baud rate
}

//****************** MAIN LOOP ********************************

void loop() {
   doSensorScan();
   lookForChange();
   saveCurrentState();
   } // end loop function

//****************** Functions ********************************
```

```
void doSensorScan() {               #C
 for(int i=0; i<8; i++){
   // select multiplexer channel
   digitalWrite(s0Pin, i & 0x1);
   digitalWrite(s1Pin, (i>>1) & 0x1);
   digitalWrite(s2Pin, (i>>2) & 0x1);
   currentState[i] = analogRead(mux1);   // dummy read to allow sample & hold capacitor
                                          //                              to charge
   currentState[i] = analogRead(mux1);   // read mux1 in first 8 array locations
   currentState[i+8] = analogRead(mux2); // dummy read to allow sample & hold capacitor
                                          //                              to charge
   currentState[i+8] = analogRead(mux2); // read mux2 in last 8 array locations
 }
}

void saveCurrentState(){            #D
  for(int i=0; i<16; i++){
    lastState[i] = currentState[i];
  }
}

void lookForChange(){               #E
  for(int i=0; i<16; i++){
    if(abs(currentState[i] - lastState[i] ) > threshold) { // if we have a sufficient change
      controlSend(channel, control[i], currentState[i]>>3);  // send control change message
    }
  }
}

void lookForChange2(){              #F
  for(int i=0; i<16; i++){
    if(abs(currentState[i] - lastState[i] ) > threshold) { // if we have a sufficient change
      controlSend(channel, control[i], currentState[i]>>3);   // send MSB
      controlSend(channel, control[i]+32, (currentState[i] &0x7) << 4);   // send LSB
    }
  }
}

 void controlSend(byte channel, byte controller, byte value) {
 byte cmd = 0xB0 | channel;  // merge channel number
 Serial.write(cmd);
 Serial.write(controller);
 Serial.write(value);
}
```

#A the analogue port for multiplexers 1 & 2 and MIDI Channel
#B set the states of the I/O pins to drive the sensor multiplexer
#C look at all the sensors
#D save the current state for comparison next time
#E the value of threshold determines if we send a new message
#F use this function if you want to send MSB and LSB CC messages

This code will monitor 16 sensor inputs connected to the multiplexers and generate Controller Change (CC) MIDI messages when the sensors change. The values read from the sensors are first read into an array, and then the array is searched to see if there has been a significant change in the readings from the last time. Only when there has been a change is a CC message sent. This tactic stops the MIDI channel from being swamped with messages showing no change or just jitter due to noise. Finally, the current readings are transferred to another array to compare the change in the next pass around the loop.

One point to mention is the double reading of the analogue input. It's not a mistake but a useful precaution when reading multiple channels on the internal multiplexer. What happens when you issue an `analogRead` command is that the internal multiplexer is switched to that channel and then the reading is taken. Sometimes, especially if you have a high impedance source, there is not enough time for the sample and hold capacitor on the input of the internal A/D to charge up to the input voltage. By taking two readings and only using the second, you give the circuit that chance to reach the right voltage. To give it even more of a chance, you can add a short delay between the two readings if needed. Just having a delay before or after the `analogRead` does absolutely nothing, although you will still see it in many programs on the Internet. This lack of time for charging the input capacitor manifests itself in the "fault" of the voltage on one input appearing to change the reading you get from another input. If you see this now, you know what to do.

The controller numbers are defined in the `control` array and you can change them to whatever you want. By arranging the numbers in this array, both in terms of what numbers are in it and in what order they appear, you effectively assign the sensor to the controller. The analogue read returns a 10-bit value, from 0 to 1023, which is a much wider range than the 0 to 127 range (seven bits) that a CC message can take. You have two options here. The first is to reduce the analogue reading to seven bits by shifting the number to the right three places (same as dividing by eight but more efficient). That is what will happen if you use the code unmodified from the listing.

The second option is to send two controller messages, one for the most significant part and the other for the least. As you saw in Chapter 3, these two-part messages normally happen on controller numbers that are apart by 32, so the alternate `lookForChange2` function has been supplied in the listing so you can substitute this for the `lookForChange` function call in the `loop` function. As a two-byte CC message has in effect 14 bits, the 10-bit reading is shuffled about a bit to make it the top ten bits of the total 14-bit CC message value.

Finally, the global variable `threshold` is used to determine how much the sensor reading has to change before triggering a new message. Note that you don't have to restrict the sensors to just pots; you can use any of the analogue sensors discussed later on in this chapter, and even those I don't mention!

So now that you can have as many analogue inputs as you like, it is time to look at the sorts of sensors you can use with these inputs.

Sensors

A *sensor* is something that converts some physical phenomena into an electrical signal. There are a wide variety of sensors out there, all begging to be used in audio applications. The conventional ones of switches, push buttons, rotary pots, and linear sliders are the stuff you will find on most commercial MIDI keyboards and controllers. However, there are many others that can add a new dimension to your creative work.

While motorized sliders look good, especially in massed ranks, they are quite expensive and appear on only top-end equipment. They are very expensive to buy as a component, so they are not so attractive for building into to your own equipment. Besides there is not much involved in using them apart from the expense. There are, however, some exotic sensors that you might like to use.

Force Sensors

Force sensors are comparatively new. These are film-resistive sensors that show a marked change in resistance as force is applied to them, the sort of force you might apply with your finger. They come in a variety of sizes and shapes. Figure 5-4 shows two such sensors—the square one is 1 3/4-inch square and the round one is 5/8-inch in diameter, just about the right size for your finger.

Figure 5-4. *Resistive force sensors*

With nothing touching the sensors, they have an almost infinite resistance, which in terms of interfacing them to the Arduino is not that helpful. The slightest touch will bring this down to about 50K, and a firm press will drop it down to 500R or lower. This untouched value is not helpful because this means that you have to connect it to a resistor in order to make a meaningful measurement and doing so reduces the range of readings you can get from them. You can wire them in several ways; Figure 5-5 shows the three most common ways.

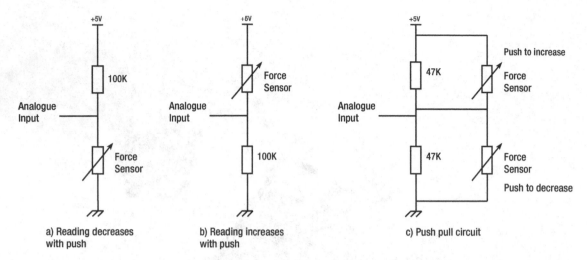

Figure 5-5. *Ways of wiring a force sensor*

In circuit a, the sensor is wired between the input and ground. This is perhaps the most conventional circuit, because as you press harder the reading decreases. Some people do not like that, although it is trivial to reverse this in software if you want; you simply subtract the reading from 1023. Circuit b has a pull-down resistor rather than a pull-up and the reading goes down as you push harder. Both of these have a 100K resistor. The higher the resistor, the more range you get out of your sensor, but also the more interference it will pick up when it is not pressed.

Circuit c is my own invention, at least I have not seen it anywhere else. It uses two force sensors. You press one and the reading increases; press the other and it decreases. Press them both and the reading will be biased toward the one you are pressing the hardest. This sort of thing is ideal for a Pitch Bend controller, because when it's not pressed, the reading will return to the middle value.

Piezo Electric Sensors

Piezo electric sensors are very cheap, flat metal discs that come in a number of different diameters. They are made from of a crystal that produces a voltage when the mechanical stress on it changes. Contrary to what some people think, they do not produce a voltage when under stress, only when that stress changes. They create a positive voltage when the stress is put on and a negative voltage when it is removed. These voltages can be in the order of hundreds of volts, yet they can be connected directly to an Arduino's input because there is almost no power behind that voltage. It is just like a spark from a firework that lands on your hand without burning it. Although the spark is very hot, there is so little mass that there is hardly any heat energy at all.

What happens with the Piezo sensor is that the internal body protection diodes kick in and stop damage from occurring. If a 1M resistor is placed across the sensor that is sufficient load to prevent the high voltage from persisting for very long. So the Piezo sensor is popular when making impact detectors, like electronic drum kits. However, there are a few problems. First of all, the pulses you get out of them are very short lived. Fortunately the Arduino by comparison is very quick and can easily scan eight sensors. But when this gets extended to many more sensors, it is possible that a pulse can be missed while the processor is looking at other sensors.

The second problem is that the output voltage rings, that is it oscillates during the pulse, which can lead to multiple detections of the same impact. The voltage output of the sensors is proportional to the impact velocity, so the difference between a hard hit and light hit can be detected. However, because an analogue reading takes longer to perform than a digital one, you can miss pulses. Sometimes a small capacitor across the sensor will hold the voltage long enough to be read. A selection of Piezo electric sensors is shown in Figure 5-6.

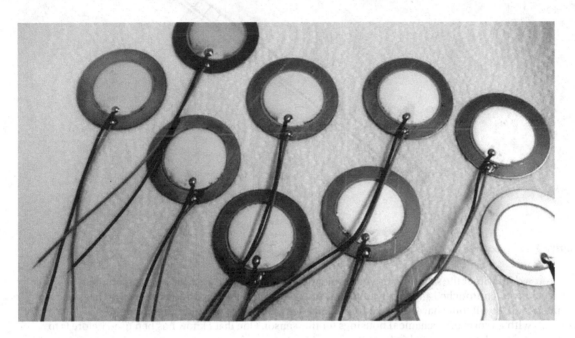

Figure 5-6. *Piezo electric sensors*

Flex Sensors

The flex sensor is similar in a way to the force sensor but, as you can guess from the name, the resistance is proportional to how much you bend it. When it's straight, it has a resistance of about 8K5 and this increases to about 15K when it is bent over at 90° in the right direction. It could suffer permanent damage if you bend it over any farther. Bending it 90° in the other direction only lowers the resistance slightly to 7K8, so basically it is a one-way bend. The bend direction is such that the light squares are on the inside radius of the bend. Figure 5-7 shows a photograph of this sort of sensor; it comes in 2.2-inch and 4.4-inch lengths.

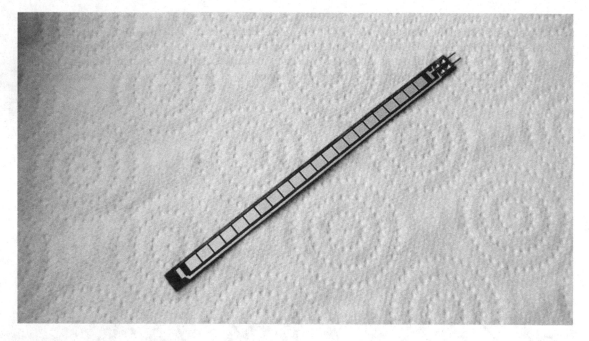

Figure 5-7. *A flex sensitive resistor*

You would wire it the same way as you would the force sensor and you don't get the problem of a large change between untouched and barely touched. You could mount two bend sensors back to back and use the push-pull circuit, but I have not tried this. It takes very little force to bend the sensor and you could come up with all sorts of mechanical housings for this sensor. One that I know has ben used before is to incorporate it in the arm of a Teddy Bear.

When wiring sensors like this and the force sensor, you can solder directly to the wires, but this might end up damaging the flexible plastic. It's much better if you can use some form of socket. I use the round turned pin 0.1-inch pitch sockets, which held the sensor firmly. For extra neatness, I used some heat shrink sleeving to stop the pin end of the sockets from getting accidentally shorted out. The results are shown in Figure 5-8.

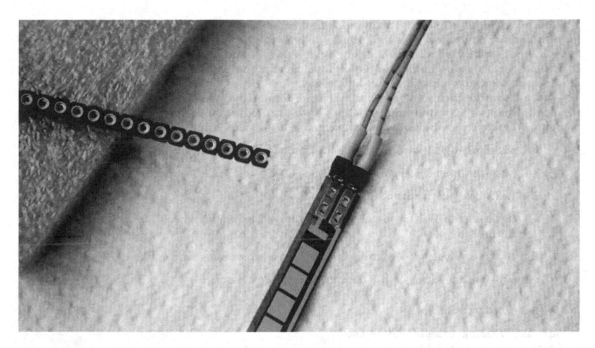

Figure 5-8. *A flex sensor with socket*

The Soft Pot

The soft pot comes in various shapes and sizes. It's basically a laminated plastic sensor rather like a linear slider potentiometer. The resistance changes the farther along the length of the sensor you press, just like a normal pot. There is a circular shaped pot as well that acts a bit like a rotational pot. These sorts of sensors are not cheap and they suffer from a problem—that is, when they are not being pressed, the wiper, the bit normally connected to the analogue input, is not connected to anything. This is known as a floating input and is subject to all sorts of pickup. This results in random values being output. In addition to this, the circular soft pot can short out the two ends of the track when you are pressing at the very ends of the circular track. As it is standard practice to wire a pot with the ends connected to the supply and ground, this can cause a short-circuit across the power supply, with the potential to damage the pot, the supply, or both.

The standard advice it to use pull-up resistors across the output rather like the force and flex sensor, but this restricts the reading and distorts the linearity of the reading especially with the resistors you need in the end stop of the circular soft pot. Instead, I have invented a way to read the soft pot without these restrictions and without the danger of damage due to the pot having its end wires shorted out.

The secret to wiring a soft pot correctly is not to wire the ends to the supply and ground but to wire them to digital output lines. You can then use these lines to switch the power to test the input. For a simple linear pot, the procedure consists of doing the following:

1. Make the two digital pins outputs.

2. Set one output to be low and the other to be high and measure the analogue input.

3. Swap over the digital outputs and measure the analogue input.

4. If the two readings, when added together, are not close to the maximum, then the reading is not valid.

The principle this works on is that by swapping over the supply voltage you will get the complement of the resistor ratio. If the reading was very high, the normal way around is by reversing the voltage applied to it, so you would get a very low reading. Add these two together and you get the maximum reading, that is 1023. If you don't get this value then the input is floating and returning a random value. In practice, you will never get the exact value, so you have to allow a little leeway.

In the case of the circular soft pot, you first have to decide if the wipers are shorting out before you make the measurements with the two outputs high and low. So in this case the digital pins are normally configured as inputs. When you want to make a measurement, you do the following:

1. Make one digital pin an input with the internal pull-up resistor enabled.

2. Make the other digital pin an output set to LOW.

3. Read the digital input pin.

4. If you see a LOW, it means the end wipers are shorted and you should abandon the measurement.

5. If you see a high, proceed to do the complementary measurements as before.

The example code for doing both of these things is shown in Listing 5-3.

Listing 5-3. Reading a Soft Pot

```
/* Soft pot reading example - Mike Cook
* Linear soft pot wired to:-
* wiper to analogue input 0
* ends to Pins 2 & 3
* Circular soft pot wired to:-
* wiper to analogue input 1
* ends to Pins 4 & 5
*/

const byte end1a = 2, end1b = 3;
const byte end2a = 4, end2b = 5;
int threshold = 40;                    #A

void setup(){
  // set up the pot end pins
  pinMode(end1a, OUTPUT);
  pinMode(end1b, OUTPUT);
  pinMode(end2a, INPUT_PULLUP);
  pinMode(end2b, INPUT_PULLUP);
  Serial.begin(9600);
}

void loop(){
  int pot1 = readLin();
  int pot2 = readCir();
  if(pot1 != -1) {
    Serial.print("Linear Pot reading ");
    Serial.println(pot1);
  }
```

```
  else {
    Serial.println("Linear Pot not touched");
  }
    if(pot2 != -1) {
    Serial.print("Circular Pot reading ");
    Serial.println(pot2);
  }
  else {
    Serial.println("Circular Pot not touched");
  }
  delay(800); // stop the display going too fast
}

int readLin(){                                #B
  digitalWrite(end1a, HIGH);
  digitalWrite(end1b, LOW);
  int read1 = analogRead(0); // read one way
  digitalWrite(end1b, HIGH);
  digitalWrite(end1a, LOW);
  int read2 = analogRead(0); // read the other way
  if( abs((read1 + read2)-1023) > threshold ) return -1; else return read1;
}

int readCir(){ // returns -1 for an invalid reading
  pinMode(end2a, INPUT_PULLUP);
  pinMode(end2b, OUTPUT);
  digitalWrite(end2b, LOW);
  if(digitalRead(end2a) == LOW){  // short across pot ends
    pinMode(end2b, INPUT_PULLUP);
    return -1; // not safe to proceed - abandon
  }
  pinMode(end2a, OUTPUT);                      #C
  digitalWrite(end2a, HIGH);
  digitalWrite(end2b, LOW);
  int read1 = analogRead(0); // read one way
  digitalWrite(end2b, HIGH);
  digitalWrite(end2a, LOW);
  int read2 = analogRead(0); // read the other way
  // return wiper pins to safe mode
  pinMode(end2a, INPUT_PULLUP);
  pinMode(end2b, INPUT_PULLUP);
  if( abs((read1 + read2)-1023) > threshold ) return -1; else return read1;
}

#A closeness of reading to be valid
#B returns -1 for an invalid reading
#C safe to proceed with reading
```

The Touch Pad

The idea of a touch pad is well established in music with the Korg's Kaoss pad. Normally, the touch pad component is quite expensive, but thanks to the success of the Nintendo handheld consoles, small touch pads are easy to get hold of as replacement items. They are great for controlling two interrelated parameters, like vibrato speed and depth, a filter's resonant frequency and Q, or frequency and volume. The Nintendo replacement screen covers are made of glass and are great for mounting behind graphic prints or artwork.

The way these resistive pads work is that there are two transparent resistive conductive plastic membranes that are not in contact. If you press on them at one point, then contact is made between the two sheets. If you apply a voltage across one of the membrane layers, the touched point forms the wiper of a potential divider, allowing you to determine how far along the axis with the voltage applied to it the touched point is. So you can determine the position in one axis.

To find the position on the other axis, you have to swap the layers you are applying the voltage to and measuring from. The schematic is shown in Figure 5-9.

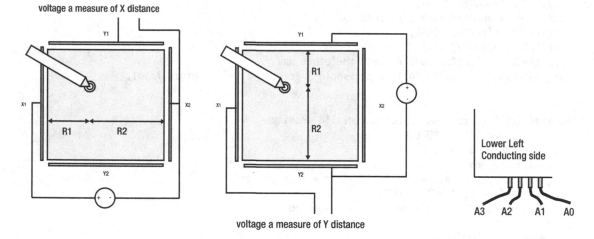

Figure 5-9. *How a resistive touch sensor works*

This involves some fancy footwork with the pins. To help detect a touch, it is best if all four pins are analogue-capable, although you could use just two in a pinch.

There are Arduino libraries that will do this sort of thing for you, but it is easy enough to write the code, as shown in Listing 5-4.

Listing 5-4. Reading a Resistive Touch Pad

```
// Touch sensor test - Mike Cook

void setup(){
  Serial.begin(9600);
}

void loop(){
  int xPos = measureX();
  int yPos = measureY();
  if(xPos != -1 && yPos !=-1){
  Serial.print("X = ");
```

```
  Serial.print(xPos);
  Serial.print(" & Y = ");
  Serial.println(yPos);
  }
  delay(100);
}

int measureX(){
 int v1,v2,v;
  pinMode(14,OUTPUT);
  pinMode(16,OUTPUT);
  digitalWrite(14,LOW);
  digitalWrite(16,LOW);
  v1 = analogRead(A3);
  digitalWrite(14,HIGH);
  digitalWrite(16,HIGH);
  v2 = analogRead(A3);
  if(v1 <60 && v2 > 990) {
  digitalWrite(16,LOW);
  digitalWrite(14,HIGH);
  v = analogRead(A3);
  }
  else {
    /*
    Serial.print(" low reading ");                        #A
    Serial.print(v1);
    Serial.print(" high reading ");
    Serial.println(v2);
   */
    v=-1;
  }
  pinMode(16,INPUT);
  digitalWrite(14,LOW);
  pinMode(14,INPUT);
  return v;
}

int measureY(){
 int v1,v2,v;
  pinMode(15,OUTPUT);
  pinMode(17,OUTPUT);
  digitalWrite(15,LOW);
  digitalWrite(17,LOW);
  v1 = analogRead(A0);
  digitalWrite(15,HIGH);
  digitalWrite(17,HIGH);
  v2 = analogRead(A0);
  if(v1 <60 && v2 > 990) {
  digitalWrite(15,LOW);
  digitalWrite(17,HIGH);
  v = analogRead(A0);
  }
```

```
else {
  /*
  Serial.print(" low reading ");                    #A
   Serial.print(v1);
  Serial.print(" high reading ");
  Serial.println(v2);
  */
   v=-1;
  }
  pinMode(15,INPUT);
  digitalWrite(17,LOW);
  pinMode(17,INPUT);
  return v;
}
```

#A Debug code to look at readings treated as no valid

Again, just like the soft pot, the problem is what to do when there is no touch. The input you are trying to measure is floating. This code solves this problem by putting both pins that are going to have a voltage across them low and taking a measurement. This should be zero if there is a touch, otherwise it will float. Then both of these pins are put high and another reading is taken. This should be the maximum reading (1023) if there is a touch. Then one of these pins is put high and the other low and the reading to measure the position is taken. In the X axis, I got readings between 82 and 940. In the Y axis, I got readings between 128 and 855.

The Nunchuck

Now you might not immediately think of Nintendo's nunchuck for the Wii controller as a music interface, but it is a bargain collection of interface devices that can be easily interface with the Arduino. It consists of two push button switches, a thumb-operated joystick, and a three-axis accelerometer. The whole thing is interfaced on the I2C bus, which you looked at in Chapter 1. There are many examples of interfacing this device to the Arduino on the Internet, but sadly most of them are wrong. There are three fundamental mistakes that are made:

- The chip in the nunchuck requires 3V3 and most places tell you to connect it to 5V.

- The I2C lines need to be pulled up to 3V3.

- The internal pull-up resistors in the Arduino are left enabled, pulling them to 5V.

While the authors of such examples will no doubt counter with "but it works" I would say "but for how long?". There is no doubt that these designs are putting voltages on the chips inside the nunchuck outside the maximum limits for the chip. The fact that they do not instantly burn out is no guarantee that the chip will work reliably and even if it does, its life will be shortened and it will fail earlier than it would have otherwise done. In any case, it's simple to correct these three faults.

The Arduino Uno and many other boards have a 3V3 output of limited current capacity, but this is enough to power the nunchuck. When it comes to physically connecting the nunchuck, you can cut off the connector, strip back the wires, and solder them directly to a row of pin headers to plug into the Arduino. However, the adaptor plugs are cheap enough so I used one of these. There are plugs that supposedly connect directly to the top four connections of the analogue input pins of the Arduino, but doing that requires you to use two of the analogue input pins to provide power. This makes all three of the mistakes I told you about. I made a lead from a nunchuck plug; the clock was connected to the A5 pin and the data was connected to the A4 with 3K pull-up resistors. The power goes to the 3V3 output, as shown in Figure 5-10.

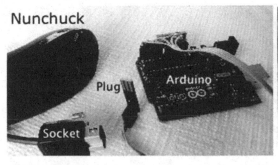 

Figure 5-10. *Wiring the nunchuck to the Arduino*

When it comes to reading, the nunchuck is at a fixed I2C address of 0x52 and you have to send it the numbers 0x40 followed by 0x00 to initialize it. Then you can read six bytes back from the device. To read any more data, you must send the number 0x00 to it again. The bytes that are returned from the nunchuck are encrypted. To get the real byte value, you must exclusive OR the byte with 0x17 and then add 0x17 to the result. Once you have done that, the data you get back has the meaning shown in Figure 5-11.

Byte

0	X7	X6	X5	X4	X3	X2	X1	X0	Joystick X - 41 to 242 - 139 middle
1	Y7	Y6	Y5	Y4	Y3	Y2	Y1	Y0	Joystick Y - 35 to 230 - 129 middle
2	AX9	AX8	AX7	AX6	AX5	AX4	AX3	AX2	Acceleration X axix - top 8 bits
3	AY9	AY8	AY7	AY6	AY5	AY4	AY3	AY2	Acceleration Y axis - top 8 bits
4	AZ9	AZ8	AZ7	AZ6	AZ5	AZ4	AZ3	AZ2	Acceleration Z axis - top 8 bits
5	AZ1	AZ0	AY1	AY0	AX1	AX0	S1	S0	Switches and lower 2 bits of Acceleration

Z button = S0

C button = S1

Figure 5-11. *The data returned from the nunchuck*

The joystick returns just 8-bit data and fits it into one byte. On the other hand, the accelerometers return 10-bit data; the top eight bits are returned in a byte and the bottom two bits are packed into the last byte along with the switch readings. This means that if you want only a crude indication of the accelerometer's data then you can just take the byte data. Otherwise, you have to glue the least significant bits on the end. The switch data is simply the lower two bits in the last byte.

There is one more thing—because the I2C lines need to have their internal pull-up resistors disabled, you either need to hack Arduino's standard library or find a library that will allow the disabling of these resistors. I have done both, but perhaps the simplest is to load a new I2C library. I found the one at http://dsscircuits.com/articles/arduino-i2c-master-library.html to be excellent and much better than the original. Using it is different from the standard library but it is simple enough. Listing 5-5 shows you how to use this and read the nunchuck.

Listing 5-5. Reading a Nunchuck

```
// Nunchuck test
#include <I2C.h>

int outbuf[6];           // array to store results
void setup () {
  Serial.begin (19200);
  I2c.begin();
  I2c.pullup(0);         // disable I2C pull ups
  I2c.timeOut(500);      // half a second to prevent lock up
  Serial.print ("Finished setup\n");
  nunchuck_init ();      // send the initialisation handshake
}

void nunchuck_init () {
  I2c.write(0x52, 0x40, 0x00);              #A
}

void send_zero () {
  I2c.write(0x52, 0x00);
}

void loop () {
 // I2c.read(address, numberBytes)
 Serial.println(" ");
 Serial.println("Raw data");
 I2c.read(0x52, 6);
 for(int j=0; j<6; j++){                      // now get the bytes one at a time
     outbuf[j] =  I2c.receive();              // receive a byte
     if(outbuf[j] < 0x10) Serial.print("0"); // print leading zero if needed
     Serial.print(outbuf[j], HEX);           // print the byte
     Serial.print(" ");
     }
     Serial.println(" ");  // new line
   printResults();
  send_zero (); // send the request for next bytes
  delay (800);
}

void printResults () {                        #B
  int z_button = 0;
  int c_button = 0;

 z_button = outbuf[5] & 1;                     #C
 c_button = 1 ^ ((outbuf[5] >> 1) & 1) ^ (outbuf[5] & 1);

 outbuf[2] = (outbuf[2] << 2) | (outbuf[5] >> 2) & 0x3; // acc x
 outbuf[3] = (outbuf[3] << 2) | (outbuf[5] >> 4) & 0x3; // acc y
 outbuf[4] = (outbuf[4] << 2) | (outbuf[5] >> 6) & 0x3; // acc x
```

```
for(int i=0; i<5; i++){
  Serial.print (outbuf[i], DEC);
  Serial.print ("\t");
}
  Serial.print (z_button, DEC);
  Serial.print ("\t");

  Serial.print (c_button, DEC);
  Serial.print ("\t");

  Serial.println(" ");
}
```

#A set up start of read
#B Print the input data we have received acceleration data is 10 bits long so we read 8 bits
   and the LS bits are in the last byte
#C byte outbuf[5] contains bits for z and c buttons it also contains the least significant
   bits for the accelerometer data so we have to check each bit of byte outbuf[5]

Note that you only get a print out of the readings when you press the Z button. That means that the Z button will always be displayed as 0, because when it is a 1, the program will not print the readings. This is so you can test how fast you can read your nunchuck. The timeBetweenReads variable governs the maximum speed and if this is too fast for the nunchuck, it will never see the Z button as 0 and so there will never be any printout on the serial monitor. I found I could set this variable to 1 and still get a reading but setting it to 0 produced no printout. Some early versions of the Nunchuck cannot read as fast as this and there are problems with the Far East nunchuck clones.

As the nunchuck is at a fixed address, you cannot simply connect more than one to the Arduino. You can connect more if you switch the I2C signals with an analogue multiplexer. You saw in Chapter 2 how to use an analogue multiplexer. Here you will need the 4052 or the 4053 to add more nunchucks, as shown in Figure 5-12.

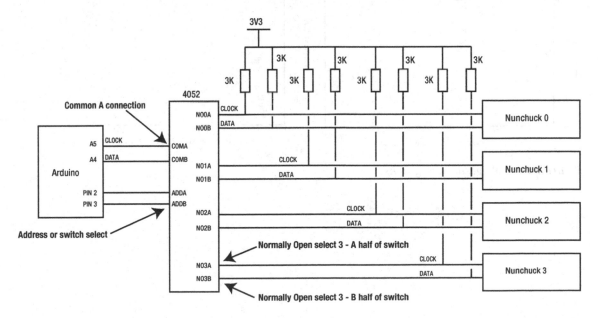

Figure 5-12. *Connecting more than one nunchuck*

Note that each Nunchuck requires its own pull-up resistor and power connections. I labeled the 4052 with the function names rather than the pin numbers so that you can easily see what is going on. There is no need to have all four nunchucks connected; you can just use two or three if you want. The switch select lines are shown coming from Arduino's pins 2 and 3, but you can use anything. Note you need to select which nunchuck you want to read by setting these multiplex select lines before sending the 0x00 number and reading back the data.

The Distance Sensor

There are several types of distance sensors—capacitive, ultrasonic, and infrared (IR)—however, in a music environment, the IR sensors are perhaps the best. This is because a capacitive distance sensor can be affected by its surroundings and an ultrasonic sensor suffers from interference when you try to use more than one.

Note that the IR distance sensor is immune from light interference, but it is the most reliable of the three. Basically they work by detecting the angle of reflected IR light. The most popular range of sensors are made by Sharp and there are two basic types—fixed distance and variable distance. The fixed distance sensors give a digital output if a reflecting object is closer than a specific distance away. This can be useful in a number of situations but for music applications is not nearly as interesting as the variable distance sensors. These have an analogue output that is in some way related to the distance. I say in some way because the reading you get out of them is not as straightforward as you might hope it to be. There are an almost bewildering variety of subtly different sensors with subtly different part numbers. The one I chose to experiment with is the GP2Y0A21YK0F, which gives useful readings up to 80cm; the distance/reading graph of this is shown in Figure 5-13.

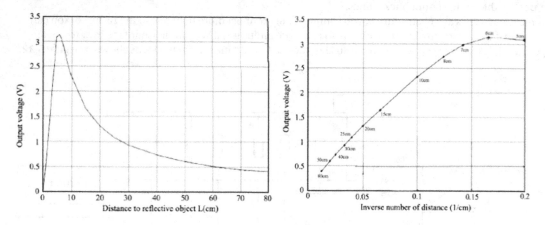

Figure 5-13. *Voltage/distance graphs*

The first thing you will notice is that the graph is not very linear. In fact at very small distances the output rises quickly as the distance increases until a distance of about 8 cm. After that, the output drops off with increasing distance, at first quickly and then slowly. If you take the reciprocal of the distance, the graph looks a lot straighter, as shown on the graph on the right, but note that this graph does not show any reading for very close distances. What this means is that simply by reading the voltage out of the sensor, you can't tell the distance. For example, suppose you read an output voltage of 1.5V. The reflecting object could be 0.3 cm or 17 cm away. This is where the fixed distance sensors come into reckoning, or you could ensure that mechanically the object you want to measure is prevented from coming any closer than 8 cm. However, for music purposes, this is not such an issue. A controller where you wave your hands and get a variable signal is many times all you need.

The maximum output is just above 3V, which means if you use the normal analogue inputs and measuring technique the maximum reading will only be about 670. You can pull a trick to increase this range, but you have to be careful. The trick is to input a voltage to the Aref pin. Because there is a 3V3 voltage output on the Arduino Uno, you can connect them directly together. However, you must tell the Arduino that there is an external voltage on this pin by including a

```
analogReference(EXTERNAL);
```

in the setup function. If you try to take an analogue reading with an external Vref voltage and that line has not been called, you could damage your Arduino by shorting out the internally generated voltage reference with the external reference voltage. With a 3V3 reference voltage, you can still put 5V into the analogue input pins without any problems. It is just that for any voltage over 3.3V you will get the same 1023 maximum reading. Doing this trick nearly doubles the resolution of the readings, but beware when switching to another sketch you have not left the Aref pin connected to the 3V3 line.

I have by no means exhausted the wide variety of sensors that you can get, but now it is time to look at some instruments you can make using some of the sensors you have seen in the last section. I encourage you to make you own variations of these projects. That is the best way to learn.

MIDI Instruments

Back in the mid 60s, solid state electronics were just beginning to emerge into the mass consumer market. One of the first musical instruments to emerge was the Stylophone. Introduced in 1968, it was affordably priced. This was a great contrast to the electronic organs of the time, which cost about as much as a small car. The Stylophone consisted of a stylus that was used to touch patches on a printed circuit board and had a raspy tone, which made it perfect for David Bowie's *Space Oddity*. Figure 5-14 shows a photograph of my parents' original Stylophone.

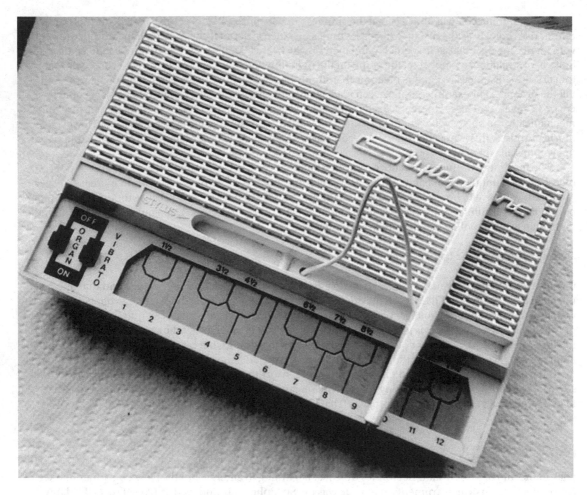

Figure 5-14. *The Stylophone*

The Stylophone used a simple saw tooth oscillator and had quite a buzzy sound. What I am going to do is to show you how to make a modern-day instrument that's inspired by the Stylophone—called the Spoon-o-Phone.

The Spoon-o-Phone

As the name implies, the Spoon-o-Phone uses a spoon to select the notes much like the stylus in the Stylophone; however, since it is a MIDI instrument, it has all the richness of tone of a modern sound generator. What is more, there are no sharps and flats on the keyboard because it is an intelligent keyboard that can play in any key you like. The secret of the Spoon-o-Phone is the keyboard made from conducting paint. I used the bare conducting paint to draw a keyboard onto a piece of MDF (medium density fiberboard), although you could use plywood. The paint is not very viscous and has a consistency like toothpaste, so the best way to apply it is to use a stencil. I made a stencil by designing my keys on the computer and printing it out onto paper. Then I covered the paper with the plastic film that you use in laminating machines and cut out where I wanted the paint using a sharp scalpel, as shown in Figure 5-15.

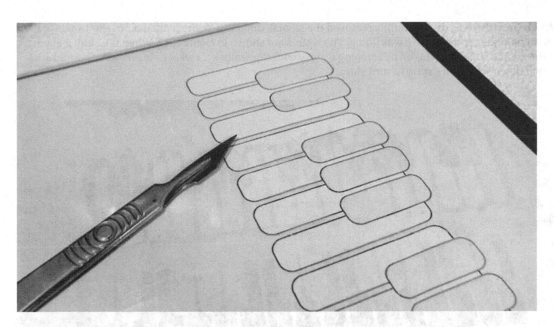

Figure 5-15. *Cutting out the stencil*

Then the stencil is fixed over the wood with masking tape and the conducting paint is applied with a brush, as shown it Figure 5-16.

Figure 5-16. *Painting through the stencil*

When the paint was dry, I carefully removed the stencil, making sure the paint did not tear by use of the scalpel on paint that looked like it was lifting. The results are shown in Figure 5-17. When the paint leaked under the stencil, I cleaned this up by scraping it away with the scalpel. If I were doing it again, I would stick the stencil down with some spray mount glue.

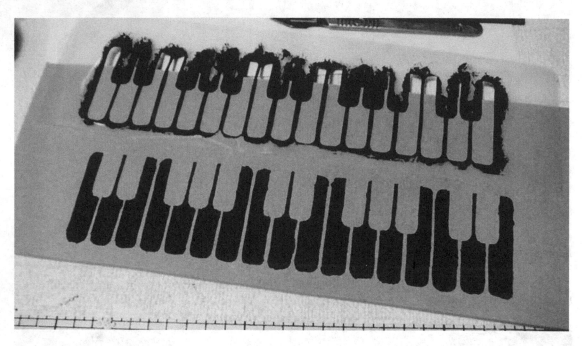

Figure 5-17. *Lifting the stencil*

The final finished instrument is shown in Figure 5-18. This shows the spoon and the way of selecting the playing key. I used a black pen to draw over the top of the keys and to draw the playing key next to the screws.

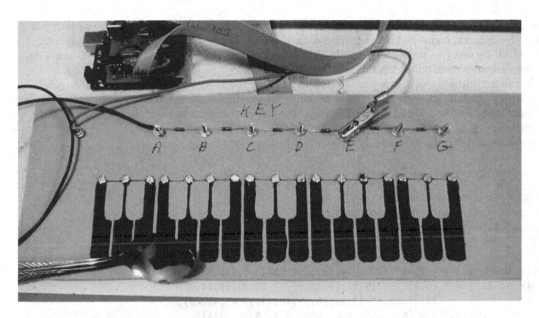

Figure 5-18. The finished Spoon-o-Phone

The schematic for connecting this to the Arduino is shown in Figure 5-19.

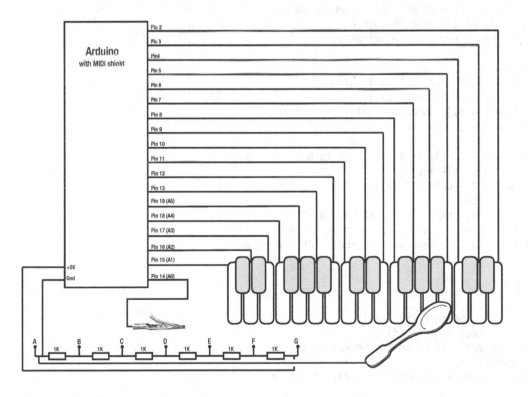

Figure 5-19. The Spoon-o-Phone schematic

Basically, it is a very simple circuit and I have pressed all but one of the analogue pins for use as digital input pins. The spoon is connected to the ground voltage and the keys are connected to an input pin with the internal pull-up resistors enabled. When the spoon touches a key, it makes the input a logic 0, which the software converts into a MIDI note ON message.

The keyboard is intelligent in that you can set it to produce any major key without actually changing the way you play from the key of C. This is done with an analogue input connected to a tapping point in a chain of resistors by a crocodile clip (or alligator clip). The software then transposes what you play into the appropriate key.

What drives all this is the software; this is shown in Listing 5-6.

Listing 5-6. The Spoon-o-Phone Software

```
/* MIDI Spoon-o-phone - Mike Cook
* simple pull down inputs for piano keys
* Alligator clip defines the key
*/

const byte keyPins[] = { 15,16,17,18,19,13,12,11,10,9,8,7,6,5,4,3,2};        #A
const byte notes[] =    {0,2,4,5,7,9,11,12,14,16,17,19,21,23,24,
                         26,28,29,31,33,35,36,38,40,41,43,45,47,48};
const int keyThreshold[] = {85, 255, 426, 596, 767, 937, 1024};
const int musicKeyPin = A0; // key select alligator clip input pin
const int numberOfKeys = 17;
boolean keyUp[numberOfKeys];
byte channel = 0;  // MIDI channel to send data on
byte octave = 3; // two below Middle C
byte lookUpOffset, keyOffset, playingKey;

void setup(){
  Serial.begin(31250); // MIDI baud rate
  for(int i=0; i<numberOfKeys; i++){
    pinMode(keyPins[i], INPUT_PULLUP);
    keyUp[i] = true;
  }
  playingKey = findKey(); // 1 to 7 is A to G
  keyOffset = notes[playingKey];
  lookUpOffset = 7+ (octave * 12);
  // setup voice to use
  controlSend(0, 0, channel); // set bank 0 MSB
  controlSend(32, 0, channel); // set bank 0 LSB
  programChange(19); // send voice number - Church organ
}

void loop(){                                                              #B
  boolean key;
  for(int i=0; i<numberOfKeys; i++){
    key = digitalRead(keyPins[i]);
    if(key != keyUp[i]){ // change in key state
      if(keyUp[i]) {
      midiSend(0x90, lookUpNote(i), 127); // note on
      }
```

```
    else {
    midiSend(0x80, lookUpNote(i), 0); // note off
    }
    keyUp[i] = key;                                          #C
  }
 }
}

void midiSend(byte cmd, byte d1, byte d2){
  cmd = cmd | channel;
  Serial.write(cmd);
  Serial.write(d1);
  Serial.write(d2);
}

byte lookUpNote(int i){
  byte note;
  note = notes[i] + lookUpOffset + keyOffset;
  return note;
}

byte findKey(){ // look up what key we are in
  int i = 0;
  int clipVoltage = analogRead(musicKeyPin);
  while(keyThreshold[i] < clipVoltage) i++;
  i++;
  return (byte) i;
}

void controlSend(byte CCnumber, byte CCdata, byte CCchannel) {
  CCchannel |= 0xB0; // convert to Controller message
  Serial.write(CCchannel);
  Serial.write(CCnumber);
  Serial.write(CCdata);
}

void programChange(byte voice){
  Serial.write((byte)0xC0 | channel);
  Serial.write(voice);
}

#A Base notes -7 (starting at G)
#B look and see if key is down - send MIDI message if it is
#C // save the new state of the key
```

This starts off by defining an array of pin numbers to be used as the inputs. I determined this from the way I had wired the instrument to the Arduino, allowing me to make the ribbon cable connections as neat as possible. You can change the way the instrument is wired simply by redefining this array. An array of threshold values for the voltage taps that determine the key are next. I calculated the voltage at each node in the resistor chain and converted that voltage into the reading I would expect by multiplying the voltage by 5/1024. Then I set the threshold as halfway between the readings of adjacent nodes. The software only looks at this on start up, so if you want to change the key then move the clip to another node and press the Reset button. You could move this findKey function into the main loop if you like, but changing a key is not something you do on a whim.

I set the voice to be a Church Organ but of course this could be any MIDI voice you like. I thought the gravitas of sound it gave was in sharp contrast with the way the note was produced. I have included the calls to write to the bank select controller channels if your sound module uses an extension to General MIDI. The other functions are the usual suspects that you have seen in other code. Note that this code is polyphonic; you can use two spoons if you want each one to be connected to a ground wire. The point about using a spoon is that it is easy to generate a trill on a note and the adjacent note by rapidly rocking the spoon backward and forward.

You might like to incorporate some of the MIDI tricks you saw in Chapter 4, like the One Finger Wonder, into this instrument's software.

The Theremin

The Theremin was named after its inventor, Léon Theremin, who patented the device in 1928. It was unique at the time, in that it required no physical contact to play it. The performer used two hands each in its own electric field to control an oscillator. One hand controlled the volume and the other controlled the pitch. You can make a passible Theremin by using the IR distance sensors you looked at in the first part of the chapter.

Now, a Theremin is not a note-based instrument, but uses a continuously variable oscillator. Although you can make it MIDI-note based using discrete positions of the hands to map to specific notes, I wanted to be true to the original design. My idea was to have a single note played at a fixed pitch triggered by the left hand's volume control and held by the sustain peddle and then have the right hand control a wide ranging pitch bend signal. Figure 5-20 shows the simple schematic of this.

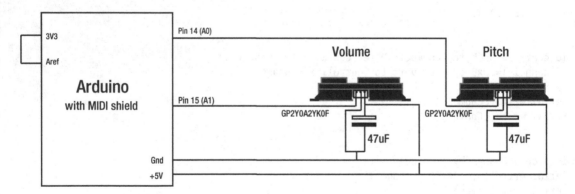

Figure 5-20. *The Arduino Theremin*

Note the 3V3 connected to the Aref. Upload the code before making this connection and remove it before uploading any other code for reasons mentioned in the "Distance Sensor" section earlier in the chapter. The only thing you might be surprised about is the 47uF capacitors across the power supply of each sensor. This is mentioned in the data sheet and is a good idea to stabilize the supply and hence the readings coming from this sensor.

These is not much to the schematic, so let's look at the software shown in Listing 5-7.

Listing 5-7. The Theremin

```
// Theremin  - Mike Cook

boolean playing = false;
const byte channel = 0;
const byte baseNote = 72;

void setup(){
  Serial.begin(31250);   // MIDI baud rate
  analogReference(EXTERNAL);
  controlSend(0, 0);      // set bank 0 MSB
  controlSend(32, 0);     // set bank 0 LSB
  programChange(52);      // send voice number
  controlSend(101, 0);                          #A
  controlSend(100, 0);
  controlSend(6,72);      // set to 6 octaves
  controlSend(38, 0);     // and zero cents
}

void loop(){
  int av1 = 1027 - analogRead(0);
  int av2 = 1027 - analogRead(1);
  if(av1 <870 && av2 < 870){
     if(!playing)noteOn();
     else {
         trackNote(av2,av1);
     }
  }
  else {
    if(playing) noteOff();
  }
}

void noteOff(){
  playing= false;
  noteSend(0x80,baseNote,127);                #B
  controlSend(64, 0);
}
void noteOn(){
 // note on + sustain on
  noteSend(0x90,baseNote,127);
  controlSend(64, 127);
  playing = true;
}

int trackNote(int freq, int volume){
  int pb = 0x2000 - (435 - freq);
  sendPB(pb);
  int vel = volume>> 3;
   controlSend(7, vel);
}
```

```
 void noteSend(byte cmd, byte data1, byte data2) {
  cmd = cmd | channel;
  Serial.write(cmd);
  Serial.write(data1);
  Serial.write(data2);
}

void controlSend(byte CCnumber, byte CCdata) {
  byte CCchannel = channel | 0xB0; // convert to Controller message
  Serial.write(CCchannel);
  Serial.write(CCnumber);
  Serial.write(CCdata);
}

void sendPB(int pb){                         #C
  Serial.write( (byte)0xE0 | channel);
  Serial.write( pb & (byte)0x7f);
  Serial.write( (pb>>7) & (byte)0x7f);
}

void programChange(byte voice){
  Serial.write((byte)0xC0 | channel);
  Serial.write(voice);
}

#A set up Pitch bend sensitivity
#B note off + sustain off
#C send pitch bend message
```

The setup function sets up the voice. This time, one of the heavenly choirs but any sustained simple voice will work well here. If the voice has too much attack on it, then I found it doesn't sound too good. You might disagree though, so I encourage you to try it. Controllers 100 and 101 set up the pitch bend range and controllers 6 and 38 set up the range—this is a whopping six octaves.

The note on is triggered by the reading from the volume and frequency sensors; when they are both triggered the MIDI note on and the sustain on messages are sent. While it is playing, the note is constantly being adjusted; the left hand controls the volume with a CC 7 message and the right hand sends out pitch bend messages.

MIDI Air Drums

Back in the sensor section I looked at the nunchuck. Using the same circuit, you can make a MIDI air drum. The nunchuck is used to trigger the drum beat and the buttons are used to determine what one of four drums sounds is produced. The code to do this is shown in Listing 5-8.

Listing 5-8. MIDI Air Drums

```
/* Nunchuck Air Drums - Mike Cook
 * plays a different drum depending on the buttons pressed
 */

#include <I2C.h>

 int outbuf[6];              // array to store results
 int z_button = 0;
 int c_button = 0;
 long timeBetweenReads = 2; // max speed to read
 long timeOfNextRead=0;
 boolean yTrig = false;
 const byte led = 13;
 byte drums[] = { 56, 49, 40, 35}; // drums to use
 byte lastDrum;

void setup () {
  Serial.begin(31250); // MIDI baud rate
  I2c.begin();
  I2c.pullup(0);                                    #A
  I2c.timeOut(500);                                 #A
  I2c.write(0x52, 0x40, 0x00);                      #A
  pinMode(led,OUTPUT);
  digitalWrite(led,LOW);
  lastDrum = drums[0]; // for first turn off
}

void loop () {
  readNunchuck();
  processResults();
}

void readNunchuck () {
  while(millis() < timeOfNextRead) { }                #B
  I2c.read(0x52, 6);          // I2c.read(address, numberBytes)
  for(int j=0; j<6; j++){    // now get the bytes one at a time
      outbuf[j] =  0x17 + (0x17 ^ I2c.receive());    // receive a byte
      }
  I2c.write(0x52, 0x00);    // send the request for next bytes
  timeOfNextRead = millis() + timeBetweenReads;
}


void processResults(){
  if( outbuf[3] < 120 && !yTrig) { // arm trigger
      digitalWrite(led,HIGH);
    yTrig = true;
    }
```

```
   if( outbuf[3] > 160 && yTrig) { // fire trigger
      digitalWrite(led,LOW);
      noteSend(0x80,lastDrum, 0);  // turn off last note
      lastDrum = drums[outbuf[5] & 0x03];
      noteSend(0x90,lastDrum, 127);                        #C
      yTrig = false;
   }
}

void noteSend(byte cmd, byte data1, byte data2) {
   cmd = cmd | (byte) 9;  // drums
   Serial.write(cmd);
   Serial.write(data1);
   Serial.write(data2);
}

// test function only
void TestProcessResults(){
   if( outbuf[3] < 120 && !yTrig) { // arm trigger
      digitalWrite(led,LOW);
      Serial.println("Armed trigger");
      yTrig = true;
   }
   if( outbuf[3] > 160 && yTrig) {   // fire trigger
      digitalWrite(led,LOW);
      Serial.println("Hit");
      Serial.print("X reading ");
      Serial.print(outbuf[2]);
      Serial.print ("\t Y reading ");
      Serial.println(outbuf[4]);
      yTrig = false;
   }
}
```

#A disable I2C pull ups set half a second time out to prevent lock up & send the
   initialisation handshake
#B hold if trying to read too fast
#C hit as hard as you can

Basically, the Y reading triggers the drum beat. When it passes a threshold, point the trigger is armed, and the hit is registered when the Y reading drops below another threshold. This ensures that the triggering requires a large excursion of the nunchuck and prevents unintended triggers. There is a TestProcessResults function that is not called; it's included in case you want to investigate the readings of the other sensors when you hit the invisible drum. You could use this to modify what drum you trigger or how you modify the sound, like applying pitch bend.

MIDI Light Show

As a final project in this chapter, I want to look at the inverse of an instrument, which is a simple MIDI light controller. This allows you to set up light sequences from your DAW by programming it just like a loop. This project is limited to just eight strips of LEDs but is easy to extend to more lights and longer strips. First look at the simple system. Figure 5-21 shows the schematic of the system.

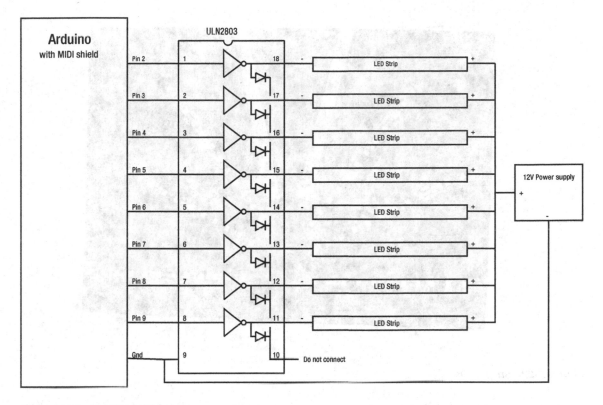

Figure 5-21. MIDI light show

You will see that it uses a ULN2803, which will allow you to drive eight 12-LED strips at the same time. The individual buffers will handle more than this, but the combination of all the strips being on at the same time will push the power dissipation of the chip. It is easy to power longer strips by replacing the ULN2803 with individual Darlington buffers like the BD679 a TIP101 or similar.

LED strips are easy to power; you just put 12V into one end and ground the other end. The flexible LED strip can be cut every three LEDs and come in a variety of colors. I arranged eight strips mounted on a base board in a fan shape, as shown in Figure 5-22.

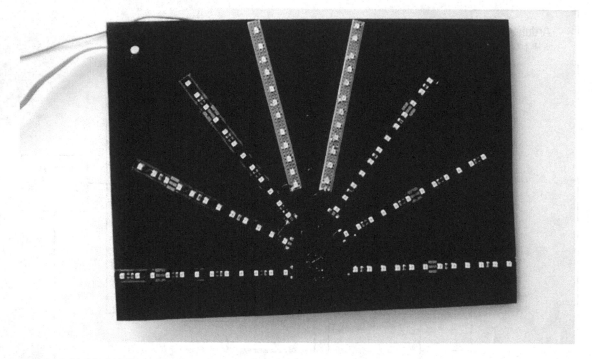

Figure 5-22. *Strip LEDs*

I covered the board in bubble wrap to act as a diffuser and it works rather well. The software is quite simple; however, for this project I have used the Arduino MIDI library as an example of how to use its callback functions. It is a lot like the Teensy system. You can get the MIDI library from `http://playground.arduino.cc/Main/MIDILibrary` and its use is shown in Listing 5-9.

Listing 5-9. MIDI Light Show

```
// MIDI Light Show - Mike Cook
#include <MIDI.h>

byte led[] = {2,3,4,5,6,7,8,9};
// pitch range to respond to
byte minPitch = 60, maxPitch = 68;
void setup()
{
  MIDI.begin(1);
  for(int i=0; i<10;i++){
  pinMode(led[i],OUTPUT);
  }

  MIDI.setHandleNoteOn(HandleNoteOn);                    #A
  MIDI.setHandleNoteOff(HandleNoteOff);
}
```

```
void loop() {
  MIDI.read();
}

void HandleNoteOn(byte channel, byte pitch, byte velocity){
    if(pitch >= minPitch && pitch <=maxPitch ){
      if(velocity == 0) digitalWrite(led[pitch - minPitch], LOW);
        else digitalWrite(led[pitch - minPitch], HIGH);
    }
 }

void HandleNoteOff(byte channel, byte pitch, byte velocity){
    if(pitch >= minPitch && pitch <= maxPitch){
    digitalWrite(led[pitch - minPitch], LOW);
    }
 }
```

#A Connect the HandleNoteOn function to the library, so it is called upon reception of a NoteOn.

The note numbers 60 to 68 are mapped to the pins in the led array. The code simply initializes the pins as outputs and sets the callback function. Then the handling routines turn on or off the LED corresponding to the appropriate notes. There is really nothing much else to it.

Summary

You have seen how a number of sensors can be pressed into service to act as MIDI instruments of various sorts. Most of these have been simple, quick-and-easy projects. To get the most out of this book, I encourage you to make your own variations and versions of these projects; it is a great way to learn. They are all suitable for a beginner. In the next chapter, we will look at a single MIDI instrument of much greater complexity, and it's definitely not suitable for beginners.

CHAPTER 6

■ ■ ■

MIDI Harp Player

This chapter covers

- What you need to do to play a real instrument
- How to construct a mechanical framework for the player
- How to control a motor powering sequence with logic gates
- The Arduino code needed to drive the player from a MIDI signal
- How to use the Harp Player in your own projects

You read in Chapter 4 how to take the information in a stream of MIDI messages and use it to light some LEDs. You also read in Chapter 2 about the structure of the MIDI messages used to control sound modules. Chapter 3 covered the ways you could get MIDI messages into an Arduino. In this chapter, we bring this all together to show you how you can use those basic concepts to play a real instrument. This is one of the major projects I talked about in Chapter 1. While you can slavishly follow what I have done here, the project's main purpose is to show you what can be done and inspire you to add your own creative input. Along the way, you will be seeing how to use logic gates and timers to automatically perform a sequence of operations to control a motor and take some of the load off the Arduino.

This project involves using workshop tools, like a saw, a drill, and a hand router. Construction of the electronic circuits will require the use of a large piece of strip board and it is moderately complex.

The instrument in question here is a medieval lute harp. However, you could, in theory, use any plucked instrument. The harp I used was a 22-string version, although it is not necessary to have a mechanism to play all the strings. In fact, the project here only plays 10 of the strings, but the hardware is designed to extend this to the full number. In that respect, this project could be considered stage one of a larger project.

The plucking mechanism for this project is rather unusual as well, because it consists of the head movement mechanism salvaged from old CD drives. It can be controlled from a MIDI sequencer like GarageBand, or you can plug it into a MIDI keyboard for direct play. It can also be used as the output from a MIDI instrument or an art installation piece.

Like all the projects in this book, this harp is not designed to be copied exactly but is a reference point for your own implementation. The design does illustrate several useful techniques for designing your own instrument player and incorporating it into your music setup. When people have seen this instrument, some have remarked about the sliding, clucking noise made by the plucking motors. Occasionally, some people have though that this is a distracting artifact, but most view it as an integral part of the instrument. Certainly the push-pull visual appearance of the plucking mechanism is fascinating to watch, and it adds much to the experience of the instrument (Figure 6-1).

Figure 6-1. *The MIDI-controlled Harp Player*

The Mechanical Design

The mechanical design is pivotal to this project and it can vary enormously depending on the design of your harp. Here, I used a medieval lute harp. Well, actually a modern instrument but built to replicate a medieval design. It is a harp designed to sit in the lap of a seated player and has thick strings mainly of clear nylon. However, the C strings are blue and the G strings are red, so you can more easily find your way about the instrument. There are many other designs for small harps, such as the Heather Harp, Celtic Harp, and Lyre Harp, as well as the large concert Welsh Harp. Fortunately, small harps are not as expensive as you might think. I picked up this Lute Harp second hand for less than $150. If you don't have perfect pitch, it is worth getting an electronic tuning indicator at the same time.

The mechanical design of this project involves several key components, and we will be going through them in detail. You need something to hold or clamp the harp to a steady base. Then you need to gather CD drives to use as the plucking mechanism. Each one needs to be mounted to the base at the right height to be able to pluck the individual strings. Finally, you need the CD drives, which have to be modified with mechanical limit sensing switches.

Building the Harp Clamp

With such an unusual shape, the first thing to do is to design a framework to hold the instrument in place. The way I chose to do this was to have the harp standing on its edge with the long bar to the bottom. The base was placed between two vertical walls and a third piece was clamped to it to hold it firm. The whole assembly was made from 12mm thick MDF. I used five M6 nutserts on the inside of one side piece to allow the clamping screws to be added, which were M6 bolts with a wing nut screwed and locked in place with an

M6 nut. A *nutsert* is a threaded insert with barbs that allow a bolt to be threaded through them. Note that these must be on the inside of the left sidepiece so that when the nuts are tightened, the force is pushing the nutsert into the MDF. These are best if they are inserted and clamped into the sidepiece before attaching it to the base.

The sides were made to stand up vertically by first routing a small slot, 5mm or so deep, in the base. Then, you set the sidepieces in this and drill five 1/4-inch holes in the base and through into the end piece. Then remove the side piece from the slot and apply woodworking glue to both pieces. Make sure a little glue is forced into the blind holes in the sidepieces. Now hammer in a piece of wooden dowel into each hole. Clamp this up while the glue dries and then add a fillet of glue between the base and the sidepiece to add extra strength (Figure 6-2).

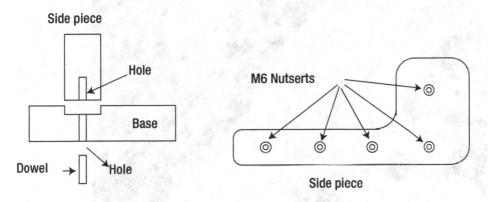

Figure 6-2. Fixing the upright sides

One side was covered in felt and the clamping piece had some 1/4-inch foam rubber glued to the side to provide a good grip without scratching the instrument. With these pieces in place, the Harp can be held quite firmly and upright. You can see in Figure 6-3 the Harp being held firmly in place. Remember not to tighten the harp clamp too much, and tighten each bolt a little at a time, just like you tighten an automobile wheel to spread the tensions evenly.

Figure 6-3. *The harp's clamping arrangement*

The Plucking Mechanism

Having fixed the Harp firmly, you can now turn your attention to the plucking mechanism. This is where ingenuity comes in. I spent a few months going through the trash at my place of work looking for old desktop computers that had been thrown out. I was after the CD drives to use on this project. When I had collected about 25, I set to dismantling them. I was after the mechanism that moves the optics across the face of the CD and not, as some people think, the draw eject mechanism. It was fascinating striping them down as I seldom found two that were identical. Even those from the same manufacturer would show design improvements and cost down revisions over several drives. It is amazing how many different designs were capable of performing the same task.

I found there were basically three different ways the optics could be driven. The first and most popular was by using a simple DC motor, which was the type I was after for this project. You can identify them in Figure 6-4 from the fact that there are only two wires coming from the motor. This sort had a limit switch at each end of the travel and sometimes a ratchet mechanism to prevent excess mechanical strain. There was a type where the optics were driven by stepping motor, shown on the left of Figure 6-4. These are not useful for this project but can come in handy for other projects I have in mind so they were put to one side. Finally there was the type where the optics were driven by a brushless motor, shown on the right. I haven't found a use for those yet, but they are in my spares drawer if inspiration ever strikes.

Figure 6-4. *Obi Wan says these are not the drives you're looking for*

The trick is to look for motors with only two wires coming from them. In addition to the motor drive, some types moved the optics on a diagonal line to the chassis (Figure 6-5). These could be used but required the mounts to be tilted to ensure that a horizontal stroke is produced perpendicular to the string. If the stroke were to slope, it could foul on the strings above or below the string you are trying to play.

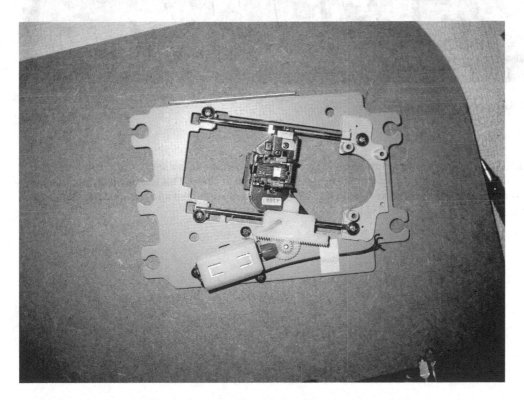

Figure 6-5. *Correct two-wire motor with a diagonal mount*

Figure 6-6 shows some of the large variety of drives I had to choose from.

Figure 6-6. *Assorted CD drive mechanisms*

Building the Staircase Drive Mounts

All the CD drive mechanisms were mounted on what can only be described as a set of stairs. The spacing of the staircase was made to match the spacing between the strings of the harp. This was again fashioned out of MDF, but this time I used 6mm thick sheet material. The outer frame was glued and clamped together using a band clamp to ensure it was square (Figure 6-7).

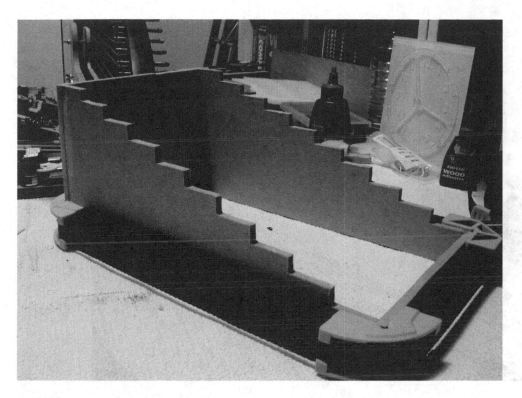

Figure 6-7. Drive mounting staircase

Then the cross pieces were glued and clamped onto the stairs. Note that on each stair I inserted two M3 nutserts to allow the mounting of the CD mechanisms (Figure 6-8). This was a bit time consuming as I had to glue and clamp each step separately and ensure the glue was dry before moving on to the next step.

Figure 6-8. *Clamping and gluing the steps*

The staircase was held in place by simply gluing a block for each corner onto the base, and then just push-fitting the staircase onto these without any glue so that they could be removed for wiring. The trick is getting the blocks exactly in the corner of the staircase. This is done by first gluing one block down and adjusting the staircase so it is in one corner. Then, when this block has set, you do the same for the opposite block. Finally, the remaining two blocks can be glued at the same time. Each time, remove the staircase while the glue dries to ensure you don't glue the staircase permanently to the base.

At this stage it is best to paint the whole assembly. Being MDF, it is very absorbent and two coats of MFD primer should be used before you attempt a topcoat of gloss. I used bright colors for the steps and gave each one two top coats of paint.

Fitting Limit Switches on the CD Drives

Next it is time to turn your attention to the CD drives. On many drives I opened up, there were no limit switches on the drive mechanisms, although there were very small switches on the disk eject mechanism. The task was to find a place where the switch could be tripped by the movement of the carriage to the end. I found that this place was different depending on the design of the drive. Some could be mounted so that the rack gear tripped the switch, whereas others were mounted so that the optical assembly tripped the switch. The recovered switches were located in the correct place and fixed using silicon rubber compound. I used the type for plumbing repairs, but any type not heavily doped with filler should do. Make sure the mechanism hits a mechanical stop before pushing the body of the switch, so that the mechanical end stop takes the force of the motor. Now you need a small piece of foam or rubber to act as a cushion on each mechanical end stop. This reduces not only the shock on the mechanism but also the noise considerably. Figure 6-9 shows two limit switches fitted to a CD drive mechanism.

Figure 6-9. Fitting limit switches

You can see the two limit switches at the top of the picture with wires attached. Note they are very different types of switches. Figure 6-10 shows a close-up of another drive with a limit switch. Note that I had to mount the switch on a small square of styrene to make it level with the drive mechanism I was trying to detect.

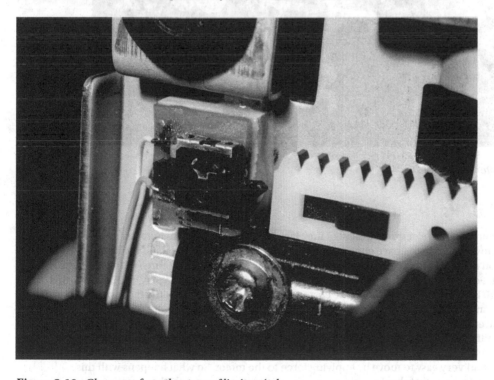

Figure 6-10. Close-up of another type of limit switch

Mounting the Motors

Finally, the striped-down CD drive mechanism is mounted on a piece of angle aluminum, which in turn is attached to each stair. If you can, make sure that each of the optic mechanisms of the CD drives is in line with a string.

Now you should attach the harp to the frame and, with lots of hot melt glue, attach a length of 5 1/2-inch long 1/4-inch thick wooden dowel to the optics. Position each one so that it just sits above the string but does not touch it. Also make sure that the dowel reaches the string at the middle of the mechanism's travel. Then hot-glue a 0.5mm thick piece of styrene to act as a plectrum on the end of each dowel. You just apply the glue to the top of the dowel to allow it a bit of flexibility. The whole assembly is shown in Figure 6-11.

Figure 6-11. *Motor assembly*

The Electronic Design

Next it's time to consider the electronic design of the Harp Player. In any design there is a trade-off between hardware and software and here I have gone for making life easy on the software and the number of input/outputs you need. The choice is between one output per string as against three outputs and two inputs per string. For a 10-string harp, that adds up to 50 I/O lines. If you want to play all 22 strings, that would require 110 I/O lines. Every compromise costs something and here it is in the more complexity required from the motor driver.

The design went through several iterations before I reached the final one, which is unusual for one of my projects. Initially I thought that the motor should be turned on, and when it hits the limit switch, it should turn off. Well, it turns out that it requires a bit more than that. When a motor is unpowered it is freewheeling and very easy to move by applying force to the motor. So what happens with this simple-minded approach is that the drive slams into the end stop and instantly the motor's power is removed. Then the recoil energy forces the drive back almost to where it came, giving a double strike. So what you need to do is detect when the drive mechanism reaches the end stop, and then delay for about 60mS and only then remove the power from the motor. This delay can be thought of as a hold time where the recoil energy is absorbed, while the drive is held firm by the still powered motor.

This needs to apply when the motor is being driven in either direction but we can't simply connect the two limit switches together as the motor would never set off moving. This is because the circuit would see the limit switch as being tripped before the motors even started. Therefore, we have to use a data select circuit to choose what limit switch our circuit looks at. This needs to be driven by a direction signal and if we arrange things correctly this can be the same signal that sets the direction of the motor. Now, normally you would have a direction signal as well as a strobe signal, which says go. However, with a bit of ingenuity, we can combine these two signals into one by using the edge of the direction signal as a strobe. The rising edge or falling edge of the direction will generate a pulse to kick the whole thing off.

Block Diagram of the System

To sum up a requirement, it is normal to generate a block diagram of the design and then work on each block specifically. Figure 6-12 shows the overall block diagram of our motor drive circuit.

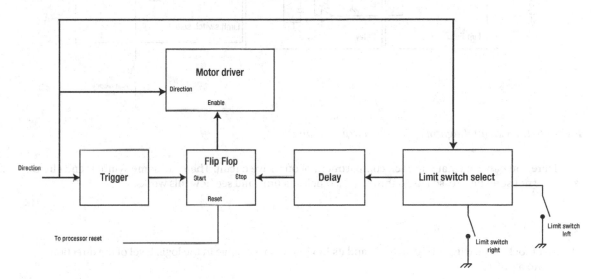

Figure 6-12. *Block diagram of the motor drive circuit*

You will see that the direction signal goes to three blocks: trigger, motor driver, and limit switch selector. The flip-flop has an extra input, that of a reset. This is common for all the motor drivers, and is connected to just one output pin on the Arduino. Its role is to hold the system steady on power up. A flip-flop is a colorful name for a bistable latch. That is a circuit that has two stable states; a pulse flips it into one state and another pulse flops it into the other. In truth this is a bit of a misnomer and should really be called a flip-flip, with a flip-flop being reserved for a monostable that you flip into one state and it flops back some time later. However, the name stuck a long time ago and that's the one everyone uses for this type of circuit. That is the name I will use here, but you and I know it's wrong.

So let's put some flesh on the bones and see how the block diagram resolves itself to be. Each block in Figure 6-12 contains some circuitry and this is reveled in Figure 6-13.

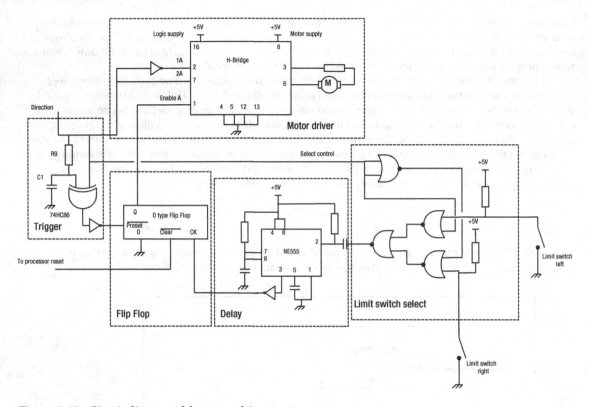

Figure 6-13. *Circuit diagram of the motor drive circuit*

Here you can see what is in each compartment of our drive circuit. There are some symbols and circuits you have not seen before, so lets go through it a block at a time and see how this works.

The Trigger

The first block is the trigger (Figure 6-14) and its job is to turn a change in the logic level of the direction signal into a pulse.

Turning a direction level change into a pulse

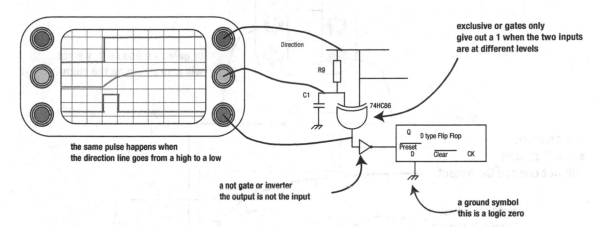

Figure 6-14. *Focus on the trigger circuit*

This uses two tricks—the exclusive OR gate and a resistor/capacitor delay circuit. An exclusive OR gate can be summed up by saying that there is a logic one on the output if the two inputs are different. If these inputs are the same, there is a logic zero output. Normally the output is a zero because the two inputs are being fed from the same signal line. One is going through a small resistor, which normally would not make any difference; however, in this case there is also a small capacitor to ground on the input as well. This means that there is small delay between the direction signal changing and that change making its way through to the output pin of the gate. The signal scope on the right shows you what is happening here. Initially, the direction signal is low and so both inputs are low and the output is low. Then the direction signal makes a transition to high, which causes the capacitor to start to charge up and the voltage begins to rise. But initially that input to the exclusive OR gate is low, with the other input being high, and because the signals don't match, the gate's output goes high. After a short time, the capacitor has charged up sufficiently for the voltage to look like a logic one on the input of the gate, and so the gate's output drops to a zero because both the inputs are the same again.

Exactly the same thing happens in reverse when the direction signal is brought low. Initially, the charge on the capacitor keeps the input looking like a logic one and so again there are different inputs on the gate producing a one on its output. After a short time, the capacitor discharges through the resistor, and the voltage drops to look like a logic zero. Both inputs are the same and a pulse has been produced on the falling edge of the direction signal. This pulse is then inverted by a NOT gate or inverting buffer before being passed to the next stage, the flip-flop. However, before we look at that, let's see where else the direction signal goes.

The Limit Switch Select Circuit

One place is the limit switch select circuit, as shown in Figure 6-15. Its job is to feed the signal from the correct limit switch to the delay to eventually turn the motor off.

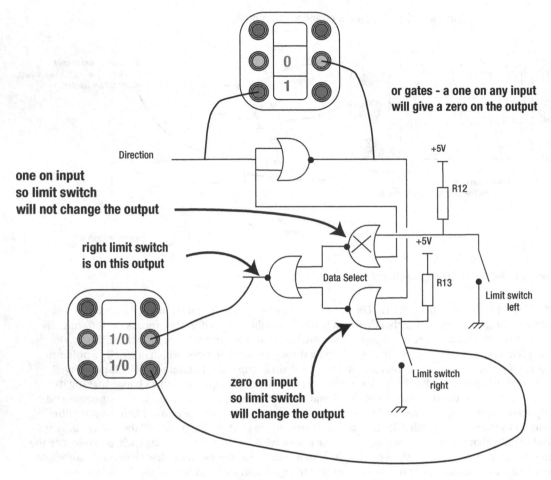

Figure 6-15. *Focus on the switch select circuit 1*

In Figure 6-15, we see the logic probe indicators showing that there is a logic one on the direction line. This time, these gates are inclusive NOR gates, which is a combination of two basic gates—the inclusive OR followed by a NOT gate or inverter. The way this gate works is that if any or both inputs are at a logic one then the output is a zero. Only when both inputs are a logic zero will the output be a logic one. The first gate the direction line sees has both inputs connected and this in effect turns it into a NOT gate. We could have used a NOT gate here but because you get four NOR gates in one package the whole of this part of the circuit fits neatly into one package. Now because the direction line is a logic one then the output of the NOR gate marked with a cross can't change, no matter what the limit switch is set to. However, the right limit switch is feeding into a gate whose other input is a logic zero; therefore, the output of this gate will be the inverse of the limit switch. This is passed to the final gate, which inverts this signal and so the final output is exactly what is being produced by the right limit switch.

Conversely, as shown in Figure 6-16, when the direction signal is low, it is the lower gate that becomes blocked and the upper gate that becomes active. This lets the logic level on the left limit switch get through to the output of the final gate.

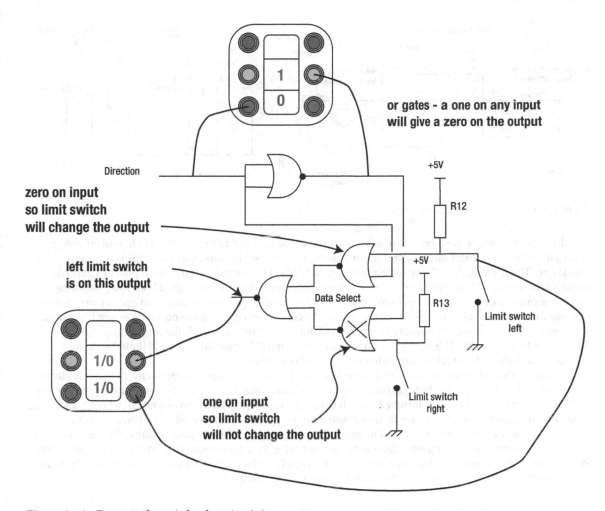

Figure 6-16. *Focus on the switch select circuit 2*

The Motor Control Block

The direction signal also goes to the motor control block, which uses half of an SN754410.

Since the motor driver chip is essentially a black box, it helps if we look at the equivalent circuit of it. An equivalent circuit is one that, while not actually being the same circuit, functions in the same way. These are often simplified, as is the case here. The chip is a quadruple half H-bridge, which means it has four half H-bridges in it. This only helps you if you know what a H-bridge is. Essentially a half H-bridge is simply two switches in series between a power supply. Turn both switches on and, poof, you have a short circuit that will cause the magic smoke to appear. So there is some logic that ensures that only one of the two switches can be closed at any time. There is also an enable input that needs to be high before any switch can turn on. If you take two of these circuits and put a load between them, in this case the motor, you get a full H-bridge, as shown in Figure 6-17.

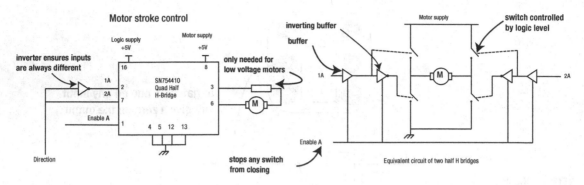

Figure 6-17. *Focus on the motor driver*

In order to control the direction of a DC motor, you need to control the direction of flow of current through it. Put the current one way and it turns clockwise, reverse that direction and it turns counter-clockwise. The inverter or NOT gate on the input of the SN754410 ensures that the two inputs (1A and 2A) always have opposite logic levels on them, no matter what level the direction signal is at. You will notice there is a resistor in series with the motor; this is only necessary if you have motors that operate on a lower voltage than that given by the motor supply voltage. Normally, this is 5V and so no such resistor is needed. However, if you want to get a bit more oomph out of the motor, you can supply the motor supply pin 8 with a bigger voltage, say 12V. This in itself might be too much for a 5V motor, so you could limit the current through the motor while still managing to give it a bit of overdrive.

Figure 6-18 shows how the current flow reversal works in an H-bridge; for simplicity, the enable circuits are omitted. On the left side, the logic probe shows a logic zero going into input 1A, which closes the bottom switch. A logic one is going into input 2A, which closes the top switch. This makes a circuit where the current flow, as indicated by the arrows, has the right connector of the motor connected to the positive motor supply and the left motor connector connected to ground. Exactly the opposite happens on the right side. The logic levels at the inputs are the opposite; this causes the opposite switches to close. You will see that now the left motor connector is connected to the motor's positive supply and the right one goes to the ground. Thus, the direction of current flow is reversed and so is the motor's rotational direction.

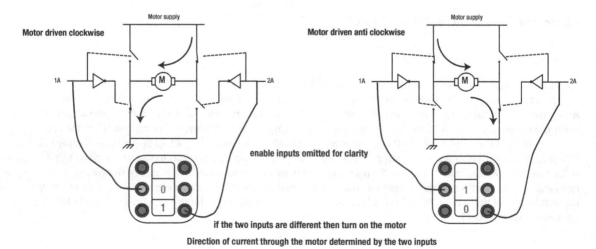

Figure 6-18. *Focus on the H-bridge*

The Delay Block

Next, we need to look at the delay section of the circuit. This takes in the signal from the selected limit switch and delays it for about 60ms so the motor is energized and resists the recoil of the CD's optics.

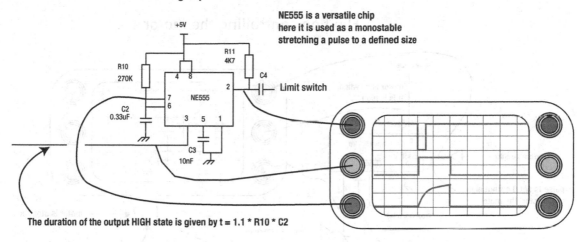

Stretching a pulse with a monostable

NE555 is a versatile chip here it is used as a monostable stretching a pulse to a defined size

The duration of the output HIGH state is given by t = 1.1 * R10 * C2

Figure 6-19. *Focus on the delay circuit*

This section uses an NE555 chip wired up to act as a monostable. A monostable is a circuit that can be triggered into an unstable state, and this is known as a quasi-stable state, and so will, after a precisely determined time interval, revert to its original state. The two states are simply the output of the circuit on pin 3, with a logic zero being stable and logic one being the quasi-stable state.

The NE555 chip is a venerable chip that has been around since 1972. It is still useful today and many books have been written about the many different applications it can be used in. Here I am using it in one of its basic modes as a monostable.

The time it is in this quasi-stable state is determined by how long it takes to charge up the capacitor C2 through the resistor R10. It often surprises beginners that you can get the units of time by multiplying the units of capacitance and resistance, but indeed that is what happens. When you do that, the number you obtain is known as the time constant. In this case, the quasi-stable state lasts for 1.1 times the time constant, which is determined by the internal design of the NE555. The input from the limit switch passes through a capacitor in a similar way as the trigger circuit to get a pulse from an edge. This pulse then triggers the monostable, shown in the top trace of the signal scope. Immediately the output, pin 3, goes high, the middle trace, and the capacitor starts to charge, bottom trace. Once the capacitor has charged to a certain level, the chip sets the output to a logic zero again and discharges the capacitor. The result is that we have a pulse on the output that lasts for the required 60ms delay. We can then use the falling edge of that pulse to stop our motor in the final stage of our drive circuit, the flip-flop.

The Flip-Flop

The flip-flop controls how long the motor runs. A basic edge triggered flip-flop transfers the logic level on the D input to the Q output on the rising edge of the clock signal. Also, the circuit has a preset and a clear input. Note that on Figure 6-20, these two inputs have a bar over their names, which means they are active low. Therefore, to preset the flip-flop, that is to set the output to a logic one, we must put a zero on the preset input. The pulse from the trigger circuit is the wrong way up, so it needs to be inverted. This is shown in

157

the top trace of the scope. This means the trigger circuit sets the output high, which turns the motor on, the middle trace. When the CD's optics reach the limit switch, the delay starts. Again, we need to invert the signal from the delay circuit to get it the right way up. When the delay finishes the rising edge of the signal transfers the logic level on the D input, which is connected to ground and so is permanently a logic zero, to the Q output, and so the motor is stopped. To make sure this circuit orchestrates the whole drive, it turns the motor on until 60ms after the limit switch is activated.

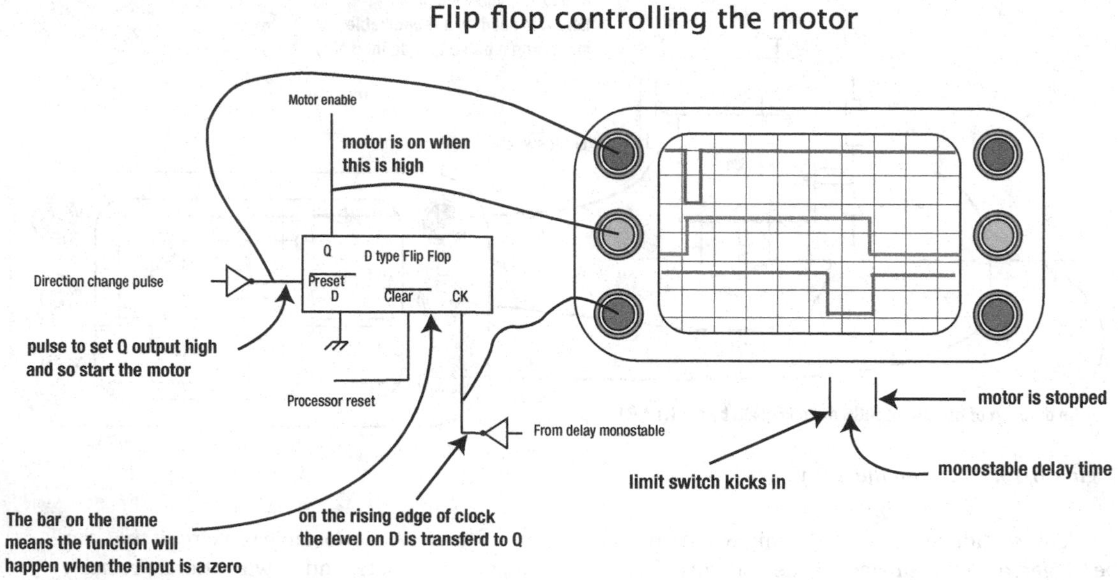

Flip flop controlling the motor

Figure 6-20. Focus on the flip-flop

Assigning Gates and Packages

Having looked at each section of the circuit in turn, it is time to see exactly how we would wire it up. Each IC has a number of identical gates in it, so rather than just having one set of ICs for one motor drive, we can have ICs shared between different motor drives, as shown in Figure 6-21.

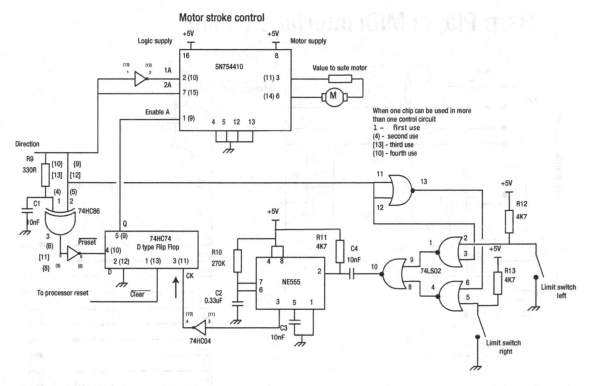

Figure 6-21. *Full motor drive schematic*

This is the full schematic for a motor drive. Remember you need one of these for each string you want to pluck. When a chip can be used in more than one drive, the alternative pin numbers are shown in brackets. For example, with the 74HC86 there are four exclusive OR gates in one package, which means the same chip can be used in four motor drive circuits. The pin numbers for the first are just shown plain, the second use is in round brackets ( ), the third use in square brackets [ ], and the fourth in curly brackets { }. Chips like the NE555 and 74LS02 can only be used in one circuit, whereas the flip-flop 74HC74 and the H-bridge SN774410 can be used in two driver circuits. This does make wiring it up a touch more complex, but also saves a lot on the number of chips you have to use.

The Arduino Controller

Now we come to the driving Arduino itself. If you are using 17 or fewer strings, you can simply use an Arduino with no additional I/O. This can be either a pucker Arduino or one you make with the separate components. Figure 6-22 shows the schematic for a homemade Arduino.

Harp Player MIDI interface wiring

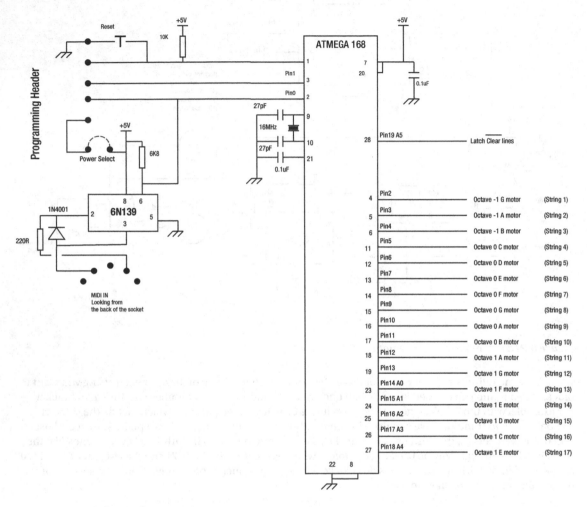

Figure 6-22. *Arduino player*

This is essentially part of the circuit you saw in the previous chapter and consists of an optically isolated MIDI input, a programming header, clock circuitry, and decoupling. The Arduino's outputs simply go to the individual motor drive circuits. If you use a real Arduino, all you need is the MIDI input part, which you can build or buy as a shield.

Power Distribution

The final part of this project's circuit is the power supply distribution. Motors, and especially DC motors, generate a lot of electrical noise. If this is not kept in check, it can end up causing temporary malfunctions in the motor drive logic or in the micro-controller itself. It is a common fault, reported by beginners on the Arduino forum, that a circuit will work until a motor is energized and then if the motor is replaced by an LED the problem goes away. This is always the result of motor noise. There are several steps that can be taken to stop this from happening. One simple-minded approach is to have a separate power supply for the logic and the motors. Although that often works, it is an expensive solution. A much better solution is to decouple the motor supply and the logic/processor supply using inductors and capacitors. Figure 6-23 shows the approach I took in this project.

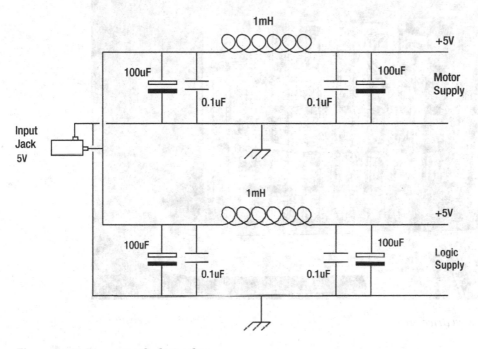

Figure 6-23. *Power supply decoupling*

I ran the project off a 5V mains supply, sometimes called a *wall wart* because they can be built into the plug that attaches to the wall. The circuit shows how this power was split between the two parts of the circuit—motor supply and logic supply. The motor supply is on pin 8 of the SN754410 chip and is separated from the logic supply by a circuit known as a pi filter, because the schematic looks a bit like the Greek letter pi ∏. It consists of a series inductor and a parallel capacitor on each side. Here, two of them are used to isolate the two supplies. The value of the inductor is not critical. Basically the higher the inductance the better, but they can get bulky. The capacitors should be a combination of a large capacitor for low frequency stabilization and small ceramic capacitor to shunt out high-frequency noise. One motor drive was considerably nosier than the rest and it caused some trouble despite the decoupling I had already. For this one I mounted extra capacitors and inductors just for that motor, actually on the CD drive itself. I built all this on strip board, surrounded it with asymmetrical aluminum channel, and mounted it on the base of the Harp board. Then I finished it off with a lid of 3mm thick styrene.

Figure 6-24. *Assembled drive circuit*

The Firmware

With all the hardware in place, it is time to write the firmware. Before you do it, it's worthwhile to test the hardware first.

Test Software

For this you do not need a MIDI input; a simple serial input from the serial monitor will do fine. The code to do this is shown in Listing 6-1.

Listing 6-1. Harp Player Test Program

```
// MIDI Harp player test by Mike Cook
void setup(){
  Serial.begin(9600);
  // make all bits outputs and low
  for(int i=2; i<20; i++){
    pinMode(i, OUTPUT); // make the pin an output
    digitalWrite(i, LOW); // set it low
    }
  while (!Serial) { } // needed for Leonardo only
  Serial.println("Harp test");
  Serial.println("type in the string number");
```

```
  delay(20);
  digitalWrite(19, HIGH); // remove motor flip flop clear
}

void loop(){
  int number = Serial.parseInt();
  if(number != 0 ){
    if(number > 17) {
      Serial.println("String number too big");
    }
    else {
      Serial.print("String number ");
      Serial.print(number);
      Serial.println(" moved");
      if( digitalRead(number+1) == HIGH) { // toggle the output pin
          digitalWrite(number+1, LOW);
        }
        else {
          digitalWrite(number+1, HIGH);
        }
    }
  }
}
```

Load this in to the Arduino and open the serial monitor. Select a baud rate of 9600 with the line ending option to New Line. Then type the string number and press Enter. You should see the motor corresponding to that string makes a transition; type in the same number and it will go back. Make sure that the motor is unpowered when it has finished moving by giving it a bit of a nudge to see that it moves freely. Remember that string 1 is connected to pin 2 and so on, so the number you are typing is not the pin number but the string number. The analogue input pins are also pressed into service as digital outputs here so string 17 will be connected to analogue pin A4, which is pin 18 when used as digital.

A quick run through the code is in order here. It consists of just the two mandatory functions—setup() and loop(). In setup() the baud rate is set and all the pins from 2 to 19 are set to be outputs and low. This includes pin 19 (labeled A5), which is the flip-flop clear common signal for all the motor drives. Then this statement:

```
while (!Serial) { }
```

Will wait until the serial port has been established inside the Arduino. Note that this is only strictly needed when using the ATmega 32u4 processor versions of the Arduino board but it does no harm if it's included in the code for other boards. After some printing and a small delay, the motor drives are enabled by removing the ~clear signal from them. Remember that a ~ in front of a signal name means it is active low, just like a bar over the name in a schematic.

The line

```
int number = Serial.parseInt();
```

looks at the input stream and returns an integer value. If nothing has been input in a second, it returns a value of zero, which is a bit of unfortunate if you want to enter a number zero. Luckily we don't here. So if the number is non-zero but is greater than our biggest string number then the program prints out an error message. Otherwise, it toggles the output corresponding to that string, by reading what it is currently set to, and then writing the inverse logic state.

The Working Software

Once you have tested the Harp motors, you can fit the Harp into the frame and play a few notes by typing in the numbers. However you need to enable the MIDI part of the circuit by writing the software to handle that.

Listing 6-2 shows the code for the MIDI Harp player.

Listing 6-2. Harp Player Program

```
// MIDI Harp by Mike Cook

   // MIDI values
  // play only notes in the key of C (that is no sharps or flats)
 // define pin numbers:-
  byte midiString[] = { 2, 0, 3, 0, 4, 5, 0, 6, 0, 7, 8, 0,    // 55 to 66
                   9, 0, 10, 0, 11, 12, 0, 13, 0, 14, 15, 0, // 67 to 78
                                       16, 0, 17, 0 };    // 79 to 82

  const int lowString =55, highString = 82;
  byte incomingByte;
  byte note;
  byte velocity;
  int state=0;        // state machine variable 0 = command waiting
                     // 1 = note waiting : 2 = velocity
  int channel = 0; // MIDI channel to respond to (in this case channel 1)
                // change this to change the channel number
                // MIDI channel = the value in 'channel' + 1

void setup() {
  Serial.begin(31250);  // for MIDI speed
    // make all bits outputs and low
  for(int i=2; i<20; i++){
    pinMode(i, OUTPUT);    // make the pin an output
    digitalWrite(i, LOW); // set it low
    }
  while (!Serial) { } // needed for Leonardo only
  delay(20);
  digitalWrite(19, HIGH); // remove motor flip flop clear
}

void loop() {
  if (Serial.available() > 0) {
    // read the incoming byte:
    incomingByte = Serial.read();
    switch (state){
      case 0:
      // look for as status-byte, our channel, note on
      if (incomingByte == (0x90 | channel)){
         state=1;
         }
         break;
```

```
    case 1:
      // get the note to play or stop
      if(incomingByte < 128) {
          note=incomingByte;
          state=2;
      }
      else{
      state = 0;  // reset state machine as this should be a note number
      }
      break;

    case 2:
      // get the velocity
      if(incomingByte < 128) {
        playNote(note, incomingByte); // turn the servo
      }
        state = 0;  // reset state machine to start
      }
    }
}

void playNote(byte note, byte velocity){
    // if velocity = 0 on a 'Note ON' command, treat it as a note off
    if (velocity == 0) return;
    if(note >= lowString && note <= highString){ // is it in the range of our strings and to
play
       note -= lowString; // start the MIDI notes in our range from zero
       if(midiString[note] !=0) { // if we have a string for this
          // move the motor
          if( digitalRead(midiString[note]) == HIGH) { // toggle output pin
             digitalWrite(midiString[note], LOW);
          }
          else {
            digitalWrite(midiString[note], HIGH);
          } // end of toggle the output pin
       } // end of if we have a string for this
    } // end of is it in the range of our strings and to play
} // end of function
```

MIDIString

The first thing to look at in this code is the array midiString, which defines the mapping between the notes that a MIDI system will send, to the Arduino pin that needs to be activated in response to those notes. We are going to use this array as an offset look-up table. The lowest string corresponds to a MIDI note number of 55; therefore, if we subtract 55 from the incoming MIDI note, we get a number that we can use to index the midiString array. If the entry in this array is zero, this means that there is no string corresponding to that MIDI note. This will happen because the Harp normally is tuned to play in one key only, whereas the MIDI note numbers represents increments of half notes. The values in this array represent the strings of the harp being tuned to the key of C, which is the normal tuning for this instrument. If you want to tune the harp in any other key, you have to change the values in this array.

Program Structure

The initialization in the setup function is virtually the same as in the test listing shown in Listing 6-1. The only difference is that now the serial speed is at the MIDI rate of 31250 baud. The loop function is basically one large state machine looking for MIDI messages. These arrive one byte at a time and advance the state machine with each byte that arrives. At the first stage, state 0, we are looking for a note on message. Due to the nature of the playing mechanism we don't care about note off messages, because there is nothing we can do with that information. Not only do we need to spot a note on message, we need to spot one for the MIDI channel our harp is set to, so our channel number is merged with the note on message number to generate the byte we expect to see. Once we spot that, we advance to the state machine by making the state variable equal to one.

Then in this state we are looking for the note to play. If this is less than 128, we know it is a note number and not a message so we can advance the state machine to state two. If it is greater than 12 then it must be another sort of MIDI message. The state is set back to zero and the state machine will start looking for the note on message again.

Finally at state two, if we receive another byte below 128, it signifies the velocity and also the end of the note on message. If it meets that criteria, the playNote function is called and the state variable is set back to zero. We wait for the next note on message.

PlayNote Function

Finally lets turn our attention to the playNote function. This takes in the note and velocity and plays the appropriate string. If the velocity is zero then this is a way that MIDI can indicate a note off action with a note on message. Therefore, all we do is return from the function with nothing more to do. That is all we do with the velocity because the hardware has no way of doing anything with that information. Next, there is a test to see if the note is within the range of our strings, and then the array is checked to see if the note number actually corresponds to a string. As mentioned before, this will depend on what key the Harp is tuned in, and is defined by the midiString array. Having passed all these tests the midiString array is used to determine exactly what Arduino pin to toggle. This is done in the same way as the test program described earlier.

Controlling the Harp Player

With the MIDI interface, this project becomes a sound generator in its own right, and as such can be controlled by any DAW to both be a solo instrument or part of an ensemble of sound generators. However, the mechanical nature of the sound generation does lend itself more to being a solo instrument. The limited range of the number of strings you can play and the fact that it is normally only playable in one key does limit the tunes you can play on it. If tunes are indeed what you are after. You can even experiment with different tuning, say a pentatonic scale, or even micro-tuning.

While getting the Harp Player to play a computer programmed sequence is fine, you can have great fun simply connecting it to a MIDI keyboard. Musicians can then adapt their playing style to suit the rhythm and tempo imposed by the fixed speed mechanical plucking arrangement. You can also use any effects the keyboard might have, such as arpeggiator or key shifter. Note that there is a limit to how rapidly any one string can be plucked, but the timing between playing different strings is as flexible as MIDI will allow. Figure 6-25 shows the finished Harp from the back.

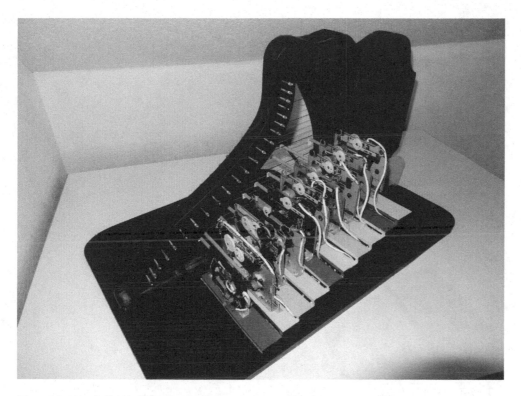

Figure 6-25. *The back of the finished project*

Finally, you don't have to have to use it as a musical instrument as such. It could be part of an art installation reacting to things around it. You might want to couple it up to some face recognition software and have notes registering how happy someone looks. It could be coupled to a staircase so a note is plucked for each stair that was trod on, a sort of stairway to heaven. It could announce a Tweet, an e-mail, or a Facebook message if coupled to the Internet. It could monitor the stock market or any other data set that you would like to sonify; the choice is yours.

■ ■ ■

CHAPTER 7

The DunoCaster

This chapter covers

- Creating a MIDI guitar

- Emulating the behaviour of the six strings

- Using I2C port expanders

- Creating touch sensors

- Using cool hidden LED construction techniques

- Using continuous rotation encoders

So far you have looked at the MIDI system and its messages. You have manipulated a MIDI stream to produce some fantastic effects and looked at simple instruments and controllers. In the last chapter, the project was a lot larger, producing a MIDI sound module that played a real harp. Now it is time to look at making a complex instrument, the DunoCaster. This is basically a MIDI instrument with the sensibility of a guitar. Sometimes these instruments are known as *keytars* because they use keys in a guitar form. However, the DunoCaster is a unique instrument in that it is easy to play and yet produces MIDI patterns reminiscent of a real guitar. Sergi Jorda, the director of the team that invented the Reactable instrument system, said to me that nothing is a real instrument unless you can play it badly. So, in that respect, the DunoCaster is definitely a real instrument. However, it is one that is very easy to learn how to play passably well.

The Concept

According to my five-year-old son, a guitar was easy to play because all you did was move your fingers at one end and hit the strings at the other end with your hand. Basically that is true, but like all things, the devil is in the details.

Exactly where you put your fingers matters enormously. You have to hold down strings at specific positions in order to generate chords. That takes a bit of mechanical dexterity and strength, not to mention a certain toughening of the fingertips. Once my son was a teenager, his desire to preserve the state of his fingertips was his excuse to get out of washing the pots for years. The other hand also has things it needs to learn. Yes, you can strum; but you can also strike individual strings in a repetitive fingerpicking fashion. There are many patterns you can use for picking, but they all need to be learned. My idea with this instrument is that the functions of the two hands should be much easer to learn. The finished instrument is shown in Figure 7-1.

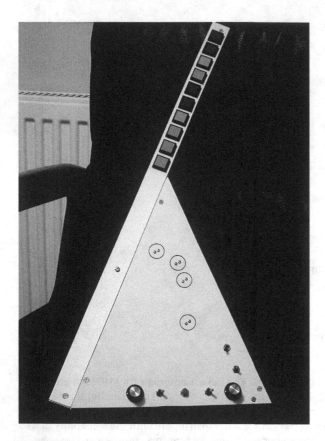

Figure 7-1. *The finished DunoCaster*

Guitar Chords

The standard guitar has six strings with a standard tuning of E, A, D, G, B, and E, from lowest (low E) to highest (high E), and while there are many other possibilities for tuning, this is regarded as the standard one. Each fret on the guitar's neck raises the pitch of a note by a semitone, and you play chords by holding down a combination of strings on specific frets. The limitations of the human hand restrict the patterns of some chords from obtaining all the correct notes for some chords and so some chords are a musical compromise. Some strings are not played for certain chords. It would be easy in an electronic instrument to get around these limitations, but in order for an electronic instrument to sound like the real thing, it is important that at least some of these limitations are reproduced.

The idea is that a number of switches on the neck of the DunoCaster will set the strings to a specific chord, E to D, so to generate a chord you simply press down the switch. So seven switches will cover all the chords. It is not quite that simple though, because there are more than seven chords. Sure there are seven major chords but another seven minor ones, not to mention major and minor sevenths chords, and that is just a start. If each chord were to have its own push button, there would be a huge number of buttons and the instrument would resemble a keyboard. In fact, the accordion has a mass of keys that do just this.

The key to this problem is to remember that you have up to four fingers free to press keys, so I came up with a unique system of setting a chord. The index finger presses a key/switch. This defines the root chord. If nothing else is pressed, you get the major version of the chord. However, if the three switches farther down the neck from the root chord are pressed, then the type of chord is modified. For example, if the next key is pressed then you get a minor version of the chord; if the second key from the root is pressed, then you get a major seventh version; if the two keys following the root are pressed, you get a minor seventh. Because there are three extra keys that can be pressed after the root chord, you can get up to eight variations of each chord, giving a total of 56 different chords. The great thing is that your fingers only have to learn what pattern of keys to hold down for one chord variation and any chord of that type can be produced by simply shifting your fingers up and down the neck. This is shown in Figure 7-2.

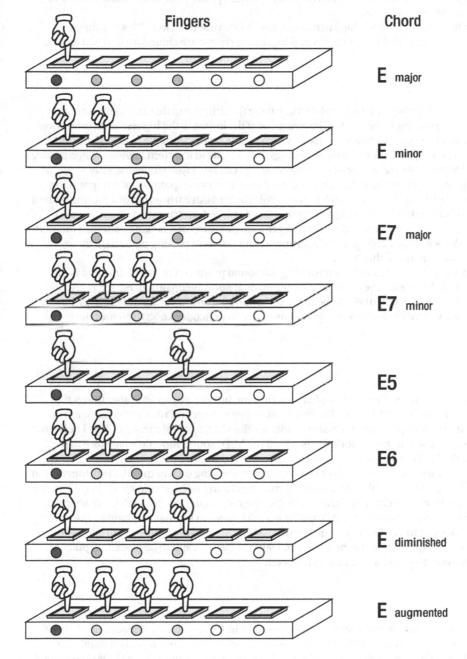

Fingers   **Chord**

E major

E minor

E7 major

E7 minor

E5

E6

E diminished

E augmented

Figure 7-2. The method of selecting a chord

This arrangement makes it easy to learn and play chords on this instrument. It also sets the number of switches you need on the neck to seven for the root chords plus three for the extension of the highest chord. In order to act as a feedback mechanism when you are holding down the keys, there are LEDs that light up. The LED against the root chord, set by the highest key up the neck, shows up as red. The three keys following this are available as chord modifiers and the LEDs against these show up as green. If any of these three keys are pressed, the green light turns yellow. So you can instantly see what pattern you are holding down and what keys are available to modify that chord.

In order to get a wider dynamic range, this instrument has an octave shift switch. This is a simple three-position switch that can select where the notes making up the chords are shifted up or down an octave.

Picking

The right hand (of a right-handed player) is responsible for striking the strings and there are quite a number of techniques to do this. The simplest is the strum. The strings from the lowest to the highest are brushed over with the thumb or a plectrum, or you can easily reverse this, striking the strings from the highest to the lowest. But there are many more ways of playing by striking the strings individually in a pattern known as *fingerpicking*. This is not just restricted to single strings either—two or more strings can be played simultaneously.

To make this operation simple to learn, I made the instrument have preset patterns of string striking automatically produced. There is a "thumb" switch that controls the repetitive triggering of a picking pattern sequence. As long as this is held down, the strings are continuously picked or strummed. There are also four (one for each finger) touch-sensitive switches that trigger a single sweep of a picking pattern, a different pattern for each switch. As that would only give the instrument four different picking patterns, a three-way *picking bank switch* is used to increase this to 12.

One of the most important parameters in determining the sound produced by the instrument is the speed of the picking pattern. If it is slow, you can hear the individual notes being produced; if it is fast, it can sound like a strum. Therefore, there needs to be some sort of picking speed control on the instrument. However, this has to have a very wide dynamic range, so I used a rotary encoder knob to control the instrument's speed.

Other Controls

The chords and picking are the two main controls of the instrument, but there are a few other things that need to be controlled in an instrument like this. The first is the volume. A second rotary encoder knob is used to define the volume or more precisely the note velocity for the MIDI note on message. This knob also serves as the voice select knob when the DunoCaster is telling the MIDI sound module what voice to use. A push button will send the MIDI Program Change message.

The other control is labelled "fret". This is has two functions, depending on whether the instrument is in playing mode or voice change mode. In playing mode, it turns on/off a fret noise sound effect, played on the next MIDI channel up, whenever the chord is changed. In the program mode, the fret switch will alternate between changing the voice and setting a capo. A "capo" is a device used on a guitar to clamp all the strings at a specific fret. This allows you to easily change the key of what you are playing. This control allows you to choose how many frets down, up to a maximum of six, you want the virtual capo to be placed. In practice, each fret down simply adds a semitone to the notes produced.

Indicators

As well as the control switches, there are a number of LEDs used as indicators. I have already talked about the LEDs on the neck used to show what chord switches are being held down, but there are a number of others. There is an LED for each of the strings that light up when the string sounds. These LEDs serve a dual function because in the change voice or program mode they act as a feedback indicator to show you what instrument number you are sending to the sound module. The voice number is shown in binary, so there is a maximum of 64 different ones the instrument can call up.

Then there are three LEDs that reflect the states of the octave shift, picking pattern shift, and the fret switch. There is also an RGB LED that color-codes the chord being held down—this is more for show than a useful function. Finally, there is an RGB LED that flashes according to the picking speed. This is useful for adjusting the picking speed rotary encoder to get it right before you ever play a single note.

One of the more interesting features of this instrument is that all the LEDs, with the exception of the chord LEDs, are hidden. This means that until they are lit there is no visible indication that there is an LED in that position. This is achieved by drilling a blind hole in the front cover and gluing the LEDs in place. When they are lit, they shine through the translucent styrene cover.

Apart from the RGB LEDs, all the other LEDs are common cathode red/green LEDs, there are two LEDs in the one package. This allows you to have three colors. You get yellow when both red and green LEDs are on. This is especially useful with hidden LEDs like this, because when they are not on, you simply cannot see them. In order to indicate one of two states, it is good to have two colors to do it with instead of just on and off.

One other thing with the instrument I wanted to avoid is the use of labels. On real guitars you don't see labels on the pickup switches saying what pickups they control, or labels on the knobs saying what part of the tone they affect, so you will see a clean interface on the DunoCaster. The one exception I made to this was the chord buttons on the neck. I used some stick on foam letters to label the chord LEDs to help beginners (like myself).

The Circuit Parts

Before you look at the full schematic of the DunoCaster, it is best to try to understand some of the component parts of the circuit. This will make it easer to understand the full circuit when you come to it in the next section. We covered some of the parts in earlier chapters, but others you will see for the first time here.

The backbone of the instrument is an Arduino running four 16-bit I2C port expanders. I chose to build a standalone Arduino here rather than a ready-built system because there are a lot of other components and one more chip for the ATmega processor chip is no great problem. However, you could use one of the prebuilt miniature Arduino boards like the Arduino Mini. You'll just need a USB adaptor board to program it, as you do with a standalone system, but the great advantage is that once you have programmed it you can use the adaptor board in your next project and the one after that. You don't have to include the now redundant USB adaptor.

The Port Expanders

The port expanders are the I2C version of the expanders used in Chapter 5 (I2C was discussed in Chapter 1). It is easy to add eight of these onto the I2C bus, but on this project you need only four of them. These port expanders handle the LEDs and the switches and push buttons.

The LEDs are driven directly but the switch inputs use some of the port expanders' features. For example, there is an optional pull-up resistor for each input bit just like there is on the Arduino. However, unlike an Arduino there is also the option of inverting the sense of the input bits. This means that you can wire the input switches "correctly" as just connecting a ground to the input and still read the action of it being pushed as a logic one. Normally, a ground on the input would be read as a logic zero, but reading it as a one makes the logic in the rest of the code slightly simpler because the action (pressing a button) can be associated with a true logic state. This enables you to write code with a more English language feel.

The other great feature of the port expanders when they're used as inputs is the interrupt triggering system. This is an output on the port expander that goes low whenever one or more of a selected group of input pins change state. This could be used to trigger an interrupt on the Arduino, but there is no need to do that here. Instead what happens on this project, is that this interrupt pin is read on a regular basis, or as we say *polled*, to see if we need to read the port expanders or not. This is a very efficient way of using the port expanders because it means the only time you need to read in all the bits is when there has been a change. Reading all the bits does not take too long (400us), but it does take some time so it is best not to do it just to find if something has changed.

Switches

There is nothing too unusual about the switches I used, but some are premade and one type we'll make on our own.

Store-Bought Switches

The chord switches in the neck are a low-profile tactile switches type made by NKK and are rather good looking and not too expensive. They come in a round or rectangular style with a variety of colored tops. For this project, I used the JF15SP1C with a red top, the JF15SP1G with the blue top, and the JF15SP1H with the grey top. There are also orange and green tops available as well. Of course, you can use any other type of switch you like, as long as it is a momentary push-to-make type.

For the toggle switches, I used three position switches. These are like the normal change-over switch, but there is a center position where the common connection is not connected to anything. This allows you to make a three state switch by connecting a ground to the common connector and an input to the other two switch contacts. So when reading this, you get no pin grounded, or the left grounded or the right grounded. The fourth combination of both the inputs being grounded is not possible.

Creating a Touch Switch

There is a very different sort of switch used here and this is a touch switch. I use these to trigger one run of a specific string-picking pattern. These are very simple to make and consist of simply two screw heads mounted close together, but not touching, on the front panel. If you place a finger across these screw heads, your skin's conductivity will cause a very tiny current to flow and this can be picked up and amplified into a logic level. The basic circuit is shown in Figure 7-3, and it uses a logic gate made using CMOS technology. These have a very high input impedance and are well suited to this sort of trickery. I say trickery because they were not designed to do this, but they can be made to do so.

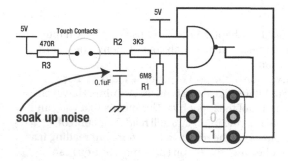
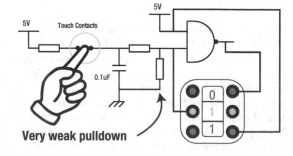

Figure 7-3. *A touch sensor made with a logic gate*

What happens is that the circuit uses a logic NAND gate. This gate will produce a logic one if any of its inputs are a logic zero; otherwise it will produce a zero. Now in the circuit you will see that one input is connected directly to 5V, so that is a logic one. The other input is connected to ground through a 6M8 resistor R1, which has a very high value of 6,800,000 ohms. This is enough for it to be considered just to be a logic zero and so the output of the gate is a logic one.

The touch contacts allow you to connect the input to +5V through some low value resistors and the resistance of the skin on your finger. This is enough to tip the logic gate into producing a logic zero on the output. The two resistors—R2 and R3—are there to protect things. First of all, R2 is there to prevent too much current being placed on the gate's input if you are charged up with static, and R3 is there to prevent too much current flowing if the touch contact is accidentally connected to anything metal that is grounded.

The capacitor is there to absorb any short but high voltage static bursts and also to act as a filter for the AC supply generated interference that your body will pick up naturally like an antenna.

The Reflective Optical Switch

The final switch is the one that keeps the finger pattern going. This is a reflective optical switch that consists of an infrared light emitting diode and sensor. The idea is that when something gets close, the infrared light is reflected off it and triggers the sensor. This is triggered by the thumb or by the cupped palm of your hand; you simply move your hand a fraction of an inch up and down over the sensor's hole. This technique is useful for shielding the sensor from strong external light. Some automatic translation services on the Internet translate the term *reflective optical switch* into *contemplative optical switch,* which while being totally incorrect is rather amusing.

Rotary Encoder

The final new component is a rotary encoder. I use two of these to provide a continuously rotational control. You use potentiometers (pots) in Chapter 4 for controlling the echo delays, and they are useful for simple control. However, they are limited in the angle that they will rotate through, normally about 240°, and the control range is limited to the resolution of the analogue to digital converter. This means that the range is limited, and if you want a wide range of control it is squashed into the small rotational angle.

To get over these problems, you can use incremental rotary shaft encoders. These produce pulses, about 8 to 16 per revolution. You can get encoders with a much higher resolution, but they are bulkier and way more expensive. The downside to using them is that you need a computer to read them, which is lucky because the Arduino is one. The way it works is that the encoder outputs two signals, A and B, that go up and down to indicate that the knob has been rotated. If you just want to know about the movement then either signal will indicate that. However, in order to tell what direction the knob is being turned, the two signals are in what is known as quadrature, that is they are 90° out of phase. This is shown in left side of Figure 7-4.

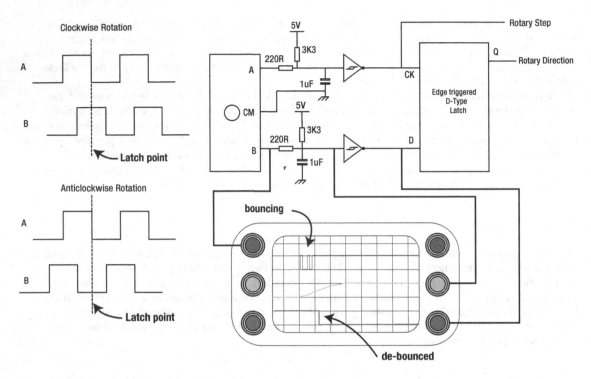

Figure 7-4. *The quadrature signal from a rotary encoder*

In order to see which direction the knob has moved, you compare the states of the signals before and after the move. From that, you can deduce if there has been a clockwise or counter-clockwise motion.

This is further complicated by the fact that, being low-cost mechanical rotary shaft encoders, they are inclined to bounce. That is, the transitions on the signals are not clean and will look like rapid switching on and off for a short time after they are changed.

There are many techniques for reading controls like this, but the one I have chosen to use here is to have Schmitt input buffers and capacitors to take out the bounce, and then a data latch to generate a direction signal from the pulses. The way this works is shown in Figure 7-4. Signals from the encoder are cleaned up, or as we say de-bounced, by passing them through a resistor/capacitor network. This means that any bouncing on the edge gets absorbed by the network. The Schmitt input buffer restores the sharpness of the signal edge, the action of it is to have a threshold where voltages above the threshold are treated as a logic one and below it as a logic zero. You might think that this is the action of a normal logic gate, and to a limited extent it is. However, the Schmitt input has a hysteresis on the threshold voltage. This means that there is a different threshold voltage for positive and negative going pulses, which prevents oscillation when slow signals with noise are going through the threshold voltage. It can also cope with much slower rising edges than normal logic gates can. So at the output of the Schmitt buffer the signal you get is just like the theoretical signal in Figure 7-4. The little symbol inside the triangular schematic symbol is supposed to indicate this hysteresis.

An edge triggered D-type latch remembers a logic level at an instant in time; the logic level on the data input (D) is transferred to the output (Q) on the rising edge of the clock signal. In other words, it takes a snapshot of the logic level on D on a transition from zero to one on the clock input. It is a sort of memory, because it keeps that logic level held on the output until another clock comes along. This is just what we need for sensing the direction from the rotary encoder, when one signal makes a specific transition (zero to one) the state of the other signal will indicate the direction of rotation. Therefore, you have a separate step and direction signal.

To use this, just keep a running total and increment or decrement the total on each step pulse according to the state of the direction signal. This method is well suited to the infrequent polling I am going to use on this project. You will notice in Figure 7-4 that the falling edge of signal A is marked as the latch point. This is because the debounce circuit also inverts the logic signal, so a falling edge on the encoder is converted to a rising edge on the latch to trigger it.

The Schematic

Unfortunately, the schematic for the DunoCaster is too big to be printed in one page of this book; even if we printed it on a fold-out section it would be too big. I have to do what the professionals do and break it down into a series of five figures. In order to help you navigate your way around them, they are drawn in what is known as a hierarchical way. This means that there is a key diagram and that contains blocks that have a specific function but are not detailed schematics as such—they are just drawn as blocks. The key point to remember is that each one of those blocks is in itself another schematic diagram. That diagram might in its turn contain other blocks with more grouped functionality further down the hierarchy. This is a much better way of drawing a schematic; better than creating a flat drawing that extends over several pages with interpage links.

The Processor

Figure 7-5 shows the top level of the hierarchy and contains, among other things, the processor. As I mentioned, this could be an Arduino of some description, but here it is shown as a standalone Arduino type system.

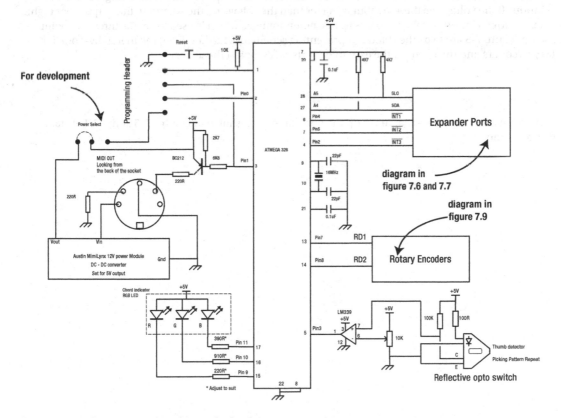

Figure 7-5. *The processor: top hierarchy level*

It contains not only the processor but also the reflective optical switch, MIDI output circuit, power regulator, and chord change RGB LED.

The MIDI output is just like you have seen in all the other projects in this book; however, for this project I used a special MIDI lead using one of the unused MIDI pins to carry the unregulated power to the instrument so that there was only one lead going into it. I made the lead using a MIDI plug (five-way DIN type plug) going to a matching cable mounting socket. Out of the back of that socket came the two wires for the power. The front of the socket was used with a normal MIDI connection cable to go to a sound module or other MIDI interface.

This 12V is then fed into a regulator to convert the 12V down to 5V. I used a switching regulator here because they are small, efficient, and run cool. There is nothing special about the one I chose, any switching regulator will do. You can even use a liner regulator if you like, although they do tend to run a bit warmer because they simply convert the excess electrical power into heat. If you use one, it is a good idea to attach it to the metal frame of the DunoCaster to act as a bit of a heat sink. There is a power select link in the circuit so you can switch the power supply from your regulator to USB power during development and testing.

The chord indicator RGB LED is driven by three of the PWM (pulse width modulation) pins on the Arduino. These produce rapidly changing on/off signals, and the ratio of the on to off time can be easily changed without requiring software intervention to keep them going. The LEDs are powered by current sinking, which means that the LED is on when the output pin is low. This allows the current to flow through the device. This results in the signal being upside down as far as the software is concerned, with an analogue write value of 255 being off and one of 0 being on. This is neatly side-stepped by subtracting the brightness value you want to use from 255.

The output from the reflective optical switch is passed through a LM339 comparator to turn the slowly varying signal from the IR sensor into a sharp on/off transition. This chip compares two voltages on its +ve and -ve inputs. If the voltage on the +ve input is higher than the voltage on the -ve input, the output goes high; otherwise, it is low. This other voltage comes from a potentiometer, which is used to set the threshold point.

Also on Figure 7-5 are two other blocks representing schematics further down the hierarchy—one for the rotary encoders and the other for the expander ports. Let's look at those next.

The Port Expanders

In fact, there are two schematics that make up the port expanders, shown in Figures 7-6 and 7-7. Lets take them one at a time.

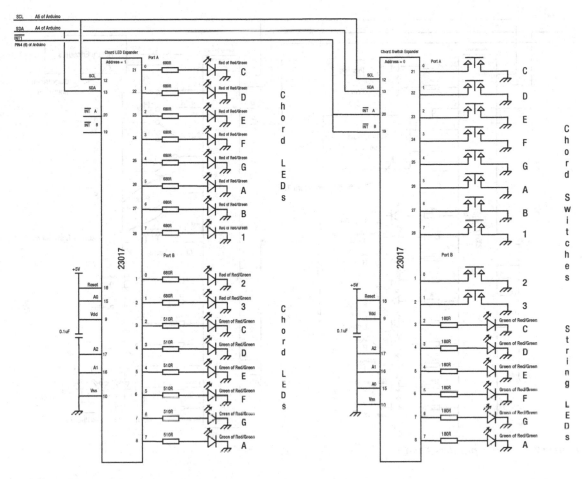

Figure 7-6. *Port expanders 0 and 1*

Figure 7-6 shows the simpler of the two diagrams of the port expanders, as they just have LEDs or switches attached to them. The port expander at address 1, the Chord LED expander, has all the red LEDs of the chord indicators and six of the green ones. The remaining four green LEDs are mopped up on port expander address 2, which is shown in Figure 7-7. This makes the programming not as easy as it might be, but because we need 10 LEDs of each color, it is not too complex to cope with. Note that the resistors for the red LEDs are a higher value than the green ones. This is because the green LEDs have a higher forward voltage and so identical resistors will not give identical brightness. What you want here is to get a nice yellow color so you might want to play around with the different values to get a good mix.

The port expander at address 0, the chord switch expander, is mainly taken up with the ten switches that define the chord to be played. As the port expanders have internal pull-up resistors, these simply need connecting to ground through the switch. The remaining six bits on this expander neatly accommodate the six green string LEDs.

The signals leaving this schematic are the two I2C lines and the two combined port interrupt signals from port address 0. These go directly into the processor. So lets turn our attention to the other pair of port expanders shown in Figure 7-7.

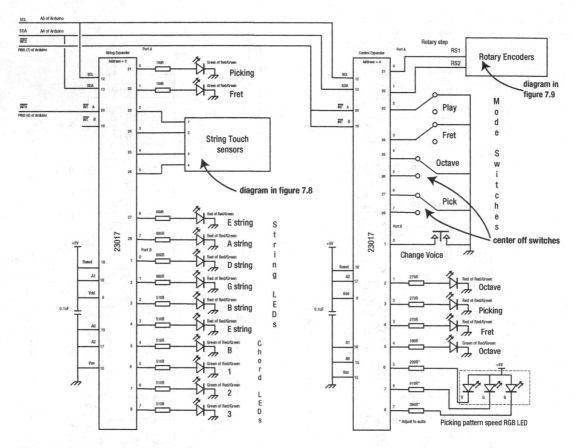

Figure 7-7. *Port expanders 2 and 4*

There is a lot more going on in Figure 7-7, because there is a bit more mopping up of signals. The string expander at address 2 has the six red string LEDs and the four remaining green chord LEDs on it. There are also the connections to the string touch sensors shown in another diagram further down the hierarchy. Finally, on this expander is the green part of the LEDs indicating the picking bank and the fret switch states. There is an interrupt signal from this expander directly to the processor to allow you to monitor when there has been a change in the state of the string touch sensors.

The control port expander at address 4 has the control switches and push button on it. The play and fret switches are simply change-over switches with one side wired up, whereas the octave shifting and pick pattern bank are three-way (center off) toggle switches. Finally, the change voice push button is a normal push to make switch.

The other inputs on this expander come from yet another diagram further down the hierarchy that monitor the rotary encoders. These are the step inputs; note that the direction inputs are wired directly to the processor. Any change in the control switches or rotary encoders is signalled by the port's two interrupt pins. Here they are connected in a wired OR configuration to signal changes from either side (port) of the expander.

The remainder of this expander is devoted to the control switch feedback LEDs and the picking speed indicator RGB LED. Note that this LED, unlike the chord LED, cannot have the brightness of the individual controlled—they are either on or off. This gives you a total of seven colors that can be obtained from this LED.

The String Touch Sensors

Figure 7-8 shows the schematic of the four string touch sensors. Essentially, they show the same circuit shown in Figure 7-3, only with four NAND gates in the same package.

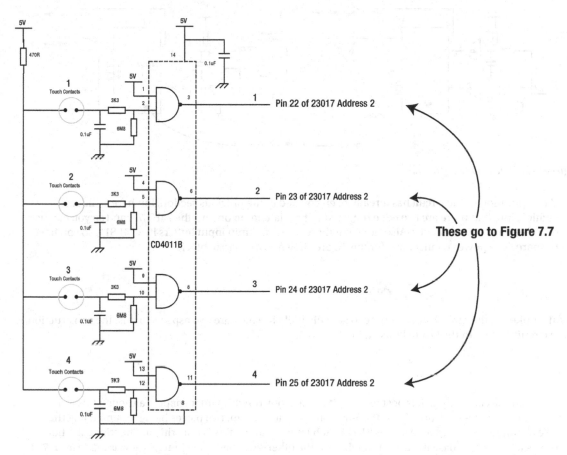

Figure 7-8. *The string touch sensors*

Note that the NAND gates are all contained inside a CD4011B integrated circuit and that the +5V connection from each sensor is protected by the same pull-up resistor. Each of the gate outputs goes to a pin on a port expander in Figure 7-7.

The Rotary Encoder

Finally, the schematic showing the circuit of the two-rotary encoder is shown in Figure 7-9.

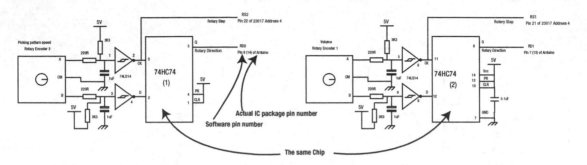

Figure 7-9. *The rotary encoders*

The operation of the circuit has already been covered in the previous section, but here is the real schematic. Note that there are two edge triggered D-type latches in one IC, the 74HC74, and so you can use just one chip for the two circuits. Also note that there are six Schmitt input buffers in a 74LS14, so you have two to spare. The power connections for this IC are shown as a separate block.

Constructing the Circuit

Having looked at the circuit, now it's time to actually build it. There are two aspects to this: the construction of the circuit itself and the box to house it in.

Building the Case

Starting with the case, I think it is best to make it at least look roughly guitar shaped, although this is not necessary. I made the neck out of 1 by 9/16-inch angled aluminium, two pieces being mounted together to make a square sectioned tube. It was 21 1/4-inch long, although this is not critical. The triangular body frame was a 8 3/4-inch base isosceles triangle with the other sides being 11 ¾ inches. It was made from 7/8 by 3/8-inch U channel aluminium, with the two pieces, neck, and triangle fixed together to be flush at the top edge. Holes were drilled along the neck to take the switches and the chord indicating the LEDs. A slot was created that aligned the triangle and the neck to pass the wires through. This is shown in Figures 7-10 and 7-11.

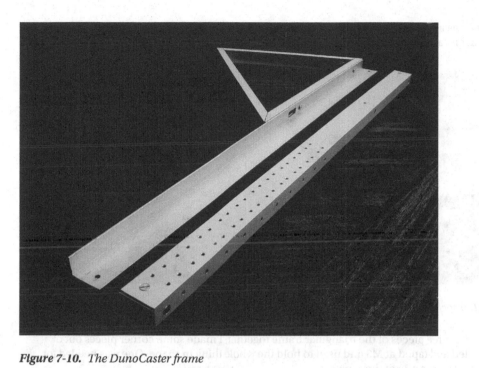

Figure 7-10. *The DunoCaster frame*

Figure 7-11. *The end fixings*

The MIDI socket was attached to the corner of the triangular frame on the same edge as the neck. It attached and fitted nicely, as shown in Figure 7-12.

Figure 7-12. The MIDI socket

In order to hold the three pieces of the triangular frame together, I made some corner pieces out of brass. These were drilled and taped at M3 and used to hold the whole thing in shape. One was needed for each corner; Figure 7-13 shows one of these pieces.

Figure 7-13. The brass corner fixings

The front cover for the triangle was made from 1/8-inch thick styrene sheet, which is just about translucent when illuminated with a strong light. The thinner the sheet the more translucent it is. The back cover was made from 1/8-inch thick grey ABS plastic sheet, although you can use styrene if you like. The back cover had recessed blind holes in it drilled with a router bit fixed in a drill press. This allowed it to sit flush over some of the fixing pan head screws holding the triangular frame together. Two of these holes are shown in Figure 7-14.

Figure 7-14. *Blind holes in the back plate*

In the neck, I over drilled the holes for the switch connectors so that they would not short out against the aluminium when I mounted them. I used a small blob of glue placed in the center of the switch to fix them. Then I placed the switch through the holes and pushed it into place. I adjusted the rotation so that it was squarely aligned with the line of the neck and made sure the legs were not touching the aluminium. Take some time with this, because there is nothing that looks worse than square switches at slightly different angles. You can use epoxy for this, but I used silicon sealant so that at a push the switches could be pried off if needed. I also glued the red/green chord indicator LEDs into the neck at the same time. Figure 7-15 shows this when the common ground for both the switches and the LEDs are in place.

Figure 7-15. *Switches and LEDs beginning to be wired up in the neck*

I wired up all the LEDs and the reflective optical switch, as shown in Figure 7-16. I painted the area around the switch inside the neck black to minimize any reflections off the aluminium.

Figure 7-16. *The optical reflective switch*

Constructing the Circuit

For construction of the logic component circuits, I used a Euro card prototype board. These are a standard size of 160 by 100 mm. I had to cut the corner off to get it to fit in the triangular C section aluminium. You can see this in Figure 7-17.

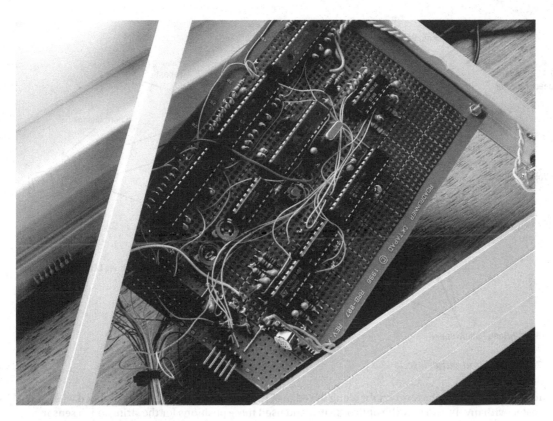

Figure 7-17. *The logic board*

Once this is wired to the chord and the switches, you can start on the front panel. You have a choice about where to put the lights and controls. Figure 7-18 shows the layout I used.

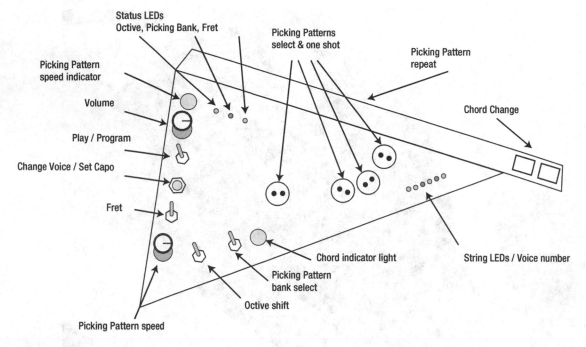

Figure 7-18. *The front panel layout*

I mounted all the switches and knobs along the edge of the triangular section. Then I marked where my fingers rested with my thumb over the optical switch and used these positions for the string touch sensor switches. I used two M2 screws mounted as close as possible without touching for the contacts. Around each pair of contacts, I took a pair of dividers set to 3/8-inch and scratched a circular line. Then I flooded the grove with black ink before quickly wiping off any that touched the surface. In that way my scored grove had a nice black line effect. Then the LEDs were mounted on the underside of the styrene top cover. I used a pillar drill and carefully drilled in three quarters of the way into the styrene, leaving a blind hole. I stood the LEDs in them and used hot melt glue to hold them in place. Figure 7-19 shows the LEDs standing in the styrene panel just after gluing.

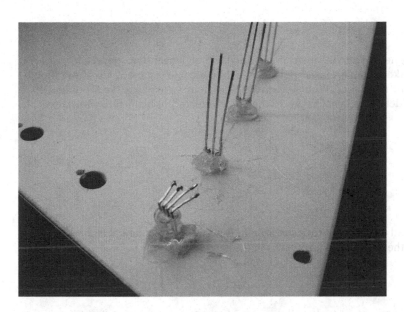

Figure 7-19. *Fixing the LEDs to the back of the front panel*

Once the front panel LEDs were in place, it was time to wire them up. At this stage there are a lot of wires and using cable ties is a good way of making them look a lot neater. A look at my wiring is shown in Figure 7-20.

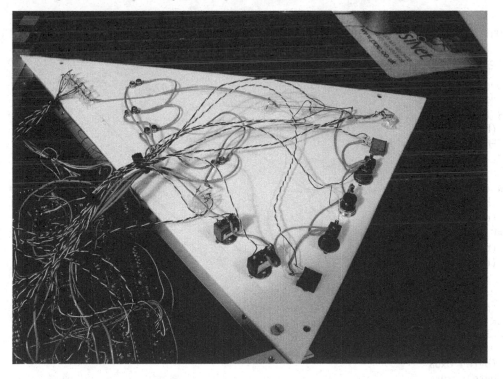

Figure 7-20. *The front panel wiring*

So, with the wiring finished, it is time for the software.

The Software

The software is the magic that breathes life into the instrument, and it is a bit longer than most code you have seen in this book so far. To make it simple, I have split some of the code into separate files. These should be included in the same folder as the main code. With your operating system, go to where the Arduino IDE stores its programs and create a folder called DunoCaster. In that folder, create four blank files with a text editor and call them:

- DunoCaster.ino
- Defines.h
- Variables.h
- Chords.h

Then open the Arduino IDE and open the DunoCaster sketch. You should see a blank sketch with four tabs. These are the places to enter the following listings.

The Header Files

These files in this section are header files; they don't contain any code for the processor to follow but instead set up names and values that the main code is going to use.

Hash Defines

So to start off, type the code in Listing 7-1 into the tab called Defines.h.

Listing 7-1. The Hash Defines

```
// hash defines
// Port expander registers
#define IODIR (byte) 0x00
#define IPOL (byte) 0x02
#define GPINTEN (byte) 0x04
#define DEFVAL (byte) 0x06
#define INTCON (byte) 0x08
#define IOCON (byte) 0x0A
#define GPPU (byte) 0x0C
#define INTF (byte) 0x0E
#define INTCAP (byte) 0x10
#define GPIO (byte) 0x12
#define OLAT (byte) 0x14

// Bits in the IOCON register
#define BANK (byte) 0x80
#define MIRROR (byte) 0x40
#define SEQOP (byte) 0x20
#define DISSLW (byte) 0x10
#define HAEN (byte) 0x08
#define ODR (byte) 0x04
#define INTPOL (byte) 0x02
```

```
// I2C device addresses
#define chordSwitchAddress   0x20  // address of chord switches
#define chordLEDaddress    0x21     // address of chord red led indicator
#define stringSwitchAddress  0x22  // address of string switches
#define controlSwitchaddress 0x24  // address of control switches & indicators
// Control Switch device bit masks
// Control Switch device bit masks
#define R1S 0x01              // rotary encoder 1 step
#define R2S 0x02              // rotary encoder 2 step
#define playSwitch 0x04       // play
#define fretSwitch 0x08       // Fret control
#define octave1Switch 0x10   // Octave 1
#define octave2Switch 0x20   // Octave 2
#define pick1Switch 0x40      // Pick 1
#define pick2Switch 0x80      // Pick 2
#define pushB   0x0100        // Push button
#define octaveLEDr 0x0200     // Octave LED red
#define octaveLEDg 0x1000     // Octave LED green
#define fretLEDr 0x0800       // Fret LED red
#define fretLEDg 0x02         // Fret LED green
#define pickingLEDr 0x0400    // Mode 2 LED red
#define pickingLEDg 0x01      // Mode 2 LED green

#define pickingSpeedLEDr 0x2000   // RGB LED 2 red
#define pickingSpeedLEDg 0x4000   // RGB LED 2 green
#define pickingSpeedLEDb 0x8000   // RGB LED 2 blue

// String Switch device bit masks
#define m2LEDg 0x01           // Mode 2 LED green
#define m3LEDg 0x02           // Mode 3 LED green
#define finger1 0x20          // Finger 1 touch switch
#define finger2 0x04          // Finger 2 touch switch
#define finger3 0x08          // Finger 3 touch switch
#define finger4 0x10          // Finger 4 touch switch
#define ddrString 0x03c       // data direction register for string switch
#define ddrChord 0x03ff       // data direction register for chord switch
#define ddrControl 0x01ff     // data direction register for control switch

// Arduino pin assignments
#define stringChange 2        // string change button
#define thumbIn 3             // Thumb optical switch
#define chordChange 4         // chord change button
#define controlChange 5       // control I2C indicator

#define R1D 7                 // rotary encoder 1 direction
#define R2D 8                 // rotary encoder 2 direction
#define chordShowLEDr 9       // RGB LED red (PWM)
#define chordShowLEDg 10      // RGB LED green (PWM)
#define chordShowLEDb 11      // RGB LED blue (PWM)
#define FRET_NOISE 52         // noise for fret slide
```

This sets up a whole bunch of predefined numbers that will be substituted for the names at compile time, making the code more readable. For example, if you want to know the bit that represents the finger 1 touch sensor, it is much easer to read this as finger1 than just reading the number 0x20.

Variable Definitions

Next there is a file that sets up all the variables the code is going to use. This is shown in Listing 7-2 and should be typed into the Variables.h tab in the Arduino IDE.

Listing 7-2. The Variable Definitions

```
// Variables setup

// The MIDI note value to be played for each string(open strings e3 a3 d4 g4 b4 e5 )
byte   note[6] = {52, 57, 62, 67, 71, 76};

int  notePlaying[6] = {0,0,0,0,0,0};    // note playing on each string - 0 for not sounding

// pattern for strum, strings 0 to 5 pattern end in a 6
const prog_uchar PROGMEM pattern[12][12] =   {
                    0,1,2,3,4,5,6,6,6,6,6,6,
                    5,4,3,2,1,0,6,6,6,6,6,6,
                    0,1,2,3,4,5,4,3,2,1,0,6,
                    5,4,3,2,1,0,1,2,3,4,5,6,

                    1,2,4,3,1,2,4,3,6,6,6,6,       // bank 2
                    2,3,5,4,2,5,3,4,6,6,6,6,
                    1,4,5,2,4,0,5,2,4,6,6,6,
                    0,4,2,5,0,4,2,5,6,6,6,6,

                    0,5,1,4,2,3,4,2,1,5,0,6,       // bank 3
                    0,2,4,1,3,5,6,6,6,6,6,6,
                    0,1,2,3,0,1,2,3,4,5,6,6,
                    0,1,2,3,4,5,3,4,5,6,6,6
                    };

// delay between the notes in the picking pattern
const prog_uchar PROGMEM patternDelay[12][12] = {
                    2,2,2,2,2,2,2,1,1,1,1,1,
                    2,2,2,2,2,2,2,1,1,1,1,1,
                    1,1,1,1,1,1,1,1,1,1,1,1,
                    1,1,1,1,1,1,1,1,1,1,1,1,

                    1,1,1,1,1,1,1,1,1,1,1,1,       // bank 2
                    1,0,1,2,1,1,1,1,1,1,1,1,
                    0,0,0,1,1,2,1,1,2,1,1,1,
                    1,1,1,1,1,1,1,1,1,1,1,1,

                    0,2,0,2,0,2,0,2,0,2,1,1,       // bank 3
                    2,2,2,2,2,2,1,1,1,1,1,1,
                    1,1,1,1,1,1,1,1,1,1,1,1,
                    1,1,1,1,1,1,1,1,1,1,1,1
                    };
```

```
byte chordColourR[8]    = {  0, 255, 196, 128,  64, 128,    0, 255 }; // red colour for chord
byte chordColourG[8]    = {  0,   0, 128,   0, 128,  32,    0, 196 }; // green colour for chord
byte chordColourB[8]    = {  0,   0,   0,  64,   0, 128, 196, 230 }; // blue colour for chord

// Time variables
int metronome = 0;
unsigned long pickTime, quench;
int currentTriggerState, lastChord = 0, currentChord, lastControl = 0, lastString = 0;

// for bit manipulation of LEDs
int redChordLED = 0, greenChordLED = 0, stringLED = 0, modeLED = 0;
int pickPat = 0;  // picking pattern number
int patShift = 0; // shift to add to the picking pattern number

// Playing
int midiChannel = 0;  // channel to use
boolean patPlaying = false, playing = true;
int playString = 0;     // string to play in picking pattern
int picksInPat = 10;   // Number of pick in this pattern
int pickNum = 0;        // How far in the pattern you have gone
int delCount = 0, lastDel =0 ;     // delay count down for spacing out time between picks
int pat = 0;            // picking pattern to use
int voice=0;         // index into the voice number to send
boolean capoMode = false;  // use the capo or not
boolean push = false;     // push button variable
int capo = 0;             // capo adding number
int octave = 0;         // octave value derived from switches

// control switch states
boolean pick2SwitchState=false, pick1SwitchState=false;
boolean octave1SwitchState=false, octave2SwitchState=false;

int rot1 = 0x40, rot2 = 100;
int rot2PlayStore = 100, rot2StoreVoice = 0;
```

First off is the array that defines what note each string will produce. This is what is changed when the chord switches are pressed, and then the array that stores the note currently playing. You need this to turn the previous note off when a new note is sounded. Then we have the arrays that define the picking patterns. The pattern[][] array defines what strings are played and in what order. A picking pattern can be any length, up to 12 notes. If you want to finish it early, all you need to do is to pad out the remaining entries in the array with sixes.

For example, the first picking pattern defined in the array is:

```
0,1,2,3,4,5,6,6,6,6,6,6,
```

This simply plays all six strings from 0 to 5, one after the other. The remaining six entries are to be ignored and so all have a value of 6. That defines what order the strings are picked in; however, the timing is defined by the patternDelay[][] array. This gives the time between each pick, which normally will be a 1 for a simple "on the next pick beat". However, sometimes you want two or more strings to be plucked together, in which case the delay value to use should be 0. If you want a longer pause in the picking, you can use other values of pick delay. I have not used anything greater than 2, but please feel free to experiment with this and with the picking patterns.

The three `chordColour` arrays define the color of the RGB chord indicator LED—these define the amount of red, green, and blue that make up a color and can be changed to colors of your choice. In order to know which LEDs have been set by other parts of the code, there are variables defined under the `for bit manipulation of LEDs` comment. Whenever a piece of code needs to change an LED, it does so by changing the bit corresponding to the required LED in one of these variables and then the variable is written out to the port expander. In that way, the code in one section does not inadvertently change the state of LEDs set by another. The rest of the variables defined are for general usage when running the sketch.

Defining the Chords

Finally, for the header files, the contents in Listing 7-3 should be typed in the `Chords.h` tab of the Arduino IDE.

Listing 7-3. Defining the Chords

```
// look up table for the string notes
const PROGMEM byte chordBank[29][6] = {
                    40, 45, 50, 55, 59, 64, // open strings
                    40, 47, 52, 56, 59, 64, // E major
        41    ,41        , 53, 57, 60, 65, // F major
                    43, 47, 50, 55, 59, 67, // G major
        33            , 45, 52, 57, 61, 64, // A major
        35            , 47, 54, 59, 63, 66, // B major
        36            , 48, 52, 55, 60, 64, // C major
        38   ,38        , 50, 57, 62, 66, // D major

                    40, 47, 52, 55, 59, 64, // E minor
        41    , 41        , 53, 56, 60, 65, // F minor
                    43, 50, 55, 58, 62, 67, // G minor
        33            , 45, 52, 57, 60, 64, // A minor
        35            , 47, 54, 59, 62, 66, // B minor
        36            , 48, 55, 60, 63, 67, // C minor
        38            , 47, 52, 55, 59, 64, // D minor

                    40, 47, 50, 56, 59, 64, // E7 major
        41 ,41            , 51, 57, 60, 65, // F7 major
                    43, 47, 50, 55, 59, 65, // G7 major
        33            , 45, 52, 57, 61, 67, // A7 major
        35            , 47, 51, 57, 59, 66, // B7 major
        36            , 48, 52, 58, 60, 64, // C7 major
        38   ,38        , 50, 57, 60, 66, // D7 major

                    40, 47, 52, 55, 62, 64, // E7 minor
                    41, 48, 51, 56, 60, 65, // F7 minor
                    43, 0, 53, 58, 62, 67, // G7 minor
                    45, 0, 55, 60, 64, 69, // A7 minor
        35            , 47, 54, 57, 62, 66, // B7 minor
        36            , 48, 55, 58, 63, 67, // C7 minor
        38            , 50, 53, 65, 62, 69, // D7 minor
                };
```

```
const PROGMEM byte soundBank[] = {
                    25,25,25,25,25,
                    26,26,26,26,26,26,
                    27,27,27,
                    28,28,
                    29,29,29,29,29,
                    30,30,
                    31,31,31,
                    32,32,32,
                    33,33,33,
                    34,34,34,34,34,34,34,
                    35,35,
                    36,36,36,36,36,36,
                    37,37,37,
                    38,38,
                    39,39,39,39,39,39,39,39,39,39,
                    40,40 };

const PROGMEM byte bankLSB[] = {
                    0,16,25,43,96,
                    0,16,35,40,41,96,
                    0,18,32,
                    0,32,
                    0,40,41,43,45,
                    0,43,
                    0,40,41,
                    0,65,66,
                    0,40,45,
                    0,18,27,40,43,45,65,
                    0,28,
                    0,32,33,34,96,97,
                    0,27,32,
                    0,43,
                    0,18,20,24,35,40,64,65,66,96,
                    0,64};
```

These arrays are stored in the processor's program memory space like the picking patterns and delay were. This is normally where the code lives but it is useful for storing tables that do not change. It is useful to do this because they take up no space in the processor's SRAM, which is where variables from your code as well as the extra code that makes the C language work are stored. On all embedded processors this is limited, so it's better not to use it. In fact, without this trick you would run out of memory and odd things would happen, such as variables losing their values.

This listing shows the 56 chords and the open string notes available from the chord keys. These numbers are the basic MIDI note numbers to send when a chord is played. This is for the chord switch and the three switches following the chord. The first two switches select the major and minor versions of chords as well as the augmented seventh of the major and minor chords. When the third switch is pressed with your little finger, there are another four chord types available to be defined. These don't fit as neatly into a scheme as the first four chord types, and you can define these however you wish. You might want them to be different from the chords I have defined, for example, putting in sharp and flat chords.

You will notice that some chords have the first one or two numbers shifted over to the left. This will not affect the array, but you might want to modify these numbers. These notes are not possible to achieve on a real guitar, either because they are lower than the open string or because your fingers simply do not bend enough to press them down. If you don't want these notes, replace these numbers with a zero.

The second half of the listing defines the MIDI voice numbers for different types of guitar. They are designed to work with the Yamaha MU10 type of sound module, where the basic MIDI voice change number is supplemented by extra variations on that sound by the LSB of the bank select CC number.

The way I have laid out this hopefully makes it clear—each line has the same MIDI program change value in the soundBank array and each line in the bankLSB array is the corresponding LSB bank select values. So the MIDI voice given by a value of 24 (Nylon String Acoustic Guitar) has five variations given by the bank numbers 0, 16, 25, 43, and 96. These can be treatments of the original sound or a new alternative sound altogether. For the first guitar sound MIDI 24 on an MU10, the variations are:

> 0 = Basic General MIDI sound
>
> 16 = Bright
>
> 25 = Release
>
> 43 = Velo Switch
>
> 96 = Alternate sound - Ukulele

These can again be customized to suit your sound module. If you have a simple one that does not take the bank parameters then the code will still work; it is just that some of the numbers will give you the same sound. In fact, the MU10 had a few more variations, but as the variation number is displayed on the string LEDs, and as there are only six of these, the maximum number of instrument voices you can select from is limited to 64. I have deliberately chosen to include only guitar sounds in this list, as I think it is in keeping with the instrument and the way that it is played. However, there is nothing to stop you choosing any other instrument in the voice list for your sound module. That said, sounds often are more realistic when the method of playing them is consistent with the sound of the natural instrument. (You don't get many fingerpicking patterns on a trumpet, do you?)

The Main Code

Now it is time to look at the main code. But before we do, it is perhaps best to look at the overall strategy and flow of the sketch.

There are basically two modes the instrument can be in: play mode, where the purpose is to produce MIDI mote messages, and program mode, where you are setting up the MIDI voice to use in the play mode. The operation of the instrument is fundamentally different in these two modes and so the first thing the main loop does is decide which mode it is in and take the appropriate action. Figure 7-21 shows the top-level flow diagram of the code.

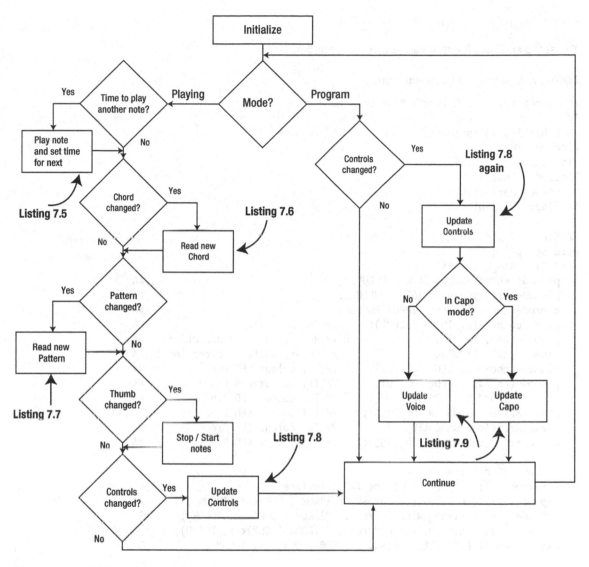

Figure 7-21. *The flow diagram of the main code*

What you see here is the order in which things are checked. It is useful when looking at the loop function to see what the code is doing. Rather than have the main code in one large indigestible lump, I have split it up into six listings. Each listing should be added to the DunoCaster tab in the Arduino IDE in the order presented here.

The Setup and Loop Functions

The setup and loop functions are shown in Listing 7-4.

Listing 7-4. Setup and Loop Functions

```
/* DunoCaster Midi Guitar - Mike Cook
*/
// Libraries to include
#include <Wire.h>
#include <Arduino.h>
#include "Chords.h"
#include "Defines.h"
#include "Variables.h"

// Start of code
void setup() {
  // I2C change inputs
  pinMode(chordChange, INPUT_PULLUP);                            #A
  pinMode(stringChange, INPUT_PULLUP);                           #A
  pinMode(controlChange, INPUT_PULLUP);                          #A
  pinMode(thumbIn, INPUT_PULLUP);      // Thumb  switch          #A
  pinMode(R1D, INPUT);                 // Rotary switch 1 direction  #A
  pinMode(R2D, INPUT);                 // Rotary switch 2 direction  #A
  pinMode(chordShowLEDr, OUTPUT);      // Tri colour LED Red     #A
  pinMode(chordShowLEDg, OUTPUT);      // Tri colour LED Green   #A
  pinMode(chordShowLEDb, OUTPUT);      // Tri colour LED Blue    #A
  analogWrite(chordShowLEDr, 255);     // Tri colour LED Red     #A
  analogWrite(chordShowLEDg, 255);     // Tri colour LED Green   #A
  analogWrite(chordShowLEDb, 255);     // Tri colour LED Blue    #A

 // Setup I2C devices
  Wire.begin();        // start the I2C interface
  expander_write(chordSwitchAddress, (MIRROR | ODR)<<8, IOCON);       #B
  expander_write(stringSwitchAddress, (MIRROR | ODR)<<8, IOCON);      #B
  expander_write(controlSwitchaddress, (MIRROR | ODR)<<8, IOCON);     #B
  expander_write(chordLEDaddress, (MIRROR | ODR)<<8, IOCON);          #B

  expander_write(chordLEDaddress, 0x0, IODIR);                 // set to all output
  expander_write(stringSwitchAddress, ddrString, IODIR);     // String triggers
  expander_write(stringSwitchAddress, ddrString, GPINTEN);   // enable interrupt on change

  expander_write(controlSwitchaddress, ddrControl, IODIR);   // Control Switches
  expander_write(controlSwitchaddress, ddrControl, IPOL);    // invert switch inputs
  expander_write(controlSwitchaddress, ddrControl, GPINTEN); // enable interrupt on change
  expander_write(controlSwitchaddress, ddrControl & 0xfffC, GPPU);  // enable pullups

  expander_write(chordSwitchAddress, ddrChord, IODIR);    // top 6 bits output rest to all inputs
```

```
    expander_write(chordSwitchAddress, ddrChord, IPOL);    // invert switch inputs so 1 = pressed
    expander_write(chordSwitchAddress, ddrChord, GPINTEN); // enable interrupt on change
    expander_write(chordSwitchAddress, ddrChord, GPPU);    // enable pullups on inputs

// set up initial state of the LEDs
    expander_write(chordLEDaddress, redChordLED, OLAT);      // turn off all LEDs
    expander_write(stringSwitchAddress, greenChordLED, OLAT);  // turn off all LEDs
    expander_write(chordSwitchAddress, stringLED, OLAT);      // turn off all LEDs
    expander_write(controlSwitchaddress, modeLED, OLAT);       // Initialize Mode red LEDs

    lastString = expander_read(stringSwitchAddress);    // get initial state of switches
    lastControl = expander_read(controlSwitchaddress);

 //  Setup serial / MIDI
    Serial.begin(31250);        // MIDI speed
 //  Serial.begin(9600);      // Debug speed
    programChange(midiChannel, 25);  // set MIDI voice to guitar
    programChange(midiChannel +1 , 120);  // set next channel voice to fret noise
    pickTime = millis() + rot2;  // initial basic tempo of notes

    // make sure software thinks all inputs have change
    lastControl = ~expander_read(controlSwitchaddress);
    doControl();
    quench = millis() + 60000UL;
}


//********************* MAIN LOOP *********************************

void loop() {
  if(playing) {
   if(millis() > quench){                                       #C
     stopNotes();                                               #C
     quench = millis() + 60000UL; // don't do anything for 60 seconds
   }
   if(millis() > pickTime){    // time to update notes or tempo LED    #D
    if(patPlaying) {
       if(delCount==0) doNextPick(); else delCount--;                  #D
     }
    else {pickTime = millis() + rot2; }     // set the next time to look at the notes
    metronome++; // Count the periods                                  #D
    if(metronome > 7){  // every 8th tick toggle the light
      // digitalWrite(LEDpin, !digitalRead(LEDpin));                   #D
       if((modeLED & pickingSpeedLEDr) == 0) modeLED ^= pickingSpeedLEDg;
       modeLED ^= pickingSpeedLEDr;                                    #D
       expander_write(controlSwitchaddress, modeLED , OLAT);          #D
       metronome = 0;                                                  #D
     //  Serial.print(" time "); Serial.println(rot2, HEX);
    }
   }
```

```
    // check for chord change                                                  #E
      if(digitalRead(chordChange) == LOW){changeChord();}                      #E
    // check for touch sensors
    if(digitalRead(stringChange) == LOW){doString();}                          #E
  // check for thumb stimulus
    if(digitalRead(thumbIn) == LOW && patPlaying == false){patPlaying = true;}  #E
    // check for change to control switches
    if(digitalRead(controlChange) == LOW){doControl();}                        #E
  }
  else {  // if not playing
      if(digitalRead(controlChange) == LOW){                                   #F
      doControl();                                                             #F
      if(!playing) { // incase mode switch has changed to playing              #F
        if(capoMode) doCapo();                                                 #F
        else doChangeSound();                                                  #F
      }
     }
    }
  } // end loop function

#A set the states of the processor's I/O pins
#B Initialise port expanders INT internal connected + open drain int
#C check for hanging notes
#D check for updating sound and update it if needed
#E update variables from control inputs
#F update variables for programming mode
```

The first thing to do is include the external libraries and the header files we have put into the other tabs when defining variables and constants. The setup function is basically split into three parts.

Initialise I/O

The first part initializes the I/O pins on the Arduino and sets up state of the chord display LED. This is straightforward and is nothing special.

Initialize I2C

The next section, however, is a bit more involved. This sets up the state of the four I2C port expanders. The way I have configured these is that the two 8-bit ports on the port expanders look to the software as if they were one 16-bit port, with port A being the least significant byte and port B the most. This minimizes the number of calls to the expander_write function. For each expander you have to set up what bits will be inputs and what outputs. This is done by writing to the Data Direction Register (DDR) with a logic one, meaning that bit will be an input and a zero meaning an output. For the bits that are inputs, there is an interrupt polarity register that inverts the reading so a logic zero on the input reads as a logic one. Then there is the register that sets up if a change on an input pin causes the interrupt output to be activated. Finally there is a register that sets up whether a pull-up resistor is enabled on an input. If you want these things to apply to all inputs, you just have to write the same bit pattern to the different registers.

Initialize External Devices

The last section of the setup function sets the serial speed, sends out the program change (voice change) messages, and sets the initial values of some variables. Note there is a commented out line for a 9600-baud speed. This is in case you want to run a debug session with the serial terminal window because this window will not run at MIDI speeds. Throughout the code there are commented out print statements that you can uncomment if you want to see the progress of the program, but make sure these are not active when you send data to your MIDI module. They will be interpreted as odd MIDI messages.

The Main loop Function

The loop function mainly follows the logic in Figure 7-20; however, not shown is the hanging note detector in the first few lines. When you play a note from a string, the previous note played from that string is sent as a note off message. But when you finish playing altogether, there is not another note to play and so your sound module never gets sent a note off message. It does not matter on some sounds because they decay away but other sounds have an infinite sustain. Therefore when you have not produced a new note within two seconds of the last one, all the notes currently sounding are turned off. The quench variable is used to do this. It is updated with the current time plus two seconds every time a note on message is sent. At the top of the loop, the code checks if this time has expired and, if it has, it calls a function to turn all the sounding notes off.

The millis system clock is also used to time when a note is due to be produced just like in the MIDI manipulation programs in Chapter 4. The time to the next pluck is the rotary encoder value plus the current state of the millis timer, so this timing can be changed on the fly. Every eight plucking time intervals the time indicator LED is changed to indicate the speed. I used a value of eight here because it looked right; it looks too fast if it goes at the same speed as the pluck indicator, especially when set to pick rapidly or as it sounds, a strum.

The rest of the code listing defines the functions, so I will split those into chunks as well. However, these could be typed in the tab in any order at the end of the DunoCaster tab.

Next Pick Function

Listing 7-5 shows the Next Pick function.

Listing 7-5. The Next Pick Function

```
void doNextPick(){  // output next note in picking pattern
    do{
      if(pgm_read_byte_near(&pattern[pat][pickNum]) != 6){        #A
        int lastString = playString;
        playString = pgm_read_byte_near(&pattern[pat][pickNum]);  // get the string to play
       if(note[playString] !=0) {        // is there a note to play in this chord
         if(notePlaying[playString]) {    // if string is sounding then turn it off
         noteSend(0x80, notePlaying[playString], 0x00, midiChannel);
         }
         if(note[playString] !=0){
         notePlaying[playString] = note[playString];
         noteSend(0x90, note[playString], rot1, midiChannel);
         quench = millis() + 2000; // 2 seconds auto note off
         // turn off other string LEDs unless last delay was zero
```

```
        if(lastDel !=0 ) stringLED &= 0xf003 ;
        stringLED |= 1 << (playString + 6);      // turn on this string LED
        expander_write(stringSwitchAddress, stringLED , OLAT);
        }
        delCount = lastDel = pgm_read_byte_near(&patternDelay[pat][pickNum]);
        }

        pickTime = millis() + rot2;                                    #B
        }
        else {  // end of sequence
          patPlaying = false;
          delCount = 0;
          lastDel = 1;    // so LED is turned off on next pick
          pickNum = -1;   // increment will take it to zero
// do not update pickTime
//so that the end of the start of the next pattern immediately follows the last pattern
        }
        pickNum++;
      } while(pgm_read_byte_near(&patternDelay[pat][pickNum]) == 0);   #C
}
A# only play a note if it is not the last note in the sequence
B# set time for next pick if there is something else in the pattern
C# keep on going until there is a delay so more than one string can be picked at a time
```

This is basically fetching the next string to play in the picking pattern, turning off the previous note, and starting the new note. If there is zero delay between the last note and this one, it keeps the note on until next time. Also the code will update the string LED so you see the picking patterns reflected on the lights. At the end of the sequence, it sets some variables so that in the next call to this function things will just be turned off. The code is written as a do ... while loop so that it is executed at least once, but in the case of zero delays, it keeps on fetching notes and playing them.

Changing a Chord

The code in Listing 7-6 shows the action of the instrument when changing chord. It has to update the LEDs and get the new set of note numbers for each string from the chord array.

Listing 7-6. Change Chord

```
// we need to change the chord
void changeChord() {
  int newState =0;
  int mask;
  int chord = 1;

  if(capoMode) {                                      #A
    noteSend(0x80, FRET_NOISE, 0x00, midiChannel + 1);
    }
  newState = expander_read(chordSwitchAddress);     // get bit pattern of chord switches
  if((newState & 0x7f) != 0){ // chord pressed
  redChordLED = 1;      // set top chord LED
  greenChordLED = 0xE; // plus light the three after it
```

```
    mask = 0xf;
    while( (newState & redChordLED) == 0) {                                #B
      redChordLED = redChordLED << 1;
      greenChordLED = greenChordLED << 1;
      mask = mask << 1;
      chord++;    // move to next chord
    }
      rgbSet(chordColourR[chord],chordColourG[chord],chordColourB[chord]);
      LEDwrite(newState & mask, greenChordLED);

      // send fret noise if enabled
      if(capoMode) {
      noteSend(0x90, FRET_NOISE, rot1, midiChannel + 1);
      }
      // add any modifier keys to base chord
      redChordLED = redChordLED << 1;
      if( (redChordLED & newState) !=0 ) chord += 7; // first modifier key
      redChordLED = redChordLED << 1;
      if( (redChordLED & newState) !=0 ) chord += 14; // second modifier key
      redChordLED = redChordLED << 1;
      if( (redChordLED & newState) !=0 ) chord += 28; // third modifier key
  } // end of chord pressed
  else { // chord released
          LEDwrite(0, 0);   // turn LEDs off
          rgbSet(0,0,0);    // turn chord colour LED off
          chord = 0;
          stopNotes();      // all notes off
      } // end of chord released
  // copy bank into current notes
      for(int j=0;j<6;j++){
      note[j]=pgm_read_byte_near(&chordBank[chord][j]);
      if(note[j] != 0) note[j] += octave + capo;                          #C
 // Serial.print(octave,DEC); Serial.print(" note number ");  Serial.println(note[j], DEC);
      }
}
#A turn off previous fret noise if enabled
#B shift the LED pattern until it matches the switch
#C don't adjust zero / non playing notes
```

This is only called when something has changed with the chord switches, so the new state of the switches are read into a variable called newState. It is checked to see that it is one of the seven chords keys that have changed and not the three supplemental keys at the end. Then the bit patterns for the red LED on the top-most key and the green LEDs for the three following are calculated by sliding the bit pattern so it matches the top bit. The chord variable will then contain the number of the root chord pressed. Knowing that, the chord indicator LED can be set.

You still need to know what variation of the chord is required, as determined by the three switches following the root chord switch. When this is done you can use the chord lookup table to copy the notes into the note array, modifying them as you copy them according to the octave and capo shifting variables. If no key is found to be held down, then the chord LEDs are turned off. This function also sends the fret noise MIDI message if that mode has been enabled.

Setting a New Picking Pattern

The next function, shown in Listing 7-7, shows the way a new fingerpicking pattern is set when one of the string touch controls is activated.

Listing 7-7. Setting a new picking pattern

```
void doString(){
      int string, stringState;
      string = expander_read(stringSwitchAddress);
 //   Serial.print(string, HEX); Serial.print(" - ");
      stringState = string ^ lastString;                    #A
      if( ( stringState & finger1) !=0 ) {
                          if(((string & finger1) == 0) && (patPlaying == false)){
                          patPlaying = true;                 #B
                          pat=patShift;                      #C
                          } }
      if( ( stringState & finger2) !=0 ) {
                          if(((string & finger2) == 0) && (patPlaying == false)){
                          patPlaying = true;
                          pat=1 + patShift;  // pattern to play
                          } }
      if( ( stringState & finger3) !=0 ) {
                          if(((string & finger3) == 0) && (patPlaying == false)){
                          patPlaying = true;
                          pat=2 + patShift;  // pattern to play
                          } }
      if( ( stringState & finger4) !=0 ) {
                          if(((string & finger4) == 0) && (patPlaying == false)){
                          patPlaying = true;
                          pat=3 + patShift;  // pattern to play
                          } }
      lastString = string;                                  #D
}
#A - filter out only the strings that have changed since last time
#B - trigger the playing of a pattern
#C - set the pattern to play
#D - remember the new state of the string for next time this function is called
```

This will change the picking pattern only if the thumb switch is not producing a continuous stream of picking. Otherwise, it will set a new pattern based on the finger switch being pressed and prime the system to send one run of the pattern. The patShift variable is taken from the pattern bank switch and is combined with the finger sensor to generate the index into the pattern and the patternDelay arrays. This code could be made a bit shorter by using arrays, but the way it is written is easier to follow.

Update Controls Function

Next we come to the update control function in Listing 7-8. The job of this function is to look at the controls when they have changed, sort out what has changed, set mode variables accordingly, and update the status LEDs. The overall flow of this function is shown in Figure 7-22.

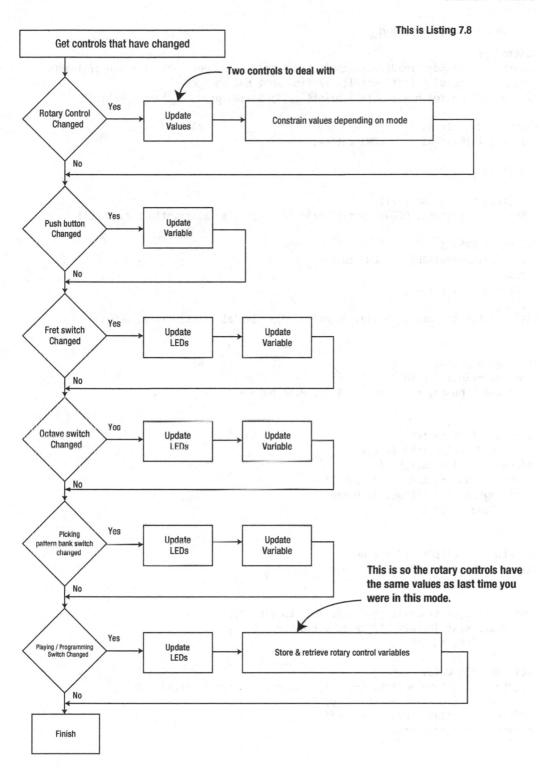

Figure 7-22. *Update Controls Flow Diagram*

Listing 7-8. Update Controls Function

```
void doControl(){
    int control = expander_read(controlSwitchaddress);    // get current state of inputs
    int change = control ^ lastControl;  // find what had changed
 // Serial.print(control,HEX); Serial.print("  "); Serial.println(change, HEX);

   if((change & R1S) != 0) {                                        #A
       if(digitalRead(R1D) == LOW) rot1++;
       else {
       if(rot1 > 0) rot1--;
       }
       if(rot1 > 127) rot1=127;
   //   Serial.print(rot1, DEC);  Serial.print(" / ");  Serial.println(rot2, DEC);
   }
   if((change & R2S) != 0) {
       if(digitalRead(R2D) == LOW) rot2++;
       else {
       if(rot2 > 0) rot2--;
       }
 //  Serial.print(rot1, DEC);  Serial.print(" / ");  Serial.println(rot2, DEC);
   }

   if( (change & pushB) !=0 ){                                      #B
   //  Serial.println("push");
   if((control & pushB) == 0) push = true; else push = false;
   }

    // sort out fret switch
    if((change & fretSwitch) != 0){
      if(control & fretSwitch) {
        modeLED &= ~fretLEDr; // red off
        stringLED |= fretLEDg; // green on
        capoMode = true;
      }
    else {
      modeLED |= fretLEDr; // red on
      stringLED &= ~fretLEDg; // green off
      capoMode = false;
      }
    expander_write(controlSwitchaddress, modeLED , OLAT);
    expander_write(stringSwitchAddress, stringLED , OLAT);
    } // end of fret switch

    // sort out the Octave switch
    if( ((change & octave1Switch) !=0 ) || ((change & octave2Switch) !=0 ) ){
        if((control & octave1Switch) == 0) {
        modeLED &= ~octaveLEDr; // red off                 #C
        octave1SwitchState =true;                          #C
          }
```

```
        else {                                                    #C
            modeLED |= octaveLEDr; // red on                      #C
            octave1SwitchState =false;                            #C
        }

    if((control & octave2Switch) == 0) {                          #C
        modeLED &= ~octaveLEDg; // green off                      #C
        octave2SwitchState =true;                                 #C
    }
  else {
      modeLED |= octaveLEDg; // green on                          #C
      octave2SwitchState =false;                                  #C
   }

    expander_write(controlSwitchaddress, modeLED , OLAT);        #D
    octave = 12;
    if(octave1SwitchState) octave = 0;                            #D
    if(octave2SwitchState) octave = 24;                          #D
    }  // end of octave switch code

// sort out picking bank switch
if( ((change & pick2Switch) !=0 ) || ((change & pick1Switch) !=0 ) ){
    if((control & pick2Switch) == 0) {
        stringLED &= ~pickingLEDg;
        pick1SwitchState =true;
    }
  else {
    stringLED |= pickingLEDg;
    pick1SwitchState =false;
}
    if((control & pick1Switch) == 0) {
        modeLED &= ~pickingLEDr;
        pick2SwitchState = true;
     }
   else {
     modeLED |= pickingLEDr;
     pick2SwitchState = false;
   }
    expander_write(stringSwitchAddress, stringLED , OLAT);
    expander_write(controlSwitchaddress, modeLED , OLAT);
    patShift=4;
    if(pick2SwitchState) patShift = 0;
    if(pick1SwitchState) patShift = 8;
    } // end of picking bank switch code

// playing programming switch
    if( (change & playSwitch) !=0 ){
//   Serial.println("switch 1");
        if((control & playSwitch) == 0) {
        playing = false;
        stopNotes();
```

```
            rot2PlayStore = rot2;                              #E
            rot2= rot2StoreVoice;
             // turn on green string LEDs as a background to the counter display
            expander_write(chordSwitchAddress, 0xfc00 , OLAT);
            stringLED &= 0xf03f;  // remove red LEDs
            stringLED |= (rot2 << 6) & 0x0fc0; // set LEDs according to the rot2 control
            expander_write(stringSwitchAddress, stringLED , OLAT); // display count
       //   Serial.print(" into voice setup "); Serial.println(rot2, HEX);
            }
            else {
              playing = true;
              expander_write(chordSwitchAddress, 0x0000 , OLAT); // turn off green LEDs
              stringLED &= 0xf03f;   // remove red LEDs
              expander_write(stringSwitchAddress, stringLED , OLAT);
              rot2StoreVoice =  rot2; // save and restore rotary 2 values
              rot2 = rot2PlayStore;
       //   Serial.print(" into play mode "); Serial.println(rot2, HEX);
             }
        }
        lastControl = control & 0x1FF;  // save state to look for change next time
}
#A Check and adjust rotary inputs
#B Check and update push switch
#C Update a three position (center off) switch
#D Update LEDs and offset values as a result of the switch states
#E Save and restore rotary 2 values for different modes
```

This is rather a long function, but then it has a lot to do. The first thing it does is get the new state of the control switches and then exclusive OR that with the last state to get a variable called change that indicates what bits have changed since the last time this function was called. The function only does things when the appropriate bits (switches) have changed.

First it checks the two rotary controls to see if they need updating. If so it increments or decrements the control's variable according to the direction pin. The code also restrains the value in the variables, with rotary control 1 not being allowed to go outside the 0 to 127 range for the note on velocity. Rotary control 2 is restrained in the lower value only with it not being allowed to go lower than zero. There is no upper limit on this control as it sets the picking speed in milliseconds and there is really no speed slow enough that you need to impose a limit.

Then the push button state is updated. Note it does nothing with the information—it just updates the variable for other functions to use. The control switches of the fret, octave shift, and picking pattern bank are checked with their status LEDs updated and variables set.

The final section checks the play/program mode switch and updates the string LEDs to reflect the controls. Note here as rotary control 2 has a different function in the two modes it saves and restores the appropriate value into the control variable called rot2. In the playing mode it controls the speed, and in the program mode it controls the voice number. By saving/restoring the values when switching modes, you isolate the control from the mode change. It feels natural when switching back from changing the voice that the picking speed is the same, but like most "natural" things in an embedded system, you have to work on it.

MIDI Functions

In the next section are the functions that handle all the MIDI messages. These are found in Listing 7-9.

Listing 7-9. MIDI Functions

```
void doChangeSound(){
  if(rot2 > 63) rot2=63;                                                  #A
  if(push){
 //  Serial.print(" sound number ");  Serial.print(pgm_read_byte_near(&soundBank[rot2]), DEC);
 //  Serial.print(" bank number ");  Serial.println(pgm_read_byte_near(&bankLSB[rot2]), DEC);
    bankChange(0,0);
    bankChange(32, pgm_read_byte_near(&bankLSB[rot2]));  // Change the bank LSB
    programChange(midiChannel, pgm_read_byte_near(&soundBank[rot2]));  // Change MIDI voice
    expander_write(chordSwitchAddress, 0x0000 , OLAT);  // turn off green LEDs

    while((expander_read(controlSwitchaddress) & pushB) ==0){ delay(10) ;}   #B

    expander_write(chordSwitchAddress, 0xFC00 , OLAT);  // turn on green LEDs
     expander_write(stringSwitchAddress, (rot2 << 6) & 0x0fc0 , OLAT); // display count
  }
  else {                                                                 #C
    stringLED &= ~0x0fc0; // clear out the red LEDs
    // display the count
    expander_write(stringSwitchAddress, ((rot2 << 6) & 0x0fc0) | stringLED , OLAT);
  }
}

//  plays a MIDI note
void noteSend(byte cmd, byte data1, byte data2, byte chan) {
  cmd = cmd | chan;  // merge channel number
  Serial.write(cmd);
  Serial.write(data1);
  Serial.write(data2);
}
//  change the voice
void programChange(byte chan, byte data1) {
  chan |= 0xC0;  // program change command
  Serial.write(chan);
  Serial.write(data1);
}
//  change the bank
void bankChange(byte cmd, byte data1) {
  Serial.write(0xB0 | midiChannel);  // control change
  Serial.write(cmd);
  Serial.write(data1);
}
```

```
// stop the notes playing on all strings
void stopNotes() {
  boolean first = false;
   for(int i=0;i<6;i++){
   if (notePlaying[i] != 0) {
      noteSend(0x80, notePlaying[i], 0x00, midiChannel);
      first = true;                          #D
      notePlaying[i] = 0;
   }
 }
  if(first) noteSend(0x80, FRET_NOISE, 0x00, midiChannel + 1);

   stringLED &= 0xf003;  // red string LEDs off
   expander_write(stringSwitchAddress, stringLED, OLAT);
}

void doCapo(){
  int bar=0;
  if(rot2 > 6) rot2=6;                       #E
  bar = (0x3f << rot2) & 0x0fc0;
  if(push){
       capo = rot2;
       expander_write(chordSwitchAddress, 0x0000 , OLAT); // turn off green LEDs
   }
   else {
     expander_write(chordSwitchAddress, 0xFC00 , OLAT); // turn on green LEDs
     stringLED &= ~0x0fc0; // clear out the red LEDs
   }
   expander_write(stringSwitchAddress, bar | stringLED, OLAT);
   if(push) {
     // do nothing while still held down
     while((expander_read(controlSwitchaddress) & pushB) ==0){ delay(10) ;}

     expander_write(chordSwitchAddress, 0xFC00 , OLAT); // turn on green LEDs
   }
}
#A needed as different to the maximum in capo mode
#B hold - do nothing while the push button is still held down
#C push button not pressed - just display rotary control on string LEDs
#D a marker to send a fret noise off as well later
#E needed as different to the maximum in change voice mode
```

The first function—doChangeSound—will send a change voice message (bank change plus a program change) when the push button is pressed. The rest of the code ensures that this function is called only when the instrument is in the program mode. The volume/voice rotary encoder is restricted to a maximum of 63 and will use the bankLSB array to recover the bank number and the soundBank array for the program (voice) number. Note that as these arrays are stored in the processor's program memory, you need to extract the number with the function pgm_read_byte_near.

When the data has been sent, the program is held in a while loop until the push button is released. This prevents multiple messages from being sent. If the push button has not been pressed yet, the current value of the volume/voice rotary encoder is displayed on the string LEDs as a binary number, or in the case of the capo mode, as a bar of increasing length representing the fret the capo is placed on. These LEDs are hidden so you can't rely on the LED being off to indicate a logic zero because of the lack of position information. The green LEDs are permanently on as a background, therefore a logic one is represented by a red LED being on, which looks orange/yellow and a logic zero shows no red LED, which looks green.

The other MIDI functions should be familiar to you if you have been following the book from the start. They simply send a MIDI message on the channel number the instrument has been set to by the global variable midiChannel.

Lightweight Functions

Next come some lightweight functions for controlling LEDs and such. These are shown in Listing 7-10.

Listing 7-10. Small Functions

```
// Output Red / Green LEDs
void LEDwrite(int r, int g) {
  int i;
  i = r | (g << 10);
  expander_write(chordLEDaddress, i , OLAT);
    stringLED &= 0x0fc3;  // leave the string LEDs alone
    stringLED |= (g << 6) & 0xf003;  /// add in the green chord LEDs
  expander_write(stringSwitchAddress, stringLED , OLAT);
}

void rgbSet(int r, int g, int b){
    analogWrite(chordShowLEDr, 255-r);
    analogWrite(chordShowLEDg, 255-g);
    analogWrite(chordShowLEDb, 255-b);
    }
```

The LEDwrite function makes it easy to cope with the fact that the red/green chord LEDs do not occupy contiguous locations on a single expander. It simply takes in the individual bit pattern for each color, then it generates a temporary variable called i that combines the bits for the two colors as if they were in a contiguous location. Because this variable is an integer (16 bits), any bits higher than this are simply removed and the resulting value is written to the chordLEDaddress. This leaves the top four bits of the green LED bit pattern to be written out to the stringSwitchAddress expander. However, this expander also has the string LEDs attached to it, so the green chord LED bits are merged with the current value of the string LEDs to produce a bit pattern that can be written to the expander without affecting any LEDs it should not change.

The other function sets the chord display LED for a current sinking configuration by simply subtracting the required brightness level from the maximum value of 255.

Expander Communication Functions

The final set of functions are called the housekeeping functions because they handle the communications between the program and the port expanders. You can configure the multiplexer's control register IOCON in two fundamentally different ways that determine the layout and addresses of the expander's registers. This can be configured either as a separate bank of registers for port A and port B, or the ports can be intertwined so that every other address swaps between the two ports. In this program, I have chosen the latter because this means that I can treat each expander as if it had 16-bit registers. This in turn makes programming easer because a lot of the hardware like the chord switches and chord LEDs take more than 8 bits, but despite this I can still access them at the same address. These functions are written to split a 16-bit quantity passed to it into two 8-bit quantities. These are fed to the expander as two separate bytes. In the IOCON register, I enabled the address increment (well, it is the default option) so that if I write two successive bytes, they will end up in two successive control registers. These functions are shown in Listing 7-11.

Listing 7-11. Expander Communication Functions

```
void expander_write(int address, int data, int reg) {
  Wire.beginTransmission(address);              #A
  Wire.write(reg);
  Wire.write(0xff & data);   //  low byte       #B
  Wire.write(data >> 8);     //  high byte      #B
  Wire.endTransmission();
}

int expander_read(int address) {
  int data = 0;
 //  Send input register address
  Wire.beginTransmission(address);
  Wire.write((byte)GPIO);
  Wire.endTransmission();
 //  Connect to device and request two bytes
  Wire.requestFrom(address, 2);
 if (!Wire.available()) { }                     #C
    data = Wire.read();
 if (!Wire.available()) { }                     #C
    data |= Wire.read() << 8;
  Wire.endTransmission();
  return data;
}
#A Set output register address
#B Connect to device and send two bytes
#C Do nothing until data arrives
```

The write function is the simplest. It takes in the address of the expander, the data you want to write, and the register you want to write it into. So you first write the register number into the expander and then split the data into two bytes using the bitwise AND operation to just leave the lower eight bits. You then the shift right operation to move the upper eight bits into the lower eight bits for sending. The expander's register number will be incremented automatically between these two writes.

The read function will in fact only read the GPIO register of the expander, but that is all you want it to do. Therefore, you only have to pass the expander's address into the function. The two bytes returned from the expander are combined to give a 16-bit integer that's returned from the function.

The Finished Instrument

You have now reached the stage where, if you have followed everything correctly, you should have a finished instrument. It is time to explore the possibilities with the range of sounds and playing styles it can create. I have a YouTube video of it in action at http://www.youtube.com/watch?v=ehy9xgl4YCs and I have been very surprised by its popularity. It has several photographs of the stages of construction as well as examples of it being "played". You will see the separate picking styles produced from each touch sensor and the continuous repeating from the thumb sensor.

A rapid picking pattern sounds like strumming and a faux flamenco style is easy to achieve. If you take some guitar music published in tabular format (sometimes called tab format), you can simply hold down the keys to give you the tab chords. Most chords, especially in the easy play editions of tab music, can be achieved by using three fingers at the most. That is a combination of major, minor, major sevenths, and minor seventh chords.

Summary

The final instrument was easy to play and produced a wide number of variations of sounds. I even learned to play "House of the Rising Sun" quite quickly. While it uses MIDI the resulting sound and playing style were anything but MIDI like. In short it achieved what I set out to make, that is an instrument that is easy to learn and struck the right balance between the skill you need to play it and the effort it takes to learn.

Things to Do

There are lots of ways you could extend this instrument. One way would be to have a solo mode where the string touch sensors just triggered one string of the chord. You could incorporate a whammy bar to add a bit of pitch bend to the notes, or add a vibrato control, or any manner of other MIDI CC controllers. You could change the string touch sensors to the force sensors you looked at in Chapter 5 and get note velocity data from them as well as the trigger data.

Another idea is to have some of the MIDI effects you looked at in Chapter 4 incorporated into the instrument, like an arpeggiator, for example. While all the I/O on the port expanders are used, there are a few spare input lines left on the processor to control these effects.

The instrument could be built in a different style housing either much smaller or larger than my design. You can even change the shape so it does not look like a guitar. I would be really interested to hear and see what you come up with.

CHAPTER 8

■■■

OSC and Friends

This chapter covers

- What is OSC

- Why use OSC

- How to use OSC on an Arduino with a serial interface

- How to use OSC with MAX and PD to talk to the Arduino

- How to use OSC over an Arduino equipped with a WiFi shield

- How to talk to your Arduino using your tablet or smartphone

- How to make an Arduino OSC keyboard

- Introduction to the Monome

In this book so far we have looked at the way you can communicate with audio equipment using MIDI messages. You have seen what MIDI is made up of and what sorts of messages can be used. You have also looked at some projects, big and small, that involve MIDI. But MIDI is not the only game in town when it comes to controlling sound and other things. There is a new kid on the block called OSC, which stands for Open Sound Control. It's faster and more flexible than MIDI and is a better fit into modern computer systems. OSC doesn't replace MIDI by a long shot at the moment—the old stager still has plenty of life in him yet—but as this century proceeds you will find MIDI gradually being replaced, especially with new forms of delivery for control messages.

OSC using apps are finding their way into all the mobile computing devices, and one of the simplest ways of getting your own custom interface on your phone or tablet is to use an OSC-based system. This chapter covers the theory and use of OSC messages in the context of an Arduino system and shows you how to use it to communicate with two major music/sound-generating languages—MAX/MSP and PD.

Finally, the chapter takes a brief look at the Monome, one of the first major groups of controllers to use OSC messages.

The Concept

OSC came about from research at UC Berkeley Center for New Music and Audio Technology (CNMAT), and they continue to develop it and host documentation on the standard. Having said that, one of OSC's more attractive features is its open, flexible nature, especially in addressing. Whereas MIDI is very much a point-to-point system with separate input and output connections, OSC is more of a network-based system with URL type address structures. It is also more flexible in terms of the data it can carry. With MIDI, data is restricted to either a 7-bit or 14-bit number; with OSC this data can be of much higher resolution and size. It can carry 4-byte integers or floating-point numbers as well as strings and blobs (a *blob* is an array of data).

OSC is designed to be transmitted over a network and this opens up the possibility of much faster communications than MIDI. This means that any delay, or latency, associated between a physical stimulus and an action can be reduced, because the time to transmit a message is not constrained by the physical method of transmitting it.

OSC messages can be sent in *bundles*, a collection of messages that must all be actioned simultaneously. It can also be sent to multiple devices and the devices can decide what parts of the message they will pay attention to. Finally, OSC can send messages to query other devices and allow systems to dynamically adjust themselves to the capabilities of the connection.

The Message

So what exactly is an OSC message and what can it convey? At the heart of it is the message, which consists basically of two parts—the address, which is the place to deliver the message, and the payload or data associated with the message. This message may be wrapped up in some other protocol for transfer, as you will see later in this chapter, but the message is the fundamental thing we want to transmit. Figure 8-1 shows the basic makeup of an OSC message.

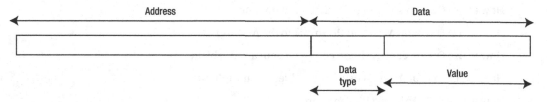

Figure 8-1. An OSC message

One of the things that complicates OSC is that the address part of the message is in normal plain text that we can read, as is the data type, whereas the data itself is in binary. Therefore, it is difficult to look at a message in a normal terminal window and make sense of it.

Let's start by examining the address part. This is a hierarchical system very similar to the URL used on the web or a path name used in computing. It consists of a sequence of addresses, starting with, and delimited by, a forward slash character. This address is totally open' you are free to make up any structure that fits your interface and organizes it in a logical way. If you are making a system to fit into an existing OSC address structure, then it is easy to pick out just the bits you want to use in your interface. To see a simple example of this, look at Figure 8-2.

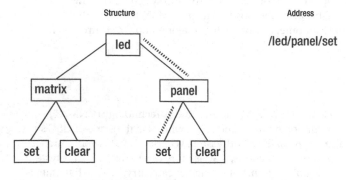

Figure 8-2. A simple OSC address structure

Here you see an address of /led/panel/set on the right side, with the left side showing the path trough a possible system that defines the message. This is showing that there are two types of LED ones in a matrix and ones on a panel. Each LED can have a further subdivision of set or clear depending on if you want the LED to be on or off. So the address shown simply turns on the LED. Note with this scheme there is no data required; the action of on or off is embedded in the address. As soon as the system receives the message /led/panel/set it knows to turn on the LED. Likewise, the message /led/panel/clear will turn it off.

This illustrates the power and flexibility of the "make it up yourself" address system, but it does put the onus on you to come up with a flexible structure. This example is not good in that respect; note it can only turn one LED on the panel on or off and likewise you might think one LED in the matrix. However, the situation is better when you consider that the message can carry data. The /led/panel/set could carry a number indicating what LED on the panel to change; more than that it could carry two numbers allowing you to specify what column and row on a matrix to change.

You can implement this example another way, by having an address for each LED and letting the number determine if it is to be turned on or off. That system might look like Figure 8-3.

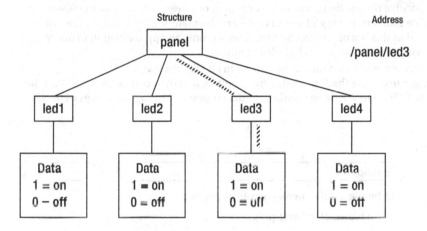

Figure 8-3. *An alternative address structure*

With this system each LED in the panel has its own address and you can turn it on or off according to the data you send. The choice is yours; there is no "correct" way although you might want to tie in with an existing system so that will dictate which sort of system you use. The way the address is parsed, or separated into its individual components, will change depending on the sort of address structure you have designed.

Adding Data

So what happens when you add data into the mix? In the last example I just slipped it in quietly, but there is a bit more to it. Each message can carry only one type of data, but it can have multiple instances of that data. For example, a message might typically carry a float or floating-point number, but it can carry more than one. To be precise, the number is a 32-bit big-endian IEEE 754 floating-point number. The structure of this is shown in Figure 8-4.

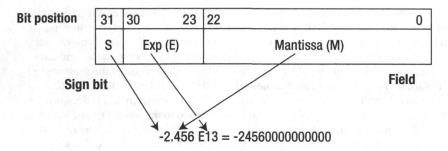

Figure 8-4. *The structure of a floating-point number*

I don't want to dwell on this structure because most of the time you don't have to bother with it, but it illustrates neatly why you can't simply look at the data in a terminal. The four bits hold three different fields—a sign bit to indicate a positive or negative number, an exponent or power of ten, and a mantissa or the details of the number. Note that only having 23 bits to represent the mantissa limits the number of decimal places you can show and as this is a binary fraction number it is only an approximation to many values anyway. This is the way virtually all computers handle big numbers.

Table 8-1 shows the five basic types of data that can be carried in an OSC message.

The data indicator is sent as a text letter that's preceded by a comma, and then comes the data. With the exception of the string type, it is difficult to see these numbers as data unless your program makes a special provision to convert them.

Table 8-1. *Basic OSC Data Types*

Type Tag	Data Type	Description
i	int32	32-bit big-endian two's complement integer
t	OSC-timetag	64-bit big-endian fixed-point time tag
f	float32	32-bit big-endian IEEE 754 floating-point number
s	OSC-string	A sequence of non-null ASCII characters followed by a null
b	OSC-blob	An int32 size count, followed by that many 8-bit bytes of arbitrary binary data

You might think that timetag is a little strange, but it follows the Internet NTP format. The first 32 bits represent the number of seconds since midnight on 1900 and the next 32 bits specify a fractional part of the second giving a precision of about 200 picoseconds. There is a special value of 63 zeros followed by a one, which means immediately.

These are not the only data types that can be used. As I mentioned, it is an open standard so you are free to make up your own types. However, when you deviate outside the standard type, you run the risk of other applications not understanding. The OSC standard has some alternative data tags that you should use for non-standard data types if they fit what you are doing, shown in Table 8-2.

Table 8-2. *Non-Standard OSC Data Types*

Type Tag	Description
h	64-bit big-endian two's complement integer
d	64-bit ("double") IEEE 754 floating-point number
S	Alternate type represented as an OSC-string (for example, for systems that differentiate "symbols" from "strings")
c	An ASCII character sent as 32 bits
r	32-bit RGBA color
m	4-byte MIDI message; bytes from MSB to LSB are `port id`, `status byte`, `data1`, and `data2`
T	True; no bytes are allocated in the argument data
F	False; no bytes are allocated in the argument data
N	Nil; no bytes are allocated in the argument data
I	Infinitum; no bytes are allocated in the argument data
[	Indicates the beginning of an array; the tags following are for data in the array until a close brace is reached
]	Indicates the end of an array

Most of the time you will be using the `float` or `integer` type of data, but this table illustrates the richness contained in the standard.

Sending a Message

You have seen the fundamental components of a message, which are the address and data, so now you need to see how this is wrapped up to form an actual message. The message as a whole must be a multiple of four bytes long; in fact each aspect of the message, address, data tag, and data must be a multiple of four bytes. This does not happen naturally and so in some cases these three parts of the message need padding out to make them the right length. This is done with what is known as null bytes, or bytes that have all bits set to zero. The data type tag is always two bytes—a comma and a letter—so to pad these out you always need to have two nulls following them. The `float` and `int` data types are four bytes long already, so there is no need to pad them, but the `blob` and `string` data types could need padding. The address will normally need padding because it is an arbitrary series of letters ending in a null, so if it is not a multiple of four, it will need one to three extra nulls after the null indicating the size of the address.

This can be confusing at first but Figure 8-5 should make things clear.

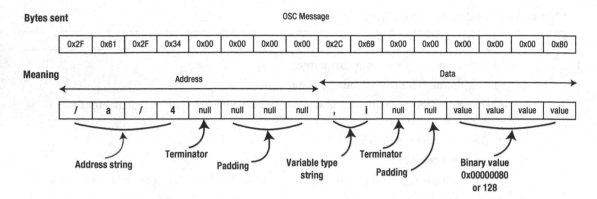

Figure 8-5. *An OSC message with padding*

You can see the actual bytes of the message in the top row of boxes in hexadecimal format, and the meaning of those bytes in the bottom row. Notice how a null byte can mean three different things—the terminator of a string, the padding to make the message segment a multiple of four bytes, or a value of zero in the number. The integer value is just a straightforward two's complement number and Figure 8-5 shows a value of 128.

So the message is already packaged and ready to send over a network. However, there are many ways to do this and all of them require that this message be wrapped up in another package to allow it to be sent.

SLIP Protocol

One way of sending a network message over a serial line is to use the SLIP (Serial Line Internet Protocol) protocol. This is good because the Arduino has a built-in serial interface so there is no extra hardware to add. Also there are network SLIP receivers built into many of the software systems you'll want to interface with. On the face of it, the SLIP protocol is very simple. The message starts and ends with the hex number 0xC0 and, to wrap up an OSC message, you simply just need to add these values to the start and end, as shown in Figure 8-6.

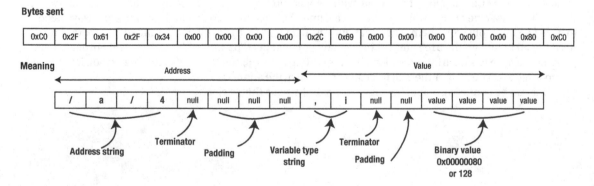

Figure 8-6. *An OSC message wrapped in a SLIP wrapper*

You might think that this is quite straightforward until you realize one thing—in order for this to work the hex number 0xC0 must not be contained in the message. This won't be the case for the address strings, as this number is a non-printing character; however, you might find this byte inside an integer or floating-point number. When this happens, the SLIP receiver software sees this value as a signal that the SLIP message has ended and passes on the message, which is now corrupted and will not work.

To get over this problem before the message is tagged with SLIP wrappers, it is searched to see if it contains the value 0xC0. If it does, that byte is replaced by the bytes 0xDB and 0xDC. But that creates another problem—what if the real message contains the byte 0xDB followed by the byte 0xDC? We don't want to confuse that with our substitution. The way around this is if we see 0xDB in our data then it is followed by an additional 0xDD. That nails it and no more confusion will occur. So a modified SLIP wrapper on an OSC message can look like Figure 8-7.

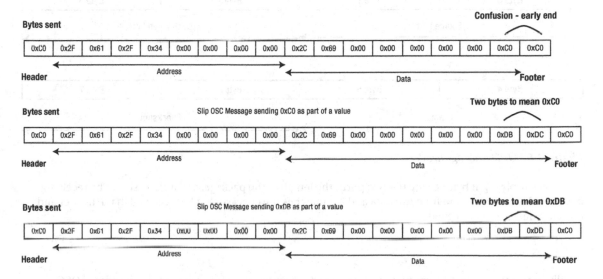

Figure 8-7. *SLIP modifications to an OSC message*

Of course, the SLIP receiver must untangle this before passing the OSC message on. Fortunately, most of the time you can avoid implementing a SLIP protocol in your own code by using libraries.

UDP Protocol

The next stage up is to use a "real" Internet protocol through a wired Ethernet socket, but in my opinion you gain very little from this because your Arduino is still tethered to your computer or OSC device through a wire. Yes, it is an Ethernet wire, not a serial (USB) wire, but it is still a wire nevertheless. So the next stage up to give you an advantage is to pass OSC messages over WiFi. To do this, you will need to attach a WiFi shield to your Arduino. The shield I use is the official Arduino one, although there are a few other good ones.

In order to send a message over either Ethernet or WiFi you need to use another protocol. The normal network protocol is TCP. This involves taking what you want to send and splitting it into separate packages, and then sending the packages one by one and assembling them at the receiving end. One of the quirks of the Internet is that packets do not always arrive in the order you sent them. Part of TCP's job is to assemble the time-stamped packets in the correct order. However, if the message you want to send is short, it will never be split up into separate packets so you can use a simpler, and thus faster, variant of TCP called UDP (User Datagram Protocol).

UDP is used for streaming media applications such as IPTV and Voice over IP (VoIP) as well online multiplayer games. It is a send and forget protocol so you never know if the message actually gets through. It could get lost on the way. However the lightweight nature makes it ideal for embedded systems like the Arduino. By cutting out the need for the receive end of the data package to acknowledge its arrival and the transmitter to retransmit a package if it is not acknowledged within a certain time, the memory footprint of this protocol as well as the time it takes to use is minimized.

A datagram is a name first used in the early 1970s and it is made up from a concatenation of the words data and telegram, and in this context it is our OSC message. You are unlikely to be involved in actually wrapping an OSC message in a UPD package with your own code; that is the sort of thing that can safely be left to a library. However, if you are curious as to what that involves, Figure 8-8 shows the header of the package.

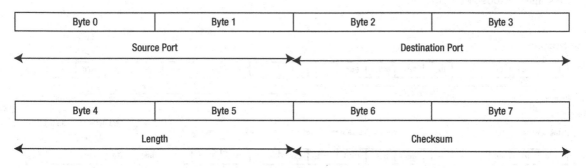

Figure 8-8. *UPD package header*

It is simply eight bytes giving the two ports, the length of the package, and a checksum. The receiving end calculates a checksum from the data and if it matches the checksum, it has received in the header and then the data is deemed good.

OSC Bundles

Finally in this theory section, we need to consider OSC bundles as so far we have only considered OSC messages. An OSC bundle is a collection of zero or more messages. It starts off with the OSC string "#bundle" followed by an OSC time tag. This is then followed by the OSC bundle elements, if there are any. A bundle element consists of a four-byte length integer followed by either an OSC message or OSC bundle. That's right, a bundle can contain another bundle, which can contain another bundle, and so on to infinity. Of course in practice there is normally an end to bundling up bundles.

Part of a bundle is shown in Table 8-3. It shows the first two elements and it could contain more.

Table 8-3. *The Start of an OSC Bundle*

Data	Size	Purpose
OSC-string "#bundle"	8 bytes	Identify this data as a bundle
OSC-timetag	8 bytes	Time tag that applies to the entire bundle
Size of first bundle element	int32 = 4 bytes	First bundle element
First bundle element's contents	As many bytes as it takes	
Size of second bundle element	int32 = 4 bytes	Second bundle element
Second bundle element's contents	As many bytes as it takes	
etc.		Additional bundle elements

Where possible, messages should be used instead of bundles. However, bundles do have the time stamp property, which means that you can specify exactly when a message should be actioned. You can even specify that something be done next year if you must.

Now that we have covered the fundamental theory of OSC, it is time to put all this into practice with a few practical examples and projects.

Practical OSC

The best way to start is to download the Berkeley OSC library for the Arduino from `https://github.com/CNMAT/OSC`. Decompress the ZIP file, rename the folder OSC, place in the Arduino's libraries folder, and restart the IDE. You are going to first use the SLIP serial interface to send and receive OSC messages on your Arduino, so you have to prepare your Arduino's hardware.

The examples I use for this first example will require the Arduino to be fitted with some switches, some LEDs, and some pots. If you have been following all the examples in this book then the setup you will need to use was shown in Figure 4-6 (Chapter 4). Note this has only one pot on the analogue inputs, and with the examples that follow you can have a pot on each input—that's six in total.

The Other End of the Link

You must have something to connect to the other end, and perhaps the most useful is an application that runs on your computer or laptop. Here there is a wide choice of applications you can use. I have chosen two of the most popular such applications in this field—PD (Pure Data) and MAX/MSP. These are in fact two very similar programming languages for generating and processing sound. PD is free and MAX/MSP is a commercial program that is most definitely not free. They share a common ancestry and do broadly similar things. They are both examples of what is known as graphical programming languages, where generating a program is done by defining or choosing functional blocks and "wiring them up" with graphic interconnections. Most musicians will have used one or other of these programs.

I will first show you how to use PD and then go on to look at MAX/MSP. So if you have not already got it, download the PD-extended package from `http://puredata.info/downloads` and have a play with the examples that come with it to get a feel about how to drive it. If you are using MAX/MSP then don't skip forward as you will miss working information that is relevant to both languages.

Using PD

With your Arduino connected to the USB lead of your computer you have in effect a serial port. When the Arduino IDE wants to program the Arduino, it switches the serial port to into the IDE, programs it, and then releases it. If you want to see what the Arduino is producing a click on the serial monitor icon will again switch the USB/serial port to the Arduino's serial window. However, it can only do these two things if the USB/serial port is not being used by another application. If it is, the computer's operating system will prevent it from connecting. If PD or MAX/MSP connects to the Arduino to read its messages, then the IDE cannot get a look at it, so you have to do a bit of juggling in the software to work on or develop an Arduino application that talks to the OSC messages. The situation is shown in Figure 8-9.

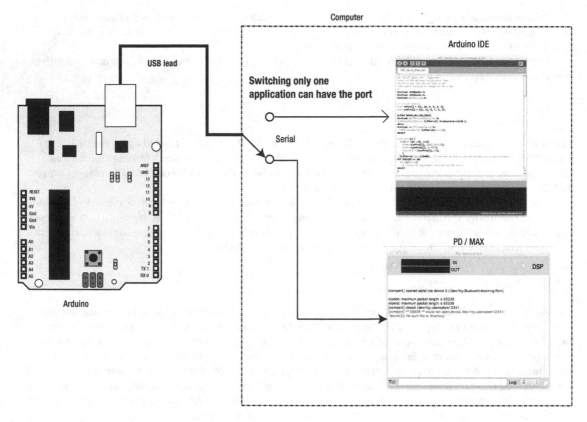

Figure 8-9. *Switching the serial port*

What you need to do is connect the serial port to PD or MAX/MSP to test the Arduino code but then disconnect it before you attempt to upload a new program into the Arduino. Connecting the serial port to PD is easy; you just double-click on the SLIP block. However, the way you get the language to give up and disconnect the serial port is to attempt to connect to a nonexistent device. With PD, this can be done with the basic o.io.slipserial.pd window. Both languages have two modes, an edit mode and a run mode. If you click the o.io.slipserial.pd in the run mode, you will get the o.io.slipserial.pd window. Then clicking the device name object in this window will disconnect the Arduino, and clicking the device name object in the main window will connect the Arduino. This is illustrated in Figure 8-10, and because this is a graphical programming language this figure also serves as the equivalent of a program listing. This program in the PD and MAX world is known as a *patch*.

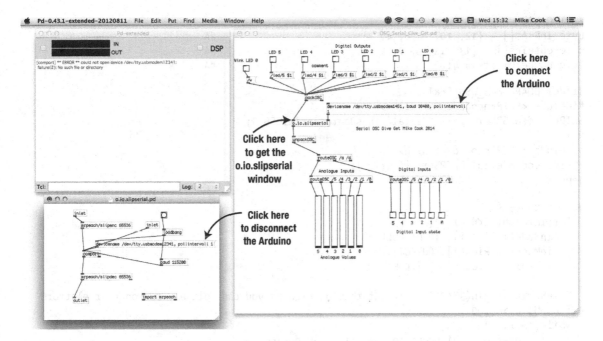

Figure 8-10. *Program listing and how to connect and disconnect the Arduino from PD*

If you don't want to construct it on screen you can also download the file or patch, as it is known, from the book's web site. The only thing you will have to change is the name in the device name box to the port name being used on your system. Put PD into Edit mode from the Edit menu to do this. For my system, this name was /dev/tty.usbmodem1451 as given in the Arduino's IDE Tools ➤ Serial Port menu. It will be different on your system.

Notice how the incoming data from the slipserial box is passed through an unpackOSC box and then sorted out by the routeOSC box into two sub-addresses, one with /a for analogue range of addresses and the other with /d for digital addresses. These are then further subdivided into the specific numbers identifying the device that sent them. Therefore, when pot 3 changes, on the Arduino the address it sends is /a/3 and when switch 3 changes, the address sent will be /d/3. In other words, the device number is in a sub-address of the device type.

On the output side, the LED box will send a specific address, for example /led/3, along with the data zero or one depending on the state of the bang box (that's the one you click). All the messages are grouped together with a packOSC box before being sent to the slipserial driver.

Having set up the PD program, you need to program the Arduino to give out and send OSC messages. For this example, upload the code in Listing 8-1.

Listing 8-1. Arduino Code for Serial_Give_Get

```
/*
OSC Serial Give & Get - Mike Cook
Sends out OSC messages and receives them
For PD or Max. See the one line in the
rxMessage() function to change for PD or Max
*/
#include <OSCBundle.h>
#include <OSCBoards.h>
#include <OSCMessage.h>
```

```
// I/O pin mapping
byte inPins[] = {12, 10, 8, 6, 4, 2};                          #A
byte outPins[] = {13, 11, 9, 7, 5, 3};                         #A
byte numberOfPots = 4;                                         #A

#ifdef BOARD_HAS_USB_SERIAL
#include <SLIPEncodedUSBSerial.h>
SLIPEncodedUSBSerial SLIPSerial( thisBoardsSerialUSB );
#else
#include <SLIPEncodedSerial.h>
 SLIPEncodedSerial SLIPSerial(Serial);
#endif

void setup() {
  for(int i=0; i<6; i++){
    pinMode(inPins[i], INPUT_PULLUP);
    pinMode(outPins[i], OUTPUT);
    digitalWrite(outPins[i],LOW);
    }
  SLIPSerial.begin(38400);    // set this as high as you can reliably run on your platform
#if ARDUINO >= 100
  while(!Serial)
     ; //Leonardo requirement to establish USB device
#endif
}

void loop(){
  // sendAutoMessage(); // simulate analogue signals         #B
  checkAnalogue(); // look at real analog ports
  if(SLIPSerial.available() > 0) rxMessage();
  checkDigital();
  delay(10);
}

void checkDigital(){                                         #C
  static boolean lastSwitchState [6];
  char messageDigital[] ="/d/3";
  boolean currentSwitchState;
  for(int i = 0; i<6; i++){
    currentSwitchState = digitalRead(inPins[i]);
   if(  currentSwitchState != lastSwitchState[i]){
     lastSwitchState[i] = currentSwitchState;
      messageDigital[3] = char( i | 0x30);
     OSCMessage mssageD(messageDigital);
     mssageD.add((int32_t)currentSwitchState & 1);
     SLIPSerial.beginPacket();
     mssageD.send(SLIPSerial); // send the bytes to the SLIP stream
     SLIPSerial.endPacket(); // mark the end of the OSC Packet
     mssageD.empty(); // free space occupied by message
   }
  }
}
```

```
void checkAnalogue(){                                             #D
  static int lastAnalogueValue [6];
  char messageAnalog[] ="/a/5";
  int currentAnalogueReading;
  for(int i=0; i<numberOfPots; i++){
    currentAnalogueReading = analogRead(i);
    if(abs(currentAnalogueReading - lastAnalogueValue[i]) > 2){
      lastAnalogueValue[i] = currentAnalogueReading;
      messageAnalog[3] = char(i + 0x30);
      OSCMessage msg(messageAnalog);
      msg.add((int32_t)currentAnalogueReading);
      // now send the message
      SLIPSerial.beginPacket();
      msg.send(SLIPSerial); // send the bytes to the SLIP stream
      SLIPSerial.endPacket(); // mark the end of the OSC Packet
      msg.empty(); // free space occupied by message
    }
  }
}

void sendAutoMessage(){
  static int count = 10, ch =0;
  char messageAnalog[] ="/a/5";
  count +=10;
  if(count> 1023) count = 0;
  ch++;
  if(ch>6) ch=0;
  messageAnalog[3] = char(ch + 0x30);
  OSCMessage msg(messageAnalog);
  msg.add((int32_t)count);
  // now send the message
  SLIPSerial.beginPacket();
  msg.send(SLIPSerial); // send the bytes to the SLIP stream
  SLIPSerial.endPacket(); // mark the end of the OSC Packet
  msg.empty(); // free space occupied by message
  }

void rxMessage(){
  // Max uses OSCBundle and PD uses OSCMessage
  OSCMessage messageIN; // comment out for MAX          #E
// OSCBundle messageIN;   // uncomment for MAX
 int sizeb =0;
 while(!SLIPSerial.endofPacket() ) {
    if( (sizeb =SLIPSerial.available()) > 0)
    {
      while(sizeb--){
        messageIN.fill(SLIPSerial.read());
      }
    }
  }
```

```
   if(!messageIN.hasError()) { // error free
     messageIN.route("/led", LEDcontrol);                    #F
     messageIN.dispatch("/w", Awink);                        #G
   }
 }
}

void LEDcontrol(OSCMessage &msg, int matched){
    boolean state = LOW;
    char whatLED[] = {'/','1',0};
     for(int i=0; i<6;i++){
        whatLED[1] = char(i | 0x30);
        if(msg.match(whatLED,matched)){
            state = LOW;
            if(msg.getInt(0) > 0) state = HIGH;
            digitalWrite(outPins[i],state);
        }
    }
}

void Awink(OSCMessage &msg) {
  for(int i=0; i<8; i++){
  wink(300,0);
  }
}

void wink(int del,byte pin){
    digitalWrite(outPins[pin],HIGH);
    delay(del);
    digitalWrite(outPins[pin],LOW);
    delay(del);
}

#A Change these to match the pins used in your Arduino
#B Uncomment to automatically send changing analogue numbers
#C Send switch message if a switch has changed
#D Send analogue values if a pot has changed
#E Max uses bundles and PD uses messages
#F Receive a message to turn on an LED
#G Receive a message to flash an LED
```

The way this code works is that it receives a message from PD whenever one of the LED boxes is clicked. This sends a message with the address of /LED/n where n is a number from 0 to 5. The data that accompanies the message is an integer variable of zero or one depending on the value in the LED box on the PD page. This will toggle on successive clicks and so will toggle the LED attached to the Arduino. Also a message with the address /w can be sent, which triggers the Arduino to wink the first LED eight times.

On the send side, the Arduino will monitor the pots and digital switches and send an OSC message whenever anything changes. These changes are then received by PD and displayed either as boxes for the digital inputs or as slider graphics for the pot values. All values are sent as integer variables from PD.

Using MAX

The almost exact same setup can be used with MAX. All that needs to be changed is the first line in the rxMessage function to use bundles, because while MAX can receive OSC messages, it is a lot easier if you let it send bundles.

MAX is a commercial application. There are various options including a full featured 30-day free trial. You can license it on a yearly basis or get a student discount; the options are listed on the company's web site at http://cycling74.com/products/max/ and while its basic functionality is similar to PD, its user interface is much slicker. It uses color and is user friendly. One of the main enhancements is the ability to do some rudimentary routing of the block's interconnections, thus making for a much neater window layout. You can see this from the MAX version of the OSC Serial Give Get code shown in Figure 8-11.

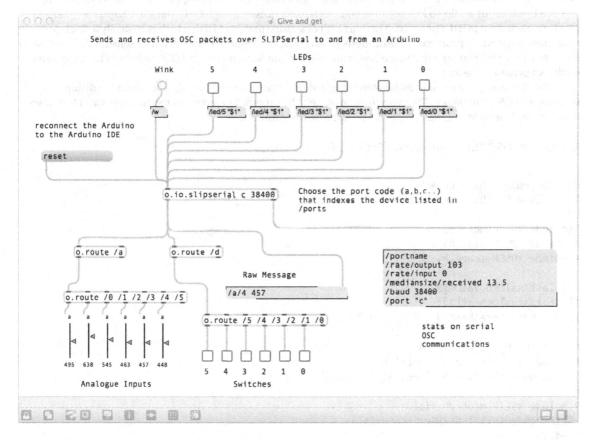

Figure 8-11. *MAX version of the OSC_Serial_Give_Get*

Notice how much neater the window is, as you have some control over how the wiring interconnections are made. However the components are virtually the same as the PD version. The main difference is the parameters used for the slipserial block and the lack of need for a packOSC block. There is a Ports menu that lists all the serial ports that the computer can see. The Arduino's port was listed as c and so the parameter to define the port therefore was simply entered as c and not the full name as you had to do in PD. It works in exactly the same way, controlling LEDs and reflecting switches and pots on the Arduino. Again this file or patch can be downloaded from the book's web site if you don't want to enter it by hand.

There are other extensions that MAX has with regard to signal processing and video processing. While PD also has some capability in this direction, its a voluntary open source project and so sometimes lags behind what you can do with paid products. While PD gives MAX a run for its money there is no doubt that MAX is the market leader and one of the most popular sound-generating applications used by professional and amateur musicians alike. The other big application in this field is Ableton Live (https://www.ableton.com/), which has a version of MAX that can run inside it. Note that MAX runs with OSC bundles when it sends data, so remember to change that line in Listing 8-1 mentioned earlier.

OSC Theremin

While turning on and off LEDs and reading pots is a great way of introducing the capabilities of a system, this is a book about audio so let's see how you can make a noise through OSC. Back in Chapter 5, I showed you how to make a MIDI Theremin. This was a bit of a fudge making MIDI, which is basically a discrete note-based system. It produced a continuous gliding note in response to two distance sensors. Now I want to show you how you can take that same hardware and use the Arduino to send OSC messages to PD so that PD itself can generate the sounds.

The first thing you need to do is write some Arduino code that will turn the data from the distance sensors into OSC messages. Then you need to make a PD program to receive those messages and turn them into sound. The code in Listing 8-2 is what I used on the Arduino.

Listing 8-2. OSC Theremin Arduino Code

```
/*
OSC Theremin - Mike Cook
Controls a PD Theremin patch
*/
#include <OSCBundle.h>
#include <OSCBoards.h>
#include <OSCMessage.h>

int lastAnalogueValue[2];
float lastValueSent[2];
float changeThreshold[] = { 0.2, 0.8 };

#ifdef BOARD_HAS_USB_SERIAL
#include <SLIPEncodedUSBSerial.h>
SLIPEncodedUSBSerial SLIPSerial( thisBoardsSerialUSB );
#else
#include <SLIPEncodedSerial.h>
 SLIPEncodedSerial SLIPSerial(Serial);
#endif

void setup() {
  analogReference(EXTERNAL);
  SLIPSerial.begin(38400);                              #A
#if ARDUINO >= 100
  while(!Serial)
    ; //Leonardo requirement to establish USB device
#endif
}
```

```
void loop(){
  checkAnalogue(); // look at analog ports 0 & 1
  delay(30); // limit the rate of change
}

void checkAnalogue(){
  char messageAnalog[] ="/a/0";
  int currentAnalogueReading;
  float value_to_send;
  for(int i=0; i<2; i++){
    currentAnalogueReading = 1027 - analogRead(i);      #B
    currentAnalogueReading = 1027 - analogRead(i);      #B
      lastAnalogueValue[i] = currentAnalogueReading;
      messageAnalog[3] = char(i + 0x30);
      OSCMessage msg(messageAnalog);
      if(i == 0){ // conditioning for right hand frequency
        value_to_send = mapfloat((float) currentAnalogueReading, 0.0, 1023.0, 100.0, 2000.0);
      }
      else {  // conditioning for left hand amplitude
       if(lastAnalogueValue[0] < 870 && lastAnalogueValue[1] < 870){
         value_to_send = mapfloat((float) currentAnalogueReading, 0.0, 870.0, 100.0, 0.0);
       }
      else {
        value_to_send = 0.0;
       }
      }
      msg.add((float)value_to_send);
      // now send the message
      if( abs(value_to_send - lastValueSent[i]) > changeThreshold[i] || ( lastValueSent[1]
      !=0.0 && value_to_send == 0.0 ) ) {
      SLIPSerial.beginPacket();
      msg.send(SLIPSerial);                      #C
      SLIPSerial.endPacket();                    #D
      msg.empty(); // free space occupied by message
      lastValueSent[i] = value_to_send;
      }
   // }
  }
}

float mapfloat(float x, float in_min, float in_max, float out_min, float out_max)
{
  return (x - in_min) * (out_max - out_min) / (in_max - in_min) + out_min;
}
#A set this as high as you can reliably run on your platform if you need to change the PD
patch as well to match.
#B Invert the sense of the readings
#C send the bytes to the SLIP stream
#D mark the end of the OSC Packet
```

The code is quite straightforward and simply involves sending a floating-point values for the left and right sensors. It contains all the elements you have seen before in the other OSC sending programs. The information from the sensors is sent with the address /a/0 and /a/1 with floating-point data. It is up to PD to do something useful with this information.

What we want the PD patch to do is take the two numbers from the distance sensors and use one to control the pitch of a sound and the other to control its amplitude. This is easy to do but not quite as easy as you might first think. First, PD has to create a wave sample that is the size of the sound at a specific instant in time, and then that sample has to be multiplied by the amplitude number with the result being fed into an DAC (Digital to Analogue Converter). This approach is covered in later chapters in much greater detail, so don't worry if this sounds too complicated for you at this time. The full PD patch is shown in Figure 8-12 and it contains a few things to give you some feedback. First of all, there are two slider indicators showing you the values given by your sensors and second there is a print block so you can see the results of the frequency sensor.

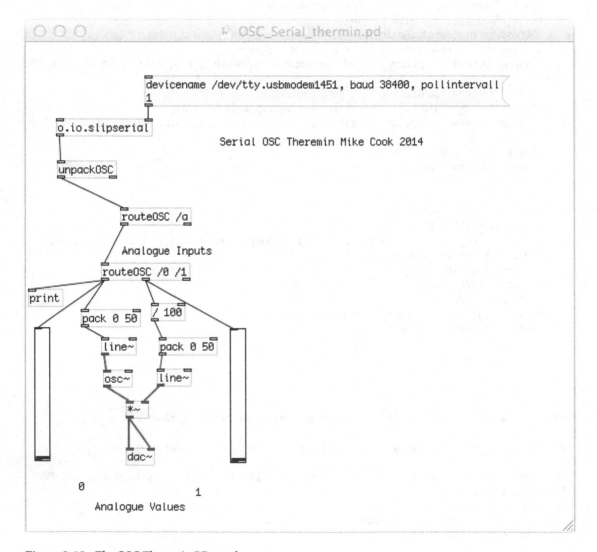

Figure 8-12. *The OSC Theremin PD patch*

The sound-generating part of this patch is shown in Figure 8-13. You can't just send the two streams of data into the sound generator (well you can, but the result would be most unsatisfactory). This is because the ear is very sensitive to discontinuities and sudden changes in sound, so the data needs to be smoothed out first. This is done with the line~ block, which generates a linear ramp between the previous data and the one you send to it. The ~ at the end of the block name in PD indicates that it is a function that does something to a waveform and you will see a few blocks with the tilde appended to the name. The line~ block takes in a list of two values. The first value is the data value and the second is the time, in milliseconds, that it will take to reach that value. You will use each of the values to control the frequency and amplitude of the sound when this ramp function is applied to them.

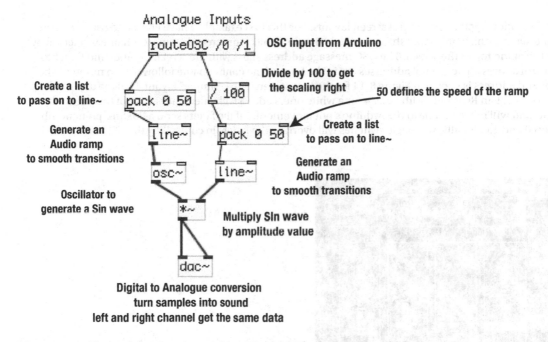

Figure 8-13. *The sound-generating section of the OSC Theremin PD patch*

The pack block generates a list from two values—the first value is initially zero but is replaced by the stream of numbers from the OSC message. The second value of 50 is fixed and attached to each list, and it determines the ramp time. The output of the line~ block is fed into the oscillator to control the frequency of the sound waveform. It is then multiplied, using the *~ block, with the volume data to control the amplitude of the waveform. Finally, the DAC turns this into an analogue signal that can be sent directly to the computer's speakers. Note that the DAC has two inputs—one for the left channel and the other for the right. The waveform is sent to both these inputs to give a mono sound output.

OSC Going Wireless

Up until now the Arduino has always been tethered to the computer by either a MIDI lead or USB connection. You can transmit OSC messages through an Ethernet connection but that is still a wire, but you can break free of that by using a WiFi shield on your Arduino. I talked about the packing of the OSC messages into UPD format earlier in this chapter, so now lets see how to do this in practice.

There are a small number of WiFi shields from different suppliers for the Arduino, but the one I used is from `http://arduino.cc/en/Main/ArduinoWiFiShield`. It is the official Arduino shield. It needs to be connected to a network and given an IP address from a DNS server, and then other devices on the same network can talk to it. Therefore, in order to use the Arduino with WiFi OSC messages, you need another device to be able to send and receive those messages. One of the most popular devices for doing this on a smartphone or tablet and that runs on all platforms is Touch OSC (`http://hexler.net/software/touchosc`) from Hexler. While you have to pay for it, the price of just under $5.00 is cheap enough. It is easy to generate your own custom layouts and assign exactly what OSC messages it sends. Therefore, that is what I will use for this section of the chapter.

Touch OSC

Touch OSC allows you to use several screen layouts. For this first example, I have chosen to use one of the example screens that comes with the app called "simple". It has four screen layouts; each one is selected by a faint tab at the top of the screen. The OSC message address starts with the screen number and then has the control address. The control addresses are in the form of the control name followed by a number. The control and address is shown in Figure 8-14 for the first screen of the "simple" layout. I will be using faders 1 to 3 to control an RGB LED, with fader 4 for a white one. Fader 5 will reflect the setting of the pot on the Arduino and will move in time to the Arduino's pot movement. All the faders send a floating-point number between 0 and 1.0. Finally, the toggle switches will override the faders in controlling the LEDs.

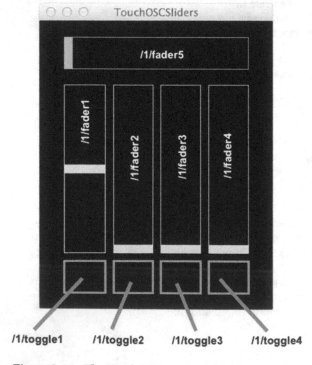

Figure 8-14. *The Touch OSC screen and addresses*

As a bonus, I also show you how to read the data from screen 3. This has a large X-Y pad that doesn't control anything on the Arduino but will simply print out a stream of readings as you adjust the pad.

The Arduino Code

The next step is to program the Arduino with the shield to communicate over WiFi. Basically, you need all the OSC message stuff you had previously plus the WiFi code. As a first example I will show you how to control some LEDs from your mobile device. You need to connect the LEDs and a pot to the Arduino as shown in Figure 8-15. Note that I used a common anode RGB LED to make things a bit more interesting. By controlling the brightness of each LED, you can mix a wide range of colors. The pot is used to show you how to send data back from the Arduino to your mobile device and shows up by affecting the bar on fader 5.

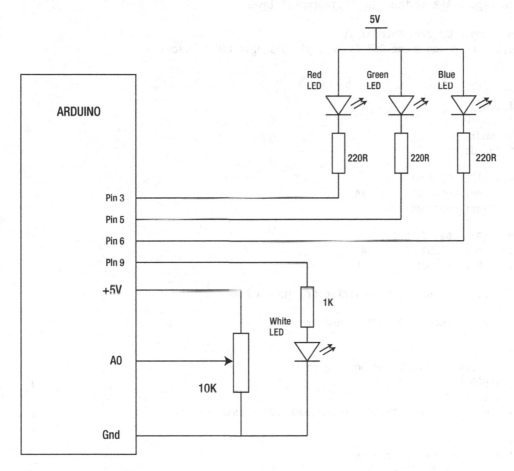

Figure 8-15. *WiFi test circuit*

Note that there is a mix of ways of powering the LEDs. The white LED is powered by current sourcing, that is the current to power is sent out of the Arduino pin through the LED. This is the most popular way in the Arduino world. However, the most popular way in the wider world is through current sinking. This is used for the common anode RGB LED and here the current comes from the 5V supply and goes to the ground through the Arduino pin. The difference between the two methods is that, with current sourcing, you have to write a logic high to turn on the LED and, with current sinking, you have to write a logic low to the pin.

The Arduino code for this example is shown in Listing 8-3.

Listing 8-3. Arduino UDP_OSC Test Code

```
/*
  Wi-Fi UDP Send and Receive OSC
  Mike Cook Jan 2014

  This sketch will wait for an OSC UDP packet on localPort using a WiFi shield.
  For use with page 1 & 3 of the "simple.touchosc" layout

  based on an example by dlf (Metodo2 srl)
  LEDs pins 3,5 & 6 common anode RGB (sink), pin 9 single LED (source)
*/

#include <SPI.h>
#include <WiFi.h>
#include <WiFiUdp.h>
#include <OSCBundle.h>
#include <OSCBoards.h>

int status = WL_IDLE_STATUS;
char ssid[] = "your network";        #A
char pass[] = "your password";       #B

IPAddress iPad(192, 168, 1, 102);  #C
unsigned int inPort = 8000;          #D
unsigned int outPort = 8001;         #E

byte leds[] = {3, 3, 5, 6, 9};  // first entry just a dummy

WiFiUDP Udp;  // instance of the WiFi handler

void setup() {
  //Initialise serial and wait for port to open:
  Serial.begin(9600);
  while (!Serial) {
    ; // wait for serial port to connect. Needed for Leonardo only
  }
  Serial.println(" ");
  // check for the presence of the shield:
  if (WiFi.status() == WL_NO_SHIELD) {
    Serial.println("WiFi shield not present");
    // don't continue:
    while(true); // hold here
  }

  // attempt to connect to WiFi network:
  while ( status != WL_CONNECTED) {
    Serial.print("Attempting to connect to SSID: ");
    Serial.println(ssid);
```

```
  // Connect to WPA/WPA2 network. Change this line if using open or WEP network:
  status = WiFi.begin(ssid, pass);

  // wait 10 seconds for connection:
  delay(10000);
}
Serial.println("Connected to wifi");
printWifiStatus();

Serial.println("\n Starting connection to server...");
// if you get a connection, report back via serial:
Udp.begin(inPort);
for(int i=1 ; i<5; i++) {
pinMode(leds[i], OUTPUT);
digitalWrite(leds[i],HIGH);         #F
    }
  delay(500);                       #F
  digitalWrite(leds[4],LOW);        #F
}

void loop() {
  checkAnalogue(); // look at real analog ports
  // if there's data available, read a packet
  OSCMessage messageIN;
  int packetSize = Udp.parsePacket();
  if(packetSize)
  {
      while(packetSize )
       messageIN.fill(Udp.read());
       if(!messageIN.hasError())
       printMessage(messageIN);
     {
        messageIN.route("/1", routeScreen1); // add others for other screens
        messageIN.route("/3", routeScreen3);
     }
 }
}

void checkAnalogue(){
  static int lastAnalogueValue;
  int currentAnalogueReading;
    currentAnalogueReading = analogRead(0);
    if(abs(currentAnalogueReading - lastAnalogueValue) > 2){
      lastAnalogueValue = currentAnalogueReading;
      OSCMessage msg("/1/fader5");
      msg.add((float)currentAnalogueReading / 1023.0);
```

```
        // now send the message to the outPort
        Udp.beginPacket(iPad,outPort);
        msg.send(Udp);
        Udp.endPacket();
        msg.empty(); // empty the bundle ready to use for new messages
    }
}

void printWifiStatus() {
  // print the SSID of the network you're attached to:
  Serial.print("SSID: ");
  Serial.println(WiFi.SSID());

  // print your WiFi shield's IP address:
  IPAddress ip = WiFi.localIP();
  Serial.print("IP Address: ");
  Serial.println(ip);

  // print the received signal strength:
  long rssi = WiFi.RSSI();
  Serial.print("signal strength (RSSI):");
  Serial.print(rssi);
  Serial.println(" dBm");
}

//incoming messages

/**
 * Route Screen 1 - OSC 5 sliders and 4 toggle switches
 *
 * called when address matched "/1"
 * expected format:
 * /1/toggle(N)
 * and
 * /1/fader(N)
 *    (N) = is 1 to 4
 *    (value) = 1.0 or 0.0 or any value in between for a fader
 */

void routeScreen1(OSCMessage &msg, int addrOffset ){
  //match input
  int match = -1;

  for(int i=1; i<5; i++){
   if(msg.match(prefixPulsNumOSCAddress("/toggle",i), addrOffset) != 0) match = i;
  }
  if(match != -1) { // if we have a match for a /toggle address
  float data = msg.getFloat(0);
  if(match == 4)
  if(data == 1.0) analogWrite(leds[match], 255); else analogWrite(leds[match], 0);
  else
```

```
      if(data == 1.0) analogWrite(leds[match], 0); else analogWrite(leds[match], 255);
    }
    else { // if not a toggle look for a fader
        for(int i=1; i<5; i++){  // don't look for fader 5
         if(msg.match(prefixPulsNumOSCAddress("/fader",i), addrOffset) != 0) match = i;
        }
        if(match != -1) { // if we have a match for a /fader address
          float data = msg.getFloat(0);
            if(match == 4)
            analogWrite(leds[match], data * 255); // set brightness
            else
            analogWrite(leds[match], 255 - (data * 255)); // set brightness
        }
    }
}


/**
 * Route Screen 3 - XY pad and 4 toggle switches (not matched for)
 *
 * called when address matched "/1"
 * expected format:
 * /3/xy
 *    (value) = two floats between 1.0 and 0.0
 * Results printed out in the serial monitor
 */
void routeScreen3(OSCMessage &msg, int addrOffset ){
  char pad[] = "/xy";
    if(msg.match(pad, addrOffset) ){
        float data = msg.getFloat(0);
        Serial.print("X = ");
        Serial.print(data);
        float data2 = msg.getFloat(1);
        Serial.print("  Y = ");
        Serial.println(data2);
        analogWrite(leds[3], data * 255); // set brightness
        analogWrite(leds[4], data2 * 255); // set brightness
    }
}

char * prefixPulsNumOSCAddress( char * prefix, int num){        #G
    static char s[12]; // space to construct the string
    int i = 11; // last location in the string
    int len = 0;
    while(prefix[len] != '\0') len++; // find the length of the prefix char array
    s[i--]= '\0';  // add a null at the end
            do
        {
            s[i] = "0123456789"[num % 10];
            --i;
            num /= 10;
        }
```

```
      while(num && i); // keep on going until num or i drop to zero
      i++;  // compensate for last --i
      for(int j=0; j<len; j++){ // add the prefix string backwards
        s[i - len + j] = prefix[j];
        }
      return &s[i-len]; // return char array and point to first byte
}
void printMessage(OSCMessage &msg){
  char address[255];
  int len = msg.getAddress(address, 0);
  for(int i=0; i<len; i++)
    Serial.print(address[i]);
    Serial.print(" with data ");
    float data = msg.getFloat(0);
    Serial.print(data);
  Serial.println(" ");
}
#A your network SSID (name)
#B your network password (use for WPA, or use as key for WEP)
#C address of iPad running OSC
#D local port to listen on needs to match OSC's outgoing port
#E local port to talk to on needs to match OSC's incoming port
#F Flash L9 on the shield and the white LED to show a connection is made
#G function to generate an address string from a number
```

To test this, you need to connect the Arduino to your computer through the USB port. This is to allow feedback messages to be displayed in the serial monitor window. Note that this code will run without the USB connection but it is an easy way to see what is happening.

The code has to cope with the fact that LED 4 is powered by current sourcing so the levels have to be inverted for just that one LED. Most of the work in using OSC is in the generation of a character string to match all the possible input messages. While you can do this with a fixed array, it is far more efficient if you can generate this in the code. That is what the function prefixPulsNumOSCAddress does; it generates a string that includes the number passed into it at the end. This makes it easy to search through all the possible messages and return a match number. Note that Touch OSC does not make much use of zero as an appended number, so in order to make the code simple I have used a dummy first element in the LED's array and it finds what pin to change in response to a matched message. Note that there is not complete freedom to change these LEDs because I am using the analogWrite function to fade the LEDs and that only works on certain pins—those shown by a ~ on next to the pin number on the Arduino board. I popped half a table tennis ball over the RGB LED to diffuse the colors and make them easy to see.

Remember that I said that the UPD was a send and forget protocol; here you might find that the odd message goes AWOL. This is especially true if your router network is carrying heavy traffic. So the toggle switches might not match the state of the LEDs. The faders send a constant stream of information as they are adjusted so those are less likely to get lost. Also, as the fader and toggle switches are controlling the same LEDs, the last message to get sent overrides any previous setting.

OSC Keyboard

As this is a book about audio, the last example in this chapter is an OSC keyboard. It requires you to generate a custom layout on the Touch OSC application and use it to send OSC messages to the Arduino, which will use the built-in tone function to generate a note. I will talk a lot more about getting the Arduino to generate audio in the next two parts of this book, but for now I will just use the simple tone function.

You can get an Arduino pin to directly drive a small loudspeaker or headphones; it will not be very loud but it is loud enough for a simple test. The best option is to feed the audio output to an amplifier. There are plenty of low-cost loudspeaker amplifiers about, and most are powered from your computer's USB port. You need a very simple circuit with a resistor to restrict the current out of the Arduino pin to a safe level, and a capacitor to prevent any DC from getting to the speaker or earphones. The circuit for this is shown in Figure 8-16.

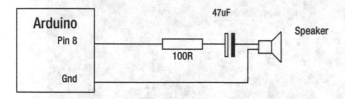

Figure 8-16. *Audio out from an Arduino*

The pin I used here is pin 8, but the tone function can use any pin. The value of the capacitor is not too critical either and anything greater than what's shown in the circuit will work just as well.

Touch OSC Screen

While some of the sample layouts have a keyboard along with some other stuff, it is easy enough to make one or copy and paste that element from another layout. You need to down load the free Touch OSC Editor and make one. If you don't fancy that then the layout file is on the book's web site to download. Make the keys out of "touch" controls with the sharps being shorter than the natural keys just like on a piano keyboard. Name the keys touch1 to touch23 and use the default values of 1.0 when touched and 0.0 when released. I used blue for the natural keys and green for the sharp keys. As an added touch, I put the note name above each key. Figure 8-17 shows what the OSC Editor looks like when I made the keyboard.

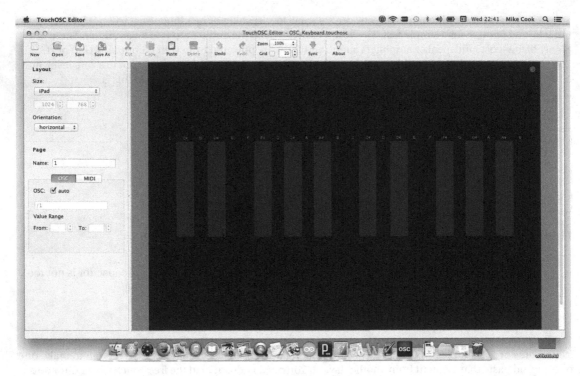

Figure 8-17. TouchOSC Editor

You can save this layout and then transfer it over to your mobile device.

Touch OSC Screen

Now you need the Arduino code to complete the project. This is a lot simpler than the other code in this chapter, as you don't need all of the debug output. It is designed as a simple standalone system. To show when it has connected to the router's network, pin 9 is set high. This can be connected to an external LED as in the previous project but there is no need. The WiFi shield contains a small green surface-mounted LED on this pin and so the green light will show that it is connected successfully and ready to go. This code is shown in Listing 8-4.

Listing 8-4. Arduino Code for the OSC Keypad

```
/*
OSC Keypad - Mike Cook Jan 2014
*/
#include <SPI.h>
#include <WiFi.h>
#include <WiFiUdp.h>
#include <OSCBundle.h>
#include <OSCBoards.h>
#define TONE_PIN 8
```

```
int notes[] = {262, 262, 277, 294, 311, 330, 349, 370, 392, 415, 440, 466, 494,      #A
              523, 554, 587, 622, 659, 698, 740, 784, 831, 880, 932, 988 } ;          #A
int status = WL_IDLE_STATUS;
char ssid[] = "myNetwork"; //  your network SSID (name)
char pass[] = "*********";     // your network password (use for WPA, or use as key for WEP)

IPAddress iPad(192, 168, 1, 102);  // address of iPad or device running OSC
unsigned int inPort = 8000;  // local port to listen on needs to match OSC's outgoing port
unsigned int outPort = 8001; // local port to talk to on needs to match OSC's incoming port

WiFiUDP Udp;  // instance of the WiFi handler

void setup() {
  pinMode(9, OUTPUT);
  digitalWrite(9,LOW); // LED off
  //Initialise serial and wait for port to open:
  Serial.begin(9600);
  while (!Serial) {
    ; // wait for serial port to connect. Needed for Leonardo only
  }
  Serial.println(" ");
  // check for the presence of the shield:
  if (WiFi.status() == WL_NO_SHIELD) {
    Serial.println("WiFi shield not present");
    // don't continue:
    while(true); // hold here
  }

  // attempt to connect to Wifi network:
  while ( status != WL_CONNECTED) {
    Serial.print("Attempting to connect to SSID: ");
    Serial.println(ssid);
    // Connect to WPA/WPA2 network. Change this line if using open or WEP network:
    status = WiFi.begin(ssid, pass);

    // wait 10 seconds for connection:
    delay(10000);
  }
  digitalWrite(9,HIGH); // show connected
  Udp.begin(inPort);
}

void loop() {                                    #B
  // if there's data available, read a packet
  OSCMessage messageIN;
  int packetSize = Udp.parsePacket();
  if(packetSize)
  {
      while(packetSize--)
       messageIN.fill(Udp.read());
       if(!messageIN.hasError())
```

243

```
        {
            messageIN.route("/1", routeScreen1);
        }
    }
}

/**
 * Route Screen 1 - OSC /push(n)
 *
 * called when address matched "/1"
 * expected format:
 * /1/push(N)
 *     (N) = is 1 to 4
 *     (value) = 1.0 for a push or 0.0 for release
 */

void routeScreen1(OSCMessage &msg, int addrOffset ){                    #C
    //match input
    int match = -1;

    for(int i=1; i<24; i++){
     if(msg.match(prefixPulsNumOSCAddress("/push",i), addrOffset) != 0) match = i;
    }
    if(match != -1) { // if we have a match for a /push address
    float data = msg.getFloat(0);
    if(data == 0.0) {
      noTone(TONE_PIN); // stop playing
    }
     else {
      tone(TONE_PIN, notes[match]); // Play note
      }
    }
}

char * prefixPulsNumOSCAddress( char * prefix, int num){                #D
    static char s[12]; // space to construct the string
    int i = 11; // last location in the string
    int len = 0;
    while(prefix[len] != '\0') len++; // find the length of the prefix char array

    s[i--]= '\0';  // add a null at the end
        do
        {
                s[i] = "0123456789"[num % 10];
                --i;
                num /= 10;
        }
    while(num && i); // keep on going until num or i drop to zero
    i++;  // compensate for last --i
    for(int j=0; j<len; j++){ // add the prefix string backwards
      s[i - len + j] = prefix[j];
      }
```

```
    return &s[i-len]; // return char array and point to first byte
}
#A Array of tone values to use for each key
#B This is the main function, checks for a message with and address starting /1
#C This function finds the number appended to the message and plays or stops the tone
#D Generates a message for testing, the same as used in Listing 8.3
```

Basically the loop function looks for message addresses starting with /1. When it finds one, it calls the routeScreen1 function. This then generates all the messages from /push1 to /push23 and sets the match variable to reflect which number was received. Then the message data is checked and if it is 1.0, a tone is started whose frequency is at the match variable index number in the array. If the data is 0.0, then any tone sounding is stopped.

If a note off OSC message is missed somehow, the note will continue to sound. This is a simple way of controlling the Arduino to make sound.

The Monome

Finally in this chapter I want to take a brief look at a controller/instrument known as a Monome that has caused somewhat of a revolution in the music world. It was created in 2006 by Brian Crabtree and Kelli Cain and at first sight seems a little underwhelming. Basically it is a simple rectangular array of illuminated push switches, that is it, no labels, no sound generation capability, no instructions, no way to play it. It is an undedicated controller whose only function is to send and receive messages in an OSC style format that tell of key presses or light LEDs. As well as buttons and switches, some Monomes also contain a tilt sensor to allow you to control things by the way you hold the instrument.

It is this very lack of specific purpose that has made the Monome such a hit, as it has been used for all sorts of applications from sequencers, to instruments, mixers to effects controllers, and even games. Also while the two inventers sell this instrument, it is also open source and many variations have been designed and built.

Part of the appeal of the original instrument is the esthetic, clean lines and sustainable wood are often a major feature as is the trademark orange LEDs illuminating the switches. But Monomes have been made using a very wide verity of switches and LED colors. There have even been some mainstream commercial versions—Akai's APC40, the Novation Launchpad, and the Livid Instruments Block and Ohm64—as examples. They are known generically as "grid-based controllers".

The use of a common control language has meant that anyone developing an application for a Monome can share it with the rest of the community, which can then improve it or simply use to create their own music. It can be fed directly into PD and MAX. While the original Monome was not built on the Arduino type processor, many variations of the Monome have been. I have designed several versions of Arduino-based Monome, which I will talk about in the next chapter.

The Monome API

There are two versions of the Monome instruction set or API (Application Protocol Interface), but both are OSC-based. The original instructions just used address-based instructions, whereas the new one uses OSC addresses with data. Table 8-4 shows some of the standard Monome OSC messages that can be sent to the Monome and Table 8-5 shows messages sent back.

Table 8-4. *Messages Sent to the Monome*

Address	Data	Description
/grid/led/set	x y s	Set led at (x,y) to state s (0 or 1)
/grid/led/all	s	Set all LEDs to state s (0 or 1)
/grid/led/map	x_offset y_offset s[8]	Set a quad (8×8, 64 buttons) in a single message
/grid/led/row x_offset	y s[..]	Set a row in a quad in a single message.
/grid/led/col	x y_offset s[..]	Set a column in a quad in a single message
/grid/led/intensity	i	Variable brightness: To be used in future set messages
/grid/led/level/set	x y l	Set the brightness for an individual LED
/grid/led/level/all	l	Set the brightness for all LEDs
/tilt/set	n s	Set active state of tilt sensor n to s - 1=active, 0= inactive

Table 8-5. *Messages Sent from the Monome*

Address	Data	Description
/grid/key	x y s	Key state change at (x,y) to s 1 = key down, 0 = key up
/tilt	n x y z	Position change on tilt sensor n, integer (8-bit) values x, y, z

A full description and examples uses can be found at http://monome.org/docs/tech:osc along with a lot more information on the same site. But after reading this chapter I am sure you can follow what the addresses mean.

Monome Variants

The grid-based Monomes come in various sizes. One of my designs is perhaps the smallest, at a grid size of 4-by-4 illuminated switches. Standard Monomes are know as "sixty four," with a grid of 8 by 8, the next up is the "one twenty eight," with a grid of 16 by 8. The largest one the company sells is a "two fifty six," being 16 by 16. However, there are many other sizes people have made. The lights also are a popular target for variations, with the original Monome having orange LEDs. People have used all the available LED colors to make their Monomes, as well as multicolored LEDs and increasingly RGB LEDs giving an almost unlimited variation on color.

As well as the original grid-based Monome, there is a newer circular based controller called the Acr and it has either two or four circles of 256 LEDs in each. One of my designs is a Monome set out in a hexagonal grid. I have called it a Hexome.

Summary

OSC is another way of getting control messages about sound and music into an out of the Arduino. It is more flexible than MIDI and can convey more precise data faster in a free format style. It has not yet reached the ubiquitous penetration of the market that MIDI has achieved but it is getting there.

As an OSC message is more network-friendly, it has found its way into many mobile devices—smartphones and tablets—and is increasingly becoming the standard to use for mobile applications. It is still under active development and I am sure the standard will continue to develop and expand well into the future.

CHAPTER 9

■ ■ ■

Some More Projects

This chapter covers

- Making a MIDI chaotic pendulum
- Controlling a child's toy glockenspiel with MIDI
- Creating a giant footswitch keyboard or controller
- Using MIDI to hit things

To round out this section of the book, this chapter looks at more projects that you can make using your Arduino to control sound. These projects are of medium complexity—harder than those discussed in Chapters 4 and 5 but simpler than those in Chapters 6 and 7.

These projects let you explore and use what you have learned in this section of the book and are the springboard to further projects of your own. There are two controllers or music generators here and two instruments or sound generators.

With the chaotic pendulum, you can make hypnotic repetitive patterns that suddenly change, with no two swings producing the same patterns. You can turn a toy glockenspiel into a MIDI-controlled instrument that you can play from a sequencer or keyboard. If you have ever wanted to create music from running about, the MIDI footsteps project shows you how. And finally, using servo motors, you can beat the living daylights out of everyday objects to create manic percussion rhythms.

The MIDI Pendulum

The MIDI pendulum creates music from the swinging of a pendulum and the results can be rather fascinating and hypnotic. This is because instead of a normal regular pendulum, you are going to make a pendulum that is driven by the laws of chaos. The result is seemingly repetitive patterns that will suddenly change in an unexpected way. Due to the pendulum's extreme sensitivity to initial conditions, the results will be different every time it is swung. There are also some software tricks you can use to increase the variability.

A pendulum is a swinging weight or mass on the end of a long string. It has a regular period that depends on the length of the string. So it might not seem likely that it would be a successful in generating interesting sounds; you might think it would be more like a metronome. This would be the case if it were not for the fact that in trying to monitor its position you disturb the movement and produce, not a regular movement, but a chaotic one. This project illustrates to great effect the scientific maxim that you cannot take a measurement of a system without disturbing that system.

In scientific terms, chaos is the state of a deterministic system becoming impossible to predict, and that is exactly the sort of system that produces interesting musical results. Basically, the pendulum you need to use has two degrees of freedom—it can swing side to side and up and down. It spends most of its time going around in some sort of ellipse. At the end of this pendulum you need to place a magnet and this magnet does two things. It is used to trigger a sensor to show that the pendulum is over a specific point and it receives a mechanical kick to subtly change the swing of the pendulum, thus producing chaotic movement.

There are a few ways of detecting a magnet but perhaps the simplest and the one that produces the maximum kick back is the reed switch. A reed switch is a sealed glass tube containing electrical contacts. These contacts are sensitive to magnetic fields and will close when a magnet is close to them. They are often used as door and window monitors in security systems where the magnet can be mounted in the swinging door and the switch mounted in the top corner of the door frame. What you are going to do is to mount reed switches on a baseboard and suspend a magnet above them. Each pass of the magnet will trigger a MIDI note and provide a mechanical kick. This kick or feedback comes from the kinetic energy removed from the pendulum in order to move the reed switch contacts. So each time a switch is triggered there is a different amount of slowing down of the pendulum and, as the angle of the approach is never the same, a small deviation in the swing.

The Sensor

Using a reed switch as a sensor is quite straightforward, but I wanted to introduce a twist and have an LED light up as the magnet passed over it. The simple way to do this is to control each LED with the Arduino and trigger it whenever the reed switch closed. However, I want this example to be a bit more sophisticated than that so I came up with a sensor circuit that included the LED and lights the LED automatically on seeing a magnetic field. This cuts down not only on the electronics but also on the amount of wiring that is needed. Figure 9-1 shows the sensor's circuit.

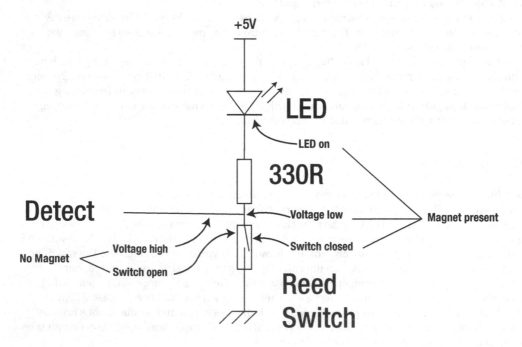

Figure 9-1. *The Reed switch sensor*

You can see that when there is no magnet, the reed switch is open and the voltage at the detect point is high because there is a path through the resistor and LED to 5V. However, as this detect line is connected to an Arduino input, there is virtually no current flowing and so the LED is not lit. Now when a magnet comes close to the reed switch, the switch closes and connects the detect point to ground. This can be detected by the Arduino as a low input, but at the same time there is a path for current to flow through the LED and resistor to ground, and lighting up the LED. So detection and feedback occur at the same time—two for the price of one—rather neat I think.

The LED needs to be a very low profile so they don't get in the way of the magnet. You can do this in two ways—you could drill a hole and mount it in the base plate, or, as I chose to do, use a surface-mount LED close to the reed switch. For this project you need to make 15 of these sensors, and to do this I mounted them on small 1.4-inch by 0.3-inch pieces of strip board, as shown in Figure 9-2.

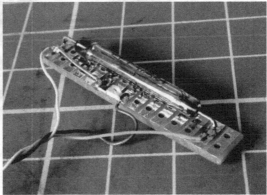

Figure 9-2. *Strip board and reed switch sensor*

Each sensor needs three wires attached to it, +5V, ground, and the detect wire. As well as the surface-mounting LED I used a surface-mounting resistor soldered between the tracks of the strip board. A close-up of the wiring is shown in Figure 9-3.

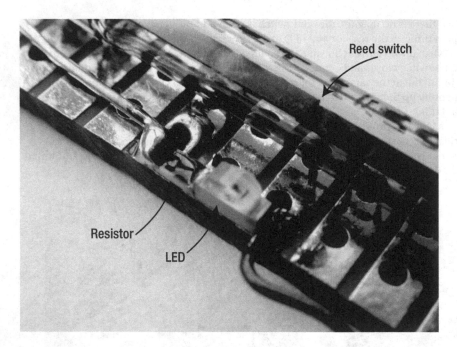

Figure 9-3. *Close-up of the wiring of the sensor*

These sensor boards should be mounted on a base plate, more or less over the area where the pendulum is going to swing. Keep the rest position directly under the pendulum clear. Before you mount them, you must first make the pendulum and the pendulum support.

The Pendulum Support

The length of the support is key to how the system will behave. Basically you need a ridged pendulum supported by a frame of some sort to suspend it above the base with the sensors. I constructed the two with 1/2-inch by 5/16-inch U channel aluminum, although you could easily use more substantial lengths of aluminum extrusion.

I made my pendulum 39-inch long with a 3/4-inch round magnet glued to the end. You have to ensure that the pendulum is long enough so that at the extremes of its swing, it is not too far away from the base to trigger the reed switches. You can test this before you do any wiring because the reed switch will click as the magnet activates it.

The pendulum support is rather like a gibbet in that an upright piece has a T-shaped top where the pendulum is attached by a thin piece of thread. It is important that this thread is as short and as flexible as possible so it does not constrict the movement of the pendulum. You can see the cross pieces of the support in Figure 9-4.

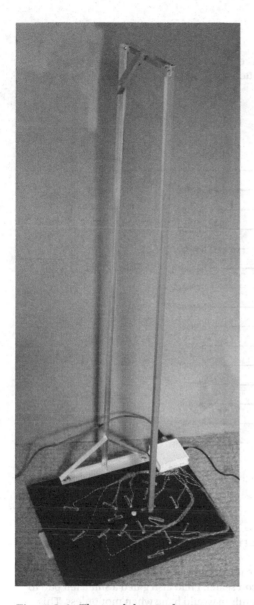

Figure 9-4. The pendulum and support

The box on the top-right of the base is where I put the Arduino. I made this from a styrene sheet and angle pieces, and the sheet made a good diffuser for the RGB LED that is used to add a bit more visual interest to the project.

The Pendulum Schematic

The schematic of the circuit is very simple and is shown in Figure 9-5. In order to make the schematic uncluttered and easy to follow, I drew the sensor board in a dotted box. You need 15 of these circuits, each one connected to one of the sensor lines.

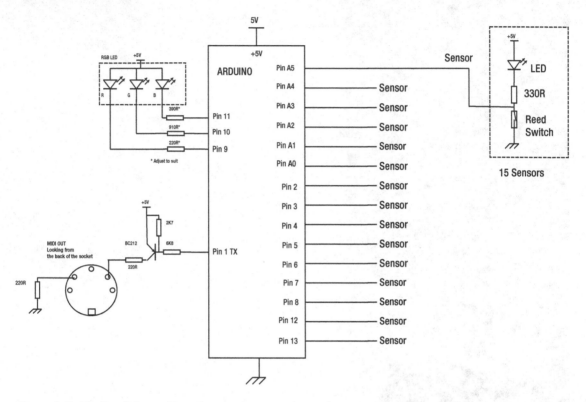

Figure 9-5. *The Pendulum schematic*

You will see on the right that there is the usual MIDI output interface and the RGB LED. So electrically there is absolutely nothing complex at all.

For the construction I made a wooden baseboard and gave it two coats of a high-gloss paint. Then I glued the sensor switches and the wiring to this plate with silicon sealer. I had also glued a small felt pad to the baseboard at exactly the center of the board where the pendulum would hang when motionless. This provided a good way of setting it up and making sure the length of thread was right to cause the pendulum to get as close to the switches as possible without hitting them.

The Pendulum Software

The movements of the chaotic pendulum provide interest and variation enough, but I wanted to add a little more. Each reed switch is assigned to a specific note. A note on MIDI message is sent when a switch is activated by the magnet. However, to add a bit of variety, I wanted that note assignment or mapping to be dynamic rather than fixed. Therefore, I assigned one sensor not only to send a note, but also to change the sensor to note mapping. I did this by having four banks of mapping defined by a two-dimensional array and used the bank switch sensor to trigger the changing of the mapping to another bank.

I also wanted a bit of a visual indication that the bank change had happened, and also feedback that a note had been sent. There is an LED on each sensor to do this, but a more colorful way is to add an RGB LED. This toggles between two colors on each note; these two colors change depending on what bank of sensor to note mapping is in force. These mappings are given in the file shown in Listing 9-1. These should be typed into a file called Defines.h and added to a file tab in the IDE.

Listing 9-1. Defines File for the Pendulum Project

```
// Arduino pin assignments
#define midiChannel (byte)0

// Define constants
#define a3 45                                                              #A
#define b3 47                                                              #A
#define c3 48                                                              #A
#define d3 50                                                              #A
#define e3 52                                                              #A
#define f3 53                                                              #A
#define g3 55                                                              #A
#define a4 57                                                              #A
#define b4 59                                                              #A
#define c4 60    // Middle C (MIDI note value 60)                         #A
#define d4 62                                                              #A
#define e4 64                                                              #A
#define f4 65                                                              #A
#define g4 67                                                              #A
#define a5 69                                                              #A
#define b5 71                                                              #A

// Variable definations
int redLED = 9, greenLED = 10, blueLED = 11;   // PWM lnes for RGB LED
int bankColourR[8]    = { 255,  0,  64, 128,  197, 128,  255, 0 };        #B
int bankColourG[8]    = { 0, 255, 128, 255,  128, 210,  255, 64 };        #B
int bankColourB[8]    = { 255,255,  255, 197,  255, 128,  64, 32 };       #B
int bankchangeSensor = 2;    // sensor for changing banks
int bank = 0;                     // bank change
const int maxSensors = 15;    // number of sensors being used
int sensorLast[maxSensors];   // the last state of the sensors
int sensor[] = {2,3,4,5,6,7,8,12,13,14,15,16,17,18,19};  // sensor pins
char notePlaying[16];
char note[16][4] = {a3, b3, c3, d3, e3, f3, g3, a4, b4, c4, d4, e4, f4, g4, a5, b5, #C
                b4, c4, d4, e4, f4, g4, a5, b5, a3, b3, c3, d3, e3, f3, g3, a4,     #C
                e3, f3, g3, a4, a3, b3, c3, d3, f4, g4, a5, b5, b4, c4, d4, e4,     #C
                b5, a5, g4, f4, e4, d4, c4, b4, a4, g3, f3, e3, d3, c3, b3, a3      #C
            };

#A - MIDI note numbers for each note of a scale
#B - Colours to use for each bank
#C - The MIDI note value to be played for each bank
```

Any of these bank-mapping arrays can be changed and I would encourage you to experiment with them. For example, you could map the notes to a scale other than C, or to a minor scale or even a pentatonic scale. The mapping of the colors are in 8-bit values (0 to 255) representing levels of those colors. The colors mix in an additive way. If they are all on full, you get white.

Now the remaining file is the one that contains the code that does all the work. This is given in Listing 9-2 and should be typed into the IDE under the name MIDI_Pendulum.

Listing 9-2. The Pendulum Sketch Code

```
/* MIDI Pendulum - Mike Cook Feb 2014
 * send MIDI serial data, for magnetic reed switch sensors
 */
#include "Defines.h"                                            #A

// #define MIDI_TEST // un-comment this line for a test to format the data for the serial
monitor

void setup() {
  //  set the states of the I/O pins:
  clearNotes();   // remove any notes playing and zero arrays
  for(int i = 0; i<maxSensors; i++){   // initialise sensor inputs
    pinMode(sensor[i],INPUT);
    sensorLast[i] = digitalRead(sensor[i]);
    }

 //  Setup serial / MIDI
#ifdef MIDI_TEST
    Serial.begin(9600);     // Debug speed
#else
    Serial.begin(31250);       // MIDI speed
#endif
  programChange(0xc0, 14);                                      #B

}

//******************* MAIN LOOP ********************************

void loop() {
  int val;
    for(int i = 0; i<maxSensors; i++){   // scan sensor inputs
    val = digitalRead(sensor[i]);
  if( val != sensorLast[i]) {
      doSensor(i,val);
      sensorLast[i] = val;
    }
  }
    } // end loop function

//******************* Functions ********************************
```

```
void doSensor(int s, int v) {                                            #C

    if( v == LOW ) {           // if we have a make on the sensor
      if(v == bankchangeSensor) {   // and it is the bank change sensor
        stopNotes();             // cycle through the sensor / note mapping banks
        bank++;
        if(bank == 4) bank = 0;
        changeLED();
      }
        // play a note
      noteSend(0x90, note[s][bank], 0x60);
      notePlaying[s] = note[s][bank];
      changeLED();       // change LED colour
      }
    else{  // sensor has released
      noteSend(0x80, note[s][bank], 0x00);    // turn off the note
      notePlaying[s] = 0;
      }
}

void changeLED(){
  static int toggle = 0;
  // toggle LED depending on the bank
    analogWrite(redLED, bankColourR[((bank << 1) + toggle)]);       #D
    analogWrite(greenLED, bankColourG[((bank << 1) + toggle)]);     #D
    analogWrite(blueLED, bankColourB[((bank << 1) + toggle)]);      #D
    toggle ^= 1;   // alternate colour for next time                #E
}

#ifdef MIDI_TEST
// This is a test so format data for viewing in the serial monitor
 void noteSend(byte cmd, byte data1, byte data2) {
  cmd = cmd | char(midiChannel);  // merge channel number
  Serial.print(((cmd >> 4) & 0xf), HEX);  // to prevent leading Fs being displayed
  Serial.print((cmd & 0xf), HEX);
  Serial.print(" ");
  Serial.print(data1, HEX);
  Serial.print(" ");
  Serial.println(data2, HEX);

}
//  change the voice
 void programChange(byte cmd, byte data1) {
   cmd = cmd | char(midiChannel);  // merge channel number
   Serial.print(((cmd >> 4) & 0xf), HEX);  // to prevent leading Fs being displayed
   Serial.print((cmd & 0xf), HEX);
   Serial.print(" ");
   Serial.println(data1, HEX);
}
```

```
#else
  // no test so send the stuff out to MIDI
 void noteSend(byte cmd, byte data1, byte data2) {
  cmd = cmd | byte(midiChannel);  // merge channel number
  Serial.write(cmd);
  Serial.write(data1);
  Serial.write(data2);
}
//   change the voice
 void programChange(byte cmd, byte data1) {
  cmd = cmd | byte(midiChannel);  // merge channel number
  Serial.write(cmd);
  Serial.write(data1);
}
#endif

// stop the notes playing on all notes
void stopNotes() {
   for(int i=0;i<16;i++){
   if (notePlaying[i] !=0) {
      noteSend(0x80, notePlaying[i], 0x00);
      notePlaying[i] = 0;
   }
 }
}

// stop all the notes playing and initialise arrays
void clearNotes() {
   for(int i=0;i<16;i++){
     noteSend(0x80, note[i][bank], 0x00);
      notePlaying[i] = 0;
 }
}
```
#A - Include the file you typed in as Listing 9-1
#B - Change the MIDI voice - this is for bells you change this to what you like
#C - Do this when a sensor change has been detected
#D - Pick the colour from the array or the one next to it
#E - The ^ operator is the "Exclusive OR" (XOR) operation and it makes this variable
alternate between zero and one.

Note that this code contains some additional functions to help you debug the output. This is switched in using the #ifdef MIDI_TEST statement. This is what is known as a compiler directive, because it changes the way the compiler generates the code. This section looks for a label called MIDI_TEST and only if it finds one will it compile the functions that follow. If it fails to find one, it will skip to the #else label and compile from there until it reaches the #endif statement. In this program, it is used to switch in an alternate set of functions that show MIDI code numbers in the serial monitor screen rather than the binary values a MIDI message needs. Using these alternate functions is triggered by uncommenting the #define MIDI_TEST line at the beginning of the program.

My final instrument is shown in Figure 9-6.

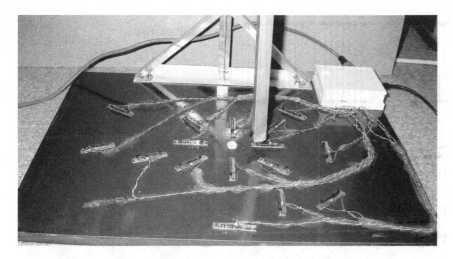

Figure 9-6. *The chaotic pendulum*

MIDI Footsteps

Have you ever wanted a giant keyboard for an exhibition or show? I needed something to trigger some Shepard tones for an exhibition. Shepard tones are a famous audio illusion rather like the never-ending staircase optical illusion used in some of the lithographs of M.C Escher, such as the 1960 print called Ascending and Descending. With Shepard tones, successive notes appear to be constantly getting higher and higher. Each note seems higher than the last. Of course, it is just an illusion and the tone stays the same. Only the mix of harmonics changes. I wanted to illustrate this point for a Maker Faire, which is why I made the MIDI footsteps controller.

It was a great success with kids running themselves silly round and round in circles, and just like the tones, getting nowhere. I also accompanied the sounds with a ball bouncing up or down (depending on the direction they were running) an Escher like staircase. What I would like to tell you about here is the MIDI controller that made all this possible.

Foot Switches

If you are going to make a foot operate switch, it needs to be sensitive and robust, as kids tend to do a lot of stomping when they see a target. You can buy pressure mat switches used in security systems, but these were a bit too big for my liking and I do like to make stuff myself. I am sure you can get smaller ones if you do want to buy a switch.

What I used for my switches was conducting foam. This is the sort of thing that is use for packing static-sensitive integrated circuits and circuit boards with protruding pins, like the Arduino WiFi shield. However, you can also use a pressure-sensitive sheet; see http://proto-pic.co.uk/pressure-sensitive-conductive-sheet-velostat-linqstat/. That web page also has a link to a great PDF file describing lots of uses for the material.

My method with the conducting foam was to rout a recess into a block of wood or MDF (Medium Density Fiberboard) for a grid of gold-plated wires in the form of a single row of 0.1-inch long pitch header pins. Then, on top of that, I placed a piece of conducting foam. When the foam was stepped on, it was compressed, lowering the resistance between adjacent bars. I cut the pins from every other bar on one side and the alternate bars on the other so that I could simply connect all the wires together on each side. This is illustrated in Figure 9-7.

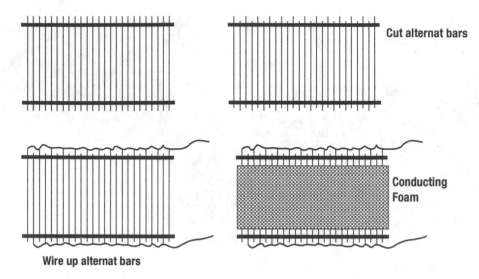

Cut alternat bars

Conducting
Foam

Wire up alternat bars

Figure 9-7. *Pressure sensor foot switch*

Then the grid and foam pad was surrounded by normal plastic foam packing material to give it some mechanical resilience. The whole thing was toped off by a piece of cloth obtained from an old curtain samples book. The stages of making the switch are shown in Figure 9-8.

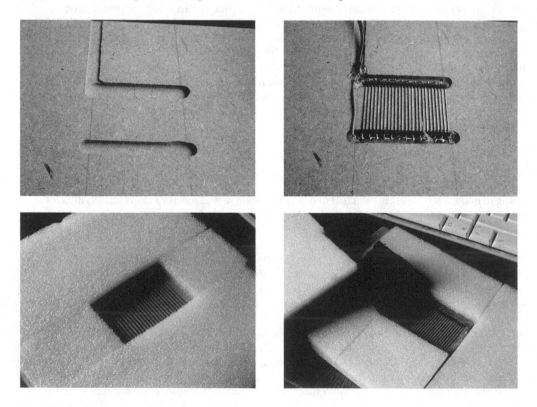

Figure 9-8. *Stages in making a foot sensor*

From the upper left, this shows the board routing to allow the bars to sit flat, then the bars being wired in. On the lower left are the bars being surrounded by packing foam and then the conducting foam being placed over them.

Footsteps Schematic

The foot switch sensors will show a lower resistance across the bars when someone stands on them. Now you have to translate this into a signal that an Arduino can understand.

So far with the projects in this book, I used an Arduino to actually build the project. This is not always the case when I do projects; often I build them as standalone systems using just the processor and a handful of components. This is an especially useful technique if the project does not require any USB communications in operation. If the only use for USB is during the programming and development stage, then it is much more economical to use a USB-to-TTL serial interface board and mount a small pin header on the board. Then you can program the project as normal and then use that interface board on the next project.

It is easy to use the schematic for an Arduino, as the pin numbers to use are shown as Pin x, where as the numbers inside the AT328 Chip circuit symbol are the actual pin numbers of the chip. Your USB-to-TTL serial interface board might not have a capacitor in series with the reset line. This allows an auto reset to occur when programming. This capacitor is shown on the schematic in series with the reset line; if you don't get an auto reset with your interface, try shorting out this capacitor. The full schematic of a standalone MIDI footsteps project is shown in Figure 9-9. Note that it contains a 5V regulator for externally powering off 9 or 12V. If you have a 5V regulated power supply you can bypass the regulator circuit completely and supply the chip directly.

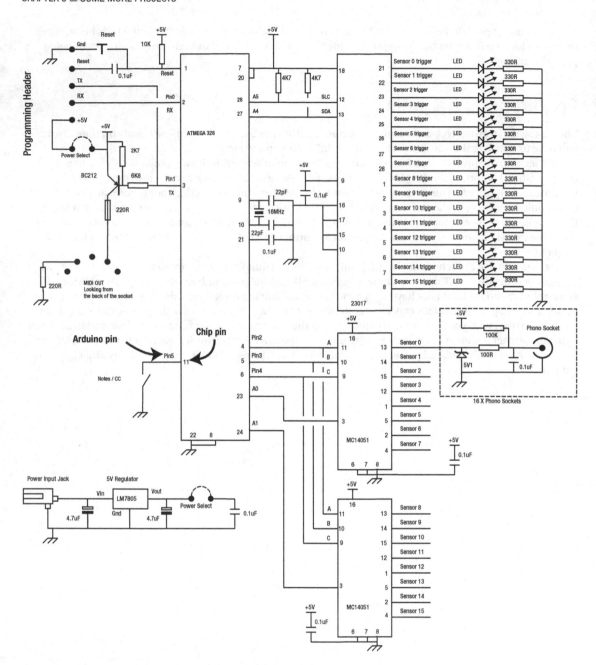

Figure 9-9. *Schematic of the MIDI footsteps project*

The foot sensors are connected to the board using phono sockets and, to simplify the schematic, the interface circuit is shown only once. However, you will need to make 16 of these, one for each sensor. The 5V1 Zener diode on the input to the multiplexer chip is there for protection in case any large static voltages are picked up on the long leads from the sensors on the floor to the unit. They do not affect the operation and can be left out if you are feeling lucky.

Each sensor feeds into an input of one of the two 4051 analogue multiplexers. These multiplexers are fed into analogue inputs A0 and A1. The Arduino pins 2 to 4 control what multiplexer input is switched to the output. The 23017 chip is a 16-bit I/O port expander and is used to provide feedback when each foot sensor is triggered. This could be completely removed from the circuit if you do not want the LED visual feedback.

The MIDI output driver is the same as you have seen before on other projects in this book. Finally, the switch on Arduino Pin 5 selects between sending note messages and CC messages. Figure 9-10 shows my finished standalone system. The LEDs are attached to the lid of the unit and the USB programming interface is in the top-right corner.

Figure 9-10. *MIDI footsteps standalone project*

Footsteps Software

What brings any hardware to life is the software. While a footfall brings a change in resistance of the sensors, you are just looking when to trigger a MIDI message, so you need to monitor the readings from the sensors until you see a level below a certain threshold value. Then you can trigger a note on, or a CC with a value of 127, message. When that sensor's reading goes above the threshold, the corresponding note off or CC with a value of 0 message is sent.

To do this, the software must be constantly looking at each of the sensors in turn and comparing the reading with what was obtained last time in order to make those decisions. Just like the previous project, this one is split into two files. The first is the Defines file shown in Listing 9-3.

Listing 9-3. Defines File from the MIDI Footsteps Project

```
// Port expander registers
#define IODIR (byte) 0x00          #A
#define IPOL (byte) 0x02           #A
#define GPINTEN (byte) 0x04        #A
#define DEFVAL (byte) 0x06         #A
#define INTCON (byte) 0x08         #A
#define IOCON (byte) 0x0A          #A
#define GPPU (byte) 0x0C           #A
#define INTF (byte) 0x0E           #A
#define INTCAP (byte) 0x10         #A
#define GPIO (byte) 0x12           #A
#define OLAT (byte) 0x14           #A

// Bits in the IOCON register
#define BANK (byte) 0x80           #A
#define MIRROR (byte) 0x40         #A
#define SEQOP (byte) 0x20          #A
#define DISSLW (byte) 0x10         #A
#define HAEN (byte) 0x08           #A
#define ODR (byte) 0x04            #A
#define INTPOL (byte) 0x02         #A

// I2C device addresses
#define ledAddress    (0x20 | 0x0)  // address of trigger LED indicators output
#define ddrTrigger 0x00000           // data direction register for trigger indictor LEDs

#define midiChannel (byte)0

// Arduino pin assignments
const int s0Pin = 2;                                #B
const int s1Pin = 3;                                #B
const int s2Pin = 4;                                #B
const int mux1 = 0;        // analogue port multiplexer 1 is read on
const int mux2 = 1;        // analogue port multiplexer 2 is read on
const int notesSelect = 5; // MIDI notes or CC

// Variable definitions
int currentState[16]; // current state of sensors
int lastState[16];    // the last state of the sensors
int threshold = 0x90;                               #C
int lastLedVal;
```

#A - Defining register & bit names in the 23017 port expander
#B - Multiplexer select pins
#C - Sets the threshold value in deciding if a sensor is pressed change this to suit your sensors

What we have here is the standard definitions of the register names and bit names for the 23017 port expander, followed by the definitions of the pin numbers that are used. Finally, the variables used by the main code are defined.

The business end of the code is shown in Listing 9-4 and should be typed into the MIDI_Footsteps tab in the IDE window.

Listing 9-4. MIDI Footsteps Code

```
s
/* Midi Footsteps - Mike Cook Feb 2014
 *
 * -----------------
 * send MIDI serial data, for multiplexed pressure pad sensors
 *
 */
#include <Wire.h>
#include "Defines.h"

char control[16] = { 16, 17, 18, 19, 20, 21, 22, 23, 24, 25, 26, 27, 28, 29, 30, 31};    #A
// key of C
char notes[16] = { 48, 50, 52, 53, 55, 57, 59, 60, 62, 64, 65, 67, 69, 71, 72, 74 };    #B

void setup() {
  //  set the states of the I/O pins to drive the sensor multiplexer:
    pinMode(s0Pin, OUTPUT);
    pinMode(s1Pin, OUTPUT);
    pinMode(s2Pin, OUTPUT);
    pinMode(notesSelect, INPUT_PULLUP);
    lastLedVal = 0;

 // Setup I2C devices
    Wire.begin();                          // start the I2C interface
     gpio_write(ledAddress, (MIRROR | ODR)<<8, IOCON);
    // Initilise registers
    gpio_write(ledAddress, ddrTrigger, IODIR);   // Make into outputs
    gpio_write(ledAddress, 0, OLAT);             // turn them all off
    doSensorScan();                              // get initial states
    saveCurrentState();
    Serial.begin(31250);       // MIDI speed
}

void loop() {
    doSensorScan();
#C
    lookForChange();
#D
    saveCurrentState();
#E
    } // end loop function


void doSensorScan() {  // look at all the sensors
 for(int i=0; i<8; i++){
    digitalWrite(s0Pin, i & 0x1);        #F
    digitalWrite(s1Pin, (i>>1) & 0x1);   #F
```

```
  digitalWrite(s2Pin, (i>>2) & 0x1);    #F
  currentState[i] = analogRead(mux1); // read mux1 in first 8 array locations
  currentState[i+8] = analogRead(mux2); // read mux2 in last 8 array locations
 }
}

void saveCurrentState(){  // save the current state for next time
  for(int i=0; i<16; i++){
    lastState[i] = currentState[i];
  }
}

// the value of threshold determines the on / off point
void lookForChange(){
  int ledVal = 0;
  int ledMask = 1;
  for(int i=0; i<16; i++){
    if(currentState[i] < threshold) ledVal |= ledMask;         #G
    ledMask = ledMask << 1;
  }
  if(lastLedVal != ledVal) {    // something has changed
  ledMask = 1;
    for(int i=0; i<16; i++){
      if((ledMask & ledVal) != (ledMask & lastLedVal)){
        if((ledMask & ledVal) == 0) {
          // note off
          if(digitalRead(notesSelect) ){                      #H
          midiSend(0xB0, control[i], 0x00);    // turn off control message
          }
          else {
            midiSend(0x80, notes[i], 0x00); // note off
          }
        }
        else{
          // note on
          if(digitalRead(notesSelect) ){                      #H
          midiSend(0xB0, control[i], 0x7f);   // turn on control message
          }
          else {
            midiSend(0x90, notes[i], velocityCalculate(currentState[i]) ); // note on
          }
        }
      }
      ledMask = ledMask << 1;
    }
    // Update the trigger LEDs
      gpio_write(ledAddress, ledVal, OLAT);
  }
  lastLedVal = ledVal;            // record current state of LEDs and MIDI notes / messages
}
```

```
byte velocityCalculate(int reading){
  int velocity;
  velocity = 95; // default velocity
  // velocity = map(reading, 0, threshold, 127, 0);    #I
  return (byte) velocity;
}

  //  send a MIDI message
 void midiSend(byte cmd, byte data1, byte data2) {
  cmd = cmd | byte(midiChannel);  // merge channel number
  Serial.write(cmd);
  Serial.write(data1);
  Serial.write(data2);
}
//  change the voice
 void programChange(byte cmd, byte data1) {
  cmd = cmd | byte(midiChannel);  // merge channel number
  Serial.write(cmd);
  Serial.write(data1);
}

void gpio_write(int address, int data, int reg) {
  //  Send output register address
  Wire.beginTransmission(address);
  Wire.write(reg);
  //  Connect to device and send two bytes
  Wire.write(0xff & data);  //  low byte
  Wire.write(data >> 8);    //  high byte
  Wire.endTransmission();
}
#A - The CC messages to send for each foot sensor
#B - The note to send for each foot sensor
#C - Read all the sensors into an array
#D - Look to see if any have changed and action them
#E - Save the new readings for next time round the loop
#F - Select multiplexer channel
#G - Mark the position of sensors below the threshold value
#H - Send a MIDI CC or note message depending on the state of the switch
#I - Uncomment for note on velocity proportional to sensor reading
```

What you see here are two arrays defining what to send for each foot sensor trigger—one array for what CC message number to send and the other for what note to send. What is actually sent is determined by the unit's note/CC switch on pin 5 of the Arduino.

The main loop() function simply looks at the new sensor readings, compares the new values with the old, and sends the appropriate MIDI messages if it has crossed the threshold value. Finally, it copies the latest readings into an array so that it can use them to test against the new data next time round the loop. The functions for sending MIDI and writing to the port expander are the same as in other projects.

As these are analogue sensors, you could do something with the analogue data it returns. There is the start of an experiment in that direction in the velocityCalculate function. This takes the actual reading and maps a note velocity for the note on message inversely proportional to the reading. As it stands this is not too successful because the note is triggered as soon as the sensor reading drops below the threshold. It takes a relatively long time, compared to the speed of the processor, for the reading to drop to its lowest value, so the range of velocities you get is quite small. This sensor must be selected again and read repeatedly until the reading stabilizes (that is, there are two same reads in a row). Then that reading will give you a much better spread of velocities. I will, as they say, leave that as an exercise to the reader.

No matter. If you want to produce a giant keyboard, make a musical staircase, or anything else involving music and feet, the MIDI footsteps project is worth looking at. If you are interested in the Shepherd tones mentioned at the start of this chapter, there is a PD (Pure Data) patch for generating them. Just look in PD under the help browser (Pure Data ➤ audio.examples ➤ D09.shepard.tone.pd).

Tripping the Light Fantastic

There is a quick extension that you can do with this project that will turn it into something totally different. Each of the foot sensors can be replaced with a light sensor, to be more specific a light-dependent resistor. This will produce a light-triggered instrument or controller.

The best way to go about this is to illuminate the sensors with a desk light and then play the instrument by waving your hands over the sensors and casting a shadow. The shadow will increase the resistance of the light-dependent resistors and the sensor reading will go up. This means you need to swap the sense that the instrument operates in. The simple way to do that is just to swap over the note on and note off MIDI messages. You will also need to adjust the threshold value.

MIDI Glockenspiel

Whereas the previous two projects in this chapter have been about using the Arduino as a controller to trigger sound, these next two are all about creating instruments with the Arduino to actually generate sound.

I created the MIDI glockenspiel project in 1993 for a BBC computer and later adapted it for an Arduino and MIDI. However, some of the electronic components I used have become obsolete and so I thought I would redesign it for this book. It has proved very popular over the years and I still get e-mails from people wanting to make one.

I used the fast real-time capability of the Arduino to simplify the electronics and used a modern Darlington driver IC. Some people would say that this is a xylophone, but they are wrong. A xylophone has wooden blocks or bars that are hit, whereas a glockenspiel has metal ones.

The basis for this instrument is a child's toy. Some of these are untuned bent sheets of metal, but you can find cheap tuned ones. The idea is to take one of these toys, arrange a solenoid under each note's bar, and have it hit the bar when activated. Figure 9-11 shows the instrument.

Figure 9-11. *The MIDI glockenspiel*

Solenoids

Solenoids are basically electro magnets with rods in their cores. When the solenoid passes current, it creates a magnetic field that pulls the rod into the core. When the current is removed, the magnetism is lost and the rod is restored to the original position due to the action of either gravity or a spring. If a small diameter extension is placed on the rod, the action of the main rod being pulled into the core causes this extension to be pushed out of the far end. This type of solenoid is known as a *push solenoid* and is the type you want to use for this project.

There are a few other important things you need to specify when looking for a solenoid for this project. The first is the voltage. You need a 12V or less powered solenoid, but you need the current for this to be as low as possible and in any case lower than 400mA so that the driver IC can handle it. The other major thing to look for is the stroke. It tells you how far the solenoid's rod will push out when activated. This doesn't have to be too far, but if it is too short you might have difficulty mounting it underneath the note. Solenoids are not particularly expensive, but remember that you need eight for this project so they do add up.

The tricky part of this project is the mechanical mounting of the solenoids. I used a sheet of *Plexiglas* (called *Perspex* in the UK) bolted to the underside of the instrument. This left a gap between the sheet and the note bar where I could fix the solenoid with a mounting nut. On top of this, I placed a screw stopper to stop the rod from dropping out. Between that and the nut, I put a piece of foam to reduce the clatter as the rod fell from the unenergized solenoid. This is shown in Figure 9-12.

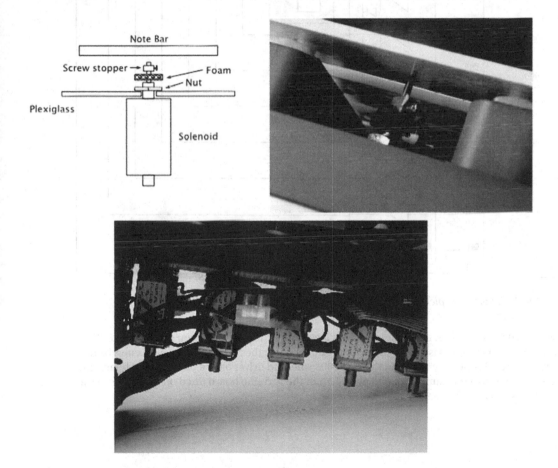

Figure 9-12. *Solenoid mounting*

To finish it off, I made end pieces from thick angle aluminum to allow the solenoids enough room to stand clear of the table top.

MIDI Glockenspiel Schematic

The schematic for this project is one of the simplest in the book. All that is required is a single chip the UNL2803. This is a Darlington driver and it sinks current through it to ground. It has built-in back EMF protection diodes for the coils; these are common on pin 10 and just need to be connected to the external 12V power supply. Note that this is not a power supply connection as such; it just suppresses the reverse voltage spikes caused when current is removed from the solenoid and the magnetic field collapses. The full schematic is shown in Figure 9-13.

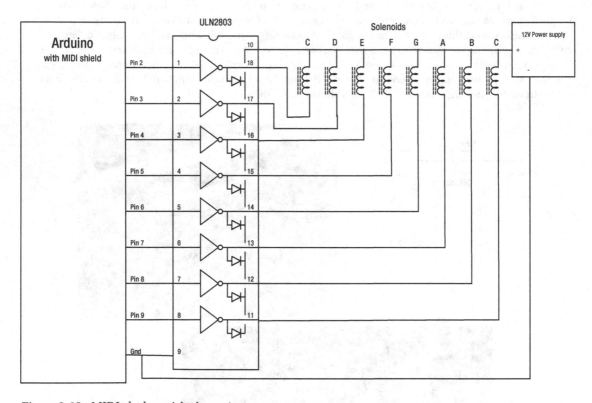

Figure 9-13. *MIDI glockenspiel schematic*

If you want to add a bit of extra glamour, or at least something to watch, you can wire an LED and resistor across each coil (that is, in parallel with the coil) so it comes on when the coil is energized.

I built the MIDI input circuitry and the ULN2803 solenoid driver onto a piece of strip board and mounted that to one of the aluminum end plates. Then the Arduino board fitted on top of this like a reverse shield. This is shown in Figure 9-14.

Figure 9-14. *The Arduino mounting*

Note that the pin spacing on the Arduino is such that you have to make special provisions to accommodate it using regular strip board.

MIDI Glockenspiel Software

The final part of the project is the software and this is where there is a clever bit of programming that allows the hardware to be simplified. My original circuit had a monostable controlling the length of pulse to the solenoid. This required a driver chip with an enable input. By controlling the duration of the solenoid pulse in the software, I could get away with using just a simple Darlington driver.

You have seen the technique for doing this in a lot of the MIDI-manipulation programs in Chapter 4. Basically the MIDI note on message will fire a solenoid, and the current value of the system time will be recorded in an array in a position corresponding to the note. Then, at the start of each loop, the system time is checked to see if it is time to turn any of the solenoids off. The length of the solenoid pulse can be set by a single variable. The full listing for this project is shown in Listing 9-5.

Listing 9-5. MIDI Glockenspiel Arduino Sketch

```
/* Midi Glock - Mike Cook Feb 2014
 * listen for MIDI serial data and fire solenoids for individual notes
 */
  byte incomingByte;
  byte note;
  byte velocity;
  int state = 0;  // state machine variable
  byte baseNote = 60;  // lowest note                              #A
```

```
  // use different values of baseNote to select the MIDI octave
  // 24 for octave 1 -- 36 for octave 2 -- 48 for octave 3 -- 60 for octave 4
  // 72 for octave 5 -- 84 for octave 6 -- 96 for octave 7

// play only notes in the key of C (that is no sharps or flats) define pin numbers:-
  byte playArray[] =    { 2,  0,  3,  0,  4,  5,  0,  6,  0,  7,  0,  8,  9 };      #B
int channel = 0; // MIDI channel

unsigned long noteOnTime[13];                                                      #C
unsigned long firingTime = 40; // time to hold the solenoid on

void setup() {
  for(int i =0 ; i<13; i++){
  if(playArray[i] !=0){
    pinMode(playArray[i],OUTPUT);        // declare the solenoid's pins as outputs
    digitalWrite(playArray[i], LOW);     // set to off
    }
  }
  Serial.begin(31250);     //start serial with MIDI baud rate
}

//loop: wait for serial data, and interpret the message
void loop () {
for(int offCheck = 0; offCheck < 13; offCheck++){                                  #D
  if((noteOnTime[offCheck] != 0) && (millis() - noteOnTime[offCheck] > firingTime) ){ #D
    noteOnTime[offCheck] = 0;                                                      #D
    if(playArray[offCheck] !=0) digitalWrite(playArray[offCheck], LOW);            #D
  }
 }
 // see if anything new has arrived
  if (Serial.available() > 0) {
    // read the incoming byte:
    incomingByte = Serial.read();
    switch (state){
      case 0:
    // look for as status-byte, our channel, note on
    if (incomingByte== (144 | channel)){
        state=1;
        }
      // consider follow on mode
      if(incomingByte< 128){
       // use same noteDown as last time
       note=incomingByte;
       state=2;
      }

      case 1:
      // get the note to play
      if(incomingByte < 128) {
          note=incomingByte;
          state=2;
      }
```

```
      else{
      state = 0;   // reset state machine as this should be a note number
      }
      break;

      case 2:
      // get the velocity
      if(incomingByte < 128) {
        playNote(note, incomingByte); // fire off the solenoid
      }
        state = 0;   // reset state machine to start
      }
   }
}

void playNote(byte note, byte velocity){
  byte playPin;
  if(velocity != 0) {  //only fire solenoids with non zero velocity
 //since we can't play all notes we only action some notes
  if(note >= baseNote && note <= (baseNote + 13)){
    playPin = playArray[note - baseNote]; // to get a pin number between 2 and 9
    if(playPin != 0) { // if it is a note in the scale
     digitalWrite(playPin, HIGH); // play it if it is one of our notes
     noteOnTime[note - baseNote] = millis(); // time we turned the note on
    }
   }
  }
}
#A - Start at middle C change this to change the octave
#B - A zero indicates do not play this note
#C - The time the solenoid was first turned on
#D - Check to see if we need to turn any solenoid off
```

The baseNote variable defines which octave the glockenspiel will respond to; here, I used middle C as the lowest note. You can easily change this to change what MIDI messages produce a solenoid activation, but obviously it won't change the actual note the glockenspiel produces. The playArray variable defines which pins fire the solenoids. Note here that for a scale of C, there are certain notes (sharps and flats) that you do not want to play. These are marked in the array with a pin number of zero.

The incoming message state machine is one I have used many times in this book and I won't dwell on that again. Finally, the playNote function generates an index for playArray by subtracting the note you need to play from the baseNote variable and, after checking that the resulting pin is a playable one (not zero), setting that pin high and recording the system time when that event occurred.

The challenge with an instrument that plays just a single octave of a single scale is to find a piece of music to play on it. Fortunately, you can find quite a few in music books for beginners and very young children.

I have seen this idea extended to 88 notes with the bars hit by an individual plastic mallet! What is more, there were two of them; a truly awe inspiring sight (and sound).

MIDI Beater

The final instrument in this chapter is one for percussion, a MIDI Beater. While you could use the Glockenspiel technique to hit things with a solenoid, a much better way is to use a *servomechanism* or *servo* for short. The idea is that you can make a percussion instrument from anything, with a collection of servos beating objects as diverse as fire extinguishers, biscuit tins, cooking pots, and even drums and symbols. This is all orchestrated from your MIDI sequencer, with note numbers defining what servo to use and the velocity value of the note defining the angle the servo moves to. So the key to understanding this instrument is understanding a servo.

Servos

Servo motors are used extensively for controlling model aircraft and animatronics; however, a servo is not a simple motor but a whole electronic sub system. There is a geared motor turning a shaft and a potentiometer the position of the shaft is monitored by reading the value of the pot. An electronics circuit is built into the servo assembly and it makes sure that the position of the shaft matches an angle set by an input signal. That input signal is normally a pulse position modulated (PPM) signal.

Fortunately, the Arduino has a library that can generate PPM signals on any of the pins. This allows you to easily set the angle you want the servo to be. If you supply that angle to the library function call, the servo will move toward that angle and stop when it reaches it. That is the best-case scenario; often it is not as simple as that.

To start with, most servos have a restricted angle of movement and if you send a signal that exceeds that, they will hit an end stop. Doing this repeatedly can damage the servo. Servos can take a lot of current and almost always need a separate power supply. They also generate a lot of electrical noise or interference. This can be so bad that often they can cause the Arduino to reset or act strangely. Finally, a typical hobby servo is designed to run off 6.5V, not a very friendly voltage. Although you can run them at 5V, you will not get the full speed and power at that voltage.

Servo motors come in many sizes. They are classed by the amount of torque they can produce and the price range is enormous—from a few dollars to thousands. Most hobby servos range from $5 to $50. The electrical connections to the vast majority of servos is the same—just three wires ground (black), power (red), and control (yellow—and they nearly all use the same 0.1-inch pitch three pin socket as well. The smaller, cheaper servos will definitely wear out quicker because of having plastic gears. Metal gears will last much longer, but be prepared to burn out some servos if you use this system a lot. A typical hobby servo is shown in Figure 9-15.

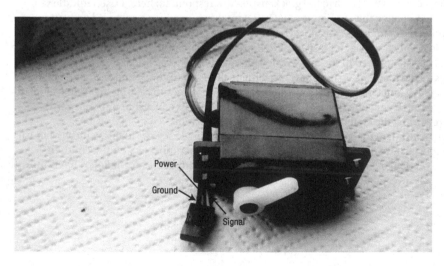

Figure 9-15. A typical hobby servo

MIDI Beater Schematic

The circuit for this instrument is quite simple. It consists of servos connected to the Arduino along with a LED to indicate there is movement on each servo, as shown in Figure 9-16. I also included a MIDI activity LED in this project. The idea is that it flashes when receiving MIDI information for the channel the instrument is set up on, even if the note numbers are not within the range of the servos.

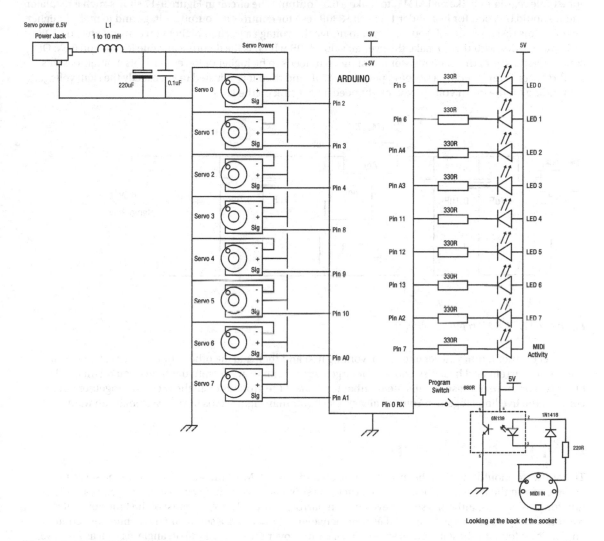

Figure 9-16. *MIDI beater schematic*

The lower-right corner shows the MIDI input circuit, as you have seen many times before in this book. There are eight LEDs that are powered by current sinking through the Arduino and on the left side are eight servos. These servos have their input signals derived from the Arduino and have the ground common to the Arduino's ground. The power for these servos comes from an external source and is wired to a power jack through an inductor for added interference suppression. The value of the inductor is not critical. There are also two capacitors—a small ceramic and a large electrolytic one—to help with the decoupling.

The power jack should be wired to a power supply with an appropriate voltage and current rating. It might be that you can't get a power supply with enough current capability to feed the exact type of servos you have, in which case you should split the positive supply into two or more groups of servos, each with its own inductor, capacitors, and power jacks.

If you cannot get a power supply with the right output voltage, then you can build a regulator. Unfortunately, there are very few fixed voltage regulators with an output of 6.5V. You can use one of the adjustable regulators, like an LM317, to make a 6.5V output. The circuit in Figure 9-17 shows such a regulator and it should be good for just under 1.5A. The 330R resistor controls the output voltage and to make it higher increase this resistor value. If you just want to nudge the voltage a fraction higher you can add an extra 10R resistor in series with this to make the over all value 340R which is the theoretical value for spot on 6.5V. Of course tolerances in the 100R resistor might mean it needs to be higher or lower than this. Sometimes this 330R resistor is replaced by a skeleton pot of say 470R and then it is adjusted to get exactly the right voltage. Depending on the input voltage, you might need a heat sink on the LM317.

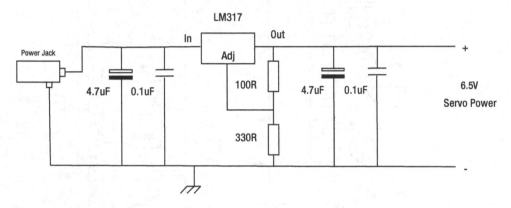

Figure 9-17. *A 6.5V regulator circuit*

I recommend that you get one servo working first and then add the others, one at a time, keeping an eye on the current and heat dissipation. For larger servos with heavy current demands, you might need to build two or more of these circuits. Remember to connect the grounds of all these circuits together but never connect the live lines together. You can always use fewer than eight servos in your system if you want.

MIDI Beater Software

The software should monitor the input for note on and note off MIDI messages and move the servo to the angle given in the note on velocity. This restricts the servo movement between 0 and 127 degrees, which is fine for most servos, although some have an even narrower angle. However, most of the time you will not want to swing the servos so far as it takes time between commanding a servo and it reaching the required angle. Therefore, it is best if there is some sort of control over the rest, or note off angle, as well as the note on angle.

This could be done by using the note off velocity, but this would not work so well with systems that use a note on message with a velocity of zero to act as a note off message. So the way I have decided to implement the reset angle is to have another note number associated with each servo that defines the note off angle. These shadow note numbers need only be sent once and the Arduino saves the note on velocity as a note off servo position. The default note off position can be predefined in the software when you initialize the note off position array. Listing 9-6 shows the Arduino code that you need.

Listing 9-6. MIDI Beater Arduino Code

```
// MIDI Beater by Mike Cook Feb 2014
#include <Servo.h>

Servo beatServo[8];  // create servo object to control a servo

byte midiActivity = 7; // activity LED
byte servoPin[] = {2, 3, 4, 8, 9, 10, 14, 15};  // define what pins the servo is on
byte ledPins[] = {5, 6, 18, 17, 11, 12, 13, 16};  // defines the pins the LEDs are on
byte servoPos[] = {0, 0, 0, 0, 0, 0, 0, 0}; // to determine if LED should be on or off
byte servoOffPos[] = {0, 0, 0, 0, 0, 0, 0, 0};                              #A
byte lowestServo = 48;                                 #B
byte lowestServoOff = 28;                              #B
int channel = 0;

void setup()
{
  for(int i =0; i<8; i++){
  beatServo[i].attach(servoPin[i]);
  pinMode(ledPins[i], OUTPUT);
  digitalWrite(ledPins[i], HIGH);   // turn off LED
  }
    for(int i =0; i<8; i++){
      beatServo[i].write(servoOffPos[i]);          #C
    }
    pinMode(midiActivity, OUTPUT);
    digitalWrite(midiActivity, HIGH); // turn off "MIDI for us" light
    Serial.begin(31250);  // for MIDI
}

void loop()
{
  checkMIDI();
}

void checkMIDI() {                                      #D
    static int state=0;
    static boolean noteDown = LOW;
    static byte note;
    byte incomingByte;

  if (Serial.available() > 0) {
    // read the incoming byte:
    incomingByte = Serial.read();
    switch (state){
      case 0:
      // look for as status-byte, our channel, note on
      if (incomingByte == (144 | channel)){
          noteDown = HIGH;
          state=1;
        }
```

```
        // look for a status-byte, our channel, note off
        if (incomingByte == (128 | channel)){
            noteDown = LOW;
            state=1;
            }
        if( ((incomingByte & 0xf) == channel) && (state == 1)) // light up command for us
            digitalWrite(midiActivity, LOW); // turn on MIDI for us light
          else
            digitalWrite(midiActivity, HIGH); // turn off MIDI for us light
          break;
        case 1:
        // get the note to play or stop
        if(incomingByte < 128) {
            note=incomingByte;
            state=2;
        }
        else{
        state = 0;   // reset state machine as this should be a note number
        digitalWrite(midiActivity, HIGH); // turn off MIDI for us light
        }
        break;

        case 2:
        // get the velocity
        if(incomingByte < 128) {
          playNote(note, incomingByte, noteDown); // turn the servo
        }
          state = 0;   // reset state machine to start
          digitalWrite(midiActivity, HIGH); // turn off MIDI for us light
      }
  }
}

void playNote(byte note, byte velocity, int down){
    byte index = note - lowestServo;
    // if velocity = 0 on a 'Note ON' command, treat it as a note off
    if ((down == HIGH) && (velocity == 0)){
      down = LOW;
        }
   if(note>= lowestServo && note < lowestServo + 8){ // is it in the range of our servos
     if(down == LOW) velocity = servoOffPos[index];   // make it the off position
       beatServo[index].write(velocity); // make servo move to angle given by velocity
       if(velocity > servoPos[index])
          digitalWrite(ledPins[index], LOW);
        else
          digitalWrite(ledPins[index], HIGH);
     servoPos[index] = velocity;
      }
```

```
    else { // set off position
      if( (note>= lowestServoOff) && (note < (lowestServoOff + 8)) ){   #E
      if(down == HIGH)servoOffPos[note - lowestServoOff] = velocity;   #F
    }
  }
}
}
```

#A - Array for the angle to go to for a note off message
#B - Defines the note and shadow note numbers for lowest servo
#C - Starting positions, move the servos to the off point
#D - MIDI input state machine
#E - Is it in the range of our off position control
#F - Save the note off position

The code should be familiar to anyone following the projects in this book so far. Many of the same functions keep making an appearance, albeit modified slightly. Here, the playNote function is changed to drive the servo. After checking that the note number is within the range specified for our servos, the beatServo[index].write(velocity) commands the servo to move. Or if the note is within the shadow range of note numbers, the velocity is simply saved in the array defining the note off position.

If you want a wider range of angles, you can do this at the expense of accuracy by doubling the value of the received velocity. I doubt you would need to do this.

MIDI Beater In Action

To use the system, the first thing you need to do is to position your servos over the object you want to hit and fix some sort of hitting object to the servo arm. I found that if the coupling between the servo and the striker had some springiness, it made a much better sound. One of my most successful arrangements was a ball from an old computer mouse wrapped up in a spring made from spiral wire used to bind sheets together into a booklet. This allowed some bounce of the ball once it hit the tin box. The use of clamps and stands makes this a lot easier; it is best to set up a temporary arrangement before making anything more permanent. Experimenting with what you can hit and with what you can hit it is great fun and leaves great scope for imagination and inventiveness.

To drive this, you need to set up a MIDI sequencer in the piano roll mode. Here, the notes are shown as blocks with the length of the block being the length of the note. You want to adjust this length so that the servo has time to make an impact. If the servo has to move too far to make a hit, there will be a delay between triggering the note and hearing the hit. If the note is too long then the two objects are in contact for too long and the sound is deadened. By carful setting of the note on time and the return position angle, you can make a variety of hit sounds from the same object. The key here is to experiment.

You are not restricted to music making only. I have a friend who made a version that played a drum roll every time a tweet with a certain hash tag was received. In fact, different hash tags triggered different sequences.

Summary

Well that about wraps up Part I of this book. You have seen how you can use your Arduino to make an instrument or a controller. You have learned about standard messages—both MIDI and OSC—and how you can use an Arduino to manipulate these messages. You have seen projects both simple and complex and I hope I have whetted your appetite for experimentation.

In the next two sections of this book, you will see how the Arduino can produce sounds of various types, by synthesizing them or manipulating existing sounds. There is a lot more to come.

PART II

■ ■ ■

Generating waveforms

The second part of the book looks at the way an Arduino can generate sound directly. We explore the techniques of waveform calculation and the production of tones. By using look up tables we can generate complex waveforms and make some unique sounds.

■ ■ ■

CHAPTER 10

The Anatomy of a Sound

This chapter covers:

- What is sound?

- How do we measure loudness and pitch?

- What makes some sounds of the same pitch and amplitude sound different?

- What is a decibel?

Part II of this book looks at synthesizing sound, but before you can do that, you need to understand what sound is made up of. There are three components to a sound—its volume, pitch, and timbre. Volume is how loud we perceive a sound to be, whereas pitch is how high it sounds. Timbre is much more complicated, and it is the quality or characters of a sound. For example, when middle C is played on a trumpet and a piano, the note has the same volume and pitch, yet you can tell one is a piano and the other is a trumpet. This is because the timbre is different.

What Makes Sound?

We are surrounded by sound but it was not until 1876 when Scottish engineer Alexander Graham Bell was awarded a U.S. patent for the first practical telephone, did we understand the nature of sound and how to copy it electrically. A year later, Thomas Edison was awarded a patent for storing sound mechanically on cylinders. Both inventors understood the nature of sound and how to make an electrical or mechanical analog of a sound. But what actually is sound?

Basically, when we hear a sound, our ears are sensing a pressure wave. The air molecules are being alternately squeezed together and pulled apart, which results in a sequence of changing air pressures. Our ear has a drum that moves in sympathy with these waves, and a large array of differently sized hairs converts those vibrations into nerve impulses. We can therefore perceive a sound. The pressure changes move in the same direction as the sound and we call this a longitudinal wave. However, this is a difficult thing for us to picture, so a wave is usually represented by a transverse wave with the displacement or pressure on the Y-axis and the direction of the wave in the X axis. Figure 10-1 shows these two ways of representing the same sound wave.

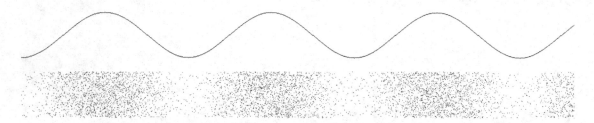

Figure 10-1. *Transverse and longitudinal waves*

The upper wave is the transverse wave. The changing pressure is represented by an up and down displacement. The lower wave consists of dots representing air molecules being squeezed together or stretched apart. Notice the correlation between the two waves. When the top wave is high, the dots in the lower wave are close together, and when the top wave is low, the dots are farther apart in the lower wave. The bottom wave is more representative of what is actually happening, but the top wave is a lot easier to understand. The actual wave shape is called a *sine wave* (pronounced sign) and is a mathematical function. It occurs in many natural phenomena, from the motion of the Earth around the Sun, to fundamental building blocks of sound. A sine wave is the purest form of sound that there is and is very close to what is produced by a flute.

When you are looking at the three characters of sound—volume, pitch, and timbre—the volume is represented by the peak-to-peak height. The bigger this is, the louder the sound. The pitch by how close the peaks are together and the timbre is the shape of the wave; in this case, it's a sine wave shape. There are a number of measures we can take of this waveform, as seen in Figure 10-2.

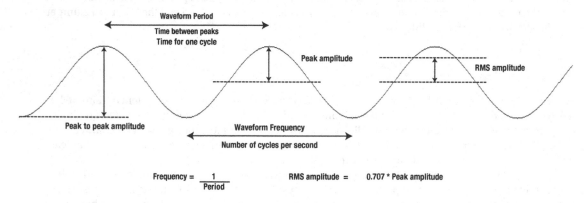

Figure 10-2. *Waveform measurements*

You can see that there are two basic types of measurements—horizontal refer to the pitch and vertical refer to the volume. But for each type, there is more than one way of specifying them. Look at the pitch measurement first; the distance between successive peaks is measuring one cycle of the waveform. You can measure how long one cycle takes, which is called the period, or how many cycles there are in a second, which is known as the frequency. Which one you choose is a matter of convention, as they both tell the same tale. The frequency used to be measured in cycles per second, but that was too easy so now it is measured in a unit called Hertz. One Hertz is one rental van per second or cycle per second if you don't have the budget for a van and have to use a cycle. The A above middle C used to be 440 cycles per second and is now 440 Hz. This frequency is used as a fixed standard for tuning, and all notes are tied to this. The two measures are simply related; the reciprocal of the period is the frequency.

The amplitude on the other hand is a bit more complicated. Basically, there are three ways of expressing the same thing. First is the peak-to-peak amplitude, which is the measure from the highest peak to the lowest peak. Then there is the peak measurement, which is the distance from the average level to the highest peak. On a sine wave the peak is half the peak-to-peak measurement. Finally, there is the RMS amplitude, which stands for Root Mean Squared and is a measure of the average height over the period of the waveform. It is related to the power in the waveform and can give comparable powers even though the waveforms might be different. For example, you might have a wave that spends most of its time on the zero line and then shoots up very high for a short time. That will not carry the same power as a wave that spends half its time high and half low. Again for a sine wave the RMS value is easy to calculate and is simply the peak amplitude multiplied by 0.707, or root 2.

Timbre: a Sound's Individuality

The characteristic of a sound is called its timbre and is basically given by the shape of the waveform making up the sound. Also, most naturally produced sounds have changing wave shapes over the duration of the sound, which is an important contribution to a sound's timbre. To make things a bit more complex it should be noted that not all different waveforms sound different. Look at the three waveforms in Figure 10-3; they all look different but all sound exactly the same.

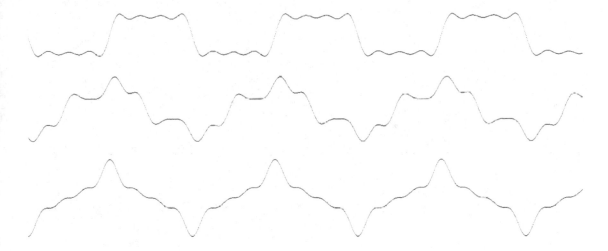

Figure 10-3. *Three waves and one sound*

So what is going on here? You might expect that a different waveform would produce different sounds and sometimes they do, but what is important is not so much the shape of the wave but what it's built from. When you have any complex waveform, it can be broken into a mixture of sine waves and it is these sine waves that define the sound we perceive. The three waveforms in Figure 10-3 are all built from the same four sine waves, yet they produce the different shape because each sine wave is phase-shifted by a different amount. A phase shift is just a sliding to the right of the start of a wave, and it affects how the waves add up to give the final wave shape. However, the human ear cannot detect phase at all, so these wave shapes all sound the same.

■ **Note**   The ear can detect when phase changes, but not a static phase between harmonics of the same sound. Phase differences between two signals, like in stereo sound, can also destroy the stereo effect. The phase between two signals affects our perception of the position of that sound, an effect used in binaural stereo.

All this was worked out in 1822 by Joseph Fourier, a French Mathematician, who was studying how heat traveled down a bar. This is exactly the mathematics needed to analyze sound, although he did not know it. He was also the person who "discovered" the greenhouse effect, in reference to heating the Earth.

Any waveform can be constructed from a sum of sine waves, but not any old sine waves. Each sine wave is harmonically related to the lowest or fundamental sine wave. The next sine wave that could be used to build another wave shape would have to have a frequency of twice the fundamental, which is known as the second harmonic. Then the next wave has a frequency of three times the fundamental and is known as the third harmonic, and so on upward. The phase of these waves is similarly restricted; they can be either in phase with the fundamental or start a quarter of the way shifted from the fundamental. This sort of wave is also known as a cosine wave, and it is said to be shifted by 90 degrees from a sine wave because one cycle represents a complete rotation or 360°. Figure 10-4 shows building a square wave from adding the contributions from four sine waves.

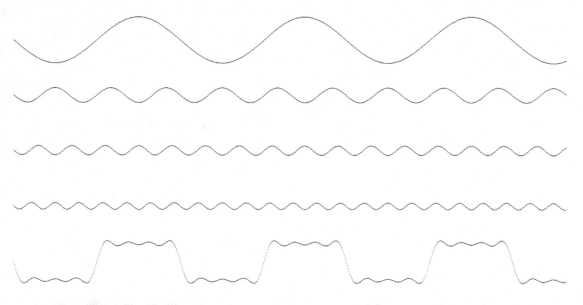

Figure 10-4. *Synthesis of a square wave*

The final bottom wave shape is generated by adding the height of each of the four waves above it together at each point. It is not a very good representation of the square wave because only four harmonics are used in its construction. The recipe for making a square wave is the fundamental plus one third of the third harmonic plus one fifth of the fifth harmonic plus one seventh of the seventh harmonic .... and so on up to infinity!

Don't worry about the infinity, that is only for a perfect shape. Once the harmonics go above the range of human hearing, you will not hear any difference. As you add more harmonics to the wave shape, the tops and bottoms get flatter and the sides get steeper until a square wave is approached. Figure 10-5 shows a square wave I made from 206 harmonics in a computer program.

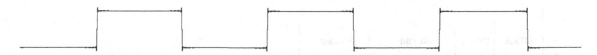

Figure 10-5. *Square wave from 206 harmonics*

By this stage it is looking very square. There is just a bit of ringing on the edges and the rise times are quite sharp.

So sounds with different wave shapes can be composed of different harmonics and it is these harmonics that contribute to the timbre of the sound.

You might think that to produce any sound, you would just have to control the mix of harmonics in that sound. That was the idea behind the church organ; these massive instruments are often built into buildings have the ability to control the exact harmonic mix through a system of stops. Each stop controls the air going to an organ pipe and each harmonic has its own pipe. The phrase "pulling out all the stops" refers to this, letting all the harmonics play. Well, first of all, this produced a massive instrument, and secondly, while it can produce many of the characters of other instruments, it always sounds like a church organ. So what is going on here?

It is not just the harmonic content that makes a sound unique; it is the fact that real instruments change their harmonic content over the duration of the note. It might start out with a high-amplitude fourth harmonic that quickly dies down, with other harmonics starting lower but lasting longer. Take a look at the plucked banjo string shown in Figure 10-6.

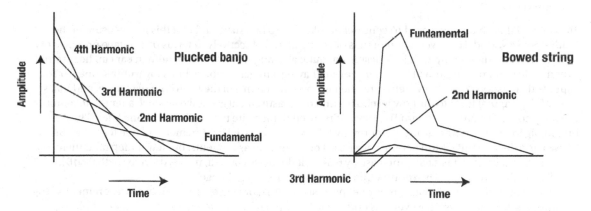

Figure 10-6. *Progression of the harmonic mix of a sound*

This figure also shows the way that the harmonics mix for a bowed string. Note how the higher harmonics are much more suppressed. These are only approximations of the real thing; in practice they are a quite a bit more complex than this. This type of analysis can be done for all instruments and will produce a fair representation of the character of the sound of a particular instrument. However, further analysis shows that these curves are different for different notes produced by an instrument. Different instrument construction changes these shapes as well, making it possible for people with good ears to distinguish between a Steinway and a Baldwin grand piano.

All this produces quite a lot of complexity to emulate if we want to generate realistic sounds. Often the compromise is to generate a wave shape and then apply an *envelope*, or time-varying volume control, to it. This envelope is often simplified into four sections and is known as an ADSR envelope. This stands for the four major stages-attack, decay, sustain, and release—which are shown in Figure 10-7.

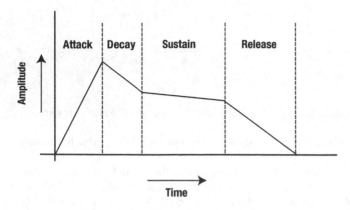

Figure 10-7. The ADSR envelope

This sort of control is often built into simple synthesizers, but you must remember it is only a crude representation of a real instrument. The four time periods can be any length as well as what the volume does during that time. For example, during the sustain time, the output could go higher, which creates sort of a swell effect.

Amplitude

To finish off this chapter, we need to consider amplitude. So far I have said that this is a measure of the loudness of a sound. However, this output is often measured objectively in terms of a voltage or power of a signal and that relationship with loudness is not quite as straight-forward. The human ear can hear sound over a wide dynamic range, and it does this by not having a linear response but a logarithmic one. So To capture this response, measurements are often expressed in terms of the logarithm of change, and that's the ratio of the original level to the new level. This unit of measurement is known as a *Bel*, after the inventor of the telephone, Alexander Graham Bell. It was first used to measure the loss in telephone lines. The Bel is a bit too big to be convenient to use, so normally things are expressed in increments of one tenth of a Bel, also known as a decibel (dB). Most people have heard of decibel measurements, but few understand them. If a signal doubles in size, it is said to increase by 6 dB; if it decreases by half, it goes down by 6 dB (-6dB).

Size in dB = $10 \times \text{Log}_{10}(\text{power now}/\text{power then})$ or = $10 \, \text{Log}_{10}(\text{change})$

At the mention of logarithms, many people just go blank, or worse, break out in a sweat remembering childhood school lessons. However, it is nothing to be afraid of. Why use such a seemingly complicated system? Because it is a way of compressing a range and it is used to make things easy. It provides a way of reducing very large numbers into ones of equal importance.

Suppose you have a stock that loses 10% of its value per day. You might think that after 10 days it will be worth nothing, after all ten times ten percent is 100%. However, that's not the case. If that stock is worth $100 on the first day, on the second it loses 10%, and so it is worth $90. On the second day, it loses 10% of $90 and so is worth $81. As the days progress, it loses fewer dollars but still decreases by the same percentage of the value it had at the start of the day. After ten days, the stock is worth $38.74. The change is a constant percentage, but that percentage is being applied to a reducing amount. Figure 10-8 shows the fall in the stock price.

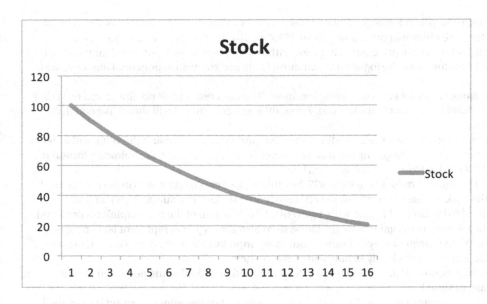

Figure 10-8. *Stock price falling at 10% per day*

This is not a straight line. This sort of curve is called an *exponential*. If the stock price falls at 10% per day, it will never reach the value of zero; however, it is very difficult to predict just from the curve what the stock price will be after 30 days. Let's take the same stock price data and plot it in dBs. Remember that a decibel is a measure of change. The results of this are shown in Figure 10-9.

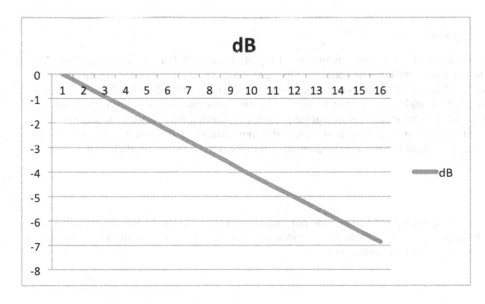

Figure 10-9. *Stock price in decibels*

Note how this time the plot is a straight line and it is very easy to continue this line to see the price at any future date. In fact, the change in price is simply -0.4575749 dBs per day. The minus sign indicates it is lower than the original reference price. Applying a logarithmic function to an exponential function has linearized it. To put it another way, the logarithmic function is the inverse of an exponential function, and vice versa.

It is exactly the same when we are considering loudness. The ear's response is not linear and by taking the logarithm of the stimulus, we can make it linear. Equal differences in the dB will sound like equal differences to our ear.

All this is with regard to the power of an audio circuit, but often you just measure the voltage of a signal. As power is voltage times current, to get the equivalent change in dBs, you can use the following formula:

Size in dB = 20 X Log_{10}(voltage now/voltage then)

Note for a 6 dB change, the ratio is actually 1.995, but this is close enough to 2 as to make no practical difference. Using dBs makes it easy to work out the effects of cascaded circuits. Suppose you have an amplifier with a gain of 6 dB followed by one with a gain of 10 dB. The gain of the two amplifiers combined would be the simple addition of the gains—16 dB. The system also allows you to represent large ranges of a physical quantity with a small range of numbers. But most important of all, it allows you to represent changes in things like sound more closely to how you perceive them.

From the study of psychoacoustics, there is the rule of thumb that to double the perceived loudness, you need a 10 dB increase in signal.

Remember that a dB measurement is the ratio of two quantities, but sometimes a sound is described as being at a certain level. For example, a subway train at 200 feet is 95 dB. The reference here is the weakest sound that can be heard—the 0dB level. Other times, signals are described with reference to a fixed quantity. A popular standard is one milliwatt (mW), also shown as dBm. So if a signal is 3 dBm, it is double or 2 mW, whereas -3dBm is half or 0.5 mW. The typical radiated output of a microwave oven is 60 dBm or 1 kW, whereas the typical signal received from a GPS satellite is -127.5 dBm or 178 aW (aW is an attowatt or 10^{-18} of a watt). The dynamic range that can be expressed in a small range of numbers is enormous.

One More Thing

It is not only loudness that is not linear; our perception of frequency is as well. For a note to sound twice as high as another note, the frequency must be doubled. This span is known as an *octave* and is well known to musicians. However, just like the stock price example, this is non-linear. A shift of 100 Hz will sound like an octave shift from the point of 100 Hz, but start at the second octave above middle C and this is just about the difference between A and A*. It is for this reason that frequencies are plotted on a logarithmic scale, so that equal distances on a graph correspond to equal perceived differences in pitch. It is not uncommon to quote the drop off in amplitude of amplifiers or other frequency-dependent circuits in terms of dBs per octave.

Summary

We have seen what makes up sound and learned the parameters we can use to define the nature of the sound. Having got that under your belt we can now go on to see how we can use the Arduino to create a sound, either from scratch or out of an existing sound.

CHAPTER 11

■■■

Square Waves

By far, the simplest way for an electronic circuit to produce an audible sound is by generating a square wave. As you saw in the previous chapter, a square wave is the infinite sum of odd harmonics. However, as far as Arduino is concerned, it is achieved by putting a pin high and then a short time after, putting it low. This will generate a signal that can be turned into a sound by putting it through a loud speaker. There are many ways of generating this signal, some are more efficient than others .

Starting Off Simply

Before we start we need to get the hardware right. In order to hear a sound it has to be passed to a sound transducer—a loud speaker, headphones, or an active speaker. You must never connect a speaker directly to an Arduino pin because this will draw too much current from the output pin and will eventually damage the Arduino. Instead, you should use a series resistor of at least 100R. Also having DC in a speaker can damage it so in addition to the resistor you need to include a series capacitor. The value is not too important, but the bigger it is, the lower the frequencies that will get through. I recommend a value of 10uF to 100uF. Note however that most of the power will go into the resistor and not the speaker, so the results will not be very loud. If you are using headphones, it will sound louder than a speaker.

By far the best way of getting sound from a single pin is to use an active speaker. The sort that is sold as a "computer speaker" is active because it contains an amplifier and speaker. You will know this by the fact that it requires batteries or needs to be plugged into an external wall adaptor or USB socket. These also tend to have volume controls on them and make the best form of output for experimenting with. If you have a stereo speaker then just connect the two inputs to the same output pin on the Arduino and remember to connect the ground. Figure 11-1 shows the general arrangement.

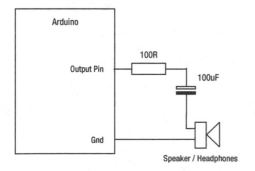
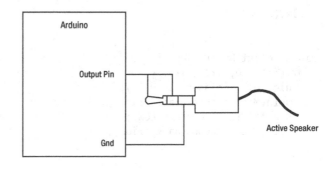

Figure 11-1. Connecting a speaker

The simplest way to generate a tone is to use something like the Arduino code shown in Listing 11-1.

Listing 11-1. Very Simple Tone

```
// Ultra simple tone
const byte soundPin = 13;
int halfPeriod = 1000;

void setup() {
  pinMode(soundPin,OUTPUT);
}

void loop() {
  digitalWrite(soundPin,HIGH);
  delayMicroseconds(halfPeriod);
  digitalWrite(soundPin,LOW);
  delayMicroseconds(halfPeriod);
}
```

This code will produce a continuous tone of about 500 Hz. This frequency is set by the variable halfPeriod, which defines the period and hence the frequency of the tone. It is not very interesting; it just produces a simple continuous tone. Let's look at something more interesting, as shown in Listing 11-2.

Something More Interesting

Listing 11-2. Robot Talk

```
// R2D2
const byte soundPin = 13;
void setup() {
  pinMode(soundPin,OUTPUT);
}

void loop() {
  for(int i; i<50; i++){
    note(random(100,2000));
  }
  delay(2000);
}

void note(int halfPeriod) {
  for (int i=0; i<20; i++) {
    digitalWrite(soundPin,HIGH);
    delayMicroseconds(halfPeriod);
    digitalWrite(soundPin,LOW);
    delayMicroseconds(halfPeriod);
  }
}
```

Here, the note-producing portion of the code has been placed into a function called note, which takes in a number to use as the half period delay. It also limits the tone produced to 20 cycles and, while this is simple, it does produce an odd effect. You see 20 cycles of a high-frequency note are going to take less time to produce than 20 cycles of a low-frequency note. This means that if you get this function to play a high-frequency note, it will be a short blip and a low-frequency note will be a longer bleep. Although you normally don't want this effect, here it used to sound like a robot. The loop function then makes 50 calls to this function, passing to it a random number for the delay. There is a two-second silence before it repeats.

Now what if you want a fixed length note regardless of the frequency? To do this, you must produce the note until a certain time has elapsed, as shown in Listing 11-3.

Listing 11-3. Equal Time Robot Talk

```
// Equal Time random tones
const byte soundPin = 13;
void setup() {
  pinMode(soundPin,OUTPUT);
}

void loop() {
  for(int i; i<30; i++){
    note(random(100,2000), 90);
  }
  delay(2000);
}

void note(int halfPeriod, long interval) {
  long startTime = millis();
  while(millis()-startTime < interval) {
    digitalWrite(soundPin,HIGH);
    delayMicroseconds(halfPeriod);
    digitalWrite(soundPin,LOW);
    delayMicroseconds(halfPeriod);
  }
}
```

By encapsulating the tone-producing part of the note function in a while loop, we keep it going until a certain time has elapsed, so in effect once per cycle we are checking if the tone has gone on for long enough. This time is passed to the tone function through a variable called interval, which defines the tone length in milliseconds. In this example, it is fixed at 90 ms, but you could try the effects of making this a random number just like the tone's frequency. Of course, the timing is not exact; it only lasts the prescribed interval plus any time up to the length of time of one period of the tone. But you don't notice this in practice. Another thing you could try is to replace the delay call in the loop function with a while loop that exits only when an external button is pushed. In that way, you can have a "conversation" with the robot, who will only answer you when you press the button.

Making a Tune

So far we have defined the tone with random numbers. If we generate data that defines the note's frequency and duration, we can play a tune. It is simplest to do this in two stages—first define the half period delay to generate a specific note in a look up table, and then define a series of notes to make the tune. For the octave of middle C, the note periods are generated by this table from a spreadsheet:

Table 11-1. *Notes Needed for the Tune*

Note	Frequency Hz	Period us	Half Period Count
C0	261.63	3822.26	1911
D0	293.66	3405.24	1702
E0	329.63	3033.73	1516
F0	349.23	2863.46	1431
G0	391.99	2551.05	1275
A0	440.00	2272.73	1136
B0	493.88	2024.77	1012
C1	523.25	1911.13	955

Having defined the notes, you now need to define the duration. There are many ways to do this. For this example, we chose to use one to represent a quarter note, meaning a whole note or minim was four and a semibreve was sixteen. These numbers need to be multiplied by some constant to get the right number of milliseconds to play each note according to the tempo of the song. Changing this multiplication constant simply changes the tempo. The code to do this is shown in Listing 11-4.

Listing 11-4. Playing a Tune

```
// Do-Re-Mi from the Sound of music
#define C_0 0
#define D_0 1
#define E_0 2
#define F_0 3
#define G_0 4
#define A_0 5
#define B_0 6
#define C_1 7
  int pitch[] = {1911, 1702, 1516, 1431, 1275, 1136, 1012, 955};
  byte melody[] = {
                C_0, 3, D_0, 1, E_0, 3, C_0, 1, E_0, 2, C_0, 2, E_0, 4,
                D_0, 3, E_0, 1, F_0, 1, F_0, 1, E_0, 1, D_0, 1, F_0, 8,
                E_0, 3, F_0, 1, G_0, 3, E_0, 1, G_0, 2, E_0, 2, G_0, 4,
                F_0, 3, G_0, 1, A_0, 1, A_0, 1, G_0, 1, F_0, 1, A_0, 8,
                G_0, 3, C_0, 1, D_0, 1, E_0, 1, F_0, 1, G_0, 1, A_0, 8,
                A_0, 3, D_0, 1, E_0, 1, F_0, 1, G_0, 1, A_0, 1, B_0, 8,
                B_0, 3, E_0, 1, F_0, 1, G_0, 1, A_0, 1, B_0, 1, C_1, 6,
                B_0, 1, B_0, 1, A_0, 2, F_0, 2, B_0, 2, G_0, 2, C_1, 2,
                G_0, 2, E_0, 2, D_0, 2,
```

```
// second verse
            C_0, 3, D_0, 1, E_0, 3, C_0, 1, E_0, 2, C_0, 2, E_0, 4,
            D_0, 3, E_0, 1, F_0, 1, F_0, 1, E_0, 1, D_0, 1, F_0, 8,
            E_0, 3, F_0, 1, G_0, 3, E_0, 1, G_0, 2, E_0, 2, G_0, 4,
            F_0, 3, G_0, 1, A_0, 1, A_0, 1, G_0, 1, F_0, 1, A_0, 8,
            G_0, 3, C_0, 1, D_0, 1, E_0, 1, F_0, 1, G_0, 1, A_0, 8,
            A_0, 3, D_0, 1, E_0, 1, F_0, 1, G_0, 1, A_0, 1, B_0, 8,
            B_0, 3, E_0, 1, F_0, 1, G_0, 1, A_0, 1, B_0, 1, C_1, 6,
            B_0, 1, B_0, 1, A_0, 2, F_0, 2, B_0, 2, G_0, 2, C_1, 10,
            C_0, 1, D_0, 1, E_0, 1, F_0, 1, G_0, 1, A_0, 1, B_0, 1,
            C_1, 2, G_0, 2, C_0, 2,
            -1, -1 };

const byte soundPin = 13;
int songTempo = 200;
void setup() {
  pinMode(soundPin,OUTPUT);
}

void loop() {
  int place = 0;
  while(melody[place] != (byte)-1){
    note(pitch[melody[place]], melody[place+1]*songTempo);
    delay(60);
    place +=2;
  }
  delay(4000); // pause before repeat
}

void note(int halfPeriod, long interval) {
  long startTime = millis();
  while(millis()-startTime < interval) {
    digitalWrite(soundPin,HIGH);
    delayMicroseconds(halfPeriod);
    digitalWrite(soundPin,LOW);
    delayMicroseconds(halfPeriod);
  }
}
```

The code starts with a series of #define commands that substitute easy-to-remember keystrokes for simple numbers. This makes it easy to separate the note from the time when it comes to the data that defines the melody. Then an array called pitch is defined that translates the note number into a half period delay value. Finally, the melody array contains the tune. For each note there are two numbers, a note number followed by a duration. This can be painstakingly extracted from sheet music. As the numbers are small in this array, it only needs to be a byte array, a marker of -1 is used to signify the end of the tune. Notice the second verse is very similar to the first, and a copy and paste will save you some time if you are typing it in. If you want to have a lot of melodies in the code, you can move them into program memory like we did with some big tables in previous chapter's projects.

The tune is played by having a pointer called place advance through the array. It will continue extracting notes and duration from this array until it fishes out a -1, which signifies the end of the tune. The note number at the array index place is used as an index into the pitch array, which actually contains the half period delay value. The duration of the note is in the index place + 1 and needs to be multiplied by the songTempo variable to get the value to use the length of the note. After the song has played, there is a four-second rest before it starts again.

A Better Way to Generate a Tone

While the previous method works well, it is rather resource hungry. While the tone is being generated, there is nothing else that the Arduino can do. This is because code of this type spends most of its time in a delay function just waiting for time to pass. This is a bit of a waste of the available processing power, so let's look at a way to generate a tone more efficiently.

The Tone Function

The Arduino has a number of built-in predefined functions and one of them is tone(). This function generates a tone on any defined pin that lasts for a specified duration, or if no duration is passed to it, it continues forever until the function noTone() is called. However, what is important here is that once the tone is started, control immediately returns to the program, which can get on with other things, like reading sensors. For details of the syntax, see the description of the function in the Arduino's reference section of the Help menu.

The tone() function accepts the pitch of the note in Hz and the duration in micro seconds. There is a Tone.h header file that defines the frequency of each note from a note name in a similar form to the last example we looked at. There is no way of altering the volume of the note produced by this function.

■ **Note**   While the tone function can output a tone on any pin, it can only output one tone at a time. You can play notes on different pins sequentially, but you have to call the noTone function first before using another pin.

The Cost of Using the Tone Function

Using the tone function comes at a price. It utilizes one of the timers in the processor. For the Uno, this is timer2 and the immediate effect you will see is that the PWM outputs on pins 3 and 11 no longer work when using tone(). This is because timer2 is used to generate those PWM waveforms and while tone is using it the PWM generation cannot do this.

There are other libraries that also use this timer and unfortunately this aspect of Arduino libraries, that of shared resources, is very poorly documented. There is no standard way that a library can declare which processor resources like the timers it is using and it is rarely mentioned in the documentation. Hence, you find that some libraries are incompatible with others. For example, libraries for IR remote controls and ultrasonic distance sensors use this timer. When a user is faced with this problem, there is little that can be done. You can look for alternate libraries, try to work around one or the other library with you own code, or try to rewrite the library using an alternative timer.

Under the Hood

The tone function is quite clever; it will adjust what it does depending on what processor it finds itself running on. When given a frequency, it will work out what timer prescale values to set up and what count down values to use in the main counter/timer. This is done so that the timer "times out" at the half period rate. When the timer "times out," an interrupt is generated. This stops whatever program is running at the time and calls another function generically known as an ISR (Interrupt Service Routine). This ISR simply toggles (inverts) the required sound output pin and then returns. ISRs do what they have to do quickly and then return to the exact point the program was at before the interrupt occurred. Thus the interrupted program is not aware that anything happened.

Timers, or counter timers to give them their full name, are complex parts of the processor's hardware peripherals. This complexity arises from the many modes that any one timer can operate in. The three timers in the Uno's processor have some unique modes as well as some common ones. All this is described in the processor's data sheet, but there is little point in going into them here when all we want to do is to generate a tone. We will need to use them later when we write code that uses them to do things that the tone() function cannot do.

A Theremin Project Using Tone

Back in Chapter 5, you saw how to make a MIDI theremin using two IR distance sensors, one for the pitch and the other for the volume. Because there is no volume control in the tone function, you only need one of the sensors to make this project. The schematic is shown in Figure 5-20 and you just need to add an output pin connected to a speaker or amplifier. Because there is no need to control the volume nor send complicated Pitch Bend messages, the program is a lot simpler. It is shown in Listing 11-5. Remember to put in the link from the 3V3 line to the AREF pin after running the program the first time.

Listing 11-5. One-Handed Theremin

```
// Tone function Theremin  - Mike Cook

const byte soundPin = 13;
void setup(){
  analogReference(EXTERNAL);
}

void loop(){
  int av1 = 1027 - analogRead(0); // pitch
  if(av1 < 870){    // if hand over sensor
    trackNote(av1);
    }
  else {
    noTone(soundPin);
  }
}

int trackNote(int freq){
  int pitch = map(freq, 100, 870, 100, 1000);
  tone(soundPin,pitch);
}
```

It simply reads the analogue input pin, and if the reading is less than 870, it will play a note based on the distance. When the reading is above this point, then it is assumed the hand has been removed from the sensor and the sound stops. As the pitch gets lower, it stops being continuously variable and breaks into individual notes. This is because the map function begins to return coarser changes. You can prevent this at the expense of the top of the frequency range by reducing the final number in the map function call.

Polyphonic Tones

When it comes to producing more than one tone at the same time, there are a few solutions out there in terms of libraries. However, a library often obscures what is happening and makes it difficult at times to integrate things. There is nothing you can do in a library that you can't do in plain sight with code, so I will show you how to generate polyphonic tones. The point is that each level of polyphony takes its toll on the processor load, and if you implement more than you need this reduces the processor's capability. By understanding your own implementation, this can be tailored to your exact needs. You will also be able to see exactly what is happening.

Theory

The theory behind this program is quite simple, it works rather like the technique in the first section of this chapter. Basically for each tone, the output pin has its own active counter. This is decremented at a fixed rate by a timer triggering an ISR. When a counter reaches zero, the pin associated with that counter is toggled and then the counter is restored to its full value from a target array. This is summarized in Figure 11-2.

Now that is for only one tone. We must do that for each tone we want to produce, and this can be done simply by duplicating the code using different variables for the active counter and target counter.

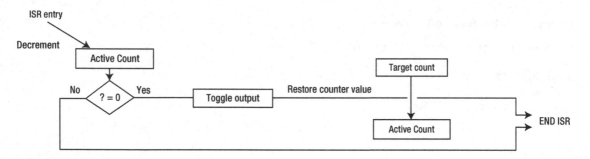

Figure 11-2. *The flow of the ISR*

Optimization

There is some optimization to be done here. Basically the trade-off is between frequency accuracy, number of polyphonic tones, and CPU usage. The more you have of the first two, the less you have of the final one. The frequency accuracy is determined by how often a counter is decremented. The more often it is, the closer to the required time period/frequency you can get. But this means that the CPU spends an increasing amount of its time in the ISR and is not available for doing other stuff. Of course, what is the limiting factor here is what the other stuff is. It could be quite intensive, like refreshing a matrix display, in which case you might see it flickering, if the processor is spending too long in the ISR. On the other hand it could be something like monitoring a push button where a user would not notice a tenth-of-a-second delay. How much frequency inaccuracy can you tolerate? If it is for a sound effect in a game, this can be quite large; on the other hand, it is more critical when playing music. This is something you can tinker with and tune to your own application because you are in control of the code.

Implementation

As an example let's see how to implement a two-tone system for signaling on telephone lines. You have heard the beeps you get when you "dial" a phone number, although we don't actually use a dial these days. You might have wondered what frequency is used; well, it is a special system where each digit is represented by two tones being played together. However, these are not any old tones but specifically designed so that there is no harmonic relationship between them. This makes turning these tones back into numbers much easier. This forms the DTMF (dual tone multifrequency) system. There are eight tones in all as shown in Table 11-2.

Table 11-2. *DTMF Frequencies*

	1209Hz	1336Hz	1477Hz	1633Hz
697Hz	1	2	3	A
770Hz	4	5	6	B
852Hz	7	8	9	C
941Hz	*	0	#	D

In order to send a 5, you must generate two tones one of 1336 Hz and the other of 770 Hz. Because these tones will be sent only when you are sending a number, you can afford to have a high interrupt rate because the processor will be waiting for the tone sequence to finish and you can turn the interrupts off when no tone is being sent. We need to turn this into a table of half period counts, but unlike the tune, this has a count rate of 10 us. This is shown in Table 11-3.

Table 11-3. *Counts for DTMF Tones*

Keys	Frequency Hz	Period us	Count@10us
1,4,7,*	1209	827.13	41
2,5,8,0	1336	748.5	37
3,6,9,#	1477	677.05	34
A,B,C,D	1633	612.37	31
1,2,3,A	697	1434.72	71
4,5,6,B	770	1298.70	65
7,8,9,C	852	1173.71	59
*,0,#,D	941	1062.70	53

At this stage in the game, the only way to send two tones is to have an output pin for each one and mix them. You must not directly connect Arduino outputs (or any other outputs for that matter) together but in this simple application it is sufficient to mix the two outputs using capacitors. Also if you are using an external speaker without volume control, it is probably prudent to include one in the mixer circuit. Figure 11-3 shows one way this can be done, using two 0.47uF capacitors and a pot. For best results, make sure the capacitors are not of the ceramic type.

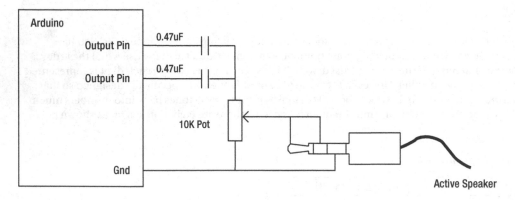

Figure 11-3. *Mixing two-tone outputs*

Again, any two Arduino outputs can be used, but this example uses output pins 12 and 13. Now this is not a perfect mixer because changes on one output pin do bleed through to the other. Figure 11-4 shows an oscilloscope measurement of the two output pins and the mixed signal at the top of the pot.

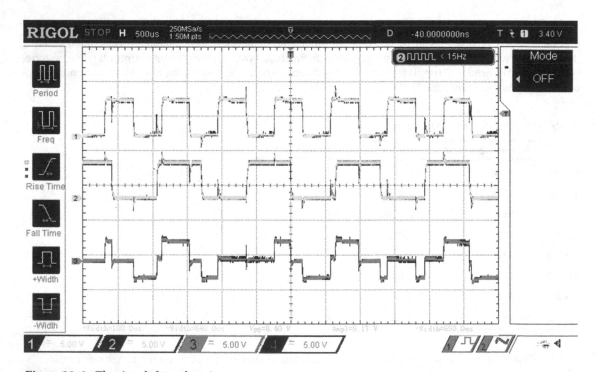

Figure 11-4. *The signals from the mixer*

The top two traces are the output pins. Note how an edge on one signal is reflected on the other with a small blip. The bottom trace is the mixture of the top two square waves. This is a complex waveform and you might be surprised by how it looks, because it is not intuitive. However, your ear can pick out two distinct tones from that signal.

The code makes use of timer2 in the processor, and it is used in its simplest mode, the counter. In this mode, the 8-bit timer simply counts up. When it reaches the top (a count of 255), it wraps around to zero. As it wraps around, it sets an interrupt flag and so can trigger an ISR (interrupt service routine). The counter increments from the processor's clock through a pre-scaler or divider. Here, we are just letting it take its input directly from the 16 MHz system clock, so it is counting as fast as it can.

This means that the counter will wrap around after 256 processor clock pulses or at a rate of once every 16us. This is not quite fast enough for the purposes required for an interrupt rate of 10us, so the first thing that needs to be done in the ISR is to load the counter with a number that means the counter will overflow in another 10us or 160 clock cycles. So to find that number, simply subtract 160 from 256 (the wrap-around point) to give 96. You must pre-load that number into the counter every interrupt. However, there is a bit of a curved ball here. Once the counter triggers an interrupt, the C language has to perform a number of functions before you get to the ISR. This preserves the state of the interrupted program so it can be resumed after the IRS, which takes some time—about 20 to 24 clock cycles normally. Therefore, you can't just load 96 into the counter; you have to add 96 to the value that you find in the counter when you enter the ISR, plus another five as fine tuning. These extra five clock cycles are needed because of this line:

```
TCNT2 = tcnt2 + TCNT2; // reload counter
```

The variable TBC2 is actually the counter accumulating the clock pulses. So to add something to it, the computer has to make a copy of the value, then fetch the data in variable TCNT2, then add them together, and finally store the result back in TCNT2. By the time it comes to storing the value back, the contents of TCNT2 are actually five greater than they were when the computer took the copy in order to add TCNT2 to it. That means we have to add five more clock cycles than we need in order to compensate. The code to do all this is shown in Listing 11-6.

Listing 11-6. DTMF Tones

```
// DTMF telephone numbers - Mike Cook
 volatile byte tone1period = 1, tone2period = 1;
 volatile byte tone1restore = 41, tone2restore = 41;
 volatile unsigned int tcnt2;
 int toneOn = 90, toneOff = 100;

byte rowTone [] = { 71, 65, 59, 53 };
byte colTone [] = { 41, 37, 34, 31 };
byte  pad[4][4] = { '1','2','3','A',
                    '4','5','6','B',
                    '7','8','9','C',
                    '*','0','#','D'  };

ISR(TIMER2_OVF_vect){  // Interrupt service routine to generate the tones
  TCNT2 = tcnt2 + TCNT2; // reload counter
  tone1period--;
  if(tone1period < 1) { // time to toggle the first pin
      tone1period = tone1restore;
      PORTB ^= _BV(5); // toggle pin 13, PB5 direct port addressing
    }
  tone2period--;
  if(tone2period < 1) { // time to toggle the second pin
      tone2period = tone2restore;
      PORTB ^= _BV(4); // toggle pin 12, PB4 direct port addressing
    }
}
```

```
void setUpTimer(){  // sets the timer going at the decrement rate
TIMSK2 &= ~_BV(TOIE2);  // Disable the timer overflow interrupt
TCCR2A &= ~(_BV(WGM21) | _BV(WGM20)); // Configure timer2 in normal mode
TCCR2B &= ~_BV(WGM22);
ASSR &= ~_BV(AS2); // Select clock source: internal I/O clock
TIMSK2 &= ~_BV(OCIE2A); //Disable Compare Match A interrupt (only overflow)
TCCR2B |= _BV(CS22) | _BV(CS20); // Set bits
TCCR2B = (TCCR2B & 0b00111000) | 0x1; // select a prescale value of 1:1
tcnt2 = 96 + 5; // give 10uS interrupt rate + adjustment
TCNT2 = tcnt2; // pre load the value into the timer
}

void setup(){
   setUpTimer();
   pinMode(13,OUTPUT); // enable the pins you want to use as tone outputs
   pinMode(12,OUTPUT);
   tone1restore = 30;
   tone2restore = 53;
   sendTones("0123 45678#"); // phone number
}

void loop() {
}

void sendTones(char *number){
   byte digit = 1, point = 0;
   while( digit != 0){
      digit = number[point];
      if( digit !=0) sendTone(digit);
      point++;
   }
}

void sendTone(byte key){
  boolean found = false;
  int i=0,j=0;
  while(j < 4 && !found){
   i=0;
   while(i<4 && !found){
      if(pad[j][i] == key) {
         tone1restore = rowTone[j];
         tone2restore = colTone[i];
         tone1period = 1;
         tone2period = 1;
       // generate tones
         TIMSK2 |= _BV(TOIE2);  // tone on
         delay(toneOn); // length of tone on
         TIMSK2 &= ~_BV(TOIE2);  // tone off
         delay(toneOff); // length of gap between tones
       found = true;
      }
```

```
  i++; // move on row
  }
  j++; // move on coloum
}
if(!found) {
  delay(toneOff); // small gap for unknown digits
}
}
```

The code has nothing in the loop function; in the setup, it makes a call to the sendTones function to make a phone call. Of course, you have to put a real telephone number in this section, but it is "dialed" only once. Hold your phone up to the speaker, get the volume right, and press the reset button to make your call.

■ **Note** Depending on where you live, this can be illegal. It is fine in the United States, but in the U.K, strictly speaking, doing this counts as "attaching a device to the phone," even though the only attachment is by sound through the air. Any equipment that is attached to a phones needs "type approval" in the UK, which is impractical and expensive for an individual.

Even if you have some experience with programming in C, the code in the setUpTimer function might look a bit odd. This is because it is setting bits in the internal registers of the processor. First of all you need to know is what these registers are and what they do. They are detailed in the ATmega 328 processor data sheet. The registers are being initialized so Timer2 works the way we want it to. In order to set or clear individual bits in the registers, there are a few tricks we can use. If we first need to set up a variable, often called a *mask*, that means a variable with the bits we want to change are set to a 1, and the bits we don't want to change are set to a 0.

Then, to set those bits in the register, you perform a logic OR with mask and register using the |= operator. If you want to clear those bits, perform a logic AND with the inverted mask and register. This is done using the &= operator and the mask is inverted using the ~ operator. To help generate the mask, we use the _BV() macro. This produces a mask with the number in the brackets determining what bit number to set. For example, if we want a mask with the most significant bit set, that is bit 7, then _BV(7) will do this. Of course, you could just write the number in hex as 0x80 or in binary b10000000 or even shift a 1 into place with 1<<7. But as the compiler has the names of the bits predefined as constants, the way we have done it here makes sense. It is only a pity that the names are a bit cryptic. If more than one bit is required to be set in the mask, you simply OR together several masks.

The interrupt service routine is called if the counter overflows (wraps around) and the timer interrupt enable mask is set. This follows the logic in Figure 11-2. When it comes to toggling the output pin, direct port addressing is used because a normal digitalWrite function call would take far too long. The toggling is done with the EOR (exclusive or) operator ^=. Turning the tone on or off is done simply by setting or clearing the timer's interrupt enable bit.

In order to pick out the right two tones to generate for any given character, a two-dimensional array is used containing the characters. So to send a specific character, the array is searched row by row until a match is found. When it is found, the row and column index it was found at is used to find the period count from the rowTone and colTone arrays. After a short delay, the interrupts are disabled and the tones stop. Note that the variables involved are all bytes, which makes the code run faster but restricts the lowest frequency to just under 200 Hz. In this application, this is no problem. You could simply change them all to integers (int type) if required.

Woops and Loops

Finally, to round things off, you can change the period counting variables on the fly to produce a number of effects. This is quite easily done by using delay and incrementing or decrementing the tone period variables. Listing 11-7 generates two tones, one going up and the other going down at the same time. To save repetition, this listing requires two functions from Listing 11-6 that are not duplicated here.

Listing 11-7. Woops

```
// Poly Tone - Mike Cook
 volatile byte tone1period = 1, tone2period = 1;
 volatile byte tone1restore = 41, tone2restore = 41;
 volatile unsigned int tcnt2;

// add function ISR(TIMER2_OVF_vect) from Listing 11-6
// add function void setUpTimer() from Listing 11-6

void setup(){
  setUpTimer();
  pinMode(13,OUTPUT); // enable the pins you want to use as tone outputs
  pinMode(12,OUTPUT);
  TIMSK2 |= _BV(TOIE2);  // tone on
}

void loop() {
  // raise tone 2 and drop tone 1 at diffrent rates
  tone1restore += 10; // lower tone 1
  if(tone1restore > 240) tone1restore = 20; // back to initial position
  tone2restore -= 28; // increase tone 2
  if(tone2restore < 20) tone2restore = 240; // back to initial position
  delay(300); // speed of note changes
}
```

By changing the value in the delay, you can drastically alter the sound from individual notes to a dynamic vibration. Changing the increment and decrement values also changes the nature of the sound. With the increment and decrement values the same, the tones stay synchronized with each other. However, by having a different value, the tones form a complex dance around each other. Small changes in the tone restore value and produce a sliding tone, whereas large changes sound like individual notes.

One extra thing you could try is ramping a tone up to a value and then ramping it back down again. Or you could see how many tones you can push this technique to.

CHAPTER 12

■ ■ ■

Other Wave Shapes

Square is by far the simplest wave shape for a digital processor to produce, as we saw it the last chapter, it was a simple matter of setting a digital pin high and then setting it low or on and off. Also we saw when mixing two such waves a third intermediate level appeared, one that was halfway between high and low. This occurred when one signal was high and the other was low. The trick to producing other wave shapes and therefore different sounding noises is to have some mechanism to generate not only one intermediate level between high and low but many. The more levels you can generate, the finer precision you can sculpt your waveform.

Not a High or a Low

The key to outputting intermediate levels is an D/A converter, which stands for digital to analogue converter. It's the way of generating voltage levels between the normal logic levels. There are a number of circuits that can do this, so before we start making noises, let's look at a few that are of interest when using an Arduino.

PWM

PWM stands for pulse width modulation and the Arduino comes ready set up to produce PWM signals. They are still digital signals in that at any instant they are either high or low, but you can easily control the proportion of the time they are high compared to the time they are low. This ratio of high to low is called the *duty cycle* of the signal, and by altering the duty cycle, you can alter the average voltage level from that pin. This is done through the misleadingly named analogWrite function. Beginners often unsurprisingly think this gives an analogue output, but it doesn't; it produces a rectangular wave, as shown in Figure 12-1.

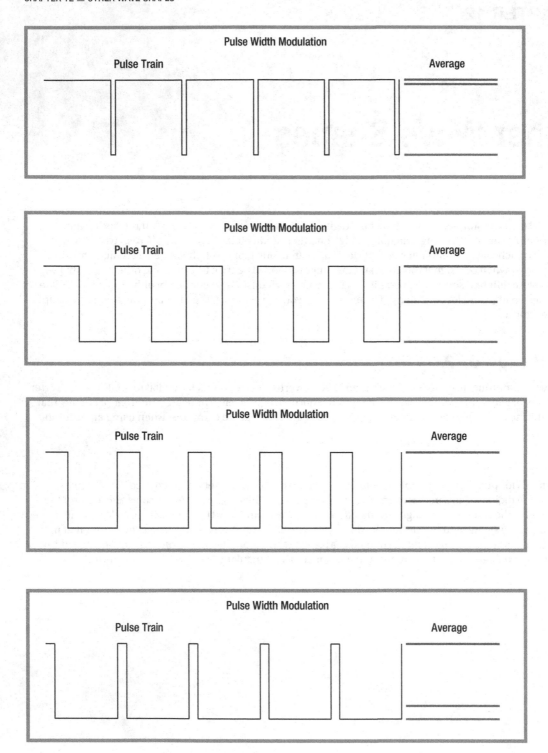

Figure 12-1. *Changing the duty cycle on PWM signals*

The trick in generating a smooth average output is to use a low-pass filter, which lets through the low-frequency average but suppresses the ripple caused by the PWM rectangular wave. Unfortunately, the default frequency for the PWM signals on the Arduino are 490Hz and 980Hz, depending on what pin you use, which is not fast enough to generate intermediate values for audio outputs. For this you have to get the PWM signal going at a speed at least twice as fast as the highest frequency you want to produce. You will see the reasons for that in later chapters, but for now, just remember this minimum speed is called the *Nyquist rate*. Fortunately, it is a simple matter to speed up the PWM signals by altering the clock's prescaler division ratio.

The design of the low-pass filter is a bit tricky as well. The cutoff frequency is the point where the filter's output drops by 3dBs. It is not the frequency where all signals above that point are eliminated; that never happens. Instead as the frequency increases above the cutoff frequency, the filter's output becomes more attenuated. It will never actually reach zero output, but keeps getting smaller and smaller. The rate of drop in signal, or rolloff as it is called, depends on the filter type and "order" of the filter. A simple RC filter has a rolloff of -6dBs per octave. Above the cutoff frequency, every doubling of frequency results in a drop off, or reduction in amplitude, of another 6dBs. This is said to be a first order filter. A simple LC filter rolls off twice as fast at -12dBs per octave and is said to be a second order filter. This is shown in Figure 12-2.

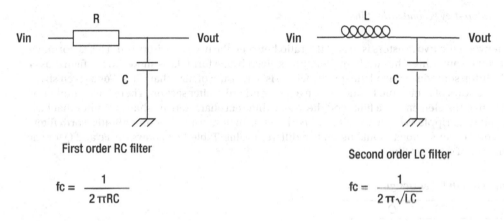

Figure 12-2. *Simple RC and LC filter circuits*

You can achieve higher-order filters by cascading lower-order filters. In fact, by designing the cutoff frequency of each stage of a multi-stage filter, you can get whatever filter shape characteristic you want. Basically, you can trade a faster initial rolloff, or steepness of slope, for a limit in how far down it ultimately goes, and you can trade steepness of slope for a ripple in the pass part of the transfer function and in the stop part of the function.

Filter design is difficult and involves using complex numbers (with real and imaginary parts) and a lot of heavy math. Whole books have been written about this subject and I don't propose to duplicate this here but just to note a few points. While a simple RC circuit looks good, when you come to cascade them, you run into trouble with input and output impedance. This sort of filter needs driving with a low impedance and has a high impedance output. Therefore, when you're cascading first order filters, it is normal to put a buffer amplifier between each section. This is rarely done, however, because if you are going to have an operational amplifier then you are better off making a second order active filter and cascading those. There are quite a few ways to implement an active filter, but one of the most popular ways is to use the Sallen–Key configuration, as shown in Figure 12-3.

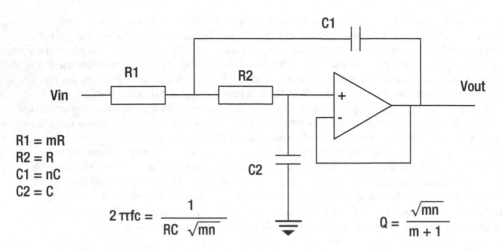

R1 = mR
R2 = R
C1 = nC
C2 = C

$$2\pi fc = \dfrac{1}{RC\ \sqrt{mn}}$$

$$Q = \dfrac{\sqrt{mn}}{m+1}$$

Figure 12-3. *A Sallen–Key second order filter*

The ratio between the two resistors is *m* and the ratio between the two capacitors is *n*. This is normally set to 1 or 2 but can be anything. The cutoff frequency *fc* is given by the formula as shown in the figure, as is the *Q*. The *Q* of a filter, sometimes called the quality factor, is a measure of how sharp it is. For a given shape and order, there are ways of setting the Fc and Q for each second order filter section. There are a number of ways you can arrange the elements in a filter and these give different characteristic shapes. A filter that has a flat pass band, that is no ripple, is known as a *Butterworth* filter. To design a higher order Butterworth filter, the Q of each second order sections should be set to a different value. Table 12-1 shows the Fc and Q for each section for a number of different filters.

Table 12-1. *Butterworth Filter Design Values*

Order	F0	Q
2 - Only section	1.0	0.707
4 - First section	1.0	0.5412
4 - Second section	1.0	1.3306
6 - First section	1.0	0.5174
6 - Second section	1.0	0.707
6 - Third section	1.0	1.9319
8 - First section	1.0	0.5098
8 - Second section	1.0	0.6013
8 - Third section	1.0	0.9000
8 - Fourth section	1.0	2.5629

Note how the F_0 (pronounced F nought) frequency is the same for each filter section, and that it is simply the frequency you want it to cut off at. It is the Q that changes with each filter section for the higher-order filters. These can all be made with the Sallen–Key circuit, but an eighth order filter will require four of these circuits each one having a different Q and hence different component values.

There are many other types of filter shapes, such as Chebyshev, Bessel, and Elliptical (sometimes called a *Cauer*). These filters all have ripple in the pass band and/or stop band, and a sharper rolloff for a given filter order. Some types even have zeros, which is a single frequency where there is a sharp null. All of which, while interesting, is not quite the subject of this book.

When designing a filter for any audio application, you have to determine how close you want the attenuated frequencies to be. The closer they are, the steeper the filter has to roll off and the higher order your filter has to be. Frequency response is not the only criteria of a filter. The phase and the impulse responses are also important. For example, for a filter with a very steep cutoff, a pulse on the input will often produce an oscillation or ringing on the output.

Resistor Tap

The resistor tap is perhaps the easiest of the D/A (digital to analogue) converters to understand; it consists of a set of resistors all in a series. At each node, or point where the resistors meet, is the input to an electric switched analogue selector. You can think of this just like a mechanical switch only with a logic signal controlling what position the switch is in. The general arrangement is shown in Figure 12-4. For simplicity it is just a four bit, that is eight-level D/A, but it is easy to imagine extending it as many bits as you want.

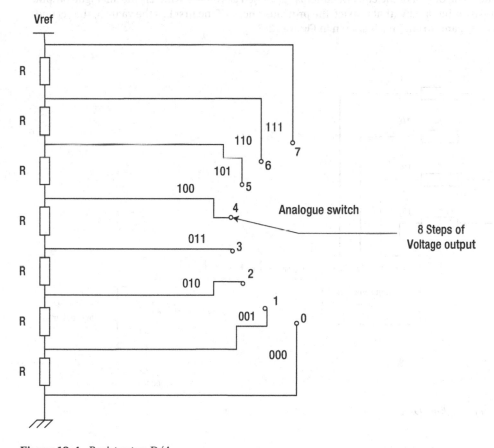

Figure 12-4. *Resistor tap D/A*

As all the resistors are in line, we are guaranteed that any change in a switch to a higher position will always produce a higher output. This property has a long and complex name, it is called *monotonicity*. With this type of converter, it is guaranteed by the design. With other types of D/A monotonicity, can be a tricky thing to achieve as it depends on the tolerance of the components used. But monotonicity is the minimum you should expect from any D/A.

While this arrangement can use a lot of resistors and analogue switches, this is no such limitation when you implement it on an integrated circuit. For an *n* bit D/A, you need $2^n - 1$ resistors, so for an 8-bit converter, you have to have 255 resistors. This is normally used to implement a digital potentiometer, because you can have access to both ends of the chain so you can feed an audio signal into it like a normal potentiometer. Note, by using unequal values of resistors, you can get a log or antilog, or indeed any other transfer characteristic you want.

The Binary-Weighted D/A

There is a way to connect outputs to resistors so that each output contributes a correct fraction of the output value according to the significance of the output bit. This is the binary weighted D/A. The logic output from a pin is passed through a resistor to produce an appropriately weighted current, which is then summed with a current adder. The output of the current adder is expressed as voltage, which is the analogue output. Each successive resistor has a value that is twice the previous one, so if the first has the value R, the second will be 2R, then 4R, 8R, and so on. This is shown in Figure 12-5.

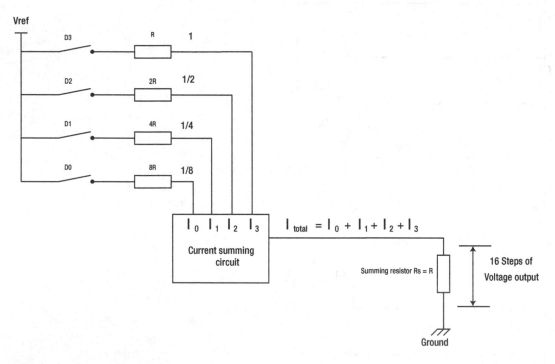

Figure 12-5. *Binary weighted D/A*

The problem with this design is that the absolute value of the resistors needs to be as precise as the number of bits. That is, for an 8-bit converter producing 256 levels, the resistors have to be within 0.39% of the nominal value. For a 12-bit converter, this increases to 0.024%. This is a very high degree of accuracy and is difficult to mass produce. You can achieve it by individually trimming the resistors' values, but they also need to be measured with this degree of accuracy. Still, for a small number of bits, it is often used as a rough-and-ready A/D. With four bits you can just get away with 5% resistors.

The R-2R Ladder

This is quite popular in hacking circles, mainly because it is misunderstood. It uses only two values of resistor—one at R and the other at 2R—therefore, there is no requirement for exact precision in their absolute value, it is only their relative value. Where this leads to a misunderstanding is that people tend to ignore the tolerance or accuracy of the relative values. For a 4-bit converter, this needs to be R/32 or just better than 3%. This accuracy doubles with each additional bit, and that is only to ensure monotonicity. I have seen circuits on the net using six or eight bits with only 1% resistors—clearly nonsense. The big advantage is that having only two values of resistor makes it much easer to manufacture. You can have two of the same resistor in a series to get 2R or two in parallel to get R. This is much easer to achieve on an integrated circuit than getting an actual precise value. A typical 4-bit ladder circuit is shown in Figure 12-6.

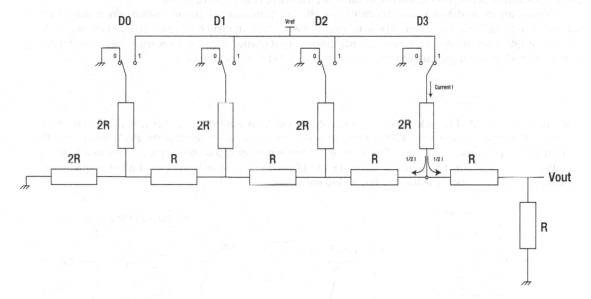

Figure 12-6. *A R-2R ladder D/A*

The way it works is that each input switches between zero volts and some voltage reference, normally 5V or whatever the output pin gives. Consider the input D3, the most significant digital output, a current of I flows down the resistor and when it reaches the node, that is the junction of the three resistors, it splits into two. Half flows to the right and half flows to the left, because the resistance looking out from each side of the node is equal. If no other inputs are switched to a one, then what appears at the output is half the current. It will then generate half the Vref voltage on the output. At each node the current into the node splits in two, so any contribution from the D2 input gets split in half twice, once at its own node and once at D3's node. The current from D2 contributes only a quarter. The farther back you go the more times the current is split in half before reaching the output. D0 only contributes 1/16 of the current to the output. Thus it adds up output currents in exactly the same weighting as a digital binary number.

The D/A Interface

The ready built D/A converters have a parallel interface or some form of serial one. With a parallel interface, all the n inputs are applied to the converter at the same time and a latch signal is used to ensure they are all presented at the same time. In the Arduino context, this takes up a lot of pins and is not a popular choice.

A serial interface, on the other hand, normally takes only two or three pins. It can be on a bus like the I2C or SPI, or it can look just like a shift register. The disadvantage of a serial interface is it takes time to shift out all the bits you need.

Generating a Waveform

Normally a waveform is generated by using an interrupt; at each entry of the ISR a new sample is generated and output to the D/A. This puts a lot of timing pressure on the processor, as the time to generate a sample affects the maximum frequency of the waveform. In any case, you have to complete it before the next interrupt comes along. That is why a simple square wave works great and is very efficient, because all that is being done is toggling or inverting the output pin. Waveforms like a triangle or a sawtooth are easy to generate as well. To generate a triangle waveform involves incrementing the output until some upper limit is reached and then switching to decrementing the output. A sawtooth is even simpler; you simply increment the output and, when it reaches the upper limit, set the output back to zero again.

Generating more than one tone is simple as well. You simply add all the current waveform samples before outputting them. Mind you, all this takes processing time and you have to be carful to ensure the maximum total output does not exceed the maximum input of your D/A. If it does, then the output wraps around and what was high instantly becomes low, thus making an awful racket.

Sawtooth Example

Using the internal PWM is the lowest component count implementation we can have, so this first example uses this. All that is needed is an RC (Resistor Capacitor) on the output to average the PWM frequency. This is often called a reconstruction filter. I used 1K and 0.1uF, which gives a cutoff frequency of about 1.5KHz. Remember that is where it starts to roll off; you will still get plenty of signal out of it at higher frequencies. Figure 12-7 shows a block diagram of what we are going to do.

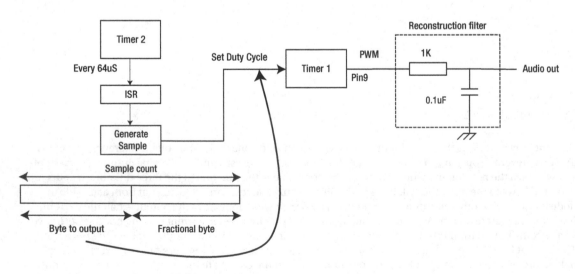

Figure 12-7. *Sawtooth waveform generation*

The figure shows that we are going to use two timers working together to produce this waveform. Timer2 is used to trigger an interrupt service routine like we did in the previous chapter. This ISR is going to generate the next sample in the waveform. This is done by adding an increment to a sample count. Both these numbers are integers—they are two bytes long. This means that they take up two bytes each. The most significant byte of these two is used to set the PWM duty cycle, leaving the least significant byte as the fractional part of the sample count. This technique is sometimes called a *fixed-point fraction* or an *accumulate and overflow* system. This is done to gain fine control over the waveform's frequency; otherwise, the size of the increment would produce too big a frequency jump for each increment value. The code to do this is shown in Listing 12-1.

Listing 12-1. Sawtooth with PWM Output

```
// Sawtooth waveform - using Timer 1's PWM as output
 volatile unsigned int sample =0;
 volatile  int increment =  0x60; // sets frequency
 volatile boolean hush = false;
 const byte hushPin = 2;

ISR(TIMER2_COMPB_vect){  // Generate the next sample and send it to the A/D
   if(!hush) { // if playing a note then output the next sample
       sample += increment;
       OCR1AL = sample >>8 ; // use sample to change PWM duty cycle
         }
}

void setPWMtimer(){
// Set timer1 for 8-bit fast PWM output to use as our analogue output
 TCCR1B = _BV(CS10);     // Set prescaler to full 16MHz for 2 cycles per sample
 TCCR1A |= _BV(COM1A1); // Pin low when TCNT1=OCR1A
 TCCR1A |= _BV(WGM10);   // Use 8-bit fast PWM mode
 TCCR1B |= _BV(WGM12);
}

void setSampleTimer(){  // sets timer 2 going at the output sample rate
  TCCR2A = _BV(WGM21) | _BV(WGM20); // Disable output on Pin 11 and Pin 3
  TCCR2B = _BV(WGM22) | _BV(CS22);
  OCR2A = 60; // defines the interval to trigger the sample generation - 30uS or 33.3KHz
  TCCR2B = TCCR2B & 0b00111000 | 0x2; // select a prescale value of 8:1 of the system clock
  TIMSK2 = _BV(OCIE2B); // Output Compare Match B Interrupt Enable
}

void setup() {
  pinMode(9, OUTPUT); // Make timer's PWM pin an output
  pinMode(hushPin,INPUT_PULLUP);
  setSampleTimer();
  setPWMtimer();
}

void loop() {
  // gate tone
  if(digitalRead(hushPin)) hush=false; else hush=true;
}
```

Timer2 is set up to generate an interrupt every 30us or 33.3KHz. This is so that the PWM is actually above the frequency range of human hearing so it will not interfere with the sawtooth. This does not mean you can get away without the reconstruction filter, as such a large high-frequency component can play havoc with audio amplifiers. The sound is muted by the hush variable and it is used in the loop function to look at the logic level on a pin to see how it is set. This means that pushing a button connected to that pin will stop the tone.

Timer1 is set up in the fast 8-bit PWM mode with a time period of 16us or a frequency of 62.5KHz. This means that even if the sample number changes every time the ISR is called, there are two cycles of the PWM to establish the analogue output level. The PWM duty cycle and hence the effective analogue output is controlled by the OCR1AL register. It is set to the sample value in the ISR. The increment variable that sets the frequency and can be calculated by using the following formula:

$$Increment = Frequency * 4.194304$$

I will leave it up to you, dear reader, to derive this if you are interested.

Triangle Wave Example

The triangle wave is very similar, but I will illustrate a different technique of outputting the waveform here. There is also a copy of the PWM output method on the book's web site. Here we are going to use the R2-R ladder method to act as a D/A converter. I have used 1K as the basic value of R; the schematic is shown in Figure 12-8.

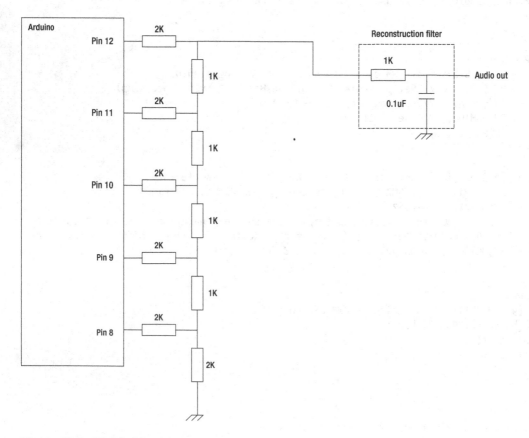

Figure 12-8. *2R-R ladder output*

Note that you still need the reconstruction filter to remove the sample noise. I have chosen to use the pins 8 to 12 for the digital outputs feeding into the ladder, because those pins are on the same port, port B, and can easily be set using direct port addressing. Thus, it forms a 5-bit or 32 level D/A converter, which we can make quite happily with 2% resistors.

This example only uses Timer2 to control the sample generation times. There is no need for PWM, as that is being handled by the resistive ladder D/A converter. Other than that, it is quite similar to the previous listing, as shown in Listing 12-2.

Listing 12-2. Triangle with 2R-R Ladder Output

```
// Triangle wave R2-R ladder output
 volatile int sample =0;
 volatile int increment =  0x200; // sets frequency
 volatile boolean hush = false;
 volatile boolean slope = false;
 const byte hushPin = 2;

ISR(TIMER2_COMPB_vect){  // Generate the next sample and send it to the A/D
   if(!hush) {            // if playing a note then output the next sample
      if (slope) sample += increment; else sample -= increment;
      if (sample < 0){  // if sample has peaked
        slope = !slope;  // reverse direction
        // do a double increment to send it in the right direction
        if (slope) sample += (increment<<1); else sample -= (increment<<1);
      }
      PORTB = (PORTB & 0xE0) | (sample >>10) ; // output to 2R-R ladder
      }
}

void setSampleTimer(){             // sets timer 2 going at the output sample rate
  TCCR2A = _BV(WGM21) | _BV(WGM20);   // Disable output on Pin 11 and Pin 3
  TCCR2B = _BV(WGM22) | _BV(CS22);
  OCR2A = 60; // defines the interval to trigger the sample generation - 30uS or 33.3KHz
  TCCR2B = TCCR2B & 0b00111000 | 0x2; // select a prescale value of 8:1 of the system clock
  TIMSK2 = _BV(OCIE2B);             // Output Compare Match B Interrupt Enable
}

void setup() {
  DDRB = (DDRB & 0xE0) | 0x1F; // set pins 8 to 12 as outputs
  pinMode(hushPin,INPUT_PULLUP);
  setSampleTimer();
}

void loop() {
  // gate tone
  if(digitalRead(hushPin)) hush=false; else hush=true;
}
```

The ISR function is the key change here. It starts off the same with the hush variable, but it also uses a Boolean variable slope to indicate if you are currently counting up or down. The sample counter this time is an int and you decide if it has overflowed or underflowed by seeing if it is negative. If it has gone outside these limits then the slope variable is toggled and twice the increment or decrement is performed. This is to remove the overflow (or underflow) and then to change the sample in the new direction.

The sample now is only five bits, but these are the most significant five bits of the sample counter. This is then moved down (shifted to the right) by one bit so that to remove the sign bit in the int and then shifted down a further nine bits to align the sample byte with the output bits. Of course, one shift instruction does both things. Figure 12-9 shows an oscilloscope trace of the waveform. I slowed the waveform down to a very low value so that you can see the individual steps in the ramp. At audio frequencies, the reconstruction filter will take these steps out and it would look smooth.

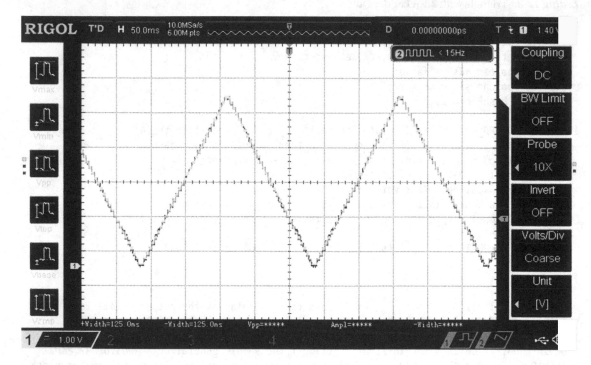

Figure 12-9. *Triangle wave output*

Wave Table Output

What happens if you want to output a more complex waveform, one that is not so easily generated? Take for example a sin wave shape. You can generate sins easily with the sin() function, but it is way too slow to be able to generate anything but the lowest frequencies. Also, what if you want to generate something more convoluted that doesn't necessarily have a trigonometric function associated with it? The answer is to use a precomputed lookup table to hold the waveform. This requires that all the sample outputs be stored in an array. The ISR will then extract the samples one at a time from the array and send them to the D/A converter.

The absolute best thing to use for an A/D converter is a specialized A/D convertor chip, and this example shows how to do this. I used an MCP4981 12 bit A/D chip. This interfaces to the Arduino through an SPI (Serial Protocol Interface), which requires only four wires. It's shown in Figure 12-10.

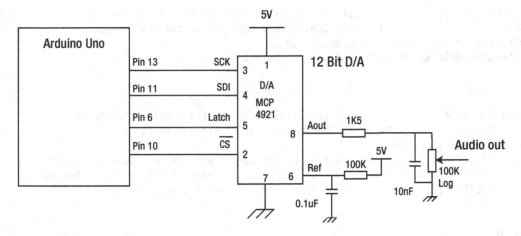

Figure 12-10. *Arduino with an SPI interface*

The way to talk to this is simple. First the chip select line (pin 2) is lowered, then the data is fed into the chip using the serial data (pin4) and clock (pin3), then the chip select is put back high. Finally, the latch (pin5) is pulsed to transfer the data to the analogue output. As it is a 12-bit converter, you need to feed it two bytes of data, but only the 12 least significant bits are used. You can either bit-bang the pins, that is setting them high and low in the right sequence, or you can use Arduino's built-in SPI hardware, which is on these pins, to transfer the data very quickly. To finish the design, a simple voltage reference of 5V is generated from the 5V supply, plus a bit of filtering.

As the D/A is using 12-bit samples, the samples we want to output must be that size but no bigger. Otherwise you will get the signal wrapping around. The size of the wave table is often made to be a power of two to make the index manipulation a bit easier, but you can make it any size you like. In this example, I used a 256 sample long wave table; note that as they are integer type variables this table will take up 512 bytes, which is a quarter of the total read/write memory in the Arduino Uno. As a demonstration I have constructed a wave table that contains two sections of waveform; the first half is filled with a sin wave and the second half with a sawtooth. What you consider to be the zero point on the waveform must in fact be the halfway point as far as the A/D is concerned. So with 12 bits, this halfway point is 2047, that is $2^{11} - 1$. If you filled the buffer with this it would be silent. With a sin function, you get -1 to +1 so that needs to be multiplied by this halfway point and then have the halfway pointed added to it to create a sample. You need to do this for angles over 2π radians spread over the length of the lookup table. The wave table code is shown in Listing 12-3.

Listing 12-3. Wave Table Output

```
// Wave table output D/A output
 #include <SPI.h>
#define CS_ADC_BAR 10
#define AD_LATCH 6

 volatile unsigned int sampleIndex =0;
 volatile int increment =  0x200; // sets frequency
 volatile boolean hush = false;
 const byte hushPin = 2;
 int waveTable [256];
```

315

```
ISR(TIMER2_COMPB_vect){          // Look up the next sample and send it to the A/D
  if(!hush) {                    // if playing a note then output the next sample
      sampleIndex += increment; // increment sample
      ADwrite(waveTable[sampleIndex >> 8])  ; // output to A/D
  }
}

void setSampleTimer(){               // sets timer 2 going at the output sample rate
  TCCR2A = _BV(WGM21) | _BV(WGM20);   // Disable output on Pin 11 and Pin 3
  TCCR2B = _BV(WGM22) | _BV(CS22);
  OCR2A = 60; // defines the interval to trigger the sample generation - 30uS or 33.3KHz
  TCCR2B = TCCR2B & 0b00111000 | 0x2; // select a prescale value of 8:1 of the system clock
  TIMSK2 = _BV(OCIE2B);              // Output Compare Match B Interrupt Enable
}

void setup() {
  // initilise control pins for A/D & SPI
  pinMode( CS_ADC_BAR, OUTPUT);
  digitalWrite(CS_ADC_BAR, HIGH);
  pinMode( AD_LATCH, OUTPUT);
  digitalWrite(AD_LATCH, HIGH);
  pinMode( hushPin, INPUT_PULLUP);
  SPI.begin();
  SPI.setDataMode(SPI_MODE3);
  SPI.setClockDivider(SPI_CLOCK_DIV2); // maximum clock speed
  generateTable();                     // calculate the lookup table
  setSampleTimer();
}

void loop() {
  // gate tone
  if(digitalRead(hushPin)) hush=false; else hush=true;
}

void generateTable(){
  const float pi = 3.1415;
  float angle;
  int sample = 2048;
  for(int i =0;i<128;i++){ // first part of the wave table is a sin
    angle = ((2.0 * pi)) / (128.0 / (float)i);
    waveTable[i] = (int)(2047.0 + 2047.0 * sin(angle));
  }
  for(int i =128;i<256;i++){       // second part of the wave table is a saw
   waveTable[i] = sample;
   sample = (sample - 64) & 0xFFF; // keep to 12 bits
  }
}
```

```
void ADwrite(int data){                 // send data to the A/D
 // digitalWrite(CS_ADC_BAR, LOW);  // replace by below
  PORTB &= ~0x4;
  SPI.transfer(((data >> 8) & 0x0f) | 0x70);
  SPI.transfer(data & 0xff);
  //digitalWrite(CS_ADC_BAR, HIGH); // replace by below
  PORTB |= 0x4;
  //digitalWrite(AD_LATCH, LOW);    // replace by below
  PORTD &= ~0x40;
  //digitalWrite(AD_LATCH, HIGH);   // replace by below
  PORTD |= 0x40;
}
```

You will see that the generateTable function uses floating-point variables to calculate the 128 sin samples in the first half of the lookup table. In the second half of the table, the sample value is decremented by 64 and ANDed with 0xFFF so that when the sample value goes below zero it automatically wraps around. The value of 64 in 128 samples ensures that there are exactly two cycles of sawtooth waveform in this section of the table.

The ADwrite function actually sends the data to the D/A. It uses direct port addressing for speed but I have kept in, but commented out, the digital write function calls it would have used. Each digital write would take about 64 times longer to perform than the direct port equivalent. The sample is output using two SPI.transfer calls; first the most significant four bits are sent along with four zeros and then the eight least significant bits are sent.

The ISR function is very simple; the sampleIndex variable has the increment added to it and then the top eight bits are used to address the wave table. So if the increment variable is smaller than 256, the actual sample accessed will not change every time the ISR is called, but only as often as needed to allow fine control over the waveform frequency. With the ISR being called every 30us and there being 256 samples in a waveform, an increment of 256 will output the whole waveform in:

$$30 * 256 = 7.68 \text{ ms or a frequency of about 130Hz}$$

Note that larger increment values will give higher frequencies, but not all the samples in the table will actually be used. However, with most increment values, successive passes through the wave table will pick up different samples each time around. Therefore, you do need the whole table. Figure 12-11 shows the output waveform on an oscilloscope.

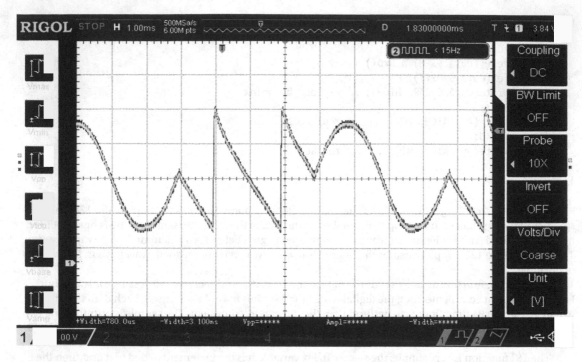

Figure 12-11. *The wave table output waveform*

Note how there is a sin wave at first, followed by two cycles of sawtooth. These are split up into half a sawtooth, followed by a whole cycle, followed by another half cycle to bring the waveform back to the zero part. When designing wave tables, it is important that they start and end at the same zero midway point to prevent any discontinuities when wrapping around the table. Note how the waveform looks like on an oscilloscope, yet it sounds like a discordant buzz.

In the next chapter, we will look at building an instrument using wave table generated sound.

CHAPTER 13

■ ■ ■

The SpoonDuino

I described the SpoonDuino, with tongue firmly in cheek, as:

The world's most sophisticated spoon-based, additive synthesized, wave table, musical instrument.

Well how many spoon-based instruments are there anyway? Okay, I know there was the spoon-o-phone in Chapter 5, but I guess not too many others. The SpoonDuino came about as a response to a competition, to design a standalone portable musical instrument run by Brunell University's Beam festival, and I only found out about the competition 10 days before the closing date. Therefore, the whole project was designed, built, and programmed in less than 10 days, and I used whatever I had in hand, as there was not much time to order stuff. In the end, I was quite pleased with the results. Others must have thought so too, as it won the competition, the prize being a Novotronic MIDI keyboard. This is the most complicated project in this book and ties in several elements explored elsewhere. It requires high levels of skill to complete.

You can see a video of the SpoonDuino in action here: https://vimeo.com/38466551.

What Is a SpoonDuino?

At the heart of the SpoonDuino is a wave table sound generator. It outputs a precalculated set of waveforms. Each waveform set consists of 16 waveforms with 256 two-byte samples in each waveform, so that is 8K of storage required per waveform set. Each waveform consists of a mix of harmonics from the fundamental to the 11th harmonic and each successive waveform in the set follows a different envelope for each harmonic.

Playing the SpoonDuino consists of placing a spoon on a conductive pad and calculating the X & Y coordinates of the contact point. The X location determines the frequency of the note and the Y location determines how quickly the waveform set is scanned through. There are several modes for interpreting the X & Y locations as sounds.

Control of the SpoonDuino is by use of an LCD displaying a menu navigated by push buttons. It has a built-in audio amplifier and volume control, along with a multi-function socket. This can be used either to add a separate extra loudspeaker for extra volume or a wave table download link. The SpoonDuino runs off eight AA batteries, which can be rechargeable if required.

The waveform set is calculated on a computer using a program written in Processing and the user interface is provided by an iPad or Android tablet running the TouchOSC app. Once a waveform set is defined, it can be saved to disc and given a text name, and then downloaded along with the name and stored in the SpoonDuino. The definition of the waveform sets can be stored from Processing and loaded back later for modification and tweaking. The first eight letters of the file name you use is automatically assigned to the waveform name. The SpoonDuino can store up to 32 wave table sets in its own non-volatile storage, so once the waveforms are stored, the SpoonDuino is completely standalone. The waveform set is selected before playing; only one waveform set can be played at any one time.

While the SpoonDuino hardware has provisions for using two spoons, currently the software only uses one of them. If you do make your own version, you could extend the software to use two spoons. Figure 13-1 shows the Processing user interface for defining the waveform set as well as a small representation of each waveform in the set on the right side.

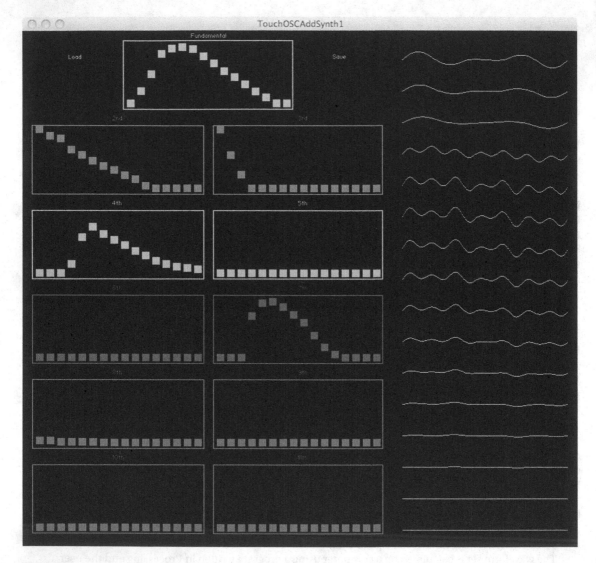

Figure 13-1. *A typical SpoonDuino waveform set*

The idea is that each harmonic has its own envelope, which is set by a slider control in the harmonic box. So, in the set in Figure 13-1, the fundamental quickly builds up to a peak and then drops away slowly. On the other hand, the second harmonic starts off at full blast and quickly fades to nothing. The third harmonic does the same but drops off even more quickly. The fourth harmonic is delayed for a time before rising to a peak and dropping away again, and the seventh harmonic does a similar thing. The wave does not contain any 5th, 6th, 8th, 9th, 10th, or 11th harmonics. The harmonic mix of a sound changing throughout its duration is something that natural sounds do, so the SpoonDuino attempts to emulate this in a rough way. Using an iPad for the interface allows you to set the sliders with one continuous natural finger movement.

SpoonDuino Building Blocks

Now that you know what a SpoonDuino does, let's see what components are needed to make it work. All the functional blocks are shown in Figure 13-2.

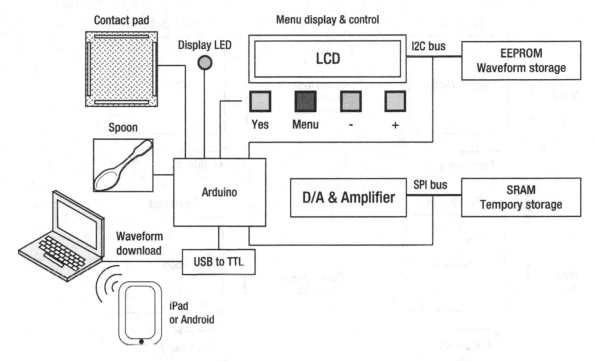

Figure 13-2. *SpoonDuino block diagram*

Figure 13-2 shows the SpoonDuino itself along with the laptop and tablet needed to define and download the waveform sets. There is a bunch of "normal" stuff connected to the Arduino, like the menu push buttons, the contact pad, spoon, and RGB display LED. Then there is the temporary stuff, like the laptop running Processing and talking to the tablet over Wi-Fi to define and download the waveform sets. Finally is the stuff that makes it work—the LCD and waveform storage EEPROM hung off the I2C bus, and the D/A and waveform storage SRAM (Static RAM).

The waveforms are downloaded into the EEPROM through the I2C bus. This is non-volatile storage, but it's way too slow to use to output an audio waveform. When you want to load a waveform set to play on the SpoonDuino, it is transferred over from the EEPROM into the SRAM ready to be read out as an audio wave. This process in electronics terms is quite slow, but as it takes only about half a second, in terms of user interaction it is almost instantaneous. This transfer is not done very often and so the I2C bus can be used also to drive the LCD, thus reducing the number of pins required on the Arduino.

The SPI bus is connected to both the D/A and the SRAM; a two-byte sample is read from the SRAM and then transferred to the D/A by an ISR when required. The output of the D/A is connected through a filter and volume control to an audio amplifier.

The contact pad works in a similar way to the touch screen used in Chapter 5; however, the spoon is used to pick up a voltage applied across the pad. By looking at what that picked up voltage is in relationship to the voltage applied, you can get a measure of how far along the pad the spoon is making contact. This gives the X measurement. The voltage is then removed from the left and right sides of the pad and applied to the top and bottom. Again, the voltage picked up from the spoon will tell you how far up the pad it is, or its Y measurement.

Playing Modes

The SpoonDuino can be played in one of four modes. Each mode makes different use of the returned X and Y spoon positions. The four modes are best summed up in Figure 13-3.

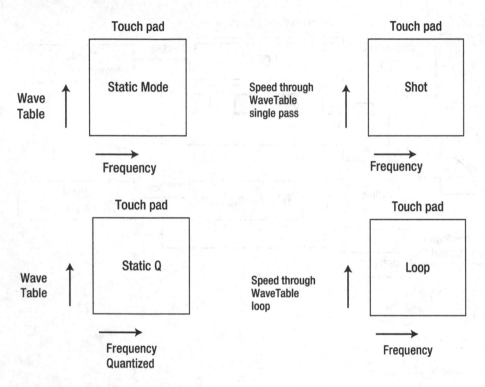

Figure 13-3. *Spoonduino playing modes*

The mode's name reflects what it does. The *static* mode simply takes the waveform from the wave table given by the Y coordinate and the frequency is given from the X value. This is a continuous change in frequency. Whereas the Static Q (Q for quantized) only outputs frequencies corresponding to whole notes. The two playing modes on the right both automatically cycle through the wave tables; the Shot mode performs a single shot through all the waveforms in the table. The speed of this shot is determined by the Y coordinate. The Loop mode is similar, except the tables are repeatedly gone through in a continuous cycle. These modes are accessed through the menu controls.

The Menu

The menu is accessed through four push buttons—Menu, Yes, - and +—and is quite simple to operate. The Menu push button cycles through the four main options—Play, Load, Save and Get Wave. Once an option is displayed, the + and - buttons cycle through the choices that option gives. The Yes button chooses that option. These options are summarized in Figure 13-4.

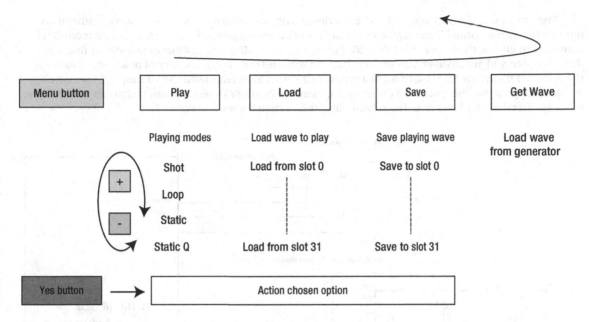

Figure 13-4. *Menu options*

The waveform table set you want to play is loaded from the bank of waveform tables in non-volatile memory or from an attached computer running the processing waveform generation program. This loads the data into fast but volatile memory to play the sound. Once in the volatile memory, it can be saved to non-volatile memory with the Save menu option. Each set of waveform tables is given an eight-character name by the computer when it is generated and this is displayed on the LCD along with the slot number where you are loading or saving it.

The Schematic

The schematic is best considered in sections in book format, but a full, scalable PDF version is available on the book's web site.

Arduino and Power

The Arduino itself is not an official Arduino but a kit or PCB from Spikenzie Labs called a Minuino. I got it in a "lucky bag" when I attended the 2011 Open hardware source conference. You can use this or build a standalone circuit or strip board. The point being that you don't need the USB-to-serial converter on the board; that was be fitted externally so it can be used on other projects. A USB-to-serial TTL lead was used and connected to the 5-pin DIN socket on the front face. This was the same type as the normal MIDI connector; again, you can use any plug. It also carried two signals from the right side of the stereo audio amplifier to allow an external speaker to be used. Note there is nothing to stop you using a "real" Arduino if you can arrange easy access to the USB socket.

The power was derived from eight AA batteries in a holder giving a 12V source. However, rather than put this through a normal linear regulator to burn away the excess power, I used a small switch mode buck converter to efficiently convert this 12V to 5V. I used the Austin MiniLynx 12V power module for this, but there are plenty of alternatives. This ensures that the batteries put every last ounce of power into supplying the system. Finally, the SRAM used for fast access to the waveform table needs a 3V3 supply. I used a A033 regulator to generate this from the 5V line. Again, there are many 3V3 linear regulators that can be used here; these are just that I had on hand. The schematic of this section is shown in Figure 13-5.

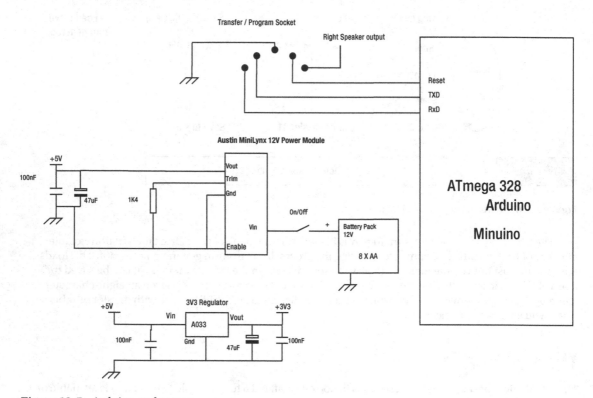

Figure 13-5. *Arduino and power*

I2C Bus

The I2C bus consists of the non-volatile EEPROM memory to permanently hold the wave table banks and the LCD to display the menu options. The schematic of this section is shown in Figure 13-6.

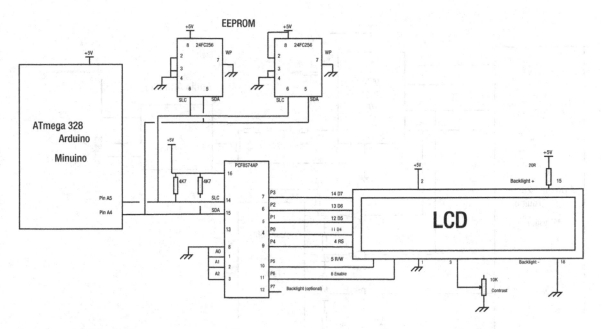

Figure 13-6. *The I2C bus components*

There are 4K7 pull-up resistors on the I2C's data and clock lines, and the LCD is connected through a PCF8574AP interface chip. You can get LCDs and I2C interfaces built together if you like; all you need to do is to use an appropriate library to access it. There is a spare line that could be used to control the LCD's backlight if required, but I didn't wire it up as I could see no reason to turn it off. The EEPROM I used was two 24FC256 chips, again because I had them. However, I only had surface mount parts, so I had to fashion a breakout board using a small strip of PCB.

SPI Bus

The SPI bus contains both the D/A converter and the SRAM memory; they take turns to be accessed. The MCP4921 is a 12-bit D/A and is fed with a reference voltage derived from the power rail. The 1K5 and 10nF reconstruction filter is fed into the input of an audio amplifier through a 50K log pot. This amplifier was from a pair of computer speakers I got at a junk sale. I took the internal amplifier out of one of the speakers and mounted the speaker on the board. It is the unusual curved pod on the right side of the SpoonDuino. The 23K256 is organized as 32K by 8-bit serial memory. This is a 3V3 device and so needs supplying with this voltage. Also, the signals going into it must not exceed 3V3. To prevent that from happening, the signals from the Arduino into this chip are passed through an open collector non-inverting buffer. The output is pulled up to 3V3 through a resistor. This is much better than the resistor potential divider method of dropping the voltage. The voltage from the memory back into the signal out (SO) goes straight into the Arduino, as it is just big enough to register in the 5V system. The schematic of this section of the circuit is shown in Figure 13-7.

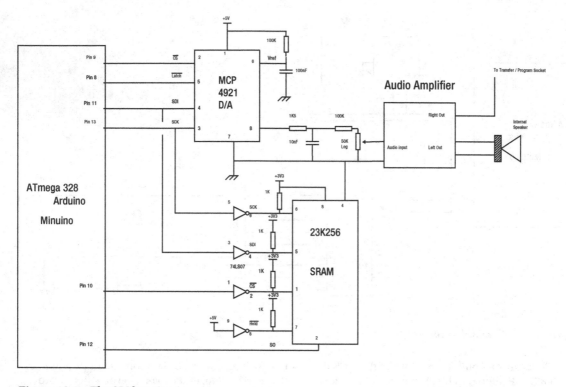

Figure 13-7. *The SPI bus circuit*

Mopping Up

The rest of the circuit consists of the conductive pad, the RGB LED, the menu buttons, and the spoons. The conductive pad is made up of a sheet of conducting plastic. This material was originally designed for plastic bags for anti-static storage of electronics boards. But you can buy this from places like Adafruit as Velostat or Linqstat. Basically, there needs to be four connections, one along each side. More details when we look at the construction in the next section. The spoons themselves are connected to two analogue inputs. Although only one spoon is activated in the present software, I made provisions for using two. I used spoons from a thrift shop at under $1 for six. The only thing you have to make sure is that the handles are insulated, that is so you can't touch any of the metal. If you do, that injects noise into the system and the software has a hard time telling whether it is in contact with the conductive pad or not.

The four menu buttons use one analogue input pin, and a binary weighted D/A is used to give a unique reading for each button. The binary weighted D/A was described in the last chapter. You might want to make the buttons different colors. I only had three different colors when I made this; they were left over from the DunoCaster project in Chapter 7. Finally, the LED indicator uses an RGB LED, although all its color potential is not used by the current software. It switches from red to blue when the spoon is in contact with the pad. These final pieces are shown in Figure 13-8.

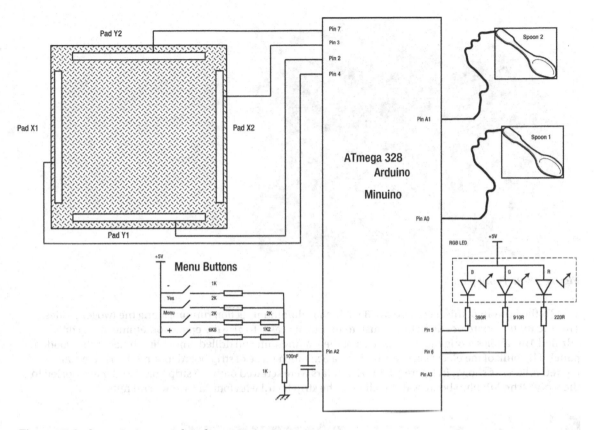

Figure 13-8. *SpoonDuino peripheral*

Construction

The whole instrument was built in a small flight case (13 x 8$^1/_2$ x 3 $^{3/4}$ inches) and constructed on a piece of 1/4-inch plywood cut so that it exactly fitted into the case. I first drilled holes for all the parts and then gave the wood two coats of light oak stain varnish. See Figure 13-9.

Figure 13-9. *Front panel*

To the bottom of this, I epoxied a 3/8 x 1-inch L aluminum section running along the two long sides. This meant the board needed a loose push to fit into the case. To give the epoxy something to grip on to, I drilled 1mm holes along the short section of the L aluminum and drilled 3mm blind holes in the wooden panel. The bulk of the electronics was built on a 5 x 3-inch piece of strip board mounted on three 10mm tapped pillars, as shown in Figure 13-10. The pillars were screwed onto the strip board and then epoxied to the wood. The Minuino board was attached to the strip board with four M3 screws and nuts.

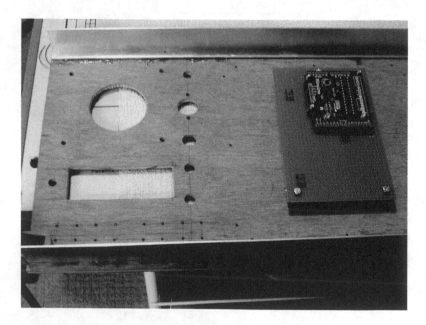

Figure 13-10. *Electronics board and aluminum runners*

Then I added the volume control, the menu switches, spoon sockets, and Din connector to the face plate. I attached the speaker and mounted the amplifier board culled from the computer speakers. At this stage, the project looked like Figure 13-11.

Figure 13-11. *Most of the front panel components*

The main circuit board was then built with small PCBs holding the surface-mount components attached to the strip board by hot-glue. Interconnections were made with 30 aw wire-wrapping wire. The main circuit strip board was constructed and was ready to be wired to the front panel components. It then looked like Figure 13-12. You can't see the 3V3 regulator because I mounted the components to the underside of the strip board.

***Figure 13-12.** Main circuit board ready to be wired*

The conducting pad was made from a piece of 1/16-inch thick 6-inch x 6-inch acrylic. Holes were drilled on each side with one at each end, and another at the center about 1/4-inch from the edge. These were 2.5mm in diameter to accommodate M2.5 screws and M3 washers. The acrylic was wrapped in the Velostat over the top face and about 1 inch was tucked under. I used some spray-on glue to try to ensure there were no creases or bubbles between the acrylic and the Velostat. I placed adhesive copper strips on the front of the panel so that it could contact each side of the conducting pad. The screw through the center on each side was used to make the electrical connection to the side of the conducting pad. Just before it was all screwed up, I used a small amount of conducting paint to act as a sort of conducting glue to form a good connection. A solder tag or wire wrapped around the nut of the screw allows the electrical connection to be made to the Arduino pin. It sounds more complicated than it actually is, as you can see from Figure 13-13.

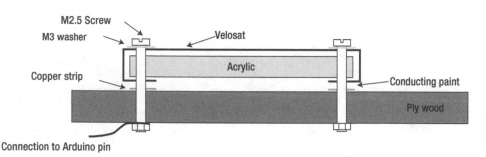

***Figure 13-13.** Cross-section through the conducting pad*

The battery holders were hot-glued to the panel and the other components wired to the main circuit board. The LCD was hot-glued in the corners. The joy of hot-glue is that while it forms a strong joint, it can always be peeled off if things need to come apart. At this stage, the underside was looking very busy, as you can see from Figure 13-14.

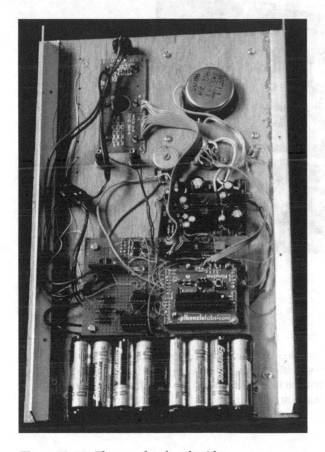

Figure 13-14. *The completed underside*

The spoons had wires attached to the handles using an M3 nut and bolt. Then to insulate them from hands, I wrapped them around in a length of self-amalgamating tape. This forms a nice tactile rubbery feel to the handles. I did try whipping the handle with orange twine and while it looked great and worked well, it didn't survive a day on show without beginning to show signs of slackening and unwinding. Figure 13-15 shows the finished instrument.

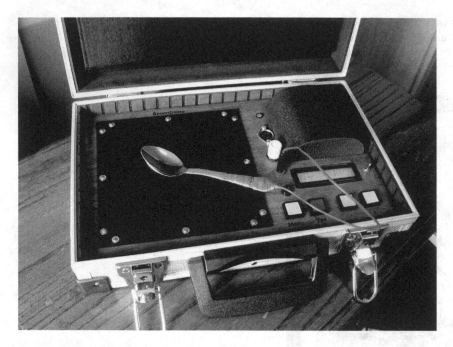

Figure 13-15. *The SpoonDuino*

The Software

The software comes in three parts. There is the embedded software in the Arduino, the software in your laptop or computer, and the software or more specifically the app on your iPad or Android device. Unfortunately, both the wave table calculations program in Processing and the code for the Arduino are quite long; however, they are given here in full so that you can reproduce what I have done.

iPad/Android App

The iPad is not that easy for everyone to write apps on, as actually getting anything onto an iPad requires Apple's approval and a long wait. Fortunately, there is a way around this problem in the form of customizable apps. The one I chose to use here is called TouchOSC and is designed to convert contact with the iPad's touch screen into OSC messages. Remember we covered OSC messages in Chapter 8. There is also a version that will work with Android devices.

As well as the app, there is also a free to download editor that allows you to make custom layouts and get them onto your device. I used this to make a bank of sliders to set the envelope for each of the harmonics in a waveform. The editor file for my layout is on the book's web site. (Being a binary file, you can't print it out.) You can find out all about this application at `http://hexler.net/blog/post/touchosc-1.9.0-for-android-and-ios-out-today`. It is quite easy to make a screen and customize the OSC messages that each predefined object sends when touched. Figure 13-16 shows the TouchOSC layout editor in action.

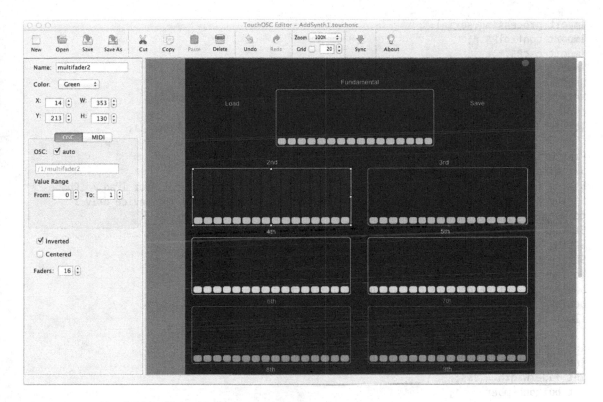

Figure 13-16. *TouchOSC editor with the SpoonDuino layout*

Wave Calculating Software

The part of the system that actually calculates the wave table will be running on your laptop or computer. It takes its input from the tablet and spits out data to the SpoonDuino. It is written in the Processing language, which is a form of Java that runs on the Windows, Mac, or Linux operating systems. It is free to download and available from https://processing.org/. It is has recently changed to Version 3 and likely not to change again for a few more years.

This program communicates with both the tablet and the Arduino and requires a couple of third-party libraries. Fortunately, the act of downloading and installing them is very much integrated into Processing 3. You will need the controlP5 and oscP5 libraries all the others are included in the default distribution of the language. The listing you need to run is shown in Listing 13-1 and is quite long.

Listing 13-1. Wave Calculating Software in Processing

```
/**
 * TouchOSC Additave Synth input 1
 *
 * For an additive synth waveforme definer
 * 16 steps per partial
 * By Mike Cook November 2015
 * Requires Processing 3
 * And a tablet running TouchOSC to change the sliders
 * If you have trouble connecting then create an adhock network and join that
 */
```

```
import processing.serial.*;
import controlP5.*;
import oscP5.*;
import netP5.*;
OscP5 oscP5;
NetAddress myRemoteLocation;
ControlP5 synth;
Textlabel loadLab, saveLab, fund, h2, h3, h4, h5, h6, h7, h8, h9, h10, h11;

PrintWriter output;
Serial port; // Create object from Serial class
String iPadIP = "169.254.46.38"; // *** change this to the address of your iPad / iPhone ***
String adaptor = "/dev/tty.usbserial-A600eudM";  // ***the name of the device driver
to use ***
String[] lines; // for input of a file
String waveName="Wave Name";
String savePath;
boolean [] buttonPressed = new boolean [2];
boolean [] multiFadeNeedsRedraw = new boolean [11];
boolean mouseHit = false, loadCallback = false, saveCallback = false;
float [][] multiFade = new float [11][17];
float incSin = TWO_PI/256.0;  // conversion for look up table x axis
int [] [] waveform = new int [16] [256];
int faderHight = 90;
int faderWidth = 245;
int buttonNumber = -1;

void setup() {
  size(850, 790);
  frameRate(30);
  background(0);
  colorMode(RGB, 255);
  for (int i =0; i<11; i++) multiFadeNeedsRedraw[i] = true;
  buttonPressed[0] = false;
  buttonPressed[1] = false;
  portConnect();
  // start oscP5, listening for incoming messages at port 8000
  oscP5 = new OscP5(this, 8000);
  // set the local IP address on the iPod to this
  myRemoteLocation = new NetAddress(iPadIP, 8080); // local IP on the iPad
  // in choosing a static IP address make sure it is in the same domain as the host
  defineLables();
  updateiPad();
}

void oscEvent(OscMessage theOscMessage) {
  String addr = theOscMessage.addrPattern();
  println(addr);    // uncomment for seeing the raw message
  int startOfNumber = addr.indexOf("/push");
  if (startOfNumber != -1) { // we have a push button message
    buttonNumber = getNumber(addr, startOfNumber + 5);
```

```
      if (theOscMessage.get(0).floatValue() != 0.0) {  // for button push
        println("press "+ buttonNumber);
        buttonPressed[buttonNumber -1] = true;
      } else {  // for button release
        // println("release "+ buttonNumber);
        buttonPressed[buttonNumber -1] = false;
      }
      multiFadeNeedsRedraw[0] = true; // just redraw fader 0
    }
    // look for fader messages
    if (addr.indexOf("/1/multifader") !=-1) {
      int fader=0;
      String list[] = split(addr, '/');
      if (list[2].length() == 12) fader = int(list[2].substring(10, 12));
      if (list[2].length() == 11) fader = int(list[2].substring(10, 11));
      fader--; // to compensate for zero based arrays
      //  println(fader);
      int x = int(list[3]);
      multiFade[fader][x]  = theOscMessage.get(0).floatValue();
      //   println(" x1 = "+multiFade[0][x]);  // uncomment to see x value
      multiFadeNeedsRedraw[fader] = true;
    }
  }
}

int getNumber(String s, int look) {
  int number = -1, i = 0;
  char p = '0';
  if (s.length() > look) {
    number = 0;
    for (int k = look; k< s.length(); k++) {
      p = s.charAt(look+i);
      i++;
      if (p >= '0' && p <= '9') number = (number * 10) + (int(p) & 0x0f);
    }
  }
  return(number);
}

void draw() {
  // see if screen needs updating
  for (int i=0; i<11; i++) {
    if (multiFadeNeedsRedraw[i] == true) {
      drawFader(i);  // only redraw the screen if we need to
      multiFadeNeedsRedraw[i] = false;
    }
  }
  // look at push buttons
  if (buttonPressed[1] || saveCallback) { // the save button
    saveCallback = false;
    calculateWaveform(); // work out the waveform tables
    displayWaveforms();
```

```
      buttonPressed[1] = false; // show we have done the action
      saveWave();                // save it to disc
   }
   if (buttonPressed[0] || loadCallback) { // the load button
      loadCallback = false;
      buttonPressed[0] = false; // show we have done the action
      loadWave();                // get it from the disc
   }
}

void calculateWaveform() {
  float sf = scaleFactor();
  float temp;
  // println("scaling factor is " + sf );
  for (int j =0; j<16; j++) {
    for (int i = 0; i<256; i++) {  // calculate entries in the table
      temp = 0;
      for (int k = 0; k<11; k++) { // for each harmonic
        temp += sf * multiFade[k][j+1] * (sin(i * incSin * (k+1)));
      }
      waveform[j][i] = int(255 * temp );
    }
  }
}

void displayWaveforms() {
  int y=48;
  fill(0, 0, 0);
  rect(580, 0, 850, 790); // blank off previous waveform
  strokeWeight(1);
  noFill();
  stroke(255, 255, 255);
  for (int table = 0; table <16; table++) {
    y = 44 + (48 * table);
    for (int x = 0; x<255; x++) {
      point(x+580, y -( waveform[table][x] / 12));
    }
  }
}

float scaleFactor() {                  // give the overall scale factor for the waveform
  float sum, maxSum = 0.0;
  for (int j = 0; j<16; j++) {         // go through each table
    sum = 0;
    for (int i = 0; i<11; i++) {
      sum += multiFade[i][j+1];        // sum the same
    }
    if (sum > maxSum) maxSum = sum;    // get the biggest amplitude
  }
  if (maxSum <= 0.0) maxSum = 1;       // prevent an infinity
  return(1.0/maxSum);
}
```

```
void drawFader(int fader) { // Update the screen image of the faders
  int xOffset = 137, yOffset = 0;
  color cFill = color(0, 200, 200); // cyan
  // draw the load / save buttons
  noStroke();
  if (buttonPressed[0]) fill(180, 180, 180);
  else fill(90, 90, 90);
  rect(65, 48, 32, 32);
  if (buttonPressed[1]) fill(180, 180, 180);
  else fill(90, 90, 90);
  rect(468, 48, 32, 32);
  // draw faders
  if (fader != 0) {
    xOffset = ((fader+1) % 2) * ( faderWidth + 30);
    yOffset = ((fader+1) / 2) * 130;
    switch(((fader+1) / 2)) {
    case 1:
      cFill = color(0, 153, 0);     // green
      break;
    case 2:
      cFill = color(200, 200, 0);   // yellow
      break;
    case 3:
      cFill = color(153, 0, 153);   // purpul
      break;
    case 4:
      cFill = color(240, 64, 0);    // orange
      break;
    case 5:
      cFill = color(250, 30, 30);   // red
      break;
    }
  }
  strokeWeight(2);
  noFill();
  stroke(cFill);
  rect(15+ xOffset, 15 + yOffset, faderWidth + 15, faderHight + 15);  // outline
  for (int x=1; x<17; x++) {
    noStroke();
    fill(40, 40, 40);
    rect( x*16+4+ xOffset, yOffset + 16, 12, faderHight + 13);        // blank rectangle
    fill(cFill); // do the solid square marking the position of the fader
    rect( x*16+4+ xOffset, yOffset + 15+(1-multiFade[fader][x])*faderHight, 12, 12);
  }
  calculateWaveform();
  displayWaveforms(); // show the wave at the side of the screen
}
```

```
void savePathCall(File selection) {
  if (selection == null) {
    // If a file was not selected
    println("No output file was selected...");
  } else {
    // If a file was selected, print path to folder
    savePath= selection.getAbsolutePath();
    waveName = savePath;
    println("save path"+savePath);
    // nibble away at the path name until we just have the file name
    while (waveName.indexOf('/') != -1) {
      waveName = waveName.substring(1, waveName.length() );
    }
    // now make it 8 long by appending spaces
    while (waveName.length() < 8) waveName = waveName + " ";
    output = createWriter(savePath+".asw"); // add file extension
    output.println(waveName);               // save the file name as part of the file
    for (int i = 0; i < 11; i++) {          // for each harmonic slider
      for (int j = 1; j <17; j++) {         // for each slider
        output.println(multiFade[i][j]);
      }
    }
    // Tidy up the file
    output.flush(); // Write the remaining data
    output.close(); // Finish the file
  }
}

void  saveWave() { // save waveform defination to disc
  selectOutput("select a place to save wavetable", "savePathCall");  // Opens file chooser
  // rest of the action handled by call back function
}

void loadWave() {   // load waveform defination from disc
  selectInput("Choose Waveform file", "doLoadWave");  // Opens file chooser
}

void doLoadWave(File selection) {
  int k=1;
  if (selection == null) {
    // If a file was not selected
    println("No file was selected...");
  } else {
    String loadPath = selection.getAbsolutePath();
    println(loadPath);
    lines = loadStrings(loadPath);
    for (int i = 0; i < 11; i++) {  // for each harmonic slider
      for (int j = 1; j <17; j++) { // for each slider
        multiFade[i][j] = Float.valueOf(lines[k]);
        k++;
      }
    }
```

```
    for (int i =0; i<11; i++) multiFadeNeedsRedraw[i] = true;
    calculateWaveform();
    displayWaveforms(); // show the wave at the side of the screen
    waveName = lines[0];
    while (waveName.length() < 8) waveName = waveName + " "; // for files with a short
    wave name
    // println("Waveform name is " + lines[0]);
    updateiPad(); // update the iPad
  }
}

void updateiPad() {                   // update the iPad
  String message, finalMessage;
  for (int i=0; i<11; i++) {          // for each fader
    message = "/1/multifader" + str(i+1);
    for (int j = 1; j<17; j++) {      // for each silder in a fader
      finalMessage = message + "/" + str(j);
      OscMessage myMessage = new OscMessage(finalMessage);
      myMessage.add(multiFade[i][j]); // add an float to the osc message
      oscP5.send(myMessage, myRemoteLocation);
      bufDelay(4);                    // make sure we don't do thing too fast
    } // end of each slider in a fader
  }   // end of for each fader
}

void portConnect() {    // Open the port that the SpoonDuino is connected to and use the
same speed
  // ***********************************
  // if the device you are looking for is
  // not avaliable the program will
  // connect to the first one in the list
  // ***********************************
  int portNumber = 99;
  String [] ports;
  // println(Serial.list()); // uncomment for full list of serial devices
  ports = Serial.list();
  for (int j = 0; j< ports.length; j++) {
    if (adaptor.equals(Serial.list()[j])) portNumber = j;
  } // go through all ports
  if (portNumber == 99) portNumber = 0; // if we haven't found our port connect to the
  first port
  String portName = Serial.list()[portNumber];
  println("Connected to "+portName);        .
  // port = new Serial(this, portName, 57600);
  port = new Serial(this, portName, 38400);
  port.bufferUntil(10);   // call serialEvent every line feed
}
```

```
void serialEvent(Serial port) {  // this gets called everytime a line feed is recieved
  String recieved = port.readString() ;
  // println(recieved + " from serial port");
  String startTransfer [] = match(recieved, "send");
  if (startTransfer != null) sendWave();
  else println(recieved);
}

void sendWave() { // send wave table to the SpoonDuino
  float sf = scaleFactor();
  float temp, maxTemp = -2, minTemp = 2;
  int entry, count=0;
  println("now sending " + waveName);
  for (int i = 0; i<8; i++) port.write(waveName.charAt(i));
  println("scaling factor is " + sf );
  for (int j =0; j<16; j++) {
    for (int i = 0; i<256; i++) { // calculate entries in the table
      temp = 0;
      for (int k = 0; k<11; k++) { // for each harmonic
        temp += sf * multiFade[k][j+1] * (sin(i * incSin * (k+1)));
      }
      if (temp > maxTemp) maxTemp = temp;
      if (temp < minTemp) minTemp = temp;
      entry = 2048 + int(2047 * temp );
      count++;
      port.write((entry >> 8) & 0xff); // send MSB
      port.write(entry & 0xff); // send LSB
    }
  }
  println(" ");
  println("Entry count is "+ count);
  println("max value "+ maxTemp + " minimum value " + minTemp);
}

void defineLables() {
  synth = new ControlP5(this);
  loadLab = synth.addTextlabel("label1")
    .setText("Load")
    .setPosition(66, 36)
    .setColorValue(0xfff0f0f0);
  saveLab = synth.addTextlabel("label2")
    .setText("Save")
    .setPosition(470, 36)
    .setColorValue(0xfff0f0f0);
  fund =  synth.addTextlabel("label3")
    .setText("Fundamental")
    .setPosition(256, 4)
    .setColorValue(0xff00c8c8);
  h2 =    synth.addTextlabel("label4")
    .setText("2nd")
    .setPosition(135, 130)
    .setColorValue(0xff009900);
```

```
    h3 =    synth.addTextlabel("label5")
      .setText("3rd")
      .setPosition(420, 130)
      .setColorValue(0xff009900);
    h4 =    synth.addTextlabel("label6")
      .setText("4th")
      .setPosition(135, 260)
      .setColorValue(0xffc8c800);
    h5 =    synth.addTextlabel("label7")
      .setText("5th")
      .setPosition(420, 260)
      .setColorValue(0xffc8c800);
    h6 =    synth.addTextlabel("label8")
      .setText("6th")
      .setPosition(135, 390)
      .setColorValue(0xff990099);
    h7 =    synth.addTextlabel("label9")
      .setText("7th")
      .setPosition(420, 390)
      .setColorValue(0xff990099);
    h8 =    synth.addTextlabel("label10")
      .setText("8th")
      .setPosition(135, 520)
      .setColorValue(0xfff04000);
    h9 =    synth.addTextlabel("label11")
      .setText("9th")
      .setPosition(420, 520)
      .setColorValue(0xfff04000);
    h10 =   synth.addTextlabel("label12")
      .setText("10th")
      .setPosition(135, 650)
      .setColorValue(0xfffa1e1e);
    h11 =   synth.addTextlabel("label13")
      .setText("11th")
      .setPosition(420, 650)
      .setColorValue(0xfffa1e1e);
}

void mousePressed() {
  int x, y;
  x = mouseX;
  y = mouseY;
  // println(x+" "+y);
  if (x>67 && x<97 && y>50 && y<82) {
    mouseHit= true;
    noStroke();
    fill(180, 180, 180);
    rect(65, 48, 32, 32);
    loadCallback = true;
  }
```

```
  if (x>470 && x< 499 && y>50 && y<82) {
    mouseHit = true;
    noStroke();
    fill(180, 180, 180);
    rect(468, 48, 32, 32);
    saveCallback = true;
  }
}
void mouseReleased() {
  if (mouseHit) {
    mouseHit = false;
    noStroke();
    fill(90, 90, 90);
    rect(65, 48, 32, 32);
    rect(468, 48, 32, 32);
  }
}
void bufDelay(long pause) {
  pause = pause + millis();
  while (pause > millis()) {
  } // do nothing
}
```

You can't just take that listing and expect it to work. You need to customize a few variables to match your hardware. This is done in these two lines:

```
String iPadIP = "169.254.46.38"; // *** change this to the address of your iPad / iPhone ***
String adaptor = "/dev/tty.usbserial-A600eudM";  // ***the name of the device driver to use ***
```

Get the IP address from the setup page of TouchOSC on your tablet device; it's labeled Local IP address. This could change if your network changes the IP address it gives the device. The adaptor device name you will get from the Arduino Tools menu when you plug in the Arduino. A lot of processing applications assume where the Arduino is on the list of serial devices and unfortunately that does not always work. This way is foolproof, providing you change the line to reflect your Arduino.

The TouchOSC app must be set up to talk on port 8000 and listen on port 8080, although you could change those two lines in the Processing listing to match the default values used by TouchOSC. Also in the TouchOSC app, the "Host" must be set to the IP address of your computer running Processing. Connection between processing and your tablet will be confirmed. When you see the sliders on the computer screen, copy the sliders as you move them on your tablet. I found on one network router I had where this setup would not immediately work. The solution was to create an ad-hoc network on another channel to my local network and let the computer and tablet connect to that.

The display of each individual wave down the right side of the screen is just a rough indication. It is scaled to the biggest sample in the set to fill the space allocated to the small wave display. Therefore, you might be altering one harmonic slider and see not that waveform get bigger but all the others getting smaller, which in effect is what is actually happening in relative terms.

The Arduino Code

Listing 13-2 shows the code to upload into the Arduino and is required if you want to reproduce my project. It is quite long in terms of pages, but just under 40% of the total memory available on a Uno. You will also need to load a special hacked about version of the LCD_I2C library called LCD_I2Cm, as well as the master I2C library again hacked by me to make it cope with a bigger buffer. These can both be found on the book's web site for this chapter.

Listing 13-2. Arduino Code

```
/* SpoonDuino - a musical instrument
*  Waveform table synthisister with spoon playing device
* By Mike Cook Nov 2015
*/
#include <SPI.h>
#include <LCD_I2Cm.h>
#include <EEPROM.h>
#include <I2C.h>

#define Xpad1 4
#define Xpad2 3
#define Ypad1 2
#define Ypad2 7
#define spoon1 0
#define blueLED 5
#define greenLED 6
#define redLED 17
#define keys 2
#define CS_BAR 9
#define LATCH 8

#define SR_CS 10  // static RAM chip select bar
#define SR_SI 12  // serial data input
int memoryAddresBase = 0x50;

// initialize the library with the I2C address
LCD_I2Cm lcd(0x20);     // send I2C address for PCF8574A with external address lines = 0
boolean button[4];      // array for menu buttons
boolean lastButton[4];
int menu =0, menuMax = 3;
String menuTitle [] = { "Play    ", "Load ", "Save ", "Get Wave"};
// autoIncDelay - delay before auto increment kicks in
// autoIncPeriod - speed of auto increment
long unsigned int autoIncDelay = 800, autoIncPeriod = 150, autoIncTrigger=0, autoInc=0;
int value[] = { 3, 0, 0, 0};        // initial values
int valueMax [] = { 3, 31, 31, 0}; // maximum value
int valueMin [] = {0, 0, 0, 0};     // mimimum value
// increment for notes C1    D1    E1    F1    G1    A1    B1    C2    D2    E2    F2
int noteLookup[] = { 0x1125, 0x133e, 0x159a, 0x16e3, 0x19b0, 0x1cd6, 0x205e, 0x224a, 0x267d,
0x2b34, 0x2dc6 }; // increments for quantised playing
String playMenu [] = { "Shot    ", "Loop    ", "Static  ", "Static Q"}; // choice of playing
options
```

```
char waveName [] = { 'b', 'l', 'a', 'n', 'k', ' ', ' ', ' ', ' '}; // array for wave name
int rawButton;
int xVal1, xVal2, yVal1, yVal2, thresh1, thresh2, key;
boolean retrigger = false;
// ISR variables
 volatile long int index = 0;
 volatile long int increment = 0x700;
 volatile boolean hush = false;
 volatile int tableOffset = 0;
 boolean tempHush = false;

void setup()
{
  // initilise control pins for A/D
  pinMode(LATCH, OUTPUT);
  digitalWrite(LATCH, HIGH);
  pinMode(CS_BAR, OUTPUT);
  digitalWrite(CS_BAR, HIGH);
    // initilise control pins for SRAM
  pinMode( SR_CS, OUTPUT);
  digitalWrite( SR_CS, HIGH);
  pinMode( SR_SI, INPUT);
   // initilise LED outputs
  pinMode(blueLED, OUTPUT);
  pinMode(greenLED, OUTPUT);
  pinMode(redLED, OUTPUT);
  digitalWrite(redLED, LOW); // turn on red light
  digitalWrite(greenLED, HIGH);
  digitalWrite(blueLED, HIGH);

  Serial.begin(38400);  // start serial for output
  I2c.begin();
  I2c.setSpeed(1);       // my hardware would only work at 800KHz
  Serial.println("SpoonDuino running");
  SPI.begin();
  SPI.setBitOrder(MSBFIRST);
  SPI.setDataMode(SPI_MODE0);
  // set status register to byte mode
   digitalWrite( SR_CS,LOW);
   SPI.transfer(0x01);  // write to status register
   SPI.transfer(0x41);  // page mode with hold disabled
   digitalWrite( SR_CS,HIGH);
   SPI.setClockDivider(SPI_CLOCK_DIV2); // maximum clock speed
   lcd.begin(8, 2);
  // Print introductory message to the LCD.
   lcd.print("SpoonDui");
   lcd.setCursor(0,1);
   lcd.print("no");
   delay(1000);
   lcd.setCursor(0,0);
   lcd.print("By Mike ");
```

```
    lcd.setCursor(0,1);
    lcd.print("Cook");
    delay(1500);
    lcd.clear();

    menuSteup(menu);  // start off the menu system
    autoIncTrigger = millis();
    hush = true;
    // automatically load in the waveform in slot zero
    romReadWave(0);
    readWaveName(0);
    // set the ISR going
    setSampleTimer();
    TIMSK2 = _BV(OCIE2B); // Output Compare Match B Interrupt Enable
}

boolean dir = true;
long tableTime=0;
long tableShiftRate = 100;

void loop(){
    doMenu();
    saveButtons();
    if(millis() > tableTime) {
      if(value[0] == 0 || value[0] == 1) { // if we are in playing modes shot or loop
      if(!hush) {   // if we are curently not playing
      if(dir) tableOffset += 512; else tableOffset -= 512;
      if(tableOffset >- 7680) {
        dir = false;
        if(value[0] == 0) hush = true; // stop going on shot mode
       }
        if(tableOffset <= 0) dir = true;
  }
    spoonRead();
    if(hush) tableTime - millis() + 100; else tableTime = millis() + tableShiftRate;
}
    else { // if we are in another mode , just static or static Q mode for the moment
    spoonRead();
    tableTime = millis() + 50; // update in another 50mS
    }
  }
}

ISR(TIMER2_COMPB_vect){  // Interrupt service routine to read the sample and send it to the
A/D
    if(!hush){ // if playing a note then output the next sample
      index += increment;
      outA_D(ramRead(tableOffset + ((index>>8) & 0x1fe)) );
    }
}
```

345

```
void setSampleTimer(){                    // sets timer 2 going at the output sample rate
  TCCR2A = _BV(WGM21) | _BV(WGM20);    // Disable output on Pin 11 and Pin 3
  TCCR2B = _BV(WGM22) | _BV(CS22);
  OCR2A = 124; // defines the frequency 120 = 16.13 KHz or 62uS, 124 = 15.63 KHz or 64uS,
  248 = 8 KHz or 125uS
  TCCR2B = TCCR2B & 0b00111000 | 0x2; // select a prescale value of 8:1 of the system clock
}

static int workingValue;
void doMenu(){
  if(readButtons()) {
    if(!button[0] && lastButton[0]){ // on menu change button
      menu ++;
      if(menu > menuMax) menu = 0;
      if(menu == 2) value[2] = value[1];
      workingValue = value[menu];
      menuSteup(menu);
    }

    if(!button[1] && lastButton[1]){ // Accept this menu choice
      value[menu] = workingValue;    // save new value
      // do the actions depending on the choice and menu
      tempHush = hush;
      hush = true;
      if(menu == 1) {
        lcd.setCursor(0, 0);
        lcd.print("Loading ");
        romReadWave(workingValue);
        readWaveName(workingValue);
        }
      if(menu == 2) {
        lcd.setCursor(0, 0);
        lcd.print("Saving ");
        romWriteWave(workingValue);
        romWaveName(workingValue);
        }
      if(menu == 3) {  // transfer wave table from Processing
        getWaveTable();
        }
      hush = tempHush;
      menuSteup(menu); // restore menu
    }

  if(!button[2] && lastButton[2]) {
    if(workingValue > valueMin[menu]) workingValue--; else workingValue = valueMax[menu];
    updateValue(menu, workingValue);
    value[menu] = workingValue;
  }
```

```
        if(!button[3] && lastButton[3]) {
         if(workingValue < valueMax[menu]) workingValue++; else workingValue = valueMin[menu];
         updateValue(menu, workingValue);
         value[menu] = workingValue;
      }
   }
}

void updateValue(int m, int v){
    if(m == 0) {lcd.setCursor(0, 1); lcd.print(playMenu[v]);}

  if(m == 1) { // load menu
    lcd.setCursor(5, 0);
    lcd.print(v);
    lcd.spc(2);
    displayLoadWaveName(v);
  }

  if(m ==2) { // save menu
    lcd.setCursor(5, 0);
    lcd.print(v);
    lcd.spc(2);
    displayWaveName();
  }

}

void menuStcup(int n){
    lcd.setCursor(0, 0);
    lcd.print(menuTitle[n]);
    if(n == 0) { lcd.spc(2); lcd.setCursor(0, 1); lcd.print(playMenu[value[0]]);
    lcd.spc(1);}
    if(n == 1){   // load menu
       lcd.print(value[1]);
       lcd.spc(2); // blank off any other value remnents
       displayLoadWaveName(value[1]);
    }

    if(n ==2){    // save menu
       lcd.print(value[2]);
       lcd.spc(2); // blank off any other value remnents
       displayWaveName();
    }
    if(n ==3){  // Get wave menu
    lcd.setCursor(0, 1);
    lcd.spc(8);  // blank off any name
    }
}
```

```
void readButton(int b){

  boolean pressed = true;
  switch (b) {
    case 0:
    if((rawButton > 0xc9) &&  (rawButton < 0xE0) ) pressed = false;
    break;
    case 1:
    if((rawButton > 0x158) &&  (rawButton < 0x168) ) pressed = false;
    break;
    case 2:
    if(rawButton >= 512) pressed = false;
    break;
    case 3:
    if((rawButton > 0x60) &&  (rawButton < 0x80) ) pressed = false;
    break;
  }
 button[b] = pressed;
}

boolean readButtons(){
  boolean change = false;
  rawButton = analogRead(keys) + 8;
  for(int i=0; i<4; i++){
  readButton(i);
   if(button[i] != lastButton[i]){
      if( ( i == 2 || i == 3) && button[i] == LOW) { // start off auto increment timer
      autoIncTrigger = millis();
      autoInc = millis();
      }
      delay(30); // debounce delay
      change= true;
    } // debounce delay if a change
  }
  // if(change)Serial.println("button change");
  if(  (button[3] == LOW || button[2] == LOW) && ( (millis() - autoIncTrigger) >
  autoIncDelay) ) { // need to auto increment
    if(millis() - autoInc > autoIncPeriod) {              // do the auto increment
      autoInc = millis();
      if(button[2] == LOW) {
      if(workingValue > valueMin[menu]) workingValue--; // don't wrap round under auto
      increment
      updateValue(menu, workingValue);
        }
      if(button[3] == LOW) {
      if(workingValue < valueMax[menu]) workingValue++; // don't wrap round under auto
      increment
      updateValue(menu, workingValue);
        }
    } // end of do the auto increment
  }
```

```
  return change;
}

void saveButtons(){
  for(int i=0; i<4; i++){
    lastButton[i] = button[i];
  }
}

void ramWrite(int add, int val){ // write val to address add of the SRAM as two bytes
  // digitalWrite( SR_CS,LOW);
   PORTB = PINB & 0xfb;
  SPI.transfer(0x02);  // write data to memory instruction
  SPI.transfer((add>>8) & 0x7f );
  SPI.transfer(add & 0xff);
  SPI.transfer(val>>8);  // write MS nibble first
  SPI.transfer(val & 0xff);
 // digitalWrite( SR_CS,HIGH);
  PORTB = PINB | 0x04;
}

void singleRamWrite(int add, uint8_t val){ // write val to address add as single byte
  // digitalWrite( SR_CS,LOW);
   PORTB = PINB & 0xfb;
  SPI.transfer(0x02);  // write data to memory instruction
  SPI.transfer((add>>8) & 0x7f );
  SPI.transfer(add & 0xff);
  SPI.transfer(val);  // write
 // digitalWrite( SR_CS,HIGH);
  PORTB = PINB | 0x04;
}

int ramRead(int add){ // read val from address as two bytes
int val;
  // digitalWrite( SR_CS,LOW); // pin 10
  PORTB = PINB & 0xfb;
  SPI.transfer(0x03);  // read data from memory instruction
  SPI.transfer((add>>8) & 0x7f);
  SPI.transfer(add & 0xff);
  val = SPI.transfer(0) << 8; // read most significant nibble
  val |= SPI.transfer(0);
//  digitalWrite( SR_CS,HIGH);
  PORTB = PINB | 0x04;
  return val;
}

uint8_t singleRamRead(int add){ // read val from address as two bytes
uint8_t val;
  // digitalWrite( SR_CS,LOW); // pin 10
  PORTB = PINB & 0xfb;
  SPI.transfer(0x03);  // read data from memory instruction
```

```
  SPI.transfer((add>>8) & 0x7f);
  SPI.transfer(add & 0xff);
  val = SPI.transfer(0);
//  digitalWrite( SR_CS,HIGH);
  PORTB = PINB | 0x04;
  return val;
}

void outA_D(int value){
  int first;
     first = ( (value >> 8) &0x0f )          | 0x40 |    0x20 |         0x10;
   //                          side A  |bufferd| gain 1 | output enabled
   // take the SS pin low to select the chip:
 // digitalWrite(CS_BAR,LOW);     // pin 9
  PORTB = PINB & 0xfd;
  SPI.transfer(first);            // control and MS nibble data
  SPI.transfer(value & 0xff);     // LS byte of data
  //  digitalWrite(CS_BAR,HIGH);
  PORTB = PINB | 0x02;
//   digitalWrite(LATCH, LOW);    // latch the output pin 8
//   digitalWrite(LATCH, HIGH);
  PORTB = PINB & 0xfe;
  PORTB = PINB | 0x01;
}

void displayWaveName(){
  // send wave name to LCD
      lcd.setCursor(0, 1);
       for(int i =0; i<8; i++){
      lcd.print(waveName[i]);
       }
  }

void getWaveTable(){  // transfer from processing into the memory
int val,address=0;
      lcd.setCursor(0, 0);
       lcd.print("Getting ");
       Serial.println("send");
       for(int numberOfBytes = 0; numberOfBytes < 8200; numberOfBytes++){ // read all the
       bytes
       while(Serial.available() == 0){ } // hold until data is in
        if(numberOfBytes < 8) {         // get the waveform name
        waveName[numberOfBytes] = Serial.read();
         }
         else {                  // get the waveform tables
         if(address & 1){        // on odd addresses write to memory
         val |= Serial.read();
         ramWrite(address-1, val); // save it in memory
         }
```

```
            else { // on even addreses just get the most significant byte
            val = Serial.read() << 8;
            }
            address++;
            }
        } // end of reading all the bytes
      menu = 2; // change to save menu
  }

void romWriteWave(int number){  // write a waveform from RAM to ROM
    int address, pg, bufferNumber=0;
    long int time;
    uint8_t buffer[255];
    for(int page= 0; page<32; page++){  // write waveform over 32 pages
    pg = (number * 32) + page;          // get absoloute point in eeprom
    address = memoryAddresBase | ( pg >> 8);
    // now fill up the buffer
    for(int i=0; i<256; i++) buffer[i] = singleRamRead(i+(bufferNumber << 8));
    bufferNumber++;
    // now write it to EEPROM
    while(I2c.write2(address, pg & 0xff, 0, buffer, 256) != 0 ) { } // repeat until command
    is taken
    }
  }

void romReadWave(int number){  // read a waveform from ROM to RAM
  int c, address, pg, ramAddress = 0;
      for(int page= 0; page<32; page++){        // write waveform over 32 pages
      pg = (number * 32) + page;                // get absoloute point in eeprom
      address = memoryAddresBase | ( pg >> 8); // create the I2C address of the chip to use
    for(int i=0; i<16; i++){                    // read 16 lines for the page
      while(I2c.write(address,pg & 0xff, i<<4) != 0) { }  // set up start of read
      I2c.read(address, 16);        // request 16 bytes from memory device ( note maximum
      buffer size is 32 bytes )
      for(int j=0; j<16; j++){    // now get the bytes one at a time
      singleRamWrite(ramAddress, I2c.receive());    // receive a byte
      ramAddress++; // move on to next address
        }
      }
    }
}

void romWaveName(int slot){
  slot = slot << 3; // make it into an eprom address
  for(int i=0; i < 8; i++){ // store the name in internal EEPROM
    EEPROM.write(slot + i, waveName[i]);
  }
}
```

```
void displayLoadWaveName(int slot){
    slot = slot << 3; // make it into an eprom address
    lcd.setCursor(0, 1);
      for(int i=0; i < 8; i++){ // get the name in internal EEPROM
      lcd.print((char)EEPROM.read(slot + i));
  }
}

void readWaveName(int slot){
    slot = slot << 3;        // make it into an eprom address
  for(int i=0; i < 8; i++){ // get the name in internal EEPROM
  waveName[i] = EEPROM.read(slot + i);
  }
}

void spoonRead(){
  key = analogRead(keys);
  if(touching()) {                  // read the spoon co-ordnates if we are touching the pad
      digitalWrite(redLED, HIGH); // LED off
      analogWrite(blueLED, xVal2 >>2);
        // take a reading
        setPads(true, false);
        xVal1 = analogRead(spoon1);
        setPads(false, false);
        yVal1 = analogRead(spoon1);

      switch(value[0]){
        case 0: // playing mode Shot or loop
        if(!retrigger) break; // exit here if we have not had a retrigger here yet
        tableOffset = 0;        // start over
        dir = true;             // going up
        retrigger = false;
        // - no I haven't missed out the break I want it to be like this
        case 1:
          hush = false;
          tableShiftRate = (yVal1 - 130)/8;
          increment = (xVal1 - 80) << 4;
        break;
        case 2: // static mode
        case 3: // static quantisation mode
        hush = false;
        tableOffset = ((yVal1 - 130)/50) << 9; // make it a whole number of tables
        if(tableOffset < 0) tableOffset =0;
        if(tableOffset > 7680) tableOffset = 7680;
        if(value[0] == 2)increment = (xVal1 - 80) << 4; else increment = quantIncrement();
        break;
        }
    }
  else {
    digitalWrite(redLED, LOW); // LED on
    analogWrite(blueLED, 255); // LED off
```

```
    switch(value[0]) {
      case 0:
      retrigger = true;
      break;
      case 1: // playing mode loop
      case 2: // static mode
      case 3: // static quantised mode
      hush = true;
      break;
    }
  }
}

long int quantIncrement(){
  int quant;
  quant = (xVal1 - 80)/88;
  return noteLookup[quant];
}

boolean touching(){
  boolean touch1 = false, touch2 = false;
  ADMUX = 0x4F; // select channel 15, this puts the input mux capacitor to ground
  // Set all te pads to outputs
   pinMode(Ypad1, OUTPUT);
   pinMode(Ypad2, OUTPUT);
   pinMode(Xpad1, OUTPUT);
   pinMode(Xpad2, OUTPUT);
   // put all the pads high
  digitalWrite(Xpad1, HIGH);
  digitalWrite(Xpad2, HIGH);
  digitalWrite(Ypad1, HIGH);
  digitalWrite(Ypad2, HIGH);
  if( analogRead(spoon1) > 980) touch1 = true;
    // put all the pads low
    digitalWrite(Xpad1, LOW);
    digitalWrite(Xpad2, LOW);
    digitalWrite(Ypad1, LOW);
    digitalWrite(Ypad2, LOW);
  if(analogRead(spoon1) < 25) touch2 = true;
  return (touch1 && touch2);
}

void setPads(boolean way, boolean pol){    // initilise xy Pads
    ADMUX = 0x4F; // select channel 15, this puts the input mux capacitor to ground
    delay(1);
  if(way){
    pinMode(Ypad1, INPUT);
    pinMode(Ypad2, INPUT);
    pinMode(Xpad1, OUTPUT);
    pinMode(Xpad2, OUTPUT);
```

```
  if(pol){
    digitalWrite(Xpad1, LOW);
    digitalWrite(Xpad2, HIGH);
  } else {
    digitalWrite(Xpad1, HIGH);
    digitalWrite(Xpad2, LOW);
  }
}
  else {
    pinMode(Xpad1, INPUT);
    pinMode(Xpad2, INPUT);
    pinMode(Ypad1, OUTPUT);
    pinMode(Ypad2, OUTPUT);
  if(pol){
    digitalWrite(Ypad1, LOW);
    digitalWrite(Ypad2, HIGH);
  } else {
    digitalWrite(Ypad1, HIGH);
    digitalWrite(Ypad2, LOW);
  }
 }
}
```

Techniques

The technique used to detect a spoon contact might need a little explanation. It is the **touching** function where this happens. The problem is that just by reading the voltage on the spoon you can't tell if it is in contact with the conducting pad, as an unconnected analogue input can read anything due to interference pickup. Therefore, we have to do something to the voltages on the conducting pad and see if the voltage picked up by the spoon is consistent with it being in contact. This is done by setting all the pins feeding the conducting pad to high and seeing if the spoon is seeing a high voltage. In this case, that would be a reading greater than 980. Then set all the pins low and see if the spoon picks up a voltage reading of less than 25. If it passes those two tests, you can assume the spoon is in contact with the pad and you can proceed to take a reading of its position.

The spoonRead function first checks that the spoon is in contact and changes the LED from red to blue to indicate this. Then two readings are taken, one with the left and right contacts having 0 and 5V on them, with the top and bottom contacts being set as a inputs so as not to affect the signal. Then the next reading is read with them swapped over, that is left and right set to inputs and top and bottom set to outputs 0 and 5V.

The setPads function actually sets up these output values as well as doing another small trick, that of selecting an input channel to the A/D converter that is wired inside the processor to ground. This discharges any voltage picked up from previous measurements that could still be lingering on the sample and hold capacitor on the input to the D/A.

When the SpoonDuino wants to get a waveform from the computer, it sends a message saying send. It then expects to get 8200 bytes back with the first eight bytes being the name of the waveform. As each sample is two bytes, it builds the sample with the most significant byte coming first, followed by the least significant. Then the sample is written to the fast SRAM memory. Note that this will happen every odd number of bytes. Once the waveform has been loaded, the menu option is automatically changed to the Save mode, where you can use the + & - keys to select a memory slot to save it into. If you save a wave table set into a slot with one already in, then it will be overwritten. Empty slots show up as eight solid squares on my display.

If you don't have a tablet device to define the waveforms you can still load the predefined waveform files found in the example waves folder on the book's web site for this chapter. Note that these are not the wave tables themselves, but the size of each harmonic required to calculate the wave tables.

Final Thoughts

I have found that prolonged use tends to wear away the conductive coating on this sort of plastic, making spoon contact more difficult. This is with bags I recovered once they had been used for packaging not the Velostat plastic, which might be more robust. However, it is possible to replace this plastic and restore the instrument's touch sensitivity. There is a vast area of potential sound waveforms I have not had time to explore myself and repeated use often brings surprises.

PART III

■ ■ ■

Signal Processing

The third part of the book looks at signal processing this is where real sounds are recorded and manipulated to produce something different. There are a number of different ways to generate sound samples on an Arduino along with real time effects like speaking backwards. Ways of creating sounds by mathematically modeling a physical system are explored along with digital filters. The Fast Forgoer transform is looked at, along with a project full of flashing colored LEDs. Waveform excitation by the introduction of extra harmonics is explains as is the use of the 32 bit class of Arduino processors.

■■■

Sampling

This third part of the book concerns signal processing, which is the input of a real audio signal and using it to produce something else. Conventional wisdom will say that you can't do much in the way of signal processing with a simple Arduino Uno, but you can do quite a lot more than you might think. By extending your processor to a Due or Teensy 3, you can do quite a bit more. So lets start off with the theory before jumping into some fun projects. Note that this is not going to be an audiophile examination of the subject, but an engineering one. That means I am not concerned with anything you can't measure with an instrument. The point of view that "the ear can pick up things that instruments can't measure" is the mumbo jumbo homeopathy approach to audio that has you buying expensive gold plated mains connectors and precious metal digital leads.

Breaking Up a Sound into Chunks

In the last section of this book we saw how you could make a sound from a wave table with each output sample being either calculated on the fly for a simple waveform like a sawtooth, or from a pre-calculated table where the calculations took too long to do in real time, like for a sin wave or multiple harmonic waves. But however they were generated, the waveform was broken into many numbers, each one being a sample.

This same thinking can be reversed and you can take a real sound as picked up from say a microphone, and make a rapid series of voltage measurements, and then output them again as a waveform. In other words record a real sound and then replay it, and in many ways that all their is to it. However, the quality of what you get depends strongly on two factors—the sample rate and the sample resolution.

Sample Rate

The sample rate is how often you sample an incoming wave and it determines how high a frequency you can record and the quality of that recording (the faster the better). Well, that is, until you reach a point where you don't get any more improvement no matter how fast you go. Like most things, there is a law of diminishing returns. At first a faster sample rate improves things greatly and then the degree of improvement drops off until doubling what you have gives you no discernable improvement.

The sample rate you should use has a strict mathematical foundation rooted in information theory, and the two names you will hear banded about are Shannon and Nyquist. The Nyquist rate, as it is most often called, is the maximum frequency signal you can sample and still recover the information it contains for any given sample rate. Put simply, you have to sample at a rate of at least two samples per cycle in order to get the fundamental frequency of a signal through a sampling process. If you try to sample a signal where there is fewer than two samples a cycle, you get what is known as aliasing, where low frequency signals are generated in the range of the frequencies you want to sample. These are extremely discordant and, once generated, cannot be filtered out.

Sampling at greater than the Nyquist rate is often called over-sampling. Normally the sample rate will be at a fixed frequency so only the top of the frequency range will approach the Nyquist rate; lower frequencies will be over-sampled. In Figure 14-1 a signal is being sampled at just over nine samples per cycle.

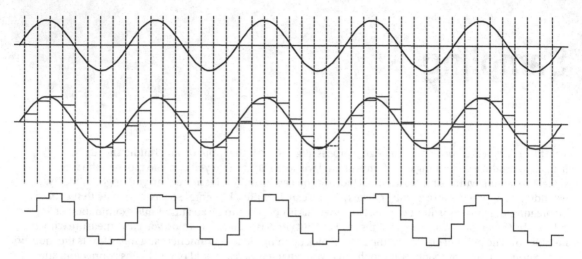

Figure 14-1. *Over-sampling a signal*

The top trace is the input signal and the vertical dotted lines show the sample times. The middle trace shows that the voltage level of the waveform at the time of the sample point is held until the next sample point. The lower trace has the original waveform removed and shows the waveform after sampling.

Take a close look at this lower waveform. Your initial thoughts could be that it looks awful and it is going to sound quite distorted. But in fact it is not so bad as it looks. However, remember what we learned about harmonics. What we have in this waveform is extra harmonics, and because the sample rate is likely to be higher than the maximum a human can hear, these extra harmonics will not be audible. If, due to the sample rate it falls within the audible range then as this distortion is harmonically related to the original signal, it will just sound a little richer. There is one other thing to note here—the sampled waveform is not exactly the same from cycle to cycle. Look especially at the peaks and troughs of the wave—they are not the same from one cycle to the next. This is because the sample rate is not synchronized with the signal that is being sampled, but information theory tells us the original signal can be recovered. It is averaged over several cycles.

There is a distortion inherent in the sampling process, and it is at its maximum when the sample rate is the Nyquist rate. When you get more samples per cycle, the distortion drops off. This is called sample *noise*, and while you can mathematically define it for a fixed waveform at a specific sample rate, it is not a very useful measurement because the ear is insensitive to some aspects of the noise. This is exactly the opposite that the audiophiles would have you believe. The match between sample noise and perceived sample noise does not correlate very well. This is in part due to the ear being less sensitive to distortions in higher frequencies.

Aliasing

There is a problem if you sample your signal at less than the Nyquist rate, which is less often than two samples per cycle. You get what is known as aliasing. This is where the reconstructed waveform is nothing like the original one, but a much lower frequency. This gets worse because a slight change in the frequency of the signal you are sampling gives you a great change in the incorrect frequency of the reconstructed waveform. The result is an awful grating like noise that seems to follow the input and sounds like severe distortion. Worse is that because the false signal is in the frequency band of the signals you are trying to digitize, no amount of filtering will remove it.

Lets see how this comes about. Figure 14-2 shows a wave being sampled at just over once per cycle.

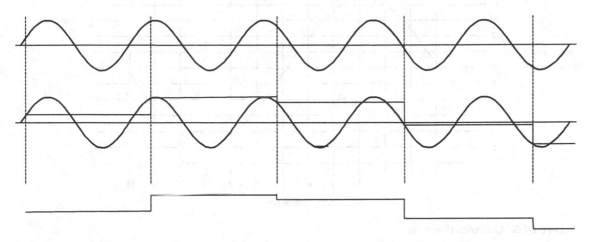

Figure 14-2. *Aliasing*

Figure 14-2 shows the same thing as Figure 14-1. You can see the top trace is the original signal, the middle trace is the voltage sample points being held from one sample time to the next, and the lower trace is the resultant waveform. Notice how the resultant waveform is actually a signal but its period is just over five times longer than the waveform we are trying to sample. You could say at this point the whole process of sampling falls in pieces.

In practice, this only happens at the top of the frequency range. When sampling speech or music, the amount energy that fall above the maximum you can successfully sample is small. Nevertheless, precautions are normally taken to ensure that this does not happen. This is done by using a low-pass filter on the audio input with a cutoff frequency below the Nyquist rate, before the signal gets to the input of the A/D converter. This is called an anti-aliasing filter. Sometimes the frequency response of the amplifiers is such that there is very little energy in these high-frequency regions, and sometimes the sample rate is so high as to be outside the human range of hearing. Still even unwanted ultrasonic signals due to interference on an audio signal can cause aliasing, which will manifest itself as audible interference.

While aliasing is a very bad thing and should be avoided, it is not always necessary to have a specific anti-aliasing filter. Its job could be effectively done by things like poor frequency response on a microphone or amplifier.

Quantization Error

In addition to sample noise, there is another source of distortion you can get when sampling a signal. Whereas sample noise is produced by the act of chopping up time into discrete lumps, the act of measuring the size of the voltage at the sample point is not perfect either, and it's known as the quantization error. Any A/D will convert an input voltage into a number, but while the input voltage is a continuously varying quantity, the number it is converted into is not. It is in discrete increments or steps. The size of these steps is dependent on the resolution of the A/D converter. We specify this resolution in terms of bits, where for N bits in a converter we have 2^N steps. This, in a similar way to the sampling error, causes distortion in the reconstituted signal. This is shown in Figure 14-3.

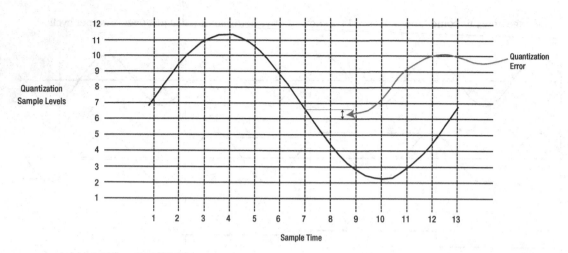

Figure 14-3. *Quantization error*

The sample time is numbered along the bottom and the reading from the A/D along the side. To make it easer to see the number of steps in the signal, height measurement is small. The way an A/D works is that it will return the highest number that the input signal is above. So, for example, at sample 7 in the diagram the number returned from the A/D will only be 6, whereas the voltage of the signal is really about 6.5. This error can be a maximum of just under one bit of A/D resolution. Table 14-1 shows the numbers returned by the A/D for Figure 14-3.

Table 14-1. *Sample Numbers Returned from Figure 14-3*

Sample Time	A/D Reading
1	7
2	9
3	11
4	11
5	10
6	8
7	6
8	4
9	2
10	2
11	2
12	4
13	6

Notice how when the waveform moves slowly—like at the peak and the trough of a sin wave, as in samples 9, 10, and 11—there is no change in what is being measured. This adds to the distortion of the reconstructed wave. This is only the quantization error for a perfect A/D converter. In practice, the step sizes will not be precisely equal, even if we have an A/D with monotonicity. This means that while quantization noise is easy enough to calculate for a perfect A/D, for real A/Ds, it will be greater. In the same way as sample noise, the theoretical noise and the perceived noise are often two different things.

My favorite academic paper ever was in the *American Journal of Audiology*, from some time in the 1960s. It was entitled "The Effects of Alcohol on Perceived Quantization Noise". Subjects were asked to judge the quality of music with precisely measured amounts of quantization noise on them and give them a numeric rating as to the sound quality. They found, to great surprise, that the more alcohol they gave the subjects, the less concerned they were about increasing levels of quantization noise. They also played back horseracing commentaries with differing levels of quantization noise and found people were less critical if they had a money bet on the outcome. Academic life is not always as dull as it is sometimes painted.

Playing Samples

Now that we have seen the theoretical background, it is time to look at some practical projects using samples with an Arduino. While we can record samples of sound on the Arduino, to start with we will look at just playing them back and what that involves. Sound samples are big, so big in fact that the read/write memory in the Arduino Uno is only sufficient for a sample lasting less than a quarter of a second. And that is only achieved by reducing the sampling rate to a meager 8K samples per second. There are ways around this by using the program memory. Even so, we are talking about something slightly over three seconds, but in some circumstances that is enough. We will use the PWM system of outputting sound from the Arduino like we saw in Chapter 12, only this time getting the samples from the program flash memory and outputting them at an 8KHz rate.

Getting the Sample

So what we need first is a way to generate samples, then we need some way of getting those samples into the Arduino's program memory. Most computers and laptops these days have a built-in microphone, an amplifier, and a A/D converter, and many programs allow you to record sounds. The best of the free ones is called Audacity and there are versions from Mac, Windows, and Linux that you can get from http://audacityteam.org/. You can do a lot of things with sounds using this program, but all we want to do here is to record short samples and trim them to size.

Set the sample rate to 8000Hz (project rate), set the recording to mono, and click the round red button to start your recording, then click the solid square to stop. You can play back the recording with the arrow and rewind buttons. Since the space in the Arduino is very limited, you need to trim the wave to minimize the silence at the start and finish. Do this by selecting portions of the wave and pressing the Delete key. When you have a sample you need, save it as a WAV file (choose File ➤ Export Audio). Then, from the Format drop-down menu, chose Other Uncompressed Files and click the Options button. From the window that pops up choose WAV (Microsoft) for the header and Signed 16-Bit PCM for the encoding. Click OK and fill in the file name you want to use. Click Save and then OK without entering any metadata. This will give you the correct format for the next step.

Creating Arduino Code

The next thing to do with this file is create a file of Arduino code ready to drop into your Arduino project. We need to create from this file some C code to define the sound data as individual bytes. While this is simple enough, it is very tedious and so I wrote a Processing program to do this.

The program reads the WAV file and goes through the data looking for the maximum and minimum values in the sound. The sound is stored in 16-bit integers, so these numbers will be positive and negative. We need them as 8-bit values, so the program will work out a scale factor so that the samples span the full range of output values. When you are only dealing with an 8-bit resolution D/A output, you need all the range you can get. Once the samples have been scaled, they are saved as .h files ready to import into the Arduino IDE. Only a rudimentary check is made on the WAV file and the program assumes the data is in the normal file position. This is why you had to save the file in a very specific WAV format version from Audacity. The Processing code to do this is shown in Listing 14-1.

Listing 14-1. Converting a .wav File to an .h File

```
/**
 * Sound Sample - Processing 3
 * by Mike Cook
 *  Converts 16 bit .wav file
 *  into 8 bit .h file for Arduino sample player
 */
PrintWriter output;
String waveName="yes";
String loadPath="blank";
String savePath="blank";

void loadFile(){                                    // load waveform definition from disc
   selectInput("Choose wav file","doLoadFile");  // Opens file chooser
 }

 void doLoadFile(File selection){
     if (selection == null) {
     println("No file was selected...");
   } else {
     loadPath = selection.getAbsolutePath();
     println(loadPath);
     saveFile();     // place to save results
    }
 }

 void saveFile(){   // load waveform definition from disc
   selectOutput("Save converted file","doSaveFile");  // Opens file chooser
 }

void doSaveFile(File selection){
     if (selection == null) {
     println("No file was selected...");
   } else {
     savePath = selection.getAbsolutePath();
      waveName = savePath;
     // nibble away at the path name until we just have the file name
     while(waveName.indexOf('/') != -1) {
        waveName = waveName.substring(1, waveName.length() );
      }
     println("wave name "+waveName);
     convertWave();
 }
}
```

```
void setup()
{
  loadFile();
}

void convertWave(){
  int lsb, msb, a;
  int max=0, min =0;
  float scale;
byte sample[] = loadBytes(loadPath);
if(sample[8] != 87 || sample[9] != 65 ||sample[10] != 86 ||sample[11] != 69){
    println("Error - "+loadPath+" is not a .wav file");
    exit();
 }
// Print each value, from 0 to 255
for (int i = 44; i < sample.length; i +=2) {
  // bytes are from -128 to 127, this converts to 0 to 255
  lsb = sample[i] & 0xff;
  msb = sample[i+1] & 0xff;
  a = lsb | (msb << 8);
  if( (a & 0x8000) != 0) a= a | 0xFFFF0000; // sign extend
  if( a > max) max = a;
  if( a < min) min = a;
  }

println("max = " + max +" min = "+min);
scale = 255.0/((float)max - (float)min);
println("scale - "+ scale);
int dataLength = (sample.length -40) / 2;
println("data length = 0x"+ hex(dataLength)+" or "+dataLength+" bytes");
msb = (dataLength >> 8) & 0xff;
lsb = dataLength & 0xff;

// output the sample file
output = createWriter(savePath+".h");
output.print("const PROGMEM byte "+waveName+"[] = { 0x" + hex((byte)lsb) + ", 0x" +
hex((byte)msb) + ", ");
for (int i = 44; i < sample.length; i +=2) {
    // Every tenth number, start a new line
  if (((i+8) % 20) == 0) {
    output.println();
  }
  // bytes are from -128 to 127, this converts to 0 to 255
  lsb = sample[i] & 0xff;
  msb = sample[i+1] & 0xff;
  a = (lsb | (msb << 8));
  if( (a & 0x8000) != 0) a= a | 0xFFFF0000;
  a = int((float)a * scale) + 128;
  if(a>255) a = 255;
  if(a<0) a = 0;
  output.print("0x"+hex(a).substring(6,8));
```

```
  if(i < sample.length - 2) output.print(", ");
   }
  // finish it off
  output.print(" };");
  output.flush(); // Write the remaining data
  output.close(); // Finish the file
  println("saved at "+savePath+".h");
  exit();
}

void draw(){  }
```

When you run this, you will see first the load file dialog come up. Choose your .wav file and then the place you want to store the .h file. On the console, under the Processing code window, you will see a little information about the file, like the wave name, maximum and minimum values, scale factor, and size of the data, along with the load and save path names. The wave name is taken from the file name and is the name of the array used to store the samples. You can look at this file with a text editor; it will look something like Listing 14-2.

Listing 14-2. A Shortened Version of the .h File

```
const PROGMEM byte yes[] = {  0xFE, 0x0B, 0x81, 0x81, 0x82, 0x82,
0x95, 0xA3, 0x9A, 0x91, 0x95, 0x8B, 0x88, 0x7D, 0x80, 0x76,
0x6E, 0x75, 0x6C, 0x6A, 0x6E, 0x70, 0x6E, 0x71, 0x7A, 0x77,
0x7B, 0x82, 0x82, 0x84, 0x88, 0x8B, 0x88, 0x89, 0x8B, 0x85,
0x84, 0x85, 0x7F, 0x7F, 0x7D, 0x7E, 0x79, 0x7C, 0x72, 0x71,
0x76, 0x65, 0x68, 0x6D, 0x65, 0x6A, 0x6B, 0x76, 0x77, 0x7A,
0x8F, 0x8A, 0x92, 0x9D, 0x9E, 0xA1, 0x9F, 0xA7, 0x9F, 0x9C,
0x80, 0x80, 0x84, 0x7E, 0x80, 0x80, 0x80, 0x81, 0x7E, 0x80,
0x81, 0x7F, 0x84, 0x7D };
```

There are a lot of numbers missing to make up a full sample, but you get the idea of what you will see. This is an array definition for a byte array called yes stored in the program memory of an Arduino. The first two bytes give you the size of the sample so the Arduino knows when it has reached the end. You can store as many samples in the Arduino as you have space for in the program memory, so let's see how to play this file.

Arduino Sample Player

The Arduino sample player uses Timer1 to generate a PWM signal on pin 9 to act as an 8-bit D/A to output the audio. Then Timer2 is used to generate an interrupt at a rate of 8KHz to feed the samples into the PWM generator, which changes the output level on pin 9. The sample is started and stopped by enabling and inhibiting the interrupts on Timer2. When the sample has finished, the ISR will inhibit the interrupts. This gives you full processing power again. You can play the sample in two modes. One is synchronously, where the sample plays until the end and does not let any other processing take place. The other is asynchronously, where the sample is started and the processor can continue doing things. This includes retriggering the sample again from the start in a sort of "Nineteen" effect (song by Paul Hardcastle). There can only be one sample playing at a time, so when a sample is triggered, any sample already playing is stopped before the next is triggered.

While an 8-bit sample with a sample rate of 8KHz is a telephone quality-type of system, it is nevertheless quite remarkable the quality you can get. And while 3 1/2 seconds does not sound so long, the example I show here with a "yes" and "no" sample sound, along with the code to play them, only takes up 23% of the program memory on an Arduino Uno. The Arduino code is shown in Listing 14-3.

Listing 14-3. Arduino Playing Samples

```
// PWM sample player - using Timer 1's PWM as output
// on pin 9 with internal flash memory holding the sample
// By Mike Cook Nov 2015

#include "no.h"  // tab containing samples saying "No"
#include "yes.h" // tab containing samples saying "Yes"

volatile int sampleCount =0;
volatile int sampleLimit =0; // number of bytes in the sample
volatile const byte *sample;
volatile boolean playing = false;
const byte play1Pin = 2, play2Pin = 3;

ISR(TIMER2_COMPB_vect){             // Generate the next sample and send it to the A/D
  sampleCount ++;
  if(sampleCount >= sampleLimit){ // have we finished
    TIMSK2 &= ~_BV(OCIE2B);        // interrupts off
    OCR1AL = 0x80;                 // leave PWM at mid point
    playing=false;
    return;
  }
  OCR1AL = pgm_read_byte_near(&sample[sampleCount]); // use sample to change PWM duty cycle
}

void setPWMtimer(){
// Set timer1 for 8-bit fast PWM output to use as our analogue output
 TCCR1B = _BV(CS10);      // Set prescaler to full 16MHz
 TCCR1A |= _BV(COM1A1); // Pin low when TCNT1=OCR1A
 TCCR1A |= _BV(WGM10);  // Use 8-bit fast PWM mode
 TCCR1B |= _BV(WGM12);
 OCR1AL = 0x80;           // start PWM going at half maximum
}

void setSampleTimer(){              // sets timer 2 going at the output sample rate
  TCCR2A = _BV(WGM21) | _BV(WGM20);   // Disable output on Pin 11 and Pin 3
  TCCR2B = _BV(WGM22) | _BV(CS22);
  OCR2A = 250; // defines the interval to trigger the sample generation - 125uS or 8.0KHz
  TCCR2B = TCCR2B & 0b00111000 | 0x2; // select a prescale value of 8:1 of the system clock
  TIMSK2 = _BV(OCIE2B);               // Output Compare Match B Interrupt Enable
}

void setup() {
  pinMode(9, OUTPUT); // Make timer's PWM pin an output
  pinMode(play1Pin,INPUT_PULLUP);
  pinMode(play2Pin,INPUT_PULLUP);
  setSampleTimer();
  setPWMtimer();
}
```

```
void loop() {                    // play samples on grounding pins
  if(!digitalRead(play1Pin)){
    playSample(&yes[0],true); // start playing and then return
  }
  if(!digitalRead(play2Pin)){
    playSample(&no[0],false); // only return when finished playing sample
  }
}

void playSample(const byte *toPlay, boolean aysync){
    TIMSK2 &= ~_BV(OCIE2B); // stop any playing
    sample = toPlay;
    sampleLimit = pgm_read_byte_near(&toPlay[0]) | (pgm_read_byte_near(&toPlay[1]) << 8);
    sampleCount =1;
    playing = true;
    TIMSK2 = _BV(OCIE2B);   // allow interrupts
    if( !aysync ) {         // play sample till the end if not aysync
        while(playing) { } // hold until finished
    }
}
```

Most of this code should be pretty familiar if you followed the examples in Chapters 11 and 12. Timer2 is set to go off at 125uS intervals triggering the ISR function. Here the samples are fetched from program memory and fed to the PWM generator in Timer1. Note the array containing the samples is not hard-coded like you might expect, because the pointer sample is set up before playing so the code knows where to fetch the samples from.

Not only do you have to have this listing, but you also need the code containing the samples. This code is placed into an extra tab in the code window by selecting the menu Sketch ➤ Add File and then finding the .h file you made with the Processing program. The two #include lines at the top of the code should reflect the actual name of the .h files you are using along with the parameters used in the calls to playSample. These two samples are played by grounding one of the two play sample pins.

Note the behavior of the two methods of playing the samples. If you press and hold down the button connected to the play2Pin and ground you will get a repeated playing of the complete word "no". Whereas if you press and hold down the play1Pin button, you will hear nothing until you release the button. This is not strange if you think about it, because you trigger the sound and set it playing, then next time around the loop the button is still seen to be pressed. The code stops the playing of the sample and starts it again. As the loop goes around much faster than the samples can be output, the result is that nothing is heard until the button is released.

You can use this system in any of your projects and, with careful juggling of program code and sample length, it should be quite flexible.

More Samples

In order to get more samples, you need to provide some extra storage space. An SD card provides the ideal answer. It can be loaded with sounds on your computer and then transferred to the Arduino system for playing in a standalone project. An ideal introduction to this is to use a commercially available product. One of the simplest, with lots of support and example projects, is the Wave Shield produced by AdaFruit at https://learn.adafruit.com/adafruit-wave-shield-audio-shield-for-arduino. This is available as a kit, or already assembled, and it slots nicely over the input pins on an Arduino Uno.

The web site contains an exhaustive tutorial on how to set it up and use it, so there is no point in going over that again here. Instead I want to show you a project I made using this shield to make a MIDI sample player. The idea is simple—a MIDI input interface is used to feed the serial input of the Arduino, and then the MIDI messages are parsed to get the MIDI note number. Each note number triggers a sample of the same name and if a sample is already playing the new sample takes over. Rather like the standalone system we have just seen, but with more samples. The Wave Shield is open source, which means that you can make your own version if you like. The basic block diagram is shown in Figure 14-4.

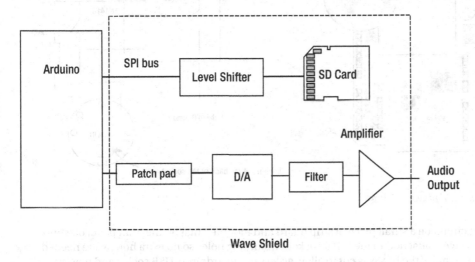

Figure 14-4. *The block diagram of the Wave Shield*

You will see that there are two main components—the SD card and the A/D converter. The SD card is fixed to the SPI bus, but the A/D converter can be wired to any pins through a small patch area on the shield. Unfortunately, the A/D converter cannot use the SPI bus because, while it is electrically compatible, when the SD card is disabled in order to use the A/D, this has the side effect of closing file that was open on the SD card. In other words, it would not hold its place reading out the file and you would have to open the file again, read through it, and find the right location for the next sample. The SD card is simply not fast enough to do this.

Instead, the A/D is talked to by bit-banging the pins connected to it. This is manipulating the individual bits connected to the A/D to emulate an SPI bus. It is slower than using dedicated hardware, but is fast enough for outputting an audio sample.

The circuit of the MIDI sample player is simple enough. First of all we need a MIDI input circuit. This was covered in Chapter 2 and the circuit shown in Figure 2-7 fits the bill nicely. Then we need an Arduino a Wave Shield, loud speaker, and a box. The schematic is shown in Figure 14-5.

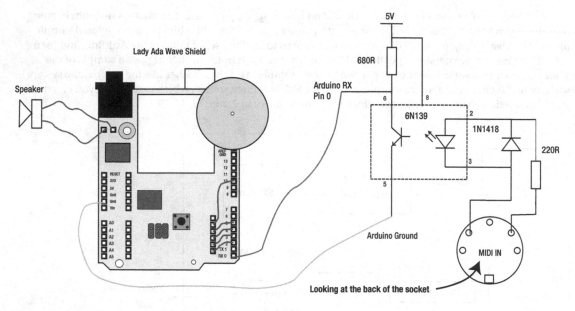

Figure 14-5. *MIDI sample player wiring*

I made the input circuit on a small piece of strip board and mounted that on the front panel on short stand-off pillars. These were attached to the MIDI socket's mounting holes so no extra holes were needed in the panel. The back panel of the box was cut to allow access to the Arduino's USB socket and power jack, and the Wave Shield's audio output, volume control, and SD card. As well as having the MIDI DIN socket, I also used a 3-inch loud speaker and drilled a decorative pattern of holes in the box. The front panel just contained a label I made from a printout of a computer drawing. I used spray glue to attach it to the aluminum panel and then gave it a coat of clear varnish to seal the ink in the paper. A photograph of my finished project is shown in Figure 14-6.

Figure 14-6. *The finished MIDI sampler*

In order to run this, the Arduino must be programmed with the code in Listing 14-4.

Listing 14-4. MIDI Sample Player Code

```
/*
   MIDI to sample player by Mike Cook Nov 2015
   This will take a byte from the serial port and play the sample corresponding to the MIDI
   note on number
   so for example if it receives a note on 34 it will play the sample file named 34.WAV
*/
#include <FatReader.h>
#include <SdReader.h>
#include "WaveUtil.h"
#include "WaveHC.h"

SdReader card;     // This object holds the information for the card
FatVolume vol;     // This holds the information for the partition on the card
FatReader root;    // This holds the information for the filesystem on the card
FatReader f;       // This holds the information for the file we're play
WaveHC wave;       // This is the only wave (audio) object, since we will only play one at a
time

// ************ Global variables  *******************
        byte incomingByte;
        byte notePlaying; // MIDI note currently playing > 128 == note off
        byte note;
        byte velocity;
```

371

```
            int noteDown = LOW;
            char toPlay[11];      // string array for file to play 00.WAV to 99999.WAV
  static int indexToWrite=0;      // For the recursive name generator
            int state=0;          // state machine variable 0 = command waiting : 1 = note
            waitin : 2 = velocity waiting
            int channel = 0;      // MIDI channel to respond to (in this case channel 1) change
            this to change the channel number
                                  // MIDI channel = the value in 'channel' + 1

void sdErrorCheck(void)
{ // freeze if there is an error
  if (!card.errorCode()) return;
  while(1);
}

void setup() {
  Serial.begin(31250);  // MIDI rate
  // Set the output pins for the DAC control.
  pinMode(2, OUTPUT);
  pinMode(3, OUTPUT);
  pinMode(4, OUTPUT);
  pinMode(5, OUTPUT);

  //  if (!card.init(true)) { //play with 4 MHz spi if 8MHz isn't working for you
  if (!card.init()) {          //play with 8 MHz spi (default faster!)
      sdErrorCheck();
  }
    card.partialBlockRead(true);

// Now we will look for a FAT partition!
  uint8_t part;
  for (part = 0; part < 5; part++) {     // we have up to 5 slots to look in
    if (vol.init(card, part))
      break;                             // we found one, lets bail
  }
  if (part == 5) {                       // if we ended up not finding one  :(
    while(1);                            // then 'halt' - do nothing!
  }
  if (!root.openRoot(vol)) { // Try to open the root directory
    while(1);                  // Something went wrong,
  }
  playfile("init.WAV");      // play a start up sound
}

void loop () {

  if (Serial.available() > 0) {      // read the incoming byte
    incomingByte = Serial.read();
    // add it to the MIDI message
```

```
    switch (state){
        case 0:  // looking for a fresh command
            if (incomingByte== (144 | channel)){   // is it a note on for our channel
            noteDown = HIGH;
            state=1; // move on to look the note to play in the next byte
            }
        if (incomingByte== (128 | channel)){ // is it a note off for our channel
            noteDown = LOW;
            state=1; // move on to look the note to stop in the next byte
            }
        case 1:
        // get the note to play or stop
        if(incomingByte < 128) {  // have we got a note number
            note=incomingByte;
            state=2;
        }
        else{     // no note number so message is screwed reset to look for a note on for
                  next byte
        state = 0;  // reset state machine as this should be a note number
        }
        break;
        case 2:
        // get the velocity
        if(incomingByte < 128) {                // is it an off velocity
            playNote(note, incomingByte, noteDown); // fire off the sample
        }
            state = 0;  // reset state machine to start
        }
    }
}

void playNote(byte note, byte velocity, int down){
    // if velocity = 0 on a 'Note ON' command, treat it as a note off
    if ((down == HIGH) && (velocity == 0)){
        down = LOW;
        }
    if(down == LOW && notePlaying == note) {
        wave.stop();       // stop it if it is the current note
        notePlaying = 255; // indicate no note is playing
        }
    if(down == HIGH) {    // play a sample with the file name based on the note number
        makeName(note,0);   // generate file name in global array toPlay
        notePlaying = note; // save note number for future stop testing
        playfile(toPlay);   // play it
        }
}
```

```
void makeName(int number, int depth){
// generates a file name 0.WAV to 9999.WAV suppressing leading zeros
  if(number > 9) {
    makeName(number / 10, ++depth); // recursion
    depth--;
    number = number % 10;   // only have to deal with the next significant digit of the
    number
    }
  toPlay[indexToWrite] = (number & 0xf) | 0x30;
  indexToWrite++;
  if(depth > 0) return; // return if we have more levels of recursion to go
  else {                 // finish off the string with the wave extension
    toPlay[indexToWrite] = '.';
    toPlay[1+indexToWrite] = 'W';
    toPlay[2+indexToWrite] = 'A';
    toPlay[3+indexToWrite] = 'V';
    toPlay[4+indexToWrite] = '\0'; // terminator
    indexToWrite = 0;              // reset pointer for next time we enter
  }
}

void playfile(char *name) {
  // see if the wave object is currently doing something
  if (wave.isplaying) wave.stop();   // something is already playing, so stop it
  // look in the root directory and open the file
    f.open(root, name);
    if (!wave.create(f)) return; // Not a valid WAV
    wave.play();                 // start playback
}
```

The MIDI input code will be familiar if you have read the first few chapters of the book. It takes the MIDI input, parses it, and gets the note on number. There is nothing we can do with the velocity or volume parameter, as all samples are played at the same volume.

What is new here is the makeName function. This uses a technique called *recursion* to convert a number into a name. Recursion involves a function calling itself, which is dangerous if it is not written correctly because you might never be able to climb out of the function. While it is debatable if you need to use recursion here, it is nevertheless interesting, efficient, and quick. Basically using recursion the code only has to cope with the numbers 0 to 9. If the number is any bigger, you just divide by 10 and call the function again. This keeps on going until the number is below 10 and then that is added to the string. Finally the .wav extension is added and the number is converted to a file name.

The playfile function simply stops any file from playing and starts a new one. You can use this as a MIDI sound generator for any of the projects in this book as well as your own.

Even More Samples

While the Wave Shield is an excellent product, I want to finish the chapter with a product that combines the function of a Wave Shield with the Arduino and then throws in quite a bit more. This is the Bare Conductive Touch Board, made by the sample people who make the conducting ink I used in the Spoon-o-Phone project in Chapter 5. This board is released under the official "Arduino at Heart" schema, whereby manufacturers can use the basic Arduino core IDE and infrastructure and add their own twist to it. This board started out as a Kickstarter campaign that I backed and I must say I was most impressed with the results.

What you have is an Arduino based on the 32u4 chip (like the Leonardo); it has a compatible pin out, but with no connectors attached. In addition, there is a 12 input touch sensor incorporated into the board along with a micro SD card reader and a VS10538 chip. This amazing chip can play MP3 files and can act as a complete general MIDI sound generator. Being a 32u4 processor chip, the board can also be made to look like a USB MIDI device. There is a lot to explore with this board and I suspect I could write a whole book about it some day. The board is shown in Figure 14-7.

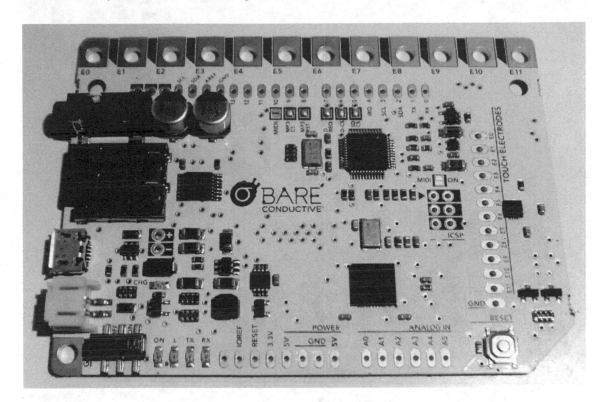

Figure 14-7. *The bare conducting's touch board*

The unexpectedly great thing about it is the initial presentation with great packaging and a fully working system programmed to give you instructions as soon as you connect it to speakers and a power source. The touch contacts are the pads at the top of the board labeled E0 to E11. You touch each one in turn for your spoken introduction to the board.

This means that right out of the box it is a sample player triggered by the touch sensors and you can make a project with it straight away. This is what I did.

First of all, I got a piece of cardboard about 14 by 6 inches, placed my hands, on it and drew an outline of my fingers. Then at the tip of each finger I pushed a paper fastener and soldered a wire to each one on the underside. Then I mounted the touch board onto the edge of the cardboard with some M3 nuts bolts and washers and connected each paper fastener wire to a separate touch sensor by wrapping the wire under the head of the bolt. I used hot-glue to fix the wires on the underside and stop them from moving about. This is important for the calibration of the touch sensors.

Finally, I got some MP3 samples on an SD card and named them "Track000" to "Track009" and I had a touch sample player. The first time you power it up, you need to press the Reset button to allow the touch sensors to calibrate. You need to adjust for the new wires on the touch sensors, and then you are good to go. A photograph of the final project, and friend, is shown in Figure 14-8.

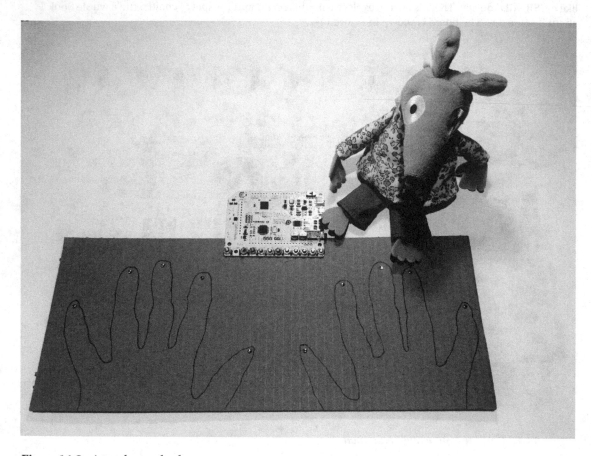

Figure 14-8. *A touch sample player*

CHAPTER 15

■■■ ■

Audio Effects

Having seen how you can use the Arduino for playing back samples, it's a good time to explore using the Arduino for doing some signal processing. This is where the Arduino takes in sound, manipulates it in some way, and then outputs the sound, all as a continuous process. While the lack of read/write memory on the Arduino Uno severely limits what can be done in this respect, with the addition of a few extra chips, you can create many startling audio effects.

First Build Your Sound Card

Before you can begin to explore how you can manipulate sound, you have to build the extra parts needed to give the Arduino the required memory storage and audio input/output capabilities.

You can't add memory that can be used to store variables and arrays with the C language, but you can add what is known as *paged* memory. You saw an example of this paged memory in the SpoonDuino project in Chapter 13. The main difference is that you have to explicitly handle memory address allocation. For example, in C if you declare a variable and give it a name, the compiler looks after allocating a memory address to store this in and makes sure no other variable uses that same address. With paged memory, your program code has to explicitly do this. So, for example, the SpoonDuino project divided the EEPROM storage into a number of "slots" to store the wave tables and its name.

For this project, you do not need permanent memory but fast access read/write memory to act as a buffer, to hold samples so that you can manipulate them. You also need to add an A/D converter as well as an input and output amplifier. In addition, in order to be able to switch between different effects, I have included a hex switch on the board. This connects to four pins and is a rotary switch with 16 positions. The block diagram of the board is shown in Figure 15-1. Note that each block is referenced to the full schematic of that block.

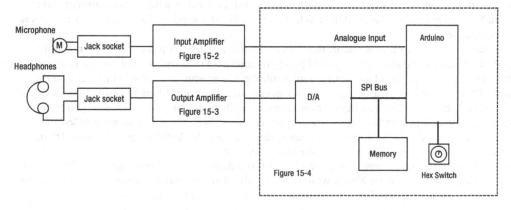

Figure 15-1. *Sound card block diagram*

377

Amplifiers

The sound card uses headphones with a built-in microphone, rather like the ones used in call centers. Surprisingly enough, these were the cheapest type of headphones in my local thrift shop. The sound card needs amplifiers to drive the headphones and to amplify the microphone signal up to the 5V needed to drive the Arduino's internal A/D converter. The schematic of the input amplifier is shown in Figure 15-2.

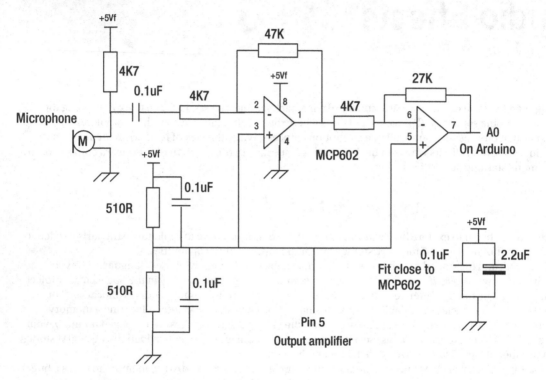

Figure 15-2. *The input amplifier*

The circuit is a two-stage amplifier using the MCP602 op-amp (operational amplifier). There are two op-amps in a package and it will work happily off 5V, in addition it is close to being rail to rail. That last bit refers to how close the output can come to the supply rails and this chip offers a linear maximum of within 0.1V of each rail. You can get within 40mV of the rail but that last little bit is not linear. Given the price, this is a very good specification.

The gain of an inverting amplifier is simply the ratio of the two resistors so you can see that the first stage has a gain of 10 and the second stage a gain of 5.7 so the total gain is the product of the two giving a gain of 57. This suited the output that I got from my microphone. If you want to change it I would alter the feedback resistor (27K) of the second amplifier. The positive input of both amplifiers is connected to a virtual signal ground, which is created by two 510R resistors, with decoupling capacitors across them. This virtual ground is also used by the output amplifier and goes to that circuit as well. The microphone is AC coupled through a 0.1uF capacitor. Note the 5V supply is not taken directly from the Arduino, but it is filtered first, hence the suffix f. The filtering circuit is shown in the last schematic.

Although the MCP602 is not a power amplifier, there is more than enough current output to drive some headphones. The output short circuit is 22mA, which is below the absolute current rating for the chip, so the headphones will not overload the amplifier. The output amplifier is shown in Figure 15-3.

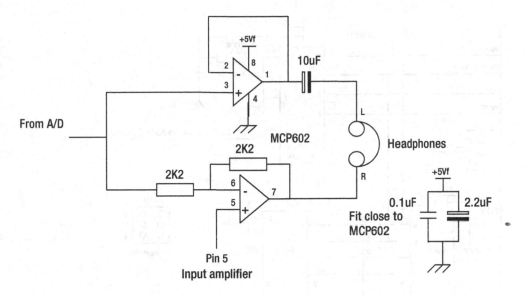

Figure 15-3. The output amplifier

This circuit might seem odd at first but it is driving the headphones with a differential signal. The ground is not connected on the output jack socket, just the left and right signals. The signal is taken from the A/D and sent to an inverting and a non-inverting amplifier both with a gain of 1. This ensures a full 10V swing at the headphones from just a 5V supply, giving the maximum volume. The 10uF capacitor ensures that DC is kept out of the headphones. Both input and output amplifiers should have a 0.1uF ceramic capacitor fitted to the power rail close to the chip. The data sheet says for best results this has to be within 2mm of the chip and the 2.2uF within 100mm. Using a surface mount ceramic capacitor means you can solder it directly onto the pins under the board.

The Digital Circuit

The remaining part of the sound card board is shown in Figure 15-4 and contains the memory, A/D, reconstruction filter, hex switch, and the power supply filtering.

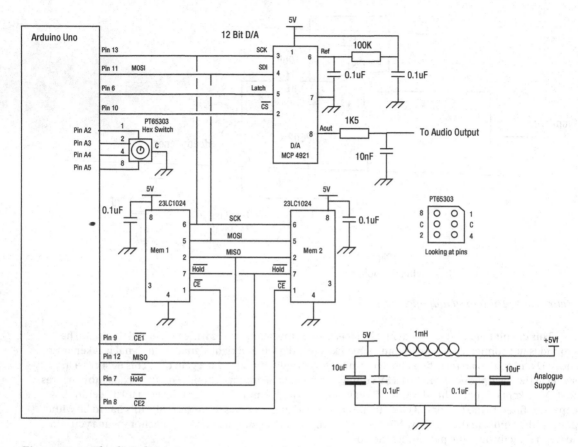

Figure 15-4. *The digital circuit*

The power filter circuit takes the 5V from the Arduino pin and filters it to reduce digital noise of the supply. It does this by using what is known as a *pi circuit*. The output of the filter is marked 5Vf and feeds the amplifier circuits. The value of the inductor is not too critical, just fit as big an inductor as you have space for. The amount of current it has to take is negligible and you will struggle to find an inductor that will not take that current. This sort of filter is known as a *pi filter*. The 0.1uF capacitors should be ceramic and handle the high frequencies, whereas the larger values are again not too critical and can be any capacitor type.

The 23LC1024 are 1Mbit memory chips organized as 128K by eight bits, so the two shown here will give you a total of 256K of memory. It is not necessary to have both chips fitted and I did most of my work here with only one chip fitted. This memory is attached to the SPI bus and shares it with the 12-bit A/D converter. The hex switch is a 16 position, four-bit rotary switch that will output a binary representation of the switch position. This is connected to four of the analogue inputs, but in the code these are just being used as normal digital inputs. There are many types of switches that give either 16 or 10 positions from a small knob to screwdriver adjustment.

Construction

I built the circuit on a strip board in the form of a shield. I used long double-sided header pins and bent over the pins for the digital connections eight and upward to cope with the extra 0.05-inch spacing on that row of connectors. I always use sockets whenever possible when using ICs and this allowed me the option of not fitting the second memory chip. Photographs of the construction are shown in Figure 15-5.

Figure 15-5. *The physical board*

Using the Sound Card

Now the A/D converter in the Arduino takes 25 clock cycles to do the first conversion and 13 clock cycles to do subsequent conversions. These are clock cycles fed to the A/D converter and are derived from the system clock through a prescale divider circuit. This is normally set to divide by 128, and with a normal Arduino system clock of 16MHz gives an A/D clock of 125KHz. That means you can get a sample rate of 125,000/13 = 9615 samples a second. However, by adjusting this prescale divider you can get it to go much faster. The data sheet warns about driving the A/D with a rate faster than 200KHz to get the full resolution from the converter but goes on to say that frequencies up to 1 MHz do not reduce the ADC resolution significantly. This gives you the green light to change the prescale divide ratio to divide by 16 and get a sample rate of just under 77K samples per second. Of course, this is only the speed you can read the A/D converter; you have to do something with that reading and that will take time as well. The number of samples you can process per second is going to be much less than this.

Basically, what you have here in the sound card is a small record/playback system; readings can be taken from the Arduino's internal 10-bit A/D converter and transferred to the 12-bit D/A output. Of course that will not be very exciting but it is a simple test of the system. The simple test is shown in Listing 15-1.

Listing 15-1. Simple Input/Output

```
// simple input / output - Mike Cook
#include <SPI.h>

#define CS1_BAR 9
#define CS2_BAR 8
#define CS_ADC_BAR 10
#define AD_LATCH 6
#define Hold_BAR 7

void setup() {
  // initialize control pins for SRAM
  pinMode( CS1_BAR, OUTPUT);
  digitalWrite( CS1_BAR, HIGH);
  pinMode( CS2_BAR, OUTPUT);
  digitalWrite( CS2_BAR, HIGH);
  pinMode( CS_ADC_BAR, OUTPUT);
  digitalWrite(CS_ADC_BAR, HIGH);
  pinMode( AD_LATCH, OUTPUT);
```

```
  digitalWrite(AD_LATCH, HIGH);
  pinMode( Hold_BAR, OUTPUT);
  digitalWrite( Hold_BAR, HIGH);

   SPI.begin();
   SPI.setDataMode(SPI_MODE3);
   SPI.setClockDivider(SPI_CLOCK_DIV2); // 8MHz clock this is the maximum clock speed
   // set up fast ADC mode
   ADCSRA = (ADCSRA & 0xf8) | 0x04;      // set 16 times division
   pinMode(2,OUTPUT);                    // for monitering sample rate
 }

void loop(){
  static int sampleIn;
  sampleIn = analogRead(0); // replace with statement below
  //sampleIn = analogRead(0) << 2;
  ADwrite(sampleIn);
  PORTD ^= 0x4;             // toggle pin each sample to check sample rate
   }

void ADwrite(int data){
 // digitalWrite(CS_ADC_BAR, LOW);   - direct addressing below
  PORTB &= ~0x4;
  SPI.transfer(((data >> 8) & 0x0f) | 0x70);
  SPI.transfer(data & 0xff);
  //digitalWrite(CS_ADC_BAR, HIGH);   - direct addressing below
  PORTB |= 0x4;
  //digitalWrite(AD_LATCH, LOW);   - direct addressing below
  PORTD &= ~0x40;
  //digitalWrite(AD_LATCH, HIGH);   - direct addressing below
  PORTD |= 0x40;
}
```

The code starts of by initializing the SPI pins for the A/D and the memory, although the memory is not used here. The setup function starts of the SPI bus and sets its speed to the maximum of 8MHz. The internal A/D speeds up by setting a 16 times division ratio.

The loop function then simply takes a reading from the A/D and outputs it to the D/A. This last job is done by the ADwrite function, which splits the data passed to it into two bytes and sends them along the SPI bus to the A/D. The chip enable and latching signals are sent by direct port access to the chip but the equivalent write commands as shown as comments. Finally with each sample processed, pin 2 is toggled. This is so that I can look at this pin on an oscilloscope and check the sample rate the program is producing. For this program, it clocks in at a very credible 44.6KHz sample rate.

There is a bit of a mismatch between the A/D and the D/A converters—you have 10 bits on the input and 12 bits on the output. As it stands, this will produce a signal that is a quarter of the maximum the D/A is capable of producing. If you replace the sample reading instruction with the commented out one below it, you effectively multiply the input by four, which makes it louder. Of course, this also makes the noise louder, but what you might not spot is that the signal's DC level also shifts to the middle of the range. This is an important thing to be aware of at times, like in the next project.

Exterminate

Now, while that code might not be so exciting there is a way to make it a lot more interesting. The second story of the then new TV program *Dr. Who* involved the Daleks with their electronically altered voices. This fascinated the 12-year-old me, and I soon found myself making a ring modulator to emulate them. With a few extra lines of code, you can make the previous listing into a ring modulator.

A ring modulator simply multiplies two signals together. The signals generated are both the sum and difference of the two signals. The name "ring modulator" was derived from how the circuit looked using audio transformers to do the modulation. The Daleks used a sin wave at 30Hz modulated with the voice signal. A slightly easier way to generate it is using a triangle waveform. It sounds much the same. So to make a Dalek voice changer, take the previous listing and replace the loop function with the code in Listing 15-2.

Listing 15-2. The Dalek Voice Changer

```
float mod = 0.5;
float increment =  0.0035;
int sampleIn, sampleOut;
int midPoint = 2048;

 void loop(){
   // make triangle wave
    mod += increment;
     if(mod > 0.90 || mod < 0.02) {
        increment = -increment;
        mod += increment;
     }
   sampleIn = (analogRead(0) <<2 ) -midPoint;
   sampleOut = (float)sampleIn * mod;
   ADwrite(sampleOut + midPoint);
   PORTD ^= 0x4; // toggle pin each sample to check sample rate
   }
```

Note the use of floating point variables. This slows things down a lot and is not normally used, but in this program you still have a sample rate of just over 16.5KHz so it is not too bad. The variable mod ramps between 0.9 and 0.02 by having a small increment added or subtracted on each sample transfer. These limits are easily changed by changing the numbers in the if statement. They test for the end of the range of the modulation variable. The size of the increment along with the time it takes to go once around the loop determines the frequency of modulation. While you could calculate this, I just looked at the output on an oscilloscope and tweaked the values until I got close to 30Hz.

The input sample is brought up to 12 bits by the shift and then it is turned into a positive/negative number by subtracting the midpoint value from it. This makes the sample range over +/- 2047 (close enough) and then multiplying by the modulation variable gives you a ring modulated "Dalek" sample. Finally, adding the midpoint value back into the sample before outputting it brings up the DC level to the midpoint of the D/A's output. Figure 15-6 shows an oscilloscope trace of a modulated whistle.

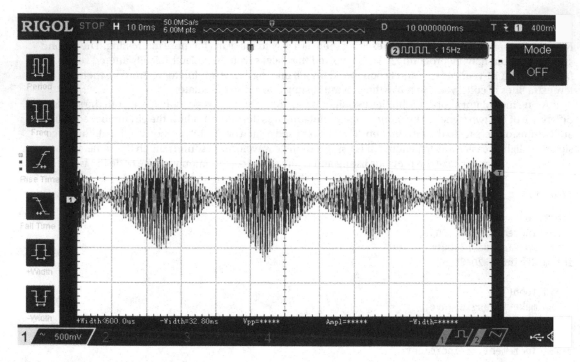

Figure 15-6. *Modulated whistle*

You might like to try changing the modulation depth by altering the ranging values in the `if` statement. You might also want to experiment with different wave shapes of modulation, like a sin wave by using a lookup table in place of generating the triangle wave, just like you did in Chapter 12.

More Effects

With the addition the extra memory, you can produce all sorts of effects. Much of the code is common to all effects, like the access to the D/A, memory, and setup. What I will to do is to look at each effect, and the short code you need to achieve it, and then bring them all together at the end of the chapter as a full listing.

But before that, you have to understand an important concept, that of FIFO memory. FIFO stands for first in, first out. That is, you place as many samples as you like into a memory buffer, and when you pull them out, the first sample you get out is the first sample you put in. In theory, what happens is that you put a sample into the input of FIFO and it shuffles along until it reaches the output and sits there waiting to be extracted. Additional sample inputs shuffle up and form an orderly queue behind the first. When one sample is extracted, the remaining samples shuffle up to fill the newly vacated space. This is shown in Figure 15-7.

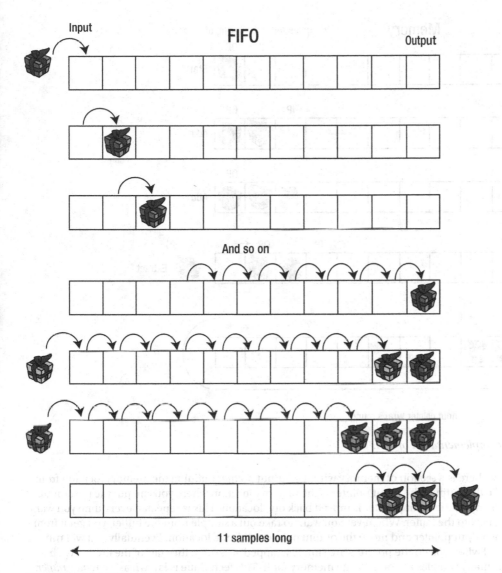

Figure 15-7. A FIFO

This forms the backbone of all the effects in this section. However, while this is the concept of how a FIFO works, it is very time consuming to implement this in practice. All that moving memory contents from one place to the next takes a lot of time, especially when you can turn the concept on its head and still have the same effect. Instead of having a fixed input and output location in the memory and shuffling the data from the input to the output, the data stays where it is and you move where you consider the input and output to be. This is shown in Figure 15-8.

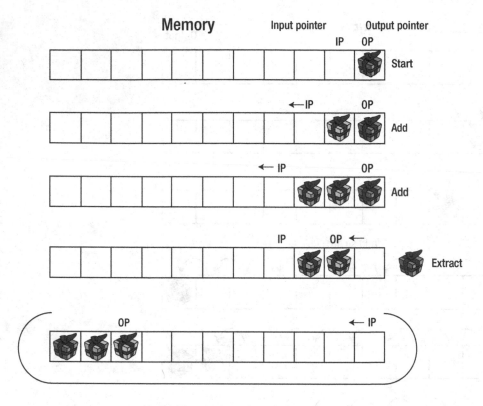

Figure 15-8. *The implementation of a FIFO*

What you have here is a section of memory with the output pointer defining the memory location from where you can take the output. The input pointer is the memory location where you can put the next input. As a new sample is input, the input pointer is moved back one location. This is repeated every time you want to add something new to the buffer. Whenever you want to take out a sample from the buffer, you get it from the location in the output pointer and move the output pointer back one location. Eventually you will run out of memory, and when you do the pointers are simply wrapped around to the start of the memory. The buffer can hold as many samples as you allocate memory for it. This technique is known as a *circular buffer*.

There are a few ways of implementing this; here the input pointer points to the next free space and the output pointer to the next output. However, note that when the input pointer is at the same place as the output pointer, the buffer is empty. Also when moving the input pointer to point at the next free space, if it becomes the same as the output buffer, the buffer is full and normally you don't move the input pointer and samples can be lost. If you did move the pointer, the whole buffer would be lost. As long as the buffer doesn't overflow, it all works fine.

Delay

The simplest effect is just a delay, which might not sound too exciting, but it can be quite funny and also therapeutic. If you feed back what a person says, with a small delay, then it can almost destroy their ability to talk. What happens is that the brain waits for the feedback and so delays saying the next word. Get someone to read a nursery rhyme from a written sheet and I guarantee that 99% of them will say the first line normally and then become all tongue tied. I have tried this at various Maker shows and it always induces a great laugh.

There is a serious side too. It can be used in training people with a stutter to ignore the feedback, and so minimize their stutter. Many people find speaking with a delayed feedback a lot easier than once was the case. This is due to mobile phones having a slight echo on the line and people, especially when they have worked in call centers, having learned to cope with this. In all the many hundreds of people who have tried my delay one stands out. She complained that it was not working, but all her friends assured her that it was. She could not perceive any delay and had no problem speaking with it on. I have no idea if this is a gift or a handicap; I suspect some researchers might be interested in what is going on in her brain.

In order to understand what you need to do to implement this, it is simplest to look at a diagram of the buffer, which is shown in Figure 15-9.

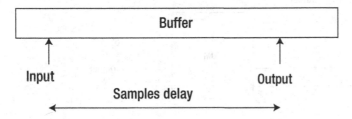

Figure 15-9. The delay algorithm

What you have here is the input buffer and the output buffer tied together. Whenever you put a sample into the buffer, you take one out. The distance between the input and output pointers coupled with the sample rate give you the delay in seconds. Note here the input and output pointers are moving from right to left. The code fragment to implement this is shown in Listing 15-3.

Listing 15-3. Simple Delay

```
void basicDelay(){  // loop time 48.2uS - sample rate 20.83 KHz
   static unsigned int bufferIn=bufferSize, bufferOut=bufferSize - bufferOffset, sample;
   while(1){
      sample = analogRead(0);
      saveSample(bufferIn, sample);
      sample = fetchSample(bufferOut);
      ADwrite(sample);
      bufferIn++;
      if(bufferIn > bufferSize) bufferIn=0;
      bufferOut++;
      if(bufferOut > bufferSize) bufferOut=0;
   }
}
```

Remember this is a code fragment and needs other functions to make it run, but you can easily see the idea. The length of the delay is set by the bufferOffset variable and is the number of samples between the input and output pointers. A sample is read from the A/D and saved at the location given by the bufferIn variable. Then a sample is taken from the memory from a location given in the bufferOut variable and sent to the A/D converter. Finally, the two pointers are incremented and, if either exceeds the total buffer size, they are wrapped around back to zero.

The bufferOffset variable is set from the outside and can implement different lengths of delay, up to the maximum size of the memory you have.

Echo

The echo effect is a bit more than just a delay; it is a delay mixed with the current input. Normally with an echo the delay is small, and when it is very small it sounds more like reverberation. Figure 15-10 shows the algorithm for an echo with three reflections.

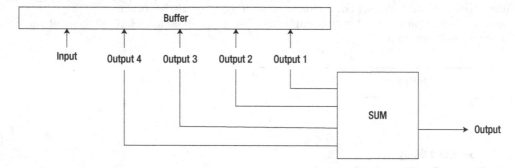

Figure 15-10. *Echo*

What you see here is one input pointer but four output pointers. You can have as many or few output pointers as you like. All the buffer pointers are all tied together so there is a fixed delay between each output pointer. The contents of all the pointers are summed together to give the final output. There is a wide variety of echo-like effects you can get with different spacing between the pointers, and I encourage you to experiment with them. A large distance gives a repeat effect where a word or phrase is repeated. As they get closer, it becomes more of an echo and, closer still, it becomes a reverberation. They don't even have to be spaced the same difference apart either. The code fragment to do this is shown in Listing 15-4.

Listing 15-4. Implementing an Echo

```
void echo4(){  // loop time 95.2uS - sample rate 10.5KHz
  // set up the initial position of the buffer pointers
   static int sample;
   static long bufferIn=bufferSize, bufferOut1=bufferSize - bufferOffset;
   static long bufferOut2=bufferSize - bufferOffset2, bufferOut3=bufferSize - bufferOffset3;
   static long bufferOut4=bufferSize - bufferOffset4;
 while(1){
    sample = analogRead(0);
    saveSample(bufferIn, sample);
    sample = fetchSample(bufferOut1);
    sample += fetchSample(bufferOut2);
    sample += fetchSample(bufferOut3);
    sample += fetchSample(bufferOut4);
    sample = sample >> 2; // so as to keep the gain down to 1 to avoid build up of noise
    ADwrite(sample); // output sample
    // adjust the buffer pointers
    bufferIn++;
    if(bufferIn > bufferSize) bufferIn=0;
    bufferOut1++;
    if(bufferOut1 > bufferSize) bufferOut1=0;
    bufferOut2++;
    if(bufferOut2 > bufferSize) bufferOut2=0;
```

```
    bufferOut3++;
    if(bufferOut3 > bufferSize) bufferOut3=0;
    bufferOut4++;
    if(bufferOut4 > bufferSize) bufferOut4=0;
  }
}
```

The buffer pointer is first set up according to the buffer size and offsets defined as global variables in the main program. Then a sample is read in and saved into the buffer. Then the sample at each of the four output pointers is fetched and summed. Then the sum is divided by four in order to keep the total gain down below one. If this were not done, then the noise in the system would ensure a full-blooded feedback howl. Finally, the buffer pointers are all incremented and wrapped around if necessary.

This effect is great fun for emulating station announcements that come from multiple speakers along the platform making them very difficult to hear. Announcements such as:

"The train now standing at platforms 5, 6, and 7, has come in sideways."

"Will passengers who have taken the 6:15 to Queens please return it, as the driver is worried."

"The train now standing in the booking office comes—as a complete surprise."

"The train now standing on platform 2 will soon be on the rails again."

I'll get my coat.

Pitch Up

This is a simulation of helium breathing where your voice goes up in pitch but does not speed up. In other words, a real-time pitch shifter. This requires a new technique with the buffer's input and output pointers. Instead of them being locked together, the output pointer is moving at twice the speed of the input pointer. If the buffer is very short, in the order of a few cycles of audio, this has the effect of doubling the output frequency. The algorithm for this is shown in Figure 15-11.

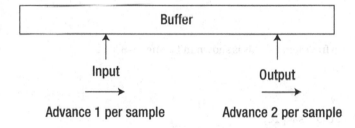

Figure 15-11. *Pitch up*

The trick is in getting the buffer the right length. Although there will be a bit of noise when the output buffer overtakes the input buffer, it is not too bad. The code fragment to implement this is shown in Listing 15-5.

Listing 15-5. Pitch Up

```
void pitchUp(){
 static unsigned int bufferIn=0, bufferOut=0, sample;
while(1){
  sample = analogRead(0);
  saveSample(bufferIn, sample);
  sample = fetchSample(bufferOut);
```

```
  ADwrite(sample);
  bufferIn++;
  if(bufferIn > bufferOffset) bufferIn=0;
  bufferOut +=2;
  if(bufferOut > bufferOffset) bufferOut=0;
  }
}
```

The code is almost identical to the delay code, the only exception being the double increment of the output buffer pointer. However, hidden in the calling code is setting up a short buffer.

Pitch Down

What goes up must come down and you can do the inverse to achieve a pitch down effect. This time it is like breathing sulfur hexafluoride, but without the toxic side-effects. It is not quite as simple as moving the output pointer at twice the speed of the input pointer, because you will be left with holes in the sample. So in addition to this, you need to fill the holes left by the input pointer moving at twice the rate by doing a double store of each sample. The algorithm is shown in Figure 15-12.

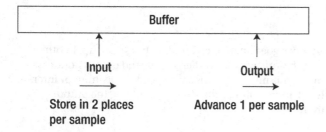

Figure 15-12. *Pitch down*

The buffer again is very short, and the code fragment for this is shown in Listing 15-6.

Listing 15-6. Pitch Down

```
void pitchDown(){
static unsigned int bufferIn=0, bufferOut=0, sample;
while(1){
   sample = analogRead(0);
   saveSample(bufferIn, sample);
   bufferIn++;
   if(bufferIn > bufferOffset) bufferIn=0;
   saveSample(bufferIn, sample);
   bufferIn++;
   if(bufferIn > bufferOffset) bufferIn=0;
   sample = fetchSample(bufferOut);
   ADwrite(sample);
   bufferOut++;
   if(bufferOut > bufferOffset) bufferOut=0;
   }
  }
```

After each increment of the pointers, you must check if the pointers need to wrap around. Anyone for a chorus of "I was born under a wandering star"?

Speaking Backward

The final effect is speaking backward in real time, and you might think that this is impossible, and if the truth be known, it is. However, you can achieve a very good facsimile by having a long buffer and moving the input pointer and output pointer in opposite directions. The effect this produces is actually a variable delay coupled with the backward playing of the sample. The result is that phrases can be heard most of the time backward if the timing is correct. Figure 15-13 shows the algorithm and Listing 15-7 shows the code fragment.

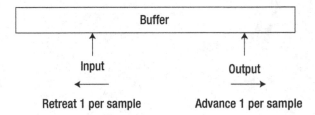

Figure 15-13. *Speaking Backward*

Listing 15-7. Speaking Backward

```
sd void reverse(){
static  long bufferIn=0, bufferOut=0, sample;
while(1){
    sample = analogRead(0);
    saveSample(bufferIn, sample);
    sample = fetchSample(bufferOut);
    ADwrite(sample);
    bufferIn++;
    if(bufferIn > bufferOffset) bufferIn=0;
    bufferOut--;
    if(bufferOut < 0 ) bufferOut=bufferOffset;
  }
}
```

Now this is almost identical to the original delay, only this time the output buffer pointer is decremented. The odd thing is then when you use this, the output sounds like you are speaking in Russian. I sometimes call it my Russian translator. When demonstrating this at a talk, I finish off by saying "hello" and it comes out as "war ler". Then I tell the audience that, without the aide of a safety net, I am about to attempt to say it backward. I say "war ler" and it comes out as "hello" this always produces a round of applause from my audience.

Putting It All Together

As I said, these code fragments need to be stitched together with common functions and also extra functions for setting the buffer lengths and clearing buffers. In order to not have to keep checking the hex switch to select the effect I want to produce, the code is written so that the switch is read, the effect program is prepared, and then the effects function is entered. You will have noticed that these are in the form of an infinite loop, so when you want to change the effect you should just select the effect number and press the Arduino's reset button. For exhibitions I made an extension cable with a physically bigger switch wired in parallel with the one on the sound card and an extra reset button. A photograph of this is shown in Figure 15-14.

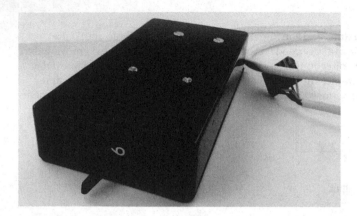

Figure 15-14. *An extended hex switch*

The final code for all the effects is shown in Listing 15-8.

Listing 15-8. All Effects

```
/* Audio effects - Mike Cook
   A 16 input switch decide the delay / effect
*/

/* the memory chip is 128K bytes - address from 0x0 to 0x1FFFF ( decimal 131071 )
and therefore 64K samples long
*/
#include <SPI.h>

#define CS1_BAR 9
#define CS2_BAR 8
#define CS_ADC_BAR 10
#define AD_LATCH 6
#define Hold_BAR 7

// All buffer sizes are in samples (2 bytes) not in bytes
// long int bufferSize = 30000;  // absolute size of circular buffer for 2 memory chips
long int bufferSize = 0xFFFF;    // maximum address of circular buffer for 1 memory chip
long int bufferOffset = 5000;    // distance between input and output points
long int bufferOffset2, bufferOffset3, bufferOffset4;
byte program = 0;

void setup()
{
  // initilise control pins for SRAM
   pinMode( CS1_BAR, OUTPUT);
   digitalWrite( CS1_BAR, HIGH);
```

```
  pinMode( CS2_BAR, OUTPUT);
  digitalWrite( CS2_BAR, HIGH);
  pinMode( CS_ADC_BAR, OUTPUT);
  digitalWrite(CS_ADC_BAR, HIGH);
  pinMode( AD_LATCH, OUTPUT);
  digitalWrite(AD_LATCH, HIGH);
  pinMode( Hold_BAR, OUTPUT);
  digitalWrite( Hold_BAR, HIGH);
  SPI.begin();
  SPI.setDataMode(SPI_MODE3);
  SPI.setClockDivider(SPI_CLOCK_DIV2); // 8MHz clock this is the maximum clock speed
  setChipMode(0x40, CS1_BAR);          // sequential mode for chip 1
  // set up fast ADC mode
  ADCSRA = (ADCSRA & 0xf8) | 0x04;     // set 16 times division
  // set input pull up pins for HEX mode switch
  for( int i= 16; i<20; i++){
    pinMode(i, INPUT_PULLUP);
  }
  // read in the HEX (or BCD) mode switch
  for(int i=19; i>15; i--){
    program = program << 1;          // move a space for the next bit
    program |= digitalRead(i) & 0x1; // add next bit
  }
  program ^= 0x0f;         // invert it
  setUpMyBuffers(program); // initilise buffer pointers
  // blank memory for initial buffer to avoid noise in phones on power up
  if( program >7) blankMemory(bufferOffset4); else blankMemory(bufferOffset);
}

void loop(){
 if(program < 5) basicDelay(); // all simple delays of differing length
 if(program == 5) pitchUp();
 if(program == 6) pitchDown();
 if(program == 7) reverse();
 if(program == 8) echo4();      // three echos and a repeat
 if(program == 9) echo4();
}
void echo4(){  // loop time 95.2uS - sample rate 10.5KHz
  // set up the initial position of the buffer pointers
    static int sample;
    static long bufferIn=bufferSize, bufferOut1=bufferSize - bufferOffset;
    static long bufferOut2=bufferSize - bufferOffset2, bufferOut3=bufferSize - bufferOffset3;
    static long bufferOut4=bufferSize - bufferOffset4;
  while(1){
    sample = analogRead(0);
    saveSample(bufferIn, sample);
    sample = fetchSample(bufferOut1);
    sample += fetchSample(bufferOut2);
    sample += fetchSample(bufferOut3);
    sample += fetchSample(bufferOut4);
    sample = sample >> 2; // so as to keep the gain down to 1 to avoid build up of noise
```

```
    ADwrite(sample); // output sample
    // adjust the buffer pointers
    bufferIn++;
    if(bufferIn > bufferSize) bufferIn=0;
    bufferOut1++;
    if(bufferOut1 > bufferSize) bufferOut1=0;
    bufferOut2++;
    if(bufferOut2 > bufferSize) bufferOut2=0;
    bufferOut3++;
    if(bufferOut3 > bufferSize) bufferOut3=0;
    bufferOut4++;
    if(bufferOut4 > bufferSize) bufferOut4=0;
  }
}

void reverse(){
 static  long bufferIn=0, bufferOut=0, sample;
while(1){
  sample = analogRead(0);
  saveSample(bufferIn, sample);
  sample = fetchSample(bufferOut);
  ADwrite(sample);
  bufferIn++;
  if(bufferIn > bufferOffset) bufferIn=0;
  bufferOut--;
  if(bufferOut < 0 ) bufferOut=bufferOffset;
  }
}

void pitchDown(){
 static unsigned int bufferIn=0, bufferOut=0, sample;
while(1){
  sample = analogRead(0);
  saveSample(bufferIn, sample);
  bufferIn++;
  if(bufferIn > bufferOffset) bufferIn=0;
  saveSample(bufferIn, sample);
  bufferIn++;
  if(bufferIn > bufferOffset) bufferIn=0;
  sample = fetchSample(bufferOut);
  ADwrite(sample);
  bufferOut++;
  if(bufferOut > bufferOffset) bufferOut=0;
  }
}
void pitchUp(){
 static unsigned int bufferIn=0, bufferOut=0, sample;
while(1){
  sample = analogRead(0);
  saveSample(bufferIn, sample);
  sample = fetchSample(bufferOut);
```

```
    ADwrite(sample);
    bufferIn++;
    if(bufferIn > bufferOffset) bufferIn=0;
    bufferOut +=2;
    if(bufferOut > bufferOffset) bufferOut=0;
    }
}

void basicDelay(){  // loop time 48.2uS - sample rate 20.83 KHz
  static unsigned int bufferIn=bufferSize, bufferOut=bufferSize - bufferOffset, sample;
while(1){
    sample = analogRead(0);
    saveSample(bufferIn, sample);
    sample = fetchSample(bufferOut);
    ADwrite(sample);
    bufferIn++;
    if(bufferIn > bufferSize) bufferIn=0;
    bufferOut++;
    if(bufferOut > bufferSize) bufferOut=0;
    }
}

void setUpMyBuffers(byte p){
    bufferSize = 30000;
    switch(p) { // depending on program mode initilise the buffer pointers
      case 0 :
          bufferOffset = 1000;  // samples between in and out 0.05 seconds
      break;
      case 1 :
          bufferOffset = 3000;  // samples between in and out 0.15 seconds
      break;
      case 2 :
          bufferOffset = 5000;   // samples between in and out 0.25 seconds
      break;
      case 3 :
          bufferOffset = 10000;  // samples between in and out 0.5 seconds
      break;
      case 4 :
          bufferOffset = 20000;  // samples between in and out 1 second
      break;
      case 5 :
          bufferOffset = 1000;   // size of buffer for pitch up
      break;
      case 6 :
          bufferOffset = 1000;  // size of buffer for pitch down
      break;
      case 7 :
          bufferOffset = 32000; // size of buffer for reverse
      break;
```

```
      case 8 :
          // bufferSize = 100000;
          bufferOffset = 3000;    // distance of input pointer to first echo 0.3 seconds
          bufferOffset2 = 6000;   // distance of input pointer to second echo 0.58 seconds
          bufferOffset3 = 9000;   // distance of input pointer to third echo  0.86 seconds
          bufferOffset4 = 22000; // distance of input pointer to fourth echo 2 seconds
        break;
      case 9 :
          // bufferSize = 100000;
          bufferOffset =  12000;  // distance of input pointer to first echo
          bufferOffset2 = 24000;  // distance of input pointer to second echo
          bufferOffset3 = 36000;  // distance of input pointer to third echo
          bufferOffset4 = 48000;  // distance of input pointer to fourth echo 5.1 seconds
        break;

      default :
      bufferOffset = 1000;
   }
}

void setChipMode(int value, int where){
  digitalWrite( where, LOW);    // CE pin
  SPI.transfer(0xff);           // reset any double or quad mode
  digitalWrite( where, HIGH);   // CE pin
  delay(2);
  digitalWrite( where, LOW);    // CE pin
  SPI.transfer(0x01);           // write to mode register
  SPI.transfer(value);          // the value passed into it
  digitalWrite( where, HIGH);   // CE pin
}
int fetchSample(long address){  // given sample address
  int data;
  address = address << 1;       // make it into byte address
  //digitalWrite(CS1_BAR, LOW); // CE pin  - direct addressing below
  PORTB &= ~0x02;
  SPI.transfer(0x03);               // read data from memory in sequence mode
  SPI.transfer((address>>16) & 0xff); // write 3 byte address most significant first
  SPI.transfer((address>>8) & 0xff);
  SPI.transfer(address & 0xff);
  data = SPI.transfer(0) << 8;
  data |= SPI.transfer(0);
  //digitalWrite(CS1_BAR, HIGH);       // CE pin  - direct addressing below
  PORTB |= 0x02;
 return data;
}

void blankMemory(long bufferLen){
  int blank = analogRead(0); // take the current input level and fill memory with it
  for(long memPoint = bufferSize - bufferLen; memPoint <= bufferSize; memPoint++){
    saveSample(memPoint,blank);
  }
}
```

```
int saveSample(long address, int data){ // given sample address
  address = address << 1;              // make it into byte address
  //digitalWrite(CS1_BAR, LOW);         // CE pin - direct addressing below
  PORTB &= ~0x02;
  SPI.transfer(0x02);                   // save data from memory in sequence mode
  SPI.transfer((address>>16) & 0xff);   // write 3 byte address most significant first
  SPI.transfer((address>>8) & 0xff);
  SPI.transfer(address & 0xff);
  SPI.transfer(data >> 8);
  SPI.transfer(data & 0xff);
  //digitalWrite(CS1_BAR, HIGH); // CE pin - direct addressing below
  PORTB |= 0x02;
}

void ADwrite(int data){
 // digitalWrite(CS_ADC_BAR, LOW);  - direct addressing below
  PORTB &= ~0x4;
  SPI.transfer(((data >> 8) & 0x0f) | 0x70);
  SPI.transfer(data & 0xff);
  //digitalWrite(CS_ADC_BAR, HIGH);  - direct addressing below
  PORTB |= 0x4;
  //digitalWrite(AD_LATCH, LOW);  - direct addressing below
  PORTD &= ~0x40;
  //digitalWrite(AD_LATCH, HIGH);  - direct addressing below
  PORTD |= 0x40;
}
```

The code to fill the memory with a mid-range sample is vital to prevent there from being a lot of loud noise when switching between effects. Remember this could be painful when wearing headphones.

This is the first time you have seen the functions that access the memory. The memory chip can operate in three modes—byte, page, and sequence. You want to use the sequence mode, so that you only have to send the address of the first byte of the sample, after successive accesses, and then read or write the address automatically to the next one. Even though the sequence of memory locations you want is only two bytes long, or one sample, there is need to send one address. With the byte mode you would have to send the address for each byte and the page mode restricts access to one addressed page, which is 32 bytes. So the setChipMode function sets up the memory's mode register for the sequential mode. The fetchSample function retrieves a sample by first converting the sampler address into a memory address by multiplying by two and then sending the three bytes of the address. Finally, the two bytes of the sample are read and combined into an integer. The saveSample function is almost identical except it writes the integer sample value by splitting it into two bytes.

The blankMemory function fills the memory with the current value seen at the A/D converter input, which will be the DC level, or silence level of the circuit, unless you happen to be shouting into it at the time. However, the worst that can happen is that there will be a click when the blank buffer starts playing.

After the hex switch has been read, the setUpMyBuffers function initializes the buffer pointers according to what effect it is going to produce. And the loop function simply calls the function for that effect. So in operation, if you want to change the effect then simply change the hex switch and press the reset button. The new effect will take place in a second or two. Some effects, like talking backward, take time to kick in. This is because at first, a long buffer has to be blanked, and then it has to be filled with samples, before any sound is heard. Others with short buffers like the pitch up start immediately.

There are only 10 effects implemented, so there is room to add your own variations for the higher numbers on the hex switch.

Finale

When I have shown these effects at exhibitions, most people who know anything about the Arduino are amazed that such things can be produced from an Arduino Uno. With the help of a bit of buffer memory, you can work wonders.

One project that is on my to-do list is a long delay so that I can watch football on the TV and listen to the radio commentary, which is normally much better. Due to the nature of digital TV these days, the radio often runs up to five seconds ahead of the TV pictures, so adding a delay to the radio should bring it back into sync, instead of thinking that the commentators can see into the future.

■ ■ ■

CHAPTER 16

Digital Filters

Having seen how you can use the Arduino for performing some digital effects, I want to look at a specific form of effect, namely the digital filter. A *filter* is a circuit that changes the amplitude of each frequency depending on what value it is. Traditionally, these filters were implemented with analogue electronics and constructed of capacitors, resistors inductors, and operational amplifiers. A new way of implementing filters with analogue circuits has been developed in recent years, and is known as a switched capacitor filter. However, the development of digital filters offers a cheap and flexible way of creating a filter that can be implemented with a processor. As CPU resources become increasingly cheap, this type of filter is becoming more useful.

Types of Filter

There are four basic sorts of filters—low pass, high bass, band pass, and band stop. There are others too, like the all pass and comb filter. As the names imply, the high pass will pass high frequencies and stop low ones whereas the low pass filter does the opposite—it passes the low and stops the high. The band pass filter lets through a range of frequencies between two points and the band stop does the opposite.

That, of course, is a gross simplification and there is the added complication of the shape of the filter or the *transfer function*, as it is known. There are many ways to design these but the three standard filter shapes are known as the Butterworth, Bessel and Cauer, or Elliptical filter as it is sometimes called. Each has its own characteristics and they are all shown in Figure 16-1.

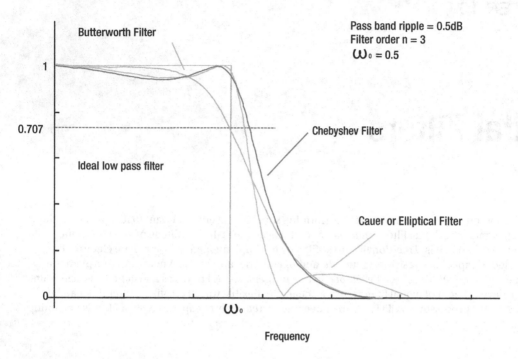

Figure 16-1. *Standard filter shapes*

The ideal filter shape is a rectangle with everything being unaffected until the *cutoff*, or break frequency, is passed and then beyond that nothing is passed. In popular parlance, this is known as a "brick wall" filter. It's not only impractical, but undesirable. This is because in practice it will not be stable and will oscillate or ring at the break frequency.

The Butterworth filter is optimally flat; that is, there is no ripple in the pass band or stop band and the filter falls off slower than the other two. The Chebysheve filter drops off faster but it has ripple in the pass band, whereas the Cauer filter drops off the quickest and has a null point in the stop band. However, you pay for this by having the stop band not going as far down as the other two. With the Chebysheve and Cauer, you can also trade more ripple in the pass band for a faster falloff.

It would take the entire book to describe how these parameters are defined. This involves lots of math with complex numbers, so I will just show you some ways to implement filters digitally.

■ **Note** *Complex* numbers are numbers that consist of two parts—one real and one imaginary. The imaginary part is a number multiplied by the square root of minus one, as no such number exists, or can exist, and so it's called *imaginary*. In fact, the imaginary parts of the numbers are just numbers that are orthogonal, or at right angles, to real numbers. When dealing with waveforms, the real number is the amplitude and the imaginary number is the phase. They have their own rules for adding, subtracting, multiplication, and division.

Low Pass Filter

One of the simplest filters to understand is called the *running average filter*. It is used to reduce rapid variations in data and show underlying trends. In finance, stocks or commodity prices are often quoted or plotted as a 200-day running average. That means the price is the average of the previous 200 days. In practice, this is a low pass filter because it removes the rapid day-to-day fluctuations. However, the prices can be considered end of the day samples of a continuously changing price, exactly like samples of audio.

Such a filter is easily implemented by adding the last *n* samples and dividing by *n,* and as such needs no special technique. But it is useful to see how this operation would be expressed in terms that can be applied to any other filter.

The code in this chapter uses the serial plotting window found in the Tools menu of the Arduino IDE. It was introduced in version 1.6.6. It allows you to see values graphically plotted. It has 500 plot positions visible before it starts to scroll and it also automatically scales the y axis, sometimes in a useful way. You can use this in order to see the contents of buffers, and hence the input and output waveforms.

The program in Listing 16-1 shows a running average filter that can be implemented on an Arduino Uno.

Listing 16-1. Running Average Filter

```
// running average filter - Mike Cook
// using byte buffers
// Open up the plot window
const int bufferSize = 250;
byte inBuffer[bufferSize], outBuffer[bufferSize];
void setup() {
Serial.begin(250000);
displayWave(); // clear display
makeWave(2);
delay(600);
runningAvfilter(20);
displayWave();
}

void loop() {
}

void makeWave(int wave){
switch(wave){
  case 0: makeTriangle();
  break;
  case 1: makeSin();
  break;
  case 2: makeSquare();
  break;
  case 3: makeNoise();
  }
}
void makeTriangle(){
  // (increment/bufferSize) determines the number of cycles
    int increment = 8, wave = 0;
  // make a triangle wave
```

```
  for(int i=0; i<bufferSize; i++){
      wave += increment;
    if(wave > (255 - increment) || wave < 0) {
      increment = -increment;
      wave += increment;
    }
    inBuffer[i] = (byte)wave;
  }
}

void makeSin(){
  // increment controls the frequency
  int count = 0, increment= 10;
  for(int i=0; i<bufferSize; i++){
    count += increment;
    if(count > 360) count -= 360;
    inBuffer[i] = (byte)(127+ (127.0*sin((float)count / 57.2957795 )));
  }
}

void makeSquare(){
  int period = 30, count = 0;
  boolean change = true;
for(int i=0; i<bufferSize; i++){
  count++;
  if(count >= period){
    count = 0;
    change = !change;
  }
  if(change){
    inBuffer[i] = 255;
  }
  else {
   inBuffer[i] = 0;
  }
 }
}
void makeNoise(){
  randomSeed(analogRead(4));
  for(int i=0; i<bufferSize; i++){
    inBuffer[i] = (byte)random(255);
  }
}

void runningAvfilter(int n){
  int acc;
   for(int i=0; i<(bufferSize-n); i++){
    acc=0;
    for(int j=0; j<n; j++){
      acc += inBuffer[i+j];
      }
```

```
  outBuffer[i]= acc/n; // save average
  }
}

void displayWave(){
  for(int i=0; i<bufferSize; i++){
    Serial.println(inBuffer[i]);
    }
  for(int i=0; i<bufferSize; i++){
    Serial.println(outBuffer[i]);
    }
}
```

This program is capable of producing a number of different waveforms, filling an input buffer with the calculated samples. Then the filter is applied to the input buffer and the results are stored in the output buffer. Finally, the input and output buffers are plotted next to each other, so that the input waveform is shown on the left and the output on the right. All the code is in the setup function, so that it runs only once.

The input waveform is determined by the number passed to the makeWave function and can be a triangle, sin, square, and random noise. Then the runningAvfilter function does the actual filtering; it is passed a number that determines the number of samples it uses to perform the averaging. Finally, the two buffers are plotted. You can change the waveform and the number of samples to averages simply by changing the numbers used when calling the functions. Changing the input waveform's frequency can be done by changing the numbers at the start of each waveform function.

The results may or may not surprise you. They are shown in Figures 16-2 to 16-5.

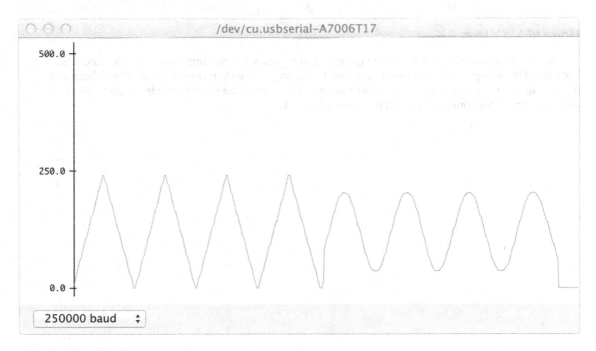

Figure 16-2. *Triangle wave*

Note that while the input is a triangle, the output is quite close to a sin wave. This is because the extra harmonics that make up the triangle are being removed, leaving you with just the fundamental.

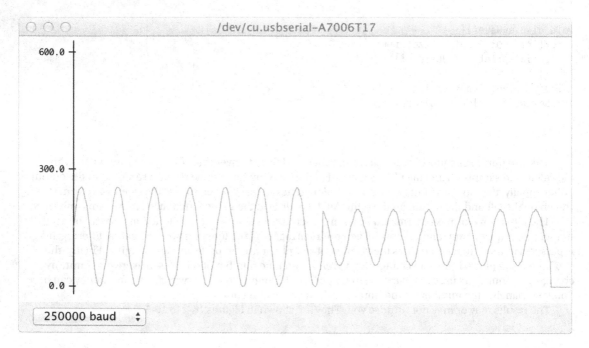

Figure 16-3. *Sin wave*

Not much change in wave shape in Figure 16-3, but notice how the amplitude is diminished. This is because of the low pass filter rolling off. See how this changes when you change the number of samples the average is taken over. If you take the average over more points than input samples in a waveform, the amplitude will drop; otherwise, it will remain unchanged.

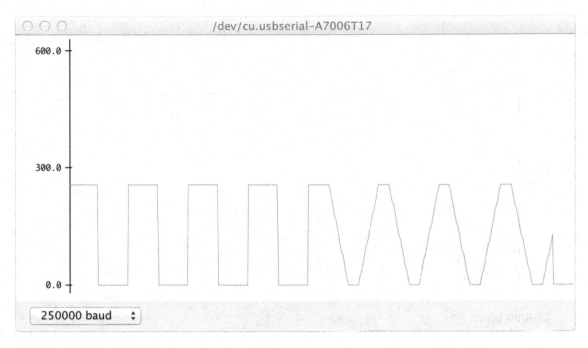

Figure 16-4. *Square wave*

Here you can see the averaging in progress. On a rapid transition, the effects of that transition take time to appear. So the output ramps up until it reaches the maximum value, and then it stops at that level until the opposite transition occurs. In other words, you get a flat top triangle wave. Altering the number of samples you average over changes the slope of this ramp up and ramp down. The fewer the averaging points, the sharper the ramp and the bigger the flat top.

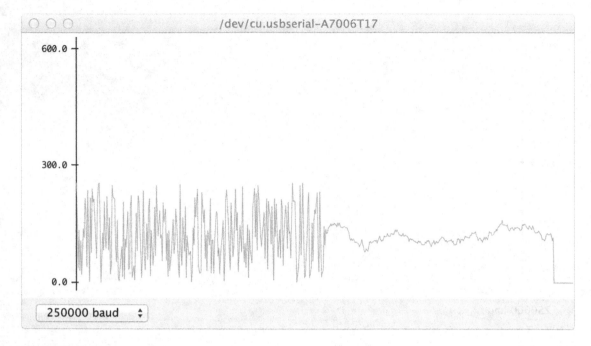

Figure 16-5. *Noise*

The input waveform in Figure 16-5 is a collection of random numbers, called *white noise*. The averaged output signal is still noise but it has a much narrower range of frequencies and amplitudes. This sort of thing is called *brown noise* because the "white" spectrum has been shifted toward the red end of the spectrum.

■ **Note** Do not confuse brown noise with Brownian noise. Brownian noise is produced by adding a small-range random number to an accumulator.

All the buffers used in this program are byte buffers, which means the dynamic range of each sample is only 0 to 255.

Describing the Filter

This can be described diagrammatically rather like a hardware schematic. There are standard symbols and notation that are used and you will encounter them in any text on digital filtering. The basic function is the delay represented by a rectangle with a T for time in it. Normally, this delay will be of one sample, when these are arranged as a chain, samples are passed from one to the other as time advances, in very much the same way as the buffer diagrams that were used in Chapter 15. A circle with a + in it is a summer circuit and one with a number in it is a multiplier. A sample that has just been taken is given the index of n and the one immediately preceding this is given index of $(n-1)$. Input samples are called X, and output samples are called Y. Figure 16-6 shows the block diagram of a running average filter.

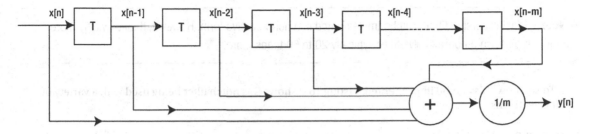

Figure 16-6. *Running the average filter block diagram*

You can see that each sample is propagated down the chain, which is as long as the number of samples you want to average over; in this case, the number is *M*. These are summed and then multiplied by 1/m, which is the same as dividing by *m*. So to get the output sample *y[n]*, you find the average of the last *m* samples.

There is a smart trick you can do to minimize the number of arithmetic operations you have to do, and that is to just keep a running total of all the samples. You then subtract the last sample and add the latest one before multiplying by 1/m. That means that no matter how many samples you average over, you only need to do two additions (subtraction is classified as a negative addition as far as processing power is concerned) and one multiplication. Normally, it is more efficient to do a multiplication than a division.

Notch Filter

While the running average filter can remove noise it can also filter the data. If you have a specific frequency of interference, for example interference from domestic AC supply, you can take out specifically that frequency and leave the others untouched. In order to do that, you need a *recursive* filter. The one you looked at previously was a nonrecursive filter, in that the output was determined by a function of previous inputs. In a recursive filter the output is determined by a function of previous inputs and previous outputs. These are potentially unstable because they are feedback systems. If you feed back too much of a signal, you just get "howl round" or oscillation. Sometimes this is simply called "feedback" and is much beloved by lead guitarists. Figure 16-7 shows the block diagram of a notch filter.

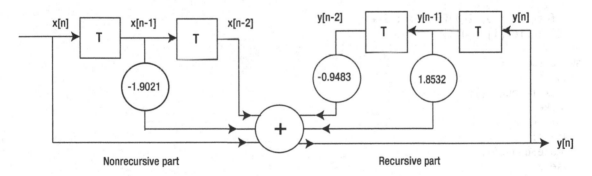

Figure 16-7. *Notch filter block diagram*

Figure 16-7 shows two short delay chains, one dealing with previous inputs and the other dealing with previous outputs. Note how three of the samples that get summed are first multiplied by a signed constant. A negative value makes the sum smaller and a positive one makes it larger.

■ **Note** Most recursive filters can be implemented in a nonrecursive form. However, it takes vastly more samples to perform a nonrecursive filter, typically 20 to 50 times more.

To see how this can be implemented, Listing 16-2 shows this notch filter being used with a variety of input waveforms.

Listing 16-2. A Notch Filter

```
// Notch filter - Mike Cook
// using int buffers
// Open up the plot window
const int bufferSize = 250;
int inBuffer[bufferSize];
int outBuffer[bufferSize];
void setup() {
Serial.begin(250000);
displayWave();   // clear display
makeWave(0);     // create input buffer wave
notchFilter();   // do the filtering
displayWave();   // to the plot window
}

void loop() {
}

void makeWave(int wave){
  // clear buffers
  for(int i=0; i<bufferSize; i++){
    outBuffer[i] = 0;
    }
    for(int i=0; i<bufferSize; i++){
    inBuffer[i] = 0;
    }
switch(wave){
 case 0:
   makeTriangle();
   makeSin();
   break;
 case 1:
   makeSquare();
 case 2:
   inBuffer[0] = 120; // inpulse
   }
}.

void makeSin(){
  // increment controls the frequency
  int count = 0;
  int increment= 18;
  for(int i=0; i<bufferSize; i++){
```

```
    count += increment;
    if(count > 360) count -= 360;
    inBuffer[i] += (int)(64.0 * sin((float)count / 57.2957795 ));
    }
}

void makeTriangle(){
  // increment/bufferSize determins the number of cycles
    int increment = 6, wave = 100;
  // make a triangle wave
  for(int i=0; i<bufferSize; i++){
      wave += increment;
    if(wave > (120) || wave < -120) {
      increment = -increment;
      wave += increment;
    }
    inBuffer[i] = wave;
  }
}

void makeSquare(){
  int count = 0, limit = 10;;
  boolean wave = true;
  for(int i=0; i<bufferSize; i++){
  if(wave) inBuffer[i] = 120; else inBuffer[i] = -120;
  count++;
  if(count >= limit){
    count = 0;
    wave = !wave;
  }
  }
}

void notchFilter(){ // for a 20 sample wave
  // prime output buffer
  outBuffer[0] = 0; // inBuffer[0]
  outBuffer[1] = 0; // inBuffer[1]
  for(int i=2; i<(bufferSize); i++){
  outBuffer[i] = ((1.8523*(float)outBuffer[i-1] - 0.94833* (float) outBuffer[i-2]
    + (float)inBuffer[i] - 1.9021*(float) inBuffer[i-1] + (float)inBuffer[i-2]));
  }
}.

void displayWave(){
  for(int i=0; i<bufferSize; i++){
    Serial.println(inBuffer[i]);
  }
  for(int i=0; i<bufferSize; i++){
    Serial.println(outBuffer[i]);
  }
}
```

Like the previous listings, all the action takes place in the setup function so that it runs only once. You can apply this notch filter to one of three input waveforms—a triangle with an interfering sin wave, a square wave, and a single sample at the start of an otherwise empty input buffer. More on this last option later. The input wave is shown on the left of the plot window with the output on the right.

The notch filter is designed to take out a signal with 20 samples in a cycle. The actual frequency that this corresponds to is determined by your sample rate. For the 60Hz supply frequency, this would be 1,200 samples per second and for 50Hz supply frequency, this would be 1,000 samples per second. Note that the buffers are integer buffers, which makes the code a bit easier. The results are shown in Figures 16-8 to 16-10.

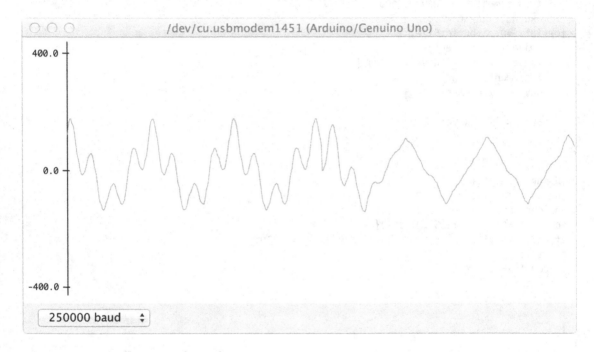

Figure 16-8. *Triangle wave with interference*

Figure 16-8 shows the classic case of an interfering signal being removed by a notch filter. The input waveform was made by adding the sin wave to the triangle and the right side shows just the triangle. Well, there are a few wobbles, but those can be removed by having a higher order filter.

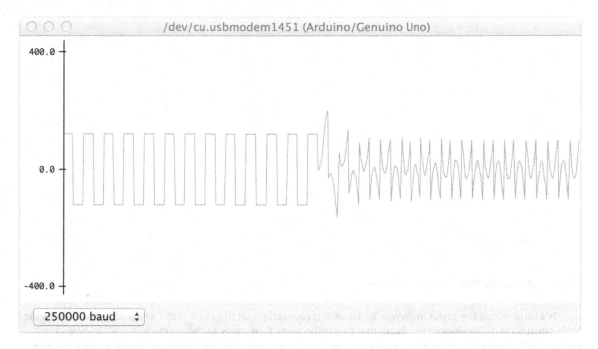

Figure 16-9. *Square wave at the notch frequency*

Figure 16-9 shows a favorite exercise of mine to give my students. You have a square wave at the notch frequency. Ignoring the bit in the middle for the moment, why would you expect this output? Well, remember the discussion in Chapter 10 about waveforms being built from a series of sin waves, and that a square wave had an infinite number of sine waves? Well, what we are doing here is removing the fundamental and leaving the infinite number of higher harmonics. It is like removing the last piece of the jigsaw. If you were to add a sine wave back into that output waveform, you would get a square wave, although the output waveform is such an odd shape.

The bit in the middle is the start of the output buffer. When you start filtering, there are no previous samples although the algorithm is calling for the last two samples. Therefore, you are not implementing the filter correctly and it takes some time for the filter to settle down and produce a steady output. This characteristic of a filter, its response to sudden change, is known as its *impulse response*. The more sharp a filter's response, the more time it takes to settle down. This is why I said previously that an ideal "brick wall" filter is not desirable because of the time it would take to settle down. You can look at the impulse response of a filter by giving it an input consisting of just one non-zero sample at the start. It is like striking a bell and seeing how it rings. This is what is shown in Figure 16-10.

411

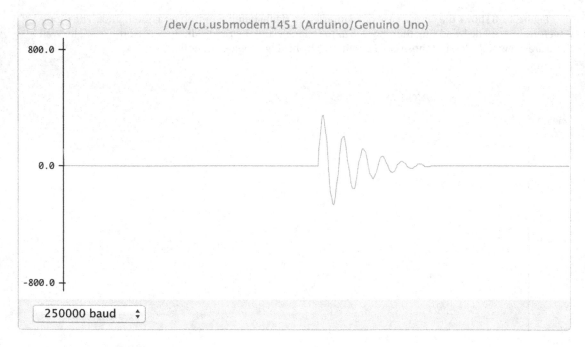

Figure 16-10. *The filter's inpulse responce*

It's hard to see the input in Figure 16-10, as it is one sample at the same point as the axis, but the ringing in the output is quite clear to see. Note that this is the same frequency as the notch. In a way, it shows how sensitive the circuit is to this frequency and how it can quickly swallow it. The bigger the impulse response, the longer it takes to settle down.

Frequency Response

So far you have looked at the input and output waveforms from a filter, but most of the time, you'll be interested in what a filter does to various frequencies, not necessarily to wave shapes. This is the transfer function, or frequency response of a filter. The program in Listing 16-3 plots the frequency response of seven filter variations, one after the other. Each filter is primed with 60 or 100 frequency waves and then each one is filtered. The input-to-output change is expressed as dB. To spread out the display a little, each point is printed four times. The filters are cycled through one at a time with a two second delay between filters.

Listing 16-3. Filter Frequency Response

```
// DSP filter plot - Mike Cook
// plots the frequency response of 7 filters
// Open up the plot window
const int bufferSize = 250;
int inBuffer[bufferSize];
int outBuffer[bufferSize];
int displayCount = 499;
float att =0.0;
```

```
void setup() {
 int steps;
 Serial.begin(250000);
  for(int k=0; k<7; k++){
    clearPlot();
    displayCount = 499;
    if(k < 3) steps = 60; else steps = 100;
    for(int i=2; i<steps; i++){
        makeWave(i); // create input buffer wave
        filter(k);   // do the filtering
        measure();   //
    }
  while(displayCount > 0){ // shift to end
    Serial.println(att);
    displayCount--;
    }
  delay(2000);
  }
}

void loop() { // do nothing
}

void makeWave(int freq){
  float count = 0.0;
  float increment= 360.0 / ((float)(bufferSize+1) / (float)freq);
  for(int i=0; i<bufferSize; i++){
   inBuffer[i] = (int)(4960.0 * sin(count / 57.2957795 ));
   outBuffer[i] = 0;
      count += increment;
   if(count > 360.0) count -= 360.0;
  }
}

void measure(){
  int point = bufferSize - 1;
  float accIn = 0.0, accOut = 0.0;
   while(point > 0){
     if(outBuffer[point] > 0) accOut += (float)outBuffer[point];
      else
       accOut -= (float)outBuffer[point];
     if(inBuffer[point] > 0) accIn += (float)inBuffer[point];
      else
       accIn -= (float)inBuffer[point];
     point --;
   }
   att = 10* log(accOut / accIn);
   for(int i=0; i<4; i++) {
    Serial.println(att);
    displayCount--;
   }
}
```

```
void filter(int f){
  switch(f){
    case 0: average(2);
    break;
    case 1: average(3);
    break;
    case 2: average(4);
    break;
    case 3: notchFilter();
    break;
    case 4: bandPass();
    break;
    case 5: highPass(1);
    break;
    case 6: highPass(-1);
  }
}

void highPass(int n){
    for(int i=1; i<(bufferSize); i++){
        outBuffer[i] = 0.3*(float)outBuffer[i-1] +(float)n*0.3*(float)inBuffer[i] -
0.3*(float)inBuffer[i-1];
    }
}

void bandPass(){
    for(int i=2; i<(bufferSize); i++){
      outBuffer[i] = (0.9*(float)outBuffer[i-1] - 0.8* (float) outBuffer[i-2]
        + (float)inBuffer[i] );
    }
}

void notchFilter(){ // for a 20 sample wave
    for(int i=2; i<(bufferSize); i++){
        outBuffer[i] = ((1.8523*(float)outBuffer[i-1] - 0.94833* (float) outBuffer[i-2]
        + (float)inBuffer[i] - 1.9021*(float) inBuffer[i-1] + (float)inBuffer[i-2]));
    }
}

void average(int n){
  int acc;
  for(int i=0; i<(bufferSize-n); i++){
    acc=0;
    for(int j=0; j<n; j++){
      acc += inBuffer[i+j];
    }
    outBuffer[i]= acc/n; // save average
  }
}
```

```
void clearPlot(){
    for(int i=0; i<500; i++){
    Serial.println(0);
  }
}
```

The `filter` function determines which filter will be used; there are seven in all. Three versions of the running average the notch filter you saw before, followed by a band pass, a high pass, and a low pass filter. If you look at the code, you will see there is not a specific low pass filter, instead the high pass filter is used but the middle term is negative. That is all it takes to turn a high pass filter into a low pass one.

The `makeWave` function creates a sin wave with the frequency set by the number passed into it. This is normally in the range of 0 to 100, but in the case of the averaging filters, it's restricted to 60 so that the averaging does not span over one cycle. If it did, the response would show an increase in the higher frequencies like the Cauer filter. Try increasing the number passed into the average function and see for yourself.

Once one frequency has been filtered, the measure function works out the relative size of the input and output. This might appear to be done in an odd way by adding up all the sample values in the buffer. Not only that, but negative values are subtracted for the total, thus making the total bigger. This is in effect what happens when you measure the RMS value of a waveform, the root of the mean squared. The squared bit is effectively removing negative values and making them positive. There is no need to take the root because all you want is a ratio of input buffer total count to the output buffer total count so in effect the roots cancel. About ten times the log of this ratio gives the response in dBs, so it is easy to see on the plot.

This function plots four points for each measurement and decrements the `displayCount` variable each plot. At the end of a complete sweep of the filter, the display is moved to within one plot point of the left side of the display. There is a bit of a quirk in the version of the IDE software that sometimes completely messes up the auto scaling if it is moved that one point farther along. That is why the `displayCount` variable is initially set to 499 and not 500. Figure 16-11 shows the band pass output from this program.

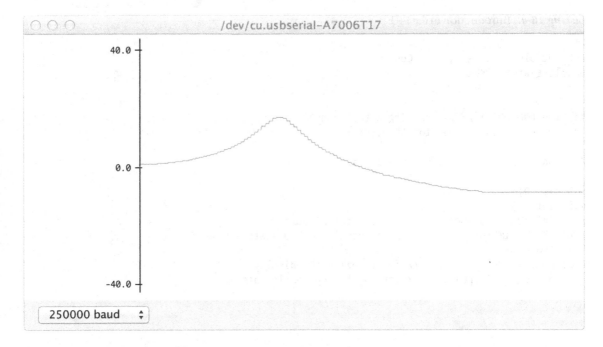

Figure 16-11. *The band pass filter responce*

These filters use floating-point arithmetic for convenience, but this is slow by comparison to integer arithmetic. Therefore, fixed-point arithmetic is often used. This is not as complex as it seems; it just involves making all numbers 1,000 or so times bigger and remembering that the answers are correspondingly 1,000 times bigger.

Fourier Transform

Chapter 10 explained any wave can be made from a collection of sin and cos waves, which is known as Fourier synthesis because you are making wave functions by adding the component harmonics. This process can be reversed. You can take a wave function and break it down into its component harmonics. This is called Fourier Analysis and it involves a set of mathematical operations collectively known as a Fourier Transform.

Furthermore, there is a short-cut method of reducing the number of calculations needed and this is known as the Fast Fourier Transform (FFT). This procedure is involved and requires some complex math, but fortunately many people have done the math and you can just treat the FFT as a black box. You just have to know a little about what you put into it and what it gives you to take out. I have found one of the best implementations of the FFT for an Arduino from Open Music Labs at http://wiki.openmusiclabs.com/wiki/ArduinoFFT?action=AttachFile&do=get&target=ArduinoFFT2.zip. Download the file and unzip the folder. In it, you will find a folder named FFT. Drag that into your Arduino libraries folder and restart the IDE.

A First Look at the FFT

One of the examples that comes with this FFT library is called fft_adc_serial and it samples a signal from the Arduino's A/D converter and prints out the results to the serial port window. However, this is not a very useful thing to do, as all you see is a mass of numbers flashing by. I have taken this example program and modified it so that it is a bit more illustrative of what an FFT can do. This is shown in Listing 16-4.

Listing 16-4. Introduction to the FFT

```
/*
fft_adc_plot_slow - by Mike Cook
Sampling at 8.88KHz
*/

#define LOG_OUT 1 // use the log output function
#define FFT_N 256 // set to 256 point fft

#include <FFT.h>  // include the library

int timer0;
void setup() {
  Serial.begin(250000);    // use the serial port
  timer0 = TIMSK0;         // save normal timer 0 state
  TIMSK0 = 0;
  pinMode(8,INPUT_PULLUP); // for freezing the display
  // pinMode(2,OUTPUT);    // for monitering sample rate
}
```

```
void loop() {
  int k;
  while(1) {                              // reduces jitter
    TIMSK0 = 0;                           // turn off timer0 for lower jitter
    cli();                                // UDRE interrupt slows this way down on arduino1.0
    // PORTD |= 0x4;                       // set pin 2 high to time 256 samples
    for (int i = 0 ; i < 512 ; i += 2) { // save 256 samples
      k = (analogRead(0) - 0x0200 )<< 6;
      fft_input[i] = k;                   // put real data into even bins
      fft_input[i+1] = 0;                 // set odd bins to 0
    }
    // PORTD ^= 0x4;                       // clear pin 2 high to time 256 samples
    fft_window();                         // window the data for better frequency response
    fft_reorder();                        // reorder the data before doing the fft
    fft_run();                            // process the data in the fft
    fft_mag_log();                        // take the output of the fft in log form
    sei();                                // enable interrupts
    TIMSK0 = timer0;                      // restart the timer
    // send out the bins to the plotter
    for (byte i = 0 ; i < FFT_N/2 ; i++) {
      for(byte j=0; j<3; j++){            // each bin three times
      Serial.println(fft_log_out[i]);     // send out the data
      //   Serial.println(fft_oct_out[i]); // send out the data
      }
    }
    for(byte j=0; j<116; j++) Serial.println(0);
      delay(2000);
      // while(digitalRead(8)) { }         // hold until this pin is low
  }
}
```

This code uses the simple digital read function and inputs samples at about 8.88KHz from the A0 analogue input. The Timer 0 is disabled and the interrupts inhibited during the sampling to reduce jitter on the sample time. Once the samples have been taken the rest of the processing can be done with normal interrupts running, which will allow the delay function to work. I also added an extra optional control in the form of a pushbutton on pin 8. This can be used to trigger another set of samples, or if implemented as a switch, can act as a run/hold switch. Each sample is displayed for two seconds before taking the next sample.

The samples are placed into a buffer, known as a bin. Into the even bins goes the real part of the sample; the imaginary parts are put in odd bins. For real samples taken from hardware, there is no imaginary part, so they are filled with zeros. There is an option, commented out, for raising pin 2 during the sampling so you can time the sample process on an oscilloscope. Once the FFT is done, the results are displayed in the serial plot window.

I took this code and applied sin wave signals from a signal generator at various frequencies. The results are shown in Figure 16-12.

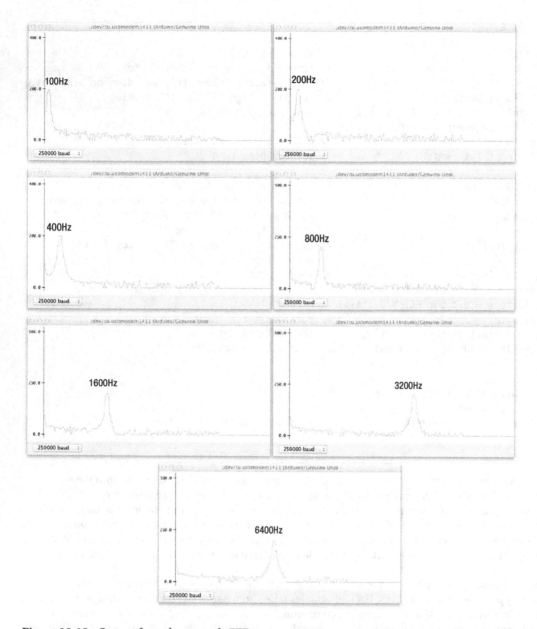

Figure 16-12. *Output from slow sample FFT*

The result of performing an FFT on a sin wave should be a single bin with a big number in it that corresponds to the signal's frequency. What you get in practice is a spreading of the peak over some adjacent bins. You can see as the frequency increases the bin with the maximum sample moves over to the right in Figure 16-12. However, look at that last output, the one for 6400Hz that is to the left of the previous one—so what is going on here? Well, remember the Nyquist rate you looked at before? At a sample rate of 8.88KHz, the highest frequency you can sample without aliasing is 4.44KHz, so that last plot has a frequency that is too fast for the sampling rate and that is an *aliased* peak.

The peak spreading and the noise outside the peak are caused by the fact that there is not a whole number of cycles of the input waveform. The Fourier Transform assumes you have an infinitely repeating signal and quite simply you do not. If you join the last sample with the first, there will be discontinuities in the waveform, and these show up as leaking and noise. In order to minimize this effect, the signal is tapered off toward the start and end of the buffer. This is known as "windowing" and the call to the function fft_window does this. There are many sorts of window functions, but this library uses just one—the Hann window. This window is basically a cos function applied across the window. Figure 16-13 shows the Hann function along with the waveform in the input buffer, before and after applying this function to the buffer.

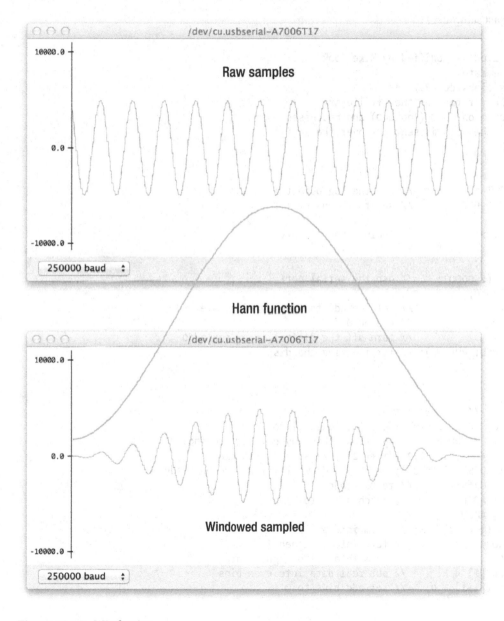

Figure 16-13. *Windowing*

The sample rate, coupled with the number of samples, defines what the bins will contain after the transform. In fact, the output of the FFT is symmetrical, consisting of positive and negative frequencies. The negative frequencies don't mean anything and aren't shown here; they are just a reflection of the positive ones. In some books, these reflections are shown.

The library example has some tricks to make the sampling faster, like letting the D/A converter run so that it can be gathering the next sample while you are manipulating and storing the previous one. In this way, the sample rate can be pushed up to 38.2KHz and the Nyquist rate is 19.1KHz. I modified this code to fit this display, as shown in Listing 16-5.

Listing 16-5. Fast sampling FFT

```
/*
fft_adc_serial.pde - Modified by Mike Cook
38.2KHz sample rate
guest openmusiclabs.com 7.7.14
example sketch for testing the fft library.
it takes in data on ADC0 (Analog0) and processes them
with the fft. the data is sent out over the serial
port at 250kb.
*/

#define LOG_OUT 1          // use the log output function
#define FFT_N 256          // set to 256 point fft

#include <FFT.h>           // include the library
int timer0;
void setup() {
  Serial.begin(250000);    // use the serial port
  timer0 = TIMSK0;
  ADCSRA = 0xe5;           // set the adc to free running mode
  ADMUX = 0x40;            // use adc0
  DIDR0 = 0x01;            // turn off the digital input for adc0
  pinMode(8,INPUT_PULLUP); // for freezing the display
}

void loop() {
  while(1) {     // reduces jitter
    TIMSK0 = 0; // turn off timer0 for lower jitter
    cli();        // UDRE interrupt slows this way down on arduino1.0
    for (int i = 0 ; i < 512 ; i += 2) { // save 256 samples
      while(!(ADCSRA & 0x10));          // wait for adc to be ready
      ADCSRA = 0xf5;       // restart adc
      byte m = ADCL;        // fetch adc data
      byte j = ADCH;
      int k = (j << 8) | m; // form into an int
      k -= 0x0200;          // form into a signed int
      k <<= 6;              // form into a 16b signed int
      fft_input[i] = k;     // put real data into even bins
      fft_input[i+1] = 0;   // set odd bins to 0
    }
```

```
fft_window();      // window the data for better frequency response
fft_reorder();     // reorder the data before doing the fft
fft_run();         // process the data in the fft
fft_mag_log();     // take the output of the fft in log form
fft_mag_octave();
sei();             // enable interrupts
TIMSK0 = timer0; // restart the timer
// send out the bins to the plotter
for (byte i = 0 ; i < FFT_N/2 ; i++) {
  for(byte j=0; j<3; j++){       // each bin three times
  Serial.println(fft_log_out[i]); // send out the data
   }
}
  for(byte j=0; j<116; j++) Serial.println(0);
  // while(digitalRead(8)) { }    // hold until this pin is low
  delay(2000);
 }
}
```

By running this code with a 400Hz sin wave input and then switching it to a square wave, you can see the harmonics all the way up to the Nyquist rate. This is shown in Figure 16-14.

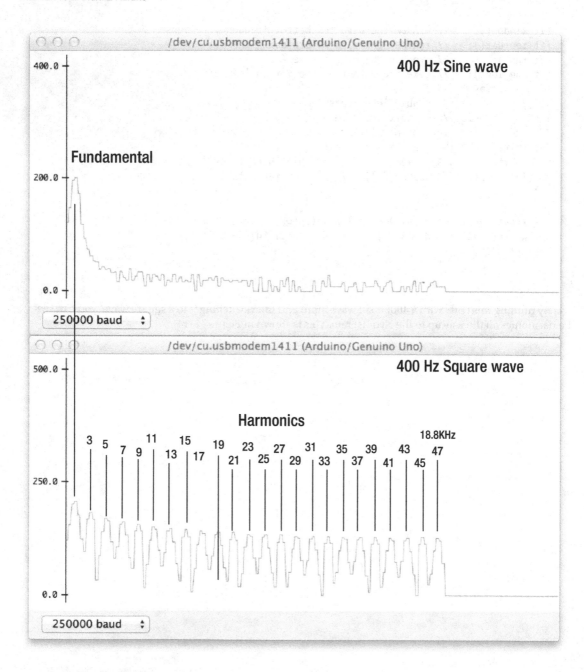

Figure 16-14. *Sin and square waves*

Summary

You have seen how to apply digital signal processing using the very modest processing power in the Arduino Uno. These can be used as filters over a restricted frequency range determined by how much processing each sample takes. Then, using an FFT library, you saw how to break up a signal into its component parts and then measure the frequency and harmonics. This can function as a tuning indicator, although it is not as simple as it sounds. With a real instrument, the harmonic content varies through the duration of the note and the fundamental is not always the strongest harmonic. The next chapter looks at some projects that use the theories in this chapter.

CHAPTER 17

■ ■ ■

DSP Projects

Having seen how you can use the Arduino for signal processing, now you'll see how you can use the much faster processor in the Due or the Zero in creating sounds and building projects. All these projects were done with the Due, but there is no reason why the Zero can't be used. Both have enough memory and processing power, along with a built-in A/D and D/A, allowing production of much better audio quality than the Uno is capable of.

There are four projects in this final chapter—using MIDI with the Due, a modeling synthesized plucked string, an audio exciter using transfer functions, and a sound to light show.

Understanding the Processor

The Due and its successor the Zero are a step up in the world of processors from the Uno and the Atmel 8-bit processor Arduinos. These models have a 32-bit core, which means that all the internal registers and memory are 32 bits wide. This means you can get what used to be multi-byte operations on a Uno done in a single instruction. This obviously uses fewer instructions even if the processor's clock were the same, which it isn't. In fact, the Due runs at 84MHz and the Zero at 48MHz.

The form factor is significant different between these two Arduinos, with the Due being the larger size along the lines of an Arduino Mega, where as the Zero is the size of an Uno. They both run at 3V3 and that makes them not exactly a beginner's model. In addition, these 3V3 system are much less robust than the Uno, meaning it is a lot easer to damage a pin by connecting it to a circuit that requires too much current or accidentally shorting a pin to the ground.

There are two types of pins on the Due—high current and low current. The high current is capable of sourcing 15mA and sinking 9mA, which is a marked contrast to the stress rating of 40mA source and sink on the Uno. The low current pins will only source 3mA and sink 6mA and are very easily damaged.

In contrast, the Zero is even more complicated in determining what the source and sink currents limits are. The maximum source current is 14mA and the sink current is 19.5mA, but this is not per pin, it's per cluster, and in the 48-pin package used in the Zero, a cluster can range from 2 to 16 pins. All this means that you have to be much more carful with the design of things.

When it comes to resources, these processors win hands down. The Due has 512K of program memory with 96K of SRAM, and the Zero has 256K of program memory and 32K of SRAM. The big advantage the Zero has over the Due is the Atmel's Embedded Debugger (EDBG), which provides a debug environment without the need for any extra hardware. This allows things like inserting breakpoints in the code so you can examine the state of the variables at any instant in the program and single stepping through the code to see how things change.

Processor Peripherals

Both processors have built-in A/D converters of a higher resolution than the 10-bit Uno. The Due has a true 12-bit D/A, whereas the Zero has a true 10 bit one, and both of these are 12-bit converters. They also both have a true 12-bit D/A, and by that I mean not a PWM generator. There are two such outputs on the Due and one on the Zero. They are both capable of outputting at a speed of 350,000 samples per second, although unfortunately they don't manage a rail-to-rail performance.

They both have three counter timers of various sizes and each one has three channels associated with them, so it is as if there were nine timers. The Zero also has a 32-bit, real-time clock timer, with a clock/calendar function. However, they are even more complex than those in the Uno having many more different modes and they are different from the Uno's counters so code on the Uno using timers will not run on these bigger processors.

There are lots of other differences from the Uno as well; for example, there is a Peripheral Touch Controller for acting as a capacitive touch sensor. A USB interface for communications with a host or client, an I2S sound controller for connecting digital sound systems together, and an Event System or DMA allowing communications directly with peripherals without CPU intervention.

Using the Due

The Due should be capable of doing everything you have done in the book so far, but one thing it won't cope with is a MIDI interface. This is because it has a low-current 3V3 interface and the MIDI is designed to be used with 5V. Therefore, you need to use a slightly different circuit if you are going to use a standard interface.

The big advantage over the Uno, however, is that, like the Mega, there are four serial ports on the Due. This means that you can keep one for communications with the USB and your programming computer, and use one of the remaining three for MIDI. This means that you can run MIDI and debug messages to the IDE console at the same time and there is no need for a programming switch to isolate the MIDI system. Figure 17-1 shows the schematic for the Due MIDI interface.

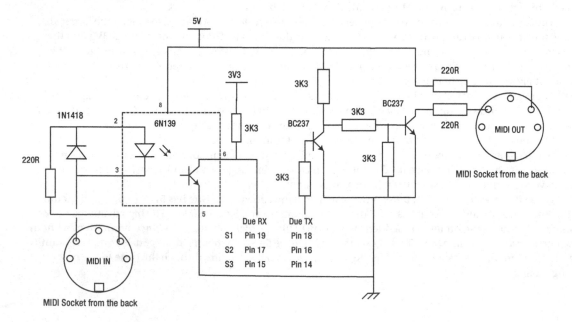

Figure 17-1. *Due MIDI interface*

The input circuit is very much like before, except that the output transistor of the opto-isolator is pulled up to the 3V3 rail. On the transmit side, the Due output goes first to an NPN switching transistor to boost the signal up to 5V, but then it is upside down, so it has to go to another transistor to turn it the right way up again. Finally, the output goes to switch in the high side, rather than the more conventional low side.

There is the choice of using serial ports 1, 2, or 3 and the diagram shows the pin connections for each port. Whatever one you use, you have to make sure that the software sends out the MIDI on that port. Listing 17-1 shows the MIDI note fire program for the Due using serial port 1.

Listing 17-1. MIDI Note Fire for the Due

```
/* Midi note fire for the Due - Mike Cook
 * using serial 1
 */
#define midiChannel (byte)0 // Channel 1

// Start of code
void setup() {
 //  Setup serial1
   Serial1.begin(31250);     // MIDI speed
}

void loop() {
   int val;
   val = random(20,100);
    noteSend(0x90, val, 127);
    delay(200);
    noteSend(0x80, val, 127);
   delay(800);
    } // end loop function

//  plays a MIDI note
 void noteSend(byte cmd, byte data1, byte data2) {
   cmd = cmd | midiChannel;  // merge channel number
   Serial1.write(cmd);
   Serial1.write(data1);
   Serial1.write(data2);
}
```

The only difference here is the use of Serial1 in place of just Serial, but as MIDI is such a slow protocol there is not a vast gain here. It can however cope with many more analogue inputs and is much faster at reading analogue values at 3.2uS per sample, as opposed to the Uno's 100uS. This makes scanning a large array of pots for a massive MIDI controller a much more responsive process.

The MIDI library works just the same, the only thing you might notice is that if you try and use the word time as a variable it will complain on completion. The solution is just to change the variable name with a search and replace. The other thing is that you will have to use the default serial port if you are using the library. As I have covered MIDI extensively in the first part of the book, let's look at some more processor intensive applications where the Due comes into its own.

Physical Modeling

The way we have looked at generating sounds so far has been in terms of defining a waveform or sampling a signal. Physical modeling involves setting up a mathematical model of an instrument and letting the computer drive it. The idea is that by varying aspects of the model, the sound produced will change in an expected way, giving a more intuitive form of sound control. For example, altering the stiffness of a membrane will change the pitch of a drum.

This topic can get very mathematical, but one of the simplest models to understand is that of a plucked string. When you pluck a string, you get an input of energy or displacement into the string, which propagates down the string to a fixed end, where the displacement gets reflected back. This happens at both ends and on each reflection some energy is lost, so the vibrations in the string get smaller as time passes. Eventually it dies out. You can also get different sounds depending whether you pluck the string at close to the fixed end or in the middle. The length of the string, along with the tension, defines the frequency it will vibrate at. All this can be modeled using differential equations to represent the string at various points along its length.

Once a model has been obtained, it can be simplified so that the calculations that need to be done are within the range of the available computing power. Perhaps the simplest model of the vibrating string is known as the *Karplus Strong algorithm* and the results are quite impressive.

The Karplus Strong Algorithm

This algorithm simulates a string through a delay line, whose length, coupled with the sample rate, determines the fundamental frequency of the output. The output of the delay line is taken as the signal output, and in addition it is filtered and fed back to the start of the delay line. The initial contents of the delay line represent the string being plucked and affect the timbre of the note. The block diagram of the process is shown in Figure 17-2.

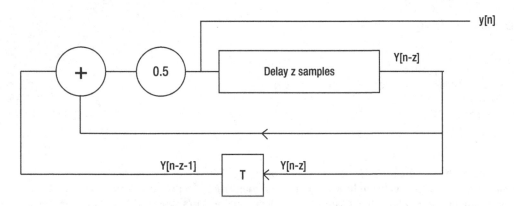

Figure 17-2. *Karplus Strong block diagram*

The delay is for *z* samples and rather than show a time delay box for each of the samples, a long box is used. The filter is a simple average of the last two samples out of the delay line. This is shown by the output sample Y[n-z] being delayed by one sample period, giving Y[n-z-], and then those two samples being averaged by summing and dividing by two. To implement this the delay line, you use a sample buffer, and the input and output pointers are moved rather than the samples themselves, as you saw in Chapter 15. The buffer representation of this algorithm is shown in Figure 17-3.

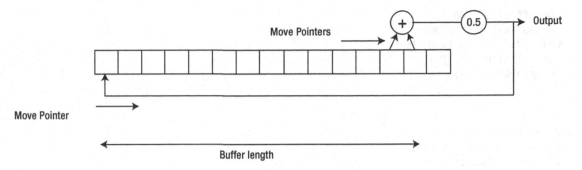

Figure 17-3. *Karplus Strong buffer implementation*

The distance between the input and output pointers determine the length of the buffer. This is not unlike the diagrams you saw in Chapter 15, but this time there is no need for external memory because the Due has enough internal memory to cope. In place of the extra delay there is simply a pointer to the last two samples in the memory, so that when the output pointer is moved, the trailing pointer picks up the same sample as the leading pointer did for the previous output.

What causes the whole system to work is the initial state of the buffer, and a short burst of random noise will kick things off. The more of the buffer that is filled the stronger is the simulated pluck. Over time the contents of the buffer get smaller and smaller and eventually die down to nothing, which causes the string to stop vibrating. To pluck the string again, you need to prime the buffer again. Listing 17-2 shows the code for this process.

Listing 17-2. Karplus Viewer

```
// Karplus viewer - Mike Cook
// using int buffers
// Open up the plot window

const int bufferSize = 500;
int outBuffer[bufferSize];
void setup() {
Serial.begin(250000);
primeBuffer();
delay(2000);
}

void loop() {
  for(int i = 0; i < bufferSize; i++){
    karplus();
  }
}

void primeBuffer(){
  // clear buffers
  int displayCount = 500;
  for(int i=0; i<480; i++){
    outBuffer[i] = random(16000) - 8000;
    Serial.println(outBuffer[i]);
    displayCount --;
  }
```

```
 //outBuffer[0] = 8000;
 // outBuffer[1] = -8000;
   while(displayCount> 0) {
     Serial.println(0);
     displayCount --;
   }
 }

void karplus(){
static int inPoint = bufferSize -1;
static int outPoint1 = 0;
static int outPoint2 = 1;

    outBuffer[inPoint] = (outBuffer[outPoint1] + outBuffer[outPoint2]) >> 1;
    Serial.println(outBuffer[inPoint]);
    // move pointers
    inPoint++;
    if(inPoint >= bufferSize -1 ) inPoint = 0;
    outPoint1++;
    if(outPoint1 >= bufferSize -1) outPoint1 = 0;
    outPoint2++;
    if(outPoint2 >= bufferSize -1) outPoint2 = 0;
    Serial.flush(); // wait until buffer empties - gives a smoother graph

}
```

This shows the output, and hence the state of the buffer. Over three or four minutes you will see the output get smoother and lower in frequency. Keep your eye on the scale and you will see the numbers on the axis getting smaller, even though the display appears to stay the same size. It takes so long to die down because it takes so long to output the buffers graphically. When you do this in real time, these notes last less than a second or two.

In order to do this for real and to hear the sound, you need to interface the Due to a speaker. The analogue output has only a very limited current output capacity of 3mA and so you must connect a 1K5 resistor in series with it in order to protect it. This gives you the opportunity to hang a capacitor on the end to act as a reconstruction filter. The hardware arrangement is shown in Figure 17-4. Note the addition of pushbuttons to trigger the sound; there is one button for each note.

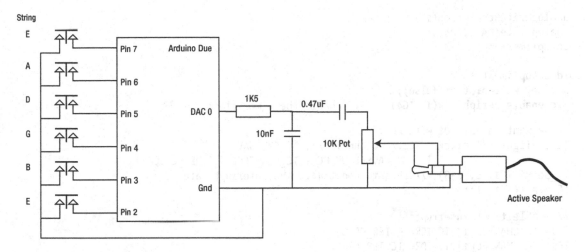

Figure 17-4. *Due sound output circuit*

The circuit is designed to trigger notes set to the frequency of the open strings on a guitar. You could use the circuit in Figure 15-3, but if you have an active speaker, this circuit is simpler.

In order to make a pitch sound you have to get the buffer length right. I used a sampling frequency of 41KHz, so the buffer length is given by:

$$\text{Buffer Length} = 41000/\text{Pitch}$$

The code in shown Listing 17-3 will produce the sound of a plucked string when a button is pushed.

Listing 17-3. Plucked String

```
// Karplus - Strong string synth for the Due - by Mike Cook
// code for the Arduino Due
// takes up 3.8uS time in the interrupt
// every 22.8 uS ( sample rate )

const int bufferMax = 550;
volatile int outBuffer[bufferMax];
volatile int bufferSize = 200;
volatile int inPoint = bufferSize -1;
volatile int outPoint1 = 0;
volatile int outPoint2 = 1;
const byte trigger[] = {7,6,5,4,3,2}; // pin to trigger the sound
// 41000 divided by frequency = buffer size required
int bufferToUse [] = {535, 401, 300, 225, 179, 134};
boolean lastPush [6];

void setup() {
  Serial.begin(250000);
  pinMode(13,OUTPUT);
  for(int i =0; i< 6; i++){
    pinMode(trigger[i], INPUT_PULLUP); // strike string
  }
```

```
  analogWriteResolution(12);
  analogWrite(DAC0,2048);
  setupTimer();
}
void setupTimer(){
  pmc_set_writeprotect(false);
  pmc_enable_periph_clk(ID_TC4);     // enable the timer clock

  // we want wavesel 01 with RC
  TC_Configure(/* clock */TC1,/* channel */1, TC_CMR_WAVE |
                       TC_CMR_WAVSEL_UP_RC | TC_CMR_TCCLKS_TIMER_CLOCK2);
  TC_SetRC(TC1, 1, 238); // sets to about 44.1 Khz interrupt rate
  TC_Start(TC1, 1);

  // enable timer interrupts
  TC1->TC_CHANNEL[1].TC_IER=TC_IER_CPCS;
  TC1->TC_CHANNEL[1].TC_IDR=~TC_IER_CPCS;

  // Enable the interrupt in the nested vector interrupt controller
  // TC4_IRQn where 4 is the timer number * timer channels (3) + the channel number
(=(1*3)+1)
  //    for timer1 channel1
  NVIC_EnableIRQ(TC4_IRQn);
}

void loop() {
  boolean push;
  for(int i=0; i<7; i++){
  push = digitalRead(trigger[i]);
  if(push == false && lastPush[i] == true){
    bufferSize = bufferToUse[i];
    primeBuffer(512,8);
    noInterrupts();
    inPoint = bufferSize -1;
    outPoint1 = 0;
    outPoint2 = 1;
    interrupts();
   }
    lastPush[i] = push;
  }
}

void primeBuffer(int energy, int stroke ){
  int primeSample = 0;
  for(int i=0; i<bufferSize/stroke; i++){
    outBuffer[i] = random(energy) - energy >> 1;
    primeSample ++;
  }
  while(primeSample < bufferMax-1) {
    outBuffer[primeSample] = 0;
    primeSample ++;
  }
 }
```

```
void TC4_Handler()
{
  // digitalWrite(13,HIGH); // time ISR - flag start
  TC_GetStatus(TC1, 1);        // clear status to allow the timer interrupt to trigger again
   outBuffer[inPoint] = (outBuffer[outPoint1] + outBuffer[outPoint2]) >> 1;
   dacc_write_conversion_data(DACC_INTERFACE, outBuffer[inPoint]+ 2048);
    // move pointers
    inPoint++;
    if(inPoint >= bufferSize -1 ) inPoint = 0;
    outPoint1++;
    if(outPoint1 >= bufferSize -1) outPoint1 = 0;
    outPoint2++;
    if(outPoint2 >= bufferSize -1) outPoint2 = 0;
  // digitalWrite(13,LOW);  //  time ISR - flag end
}
```

This works very similarly to other programs in this book; the only complication is that this time it is the Due's timers that have to be used and these work rather differently from the timers in the Uno. Basically the timers are set up so that Timer/Counter 1 produces an interrupt at 41KHz, which calls the TC4_Handler() function, this is where the Karplus Strong algorithm is implemented. There is first a bit of housekeeping, where a status flag bit has to be cleared. This, in effect, acknowledges the interrupt and thus allows the function to be triggered again. Then the buffer is updated and the output written to the internal D/A converter. The rest of the code just involves moving the pointers and making sure they wrap around when they reach the end. Finally, this function is surrounded by an optional set of instructions to raise and lower a bit to allow measuring the time taken in the ISR to be measured externally.

The primeBuffer function initializes the buffer and is akin to striking the string. This is passed two parameters—energy and stroke. The stroke defines how much of the buffer is filled with random numbers, and the energy defines the range of these random numbers. Both have a different effect on the timbre produced and I would encourage you to modify them and hear the change. Note that the interrupts are always running, and what stops the note is just that the disturbance in the buffer dies down to nothing.

The only problem is that the program is monophonic, that is it can only produce one note at a time. So encouraged by how little time this took in the ISR, I wrote a polyphonic version of this code. Basically what you need to do is turn what were single variables into arrays and access them appropriately. This is shown in Listing 17-4.

Listing 17-4. Polyphonic Strings

```
// Polyphonic Karplus - Strong string synth for the Due - by Mike Cook
// code for the Arduino Due
// takes 11.7uS time in the interrupt
// every 22.8 uS ( sample rate )

const int bufferMax = 550;
volatile int outBuffer[6][bufferMax];
volatile int inPoint [6];
volatile int outPoint1[6];
volatile int outPoint2[6];
volatile int bufferSize[] = {535, 401, 300, 225, 179, 134};
const byte trigger[] = {7,6,5,4,3,2}; // pin to trigger the sound
boolean lastPush [6];
```

```
void setup() {
  pinMode(13,OUTPUT);
  for(int i =0; i< 6; i++){
    pinMode(trigger[i], INPUT_PULLUP); // strike string
    inPoint [i] = bufferSize[i] -1;
    outPoint1[i] = 0;
    outPoint2[i] = 1;
  }
  analogWriteResolution(12);
  analogWrite(DAC0,2048);
  setupTimer();
}

void setupTimer(){
  pmc_set_writeprotect(false);
  pmc_enable_periph_clk(ID_TC4);      // enable the timer clock

  TC_Configure(TC1,1, TC_CMR_WAVE |
                       TC_CMR_WAVSEL_UP_RC | TC_CMR_TCCLKS_TIMER_CLOCK2);
  TC_SetRC(TC1, 1, 238); // sets to about 44.1 Khz interrupt rate
  TC_Start(TC1, 1);
  TC1->TC_CHANNEL[1].TC_IER=TC_IER_CPCS;
  TC1->TC_CHANNEL[1].TC_IDR=~TC_IER_CPCS;
  NVIC_EnableIRQ(TC4_IRQn);
}

void loop() {
  boolean push;
  for(int i=0; i<7; i++){
  push = digitalRead(trigger[i]);
  if(push == false && lastPush[i] == true){
    primeBuffer(512,16,i);
    noInterrupts();
    inPoint[i] = bufferSize[i] -1;
    outPoint1[i] = 0;
    outPoint2[i] = 1;
    interrupts();
   }
    lastPush[i] = push;
  }
}

void primeBuffer(int energy, int stroke, int bufferNo ){
  int primeSample = 0;

  for(int i=0; i<bufferSize[bufferNo]/stroke; i++){
    outBuffer [bufferNo][i] = random(energy) - energy >> 1;
    primeSample ++;
  }
```

```
   while(primeSample < bufferMax-1) {
    outBuffer[bufferNo][primeSample] = 0;
    primeSample ++;
   }
 }

void TC4_Handler()
{
  // digitalWrite(13,HIGH); // time ISR - flag start
  TC_GetStatus(TC1, 1);     // clear status to allow the timer interrupt to trigger again
  int acc = 0;
  for(int b=0; b <6; b++) {
     outBuffer[b][inPoint[b]] = (outBuffer[b][outPoint1[b]] + outBuffer[b][outPoint2[b]]) >> 1;
     acc += outBuffer[b][inPoint[b]];
     // move pointers
     inPoint[b]++;
     if(inPoint[b] >= bufferSize[b] -1 ) inPoint[b] = 0;
     outPoint1[b]++;
     if(outPoint1[b] >= bufferSize[b] -1) outPoint1[b] = 0;
     outPoint2[b]++;
     if(outPoint2[b] >= bufferSize[b] -1) outPoint2[b] = 0;
  }
  dacc_write_conversion_data(DACC_INTERFACE, acc + 2048);
  // digitalWrite(13,LOW);  //  time ISR - flag end
}
```

The results are rather pleasing, as you can hear one note fade away while another starts. While I did not hear anything odd about the monophonic version at first, when I went back to it after using the polyphonic version I could hear the previous string being cut off when a new one started.

Also note that the time taken in the ISR is not six times greater than the monophonic version. This is because raising and lowering the timing pin with the digitalWrite function takes quite a bit of time and with them commented out there is even more processor resource than the measurements would have you believe.

There are other ways of modeling a plucked string using two buffers and extracting the sample from the middle of the delay line. They produce even more realistic sounds but take more memory and processing power. I encourage you to search online for the details and try them out.

Audio Excitation

Back in the 1970s there was a company that produced an audio exciter effects box for professional recording studios. You could not buy it; you rented it by the hour and it came with its own technician to operate it. It was shrouded in secrecy as to what it did, but it could give that "wow" factor to a final mix and was used on many hits. What it in fact did was introduce extra harmonics into a sound, a sort of harmonically controlled distortion. You'll see how this was done and learn how to produce your own version on the Due.

The trick is to use a controllable transfer function, sometimes known as *wave shaping*. A transfer function is simply the relationship between the input and output of a system, and normally you want that function to be a simple straight line with a slope of 1, which is what you put in you get out. This might seem obvious, but bear with me for a moment and consider Figure 17-5, which shows a straight-line transfer function.

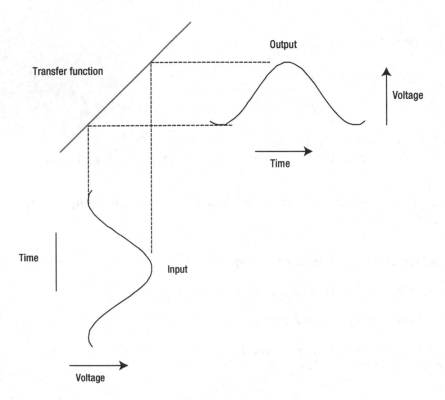

Figure 17-5. *A one-to-one transfer function*

What you see here is an input voltage being transferred to the output through a function, which is a straight line. Each point on the input maps to an identical point on the output. Imagine if that line was steeper, then what would happen is that the peak on the input waveform would map to a higher peak on the output waveform. In other words, the output signal would be bigger in amplitude. If the slope were smaller then the output would be smaller than the input. Therefore, a volume control can be thought of as a variable slope linear transfer function, with the volume knob controlling the transfer function's slope.

Now consider what would happen if this transfer function was not a straight line but a curve. This is shown in Figure 17-6.

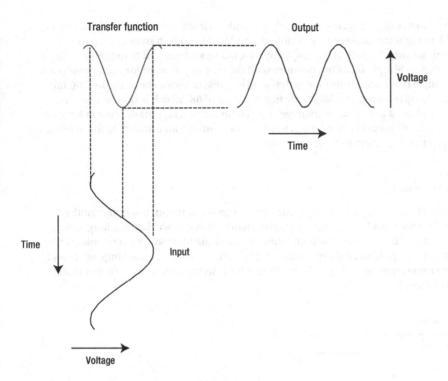

Figure 17-6. A curved transfer function

Here the transfer function has two peaks, one when the input signal is low and one when it is high. When the input wave is midway the output will be at its minimum. You can see how the output waveform has double the frequency of the input waveform. Note that this is only true for a waveform that covers the full amplitude range of the transfer function.

So how can you implement such a thing in a processor? Well, remember that the input waveform is simply a sequence of samples and a sample is just a number. To implement an arbitrary transfer function, you use that number to address a lookup table, and the contents of that address are used as the value of the output. Therefore, the transfer function is defined by the memory contents in the lookup table. This is shown in Figure 17-7.

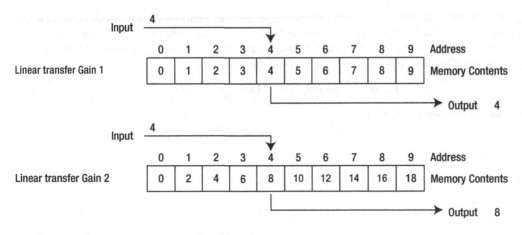

Figure 17-7. Lookup table transfer function

With the top table, the contents of an address are simply the address itself, so whatever is input is output. However, in the second lookup table the contents are double the address, giving a transfer function with a gain of two. Yes, I know you can simply multiply the input by two, but this allows you to implement any transfer function you can imagine. Simply fill in the memory with the output you want for each input point you can get. With a 12-bit sample resolution, this means that it takes 4,098 entries to be in the lookup table, and with two bytes per entry this gives a total lookup table memory size of 8K, which is fine on the Due.

Incidentally, this is exactly how a car's engine management computer works. Lots of sensors form an address to a lookup table, and the contents control the actuators. For example, an input from the accelerator pedal outputs to the carburetor and ignition timing.

What Transfer Function to Use?

It is one thing to have a mechanism for implementing an arbitrary transfer function, but quite another thing to know what transfer function produces what effect. Fortunately, this was worked out long ago by Chebysheve. You might remember that his name was attached to one of the filter shapes you looked at in Chapter 16. He produced a series of polynomial expressions, which when taken over the range of -1 to +1, produces a transfer function to generate only a specific harmonic from an input fundamental frequency. The functions are shown in Table 17-1.

Table 17-1. *Polynomial Functions*

Harmonic	Polynomial
Fundamental	X
Second	$2X^2 - 1$
Third	$4X^3 - 3X$
Fourth	$8X^4 - 8X^2 + 1$
Fifth	$16X^5 - 20X^3 + 5X$
Sixth	$32X^6 - 48X^4 + 18X^2 - 1$
Seventh	$64X^7 - 112X^5 + 56X^3 - 7X$
Eighth	$128X^8 - 256X^6 + 160X^4 - 32X^2 + 1$

If you don't want to be as drastic as to turn a wave completely into a harmonic, you can mix and match these polynomials. You just need to add a multiplication factor to each one to determine how much you have. Their multiplication factors must add up to 1, so to have an output waveform consisting of half the third harmonic and half seventh, you need to have a transfer function of:

$$F = 0.5(4X^3 - 3X) + 0.5(64X^7 - 112X^5 + 56X^3 - 7X)$$

This is shown plotted out in Figure 17-8.

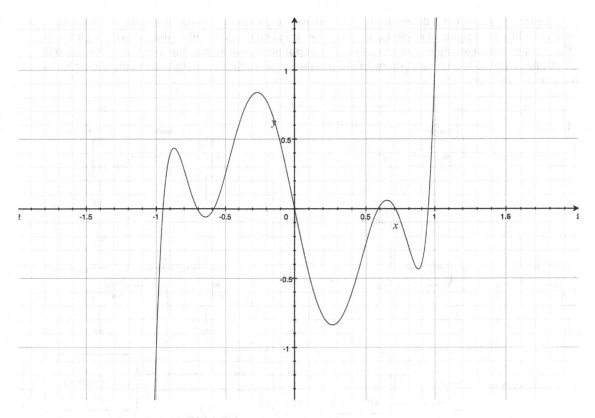

Figure 17-8. *Transfer function half third and half seventh*

This harmonic mix can be set using a potentiometer to control each harmonic, although even for a Due, the 4098 calculations of a mixture of eight harmonic polynomials does take about seven seconds. Therefore, when you want to change the lookup table, you must trigger the change with a pushbutton.

In order to get a signal into the Due, you can use the amplifier circuit in Figure 15-2, but you will have to connect the amplifier's power supply to 3V3 not 5V. The amplifier will just about work with this voltage input. This ensures that the input signal will not go outside the Due's power rails. However, if you do not need the gain of this circuit, you can use either of the circuits shown in Figure 17-9.

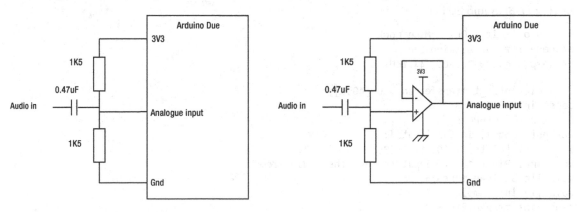

Figure 17-9. *Audio input circuits*

The circuit on the left is the minimum you can use and just biases the signal at halfway. This is useful if you have a line level signal or a signal generator. The circuit on the right buffers the audio through a voltage follower operational amplifier and provides a bit of input protection for the Due. You can, of course, make this supply a little gain with the addition of two resistors. The whole schematic of the audio exciter is shown in Figure 17-10.

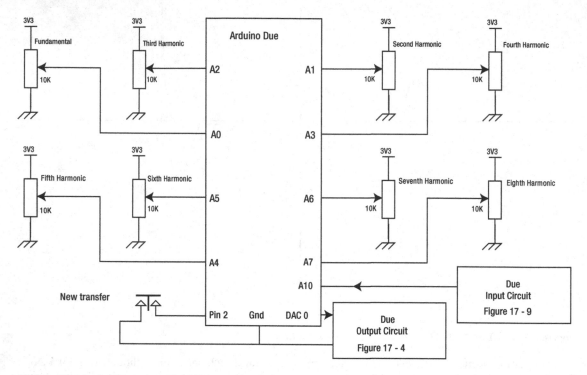

Figure 17-10. *Audio exciter schematic*

The circuit is basically eight pots connected to the first eight analogue inputs, and the Audio input is being fed into A10. The audio output is taken from DAC 0 through an output circuit. The code to drive the exciter is shown in Listing 17-5.

Listing 17-5. Audio Exciter

```
// Audio Exciter Due - Mike Cook
// code for the Arduino Due
// sample every 22.8uS   44.1KHz

volatile int16_t transferFunction[4096];
const int nPots = 8;
float potPram[nPots];
int pot[nPots], lastPot[nPots];
int potPin[nPots] = {0, 1, 2, 3, 4, 5, 6, 7};
int samplePin = 10; // input to take the audio from
volatile boolean taken = true;
volatile int sample = 0;
const int triggerPin = 2;
const int timePin = 13;
```

```
void setup() {
  Serial.begin(250000);
  REG_ADC_MR = (REG_ADC_MR & 0xFFF0FFFF) | 0x00020000; // master A/D clock
  adc_init(ADC, SystemCoreClock, ADC_FREQ_MAX, ADC_STARTUP_FAST);
  pinMode(timePin,OUTPUT);
  pinMode(triggerPin,INPUT_PULLUP); // trigger new lookup
  analogWriteResolution(12);
  analogReadResolution(12);
  analogWrite(DAC0,2048);
  getPots();
  displayTransfer(); // remove if not displaying plot
  setupTimer();       // go
}

void setupTimer(){
  pmc_set_writeprotect(false);
  pmc_enable_periph_clk(ID_TC4);     // enable the timer clock

  /* we want wavesel 01 with RC */
  TC_Configure(/* clock */TC1,/* channel */1, TC_CMR_WAVE | TC_CMR_WAVSEL_UP_RC |
  TC_CMR_TCCLKS_TIMER_CLOCK2);
  TC_SetRC(TC1, 1, 238); // sets to about 44.1 Khz interrupt rate
  TC_Start(TC1, 1);

  // enable timer interrupts
  TC1->TC_CHANNEL[1].TC_IER=TC_IER_CPCS;
  TC1->TC_CHANNEL[1].TC_IDR=~TC_IER_CPCS;

  /* Enable the interrupt in the nested vector interrupt controller */
  /* TC4_IRQn where 4 is the timer number * timer channels (3) + the channel number
  (=(1*3)+1) for timer1 channel1 */
  NVIC_EnableIRQ(TC4_IRQn);
}

void TC4_Handler() // measured at 3.2uS
{
  //digitalWrite(timePin,HIGH); //  time ISR - flag start
  TC_GetStatus(TC1, 1);  // clear status to allow the timer interrupt to trigger again
  sample = transferFunction[sample];
  dacc_write_conversion_data(DACC_INTERFACE, sample);
  taken = true;
  //digitalWrite(timePin,LOW);  //  time ISR - flag end
}

void loop() {
 if(taken) sample = {
      analogRead(samplePin);
      taken = false;
  }
```

```
 if(!digitalRead(triggerPin)){
  noInterrupts();
  getPots();
  interrupts();
  displayTransfer(); // remove for faster update
 }
}
void getPots(){
      float sum = 0.0;
  for(int i=0; i<nPots; i++){
    pot[i]=analogRead(potPin[i]);
  }
 // work out pot paramaters
    for(int i=0; i<nPots; i++){
       sum += (float)(pot[i]) / 1023.0;
    }
    for(int i=0; i<nPots; i++){
       potPram[i] = ((float)(pot[i]) / 1023.0) / sum ;
    }
    makeLookup(); // create new lookup table
 }

void makeLookup(){
  float res = 2.0 / 4096.0 ;
  float n = -1;
  float value = 0;
  for(int i = 0; i<4096 ; i++){
    value = potPram[0]*fundmental(n) + potPram[1]*secondH(n) + potPram[2]*thirdH(n) +
             potPram[3]*forthH(n) + potPram[4]*fifthH(n) + potPram[5]*sixthH(n) +
            potPram[6]*seventhH(n) + potPram[7]*eighthH(n);
    transferFunction[i] = (int16_t)(value*2047 + 2047);
    n += res;
  }
}

float fundmental(float n){
  return n;
}

float secondH(float n){
    n = 2*pow(n,2.0) - 1;
  return n;
}

float thirdH(float n){
    n = 4*pow(n,3.0) - 3*n;
  return n;
}
```

```
float forthH(float n){
    n = 8*pow(n,4.0) - 8*pow(n,2.0) + 1;
   return n;
}

float fifthH(float n){
    n = 16*pow(n,5.0) - 20*pow(n,3.0) + 5*n;
   return n;
}
float sixthH(float n){
    n = 32*pow(n,6.0) - 48*pow(n,4.0) + 18*pow(n,2.0) - 1;
   return n;
}

float seventhH(float n){
    n = 64*pow(n,7.0) - 112*pow(n,5.0) + 56*pow(n,3.0) - 7*n;
   return n;
}
float eighthH(float n){
    n = 128*pow(n,8.0) - 256*pow(n,6.0) + 160*pow(n,4.0) - 32*pow(n,2.0) + 1;
   return n;
}

void displayTransfer(){
   for(int i=0; i<500; i++){
     Serial.println(transferFunction[i*8]);
   }
   for(int i=0; i<96; i++){
     Serial.println(0);
   }
}
```

The big problem here is that you cannot take a sample from the A/D using the analogRead function from within an interrupt service routine. Therefore, you have to resort to a little trick. A flag called taken is set once the ISR routine has used an input sample. Then, in the loop function, if taken is found to be true, an analogRead is used to get the next sample. In that way, the sample rate is tied to the ISR, which handles the output. Note that the input sample is used as an index to access the transferFunction array to get the output sample.

The loop function just takes a sample when needed and looks at the new transfer function button. When this is pressed, the getPots function reads the potentiometers, but you are not interested in the absolute value here only their relative values. That is the potentiometers indicate the proportion of each harmonic, so as you turn one harmonic up, all the other values go down so that the overall sum is still one. This is done in several stages—first all the pots are read, then they are normalized and all added up. Finally, the normalized values are divided by the sum to get the multiplication factor for each harmonic. Finally, the makeLookup function calculates the lookup table using a separate function for each harmonic's polynomial. As the polynomial has to range between X values of -1 to +1 the value is incremented in steps of 2/ 4098, starting at –1, to cover the whole range of the digitized input signal.

This function takes about seven seconds to run and while it is updating the lookup table, you don't want anything accessing it. If you do the output will be somewhat random, and a high-frequency noise appears on the output pin. To stop this from happening, the interrupts are turned off during the update and back again when the process is over. The displayTransfer function shows the lookup table in the plot window when it has been updated, but this can be omitted if you don't require this.

The input and output waveforms of a fourth harmonic transfer function, can be seen in Figure 17-11.

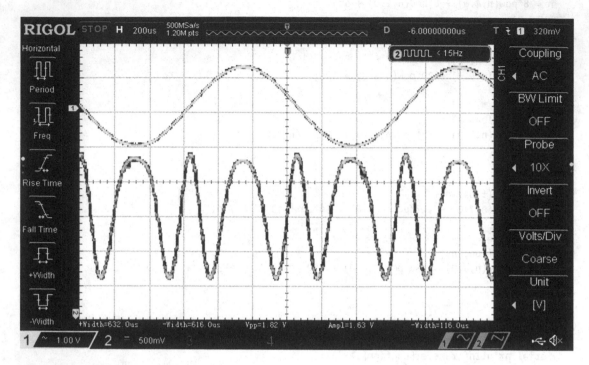

Figure 17-11. *Input with fourth harmonic output*

Notice how the harmonic output is not a pure sin wave, indicating that there is some other harmonic content in the output as well. The audio exciter should be used sparingly in normal audio mixes, because the ears soon get tired and quickly adapt if the effect is overused. However, if it is used in an effects unit, say a guitar pedal, it can be used permanently. You can experiment with other transfer functions too; remember you only get the full effect of a transfer function when the input signal covers all the input range of values.

Music Light Show

Turning sound into lights is something I began doing back in the 1960s, with today's processors and LED technology some quite startling effects can be generated. This is also a very popular project and it has a certain "wow" factor. The recent introduction of RGB LEDs with a built-in controller in the form of WS2812b LED strips has been a game-changer as far as large-scale LED projects are concerned. This project uses a Due running an FFT to drive a matrix of LEDs made from WS2812b LED strips in order to display a real-time changing spectrum of the music.

The WS2812b LED strips come in three LED densities—30, 60, and 120 LEDs per meter—and I think the 60 LEDs per meter version are the right sort of spacing for this project. Typically they are sold in 4M lengths and this gives a total of 240 LEDs. These can be made into a matrix by cutting the strip up into lengths and laying them side by side, mounted on a board, or creating "Venetian blind" like strips mounted on fabric so it can be rolled up. You have a choice of dimension and perhaps it is better to get the project working on a continuous strip before deciding on what dimensions to use.

The strips are available in two types—waterproof and bare PCB—for this project you would not expect to use the waterproof type, the non-waterproof ones are cheaper. You can cut the PCB with a sharp knife at every LED interval, and as long as you wire the three wires from the end of one cut to the beginning of the next, it will work fine. For this project, I decided to make a matrix 20 strips wide with each strip having 12 LEDs in it. This is shown in Figure 17-12.

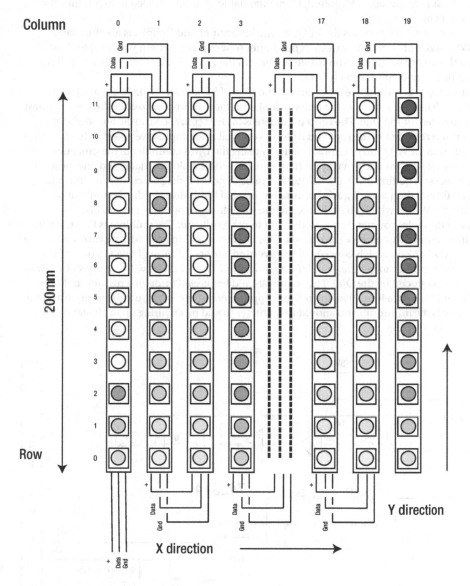

Figure 17-12. *Wiring up the matrix*

Note how the wiring goes from the top of one column to the top of the next, and from the bottom of one to the bottom of the next. This is known as a *serpentine raster* and is the best way to wire things because it minimizes the wiring you need. That means the signal does not deteriorate as much as wiring it the other way. However, the LEDs are numbered from the start of the strip to the end in increasing numbers; therefore

445

you need to use a bit of math to convert a pixel's position in terms of its X, Y coordinates in the matrix into its position from the start of the strip. For odd columns, this is simple. The LED position is given by the value of the Y coordinate, plus the X coordinate multiplied by the number of LEDs in a column. For even columns, however, the Y value must be subtracted from the number of LEDs in the column minus one, before being added to the X coordinate multiplied by the number of LEDs in a column. Fortunately, once a conversion function has been written this can be safely forgotten. Understandable coordinates feed in to produce the position of the LED in the continuous strip.

The Neopixel library from AdaFruit treats the LEDs as one long buffer and Neopixels are the brand name for the generic WS2812b LEDs. You set values in this buffer to set up any pattern you want and then use the show method of the library to transfer the whole buffer into the LEDs. Each LED has an 8-bit value that determines the brightness and color of each LED.

The other side of the project is turning the input sound into a list of frequencies, which, as you saw in Chapter 16, can be done with an FFT. However, the one you looked at there was optimized for the Uno, For best results, you need one optimized for the Due. The one I used here is from https://coolarduino.wordpress. com/2014/09/25/splitradixreal-fft-library/ and it works very well at an impressive speed. What is more, there is a system for reading in the A/D converter automatically using the DMA controller in the processor. DMA stands for Direct Memory Access and is a way for hardware to transfer a block of data from one location to another, without the processor getting involved. All that has to be done is for the source, destination, and number of bytes to be set up and then away it goes. Fortunately, most of this is done by the demonstration program that comes with the library, which I have hacked about mercilessly to produce this project.

So before you look at the code, you need an introduction to the hardware. The problem is that the Due has a 3V3 output and the Neopixels need a 5V data signal. This is a fast signal so any old transistor will not be fast enough. Instead I used a 74LS14, which consists of six inverting buffers. Of those, I need to use only two, one to boost the signal and the other to get the signal the right way up. These buffers will happily switch from the smaller voltage signals produced by the Due. The output should be passed through a resistor to damp down any reflections from LED's data line. Also, the power supply needs some extra bulk decoupling and the capacitor in the schematic is the minimum you should use—better would be anything up to 10,000uF. This schematic is shown in Figure 17-13.

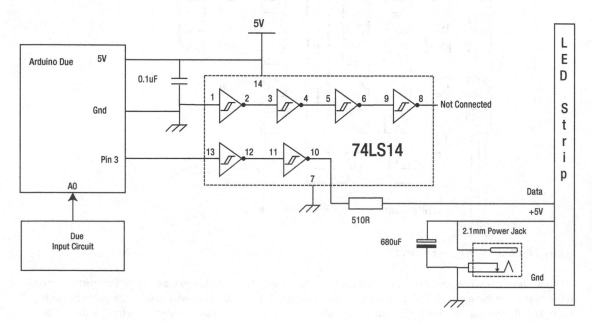

Figure 17-13. *Light show schematic*

Each LED, when all three colors are on at the brightest, will consume 60mA. So for a strip of 240 LEDs, this is a total current of 14.4Amps. This sort of power supply is expensive and on some projects it is simply not necessary. If you make the assumption that no LED will be set to white, that limits the current between a maximum of 20 to 40mA per LED (that is, a touch under 5 to 10A top). Then factor into the equation that not all the LEDs will be on at any one time (let's say only three quarters are on), which brings down the current requirement even further. In fact, I use a 4Amp 5V supply, which is about the smallest you can get away with on this project. This should be supplied from an external separate regulated power supply.

So with all the pieces in place, it is time for the code—it's shown in Listing 17-6.

Listing 17-6. The Light Show

```
/*
 * Light spectrum - FFT by Mike Cook
 * for Arduino Due & Neopixel strip
 * Each bin covers 23.4375 Hz
 */
#include <SplitRadixRealP.h>
#include <Adafruit_NeoPixel.h>

#define NEOPIXEL_PIN   3 // pin connected to the NeoPixels
#define NUMPIXELS    240  // number of LEDs 240 LEDs in 4 meters
#define xMax 20          // maximum number of coloumns
#define yMax 12          // maximum number of rows

#define   SMP_RATE            48000UL
#define   CLK_MAIN           84000000UL
#define   TMR_CNTR           CLK_MAIN / (2 *SMP_RATE)

// FFT_SIZE IS DEFINED in Header file Radix4.h
// #define   FFT_SIZE   2048

#define   MIRROR    FFT_SIZE / 2  // mirror image of bins
#define   INP_BUFF FFT_SIZE       // input buffer for samples

volatile   uint16_t   sptr = 0 ;
volatile   int16_t    flag = 0 ;
 uint16_t  inp[2][INP_BUFF]   = { 0};      // DMA likes ping-pongs buffer
      int  f_r[FFT_SIZE]   = { 0};
      int  out1[MIRROR]    = { 0};      // Magnitudes
      int  out2[MIRROR]    = { 0};      // Magnitudes
const int  dc_offset       = 2047;      // vertual ground

Adafruit_NeoPixel pixels = Adafruit_NeoPixel(NUMPIXELS, NEOPIXEL_PIN, NEO_GRB + NEO_KHZ800);
SplitRadixRealP       radix;

//const int binSplit[] = {1,4,9,13,17,22,26,30,35,38,43,85,128,171,213,256,299,341,384,
469,512};
// Alternative bin split
const int binSplit[] ={1,4,5,7,9,12,15,20,25,32,43,55,71,92,119,154,196,252,324,427,
555,713};
```

```
int binTotal[20];
int angleInc = 360 / (xMax / 2);
int partAngleInc = angleInc / yMax;
// cosmetic value to scale bins by - set to taste
int scale[] = {1,1,1,1,1,1,1,1,1,1,1,1,1,1,1,1,1,1,1,1};

void pio_TIOA0 () { // Configure Ard pin 2 as output from TC0 channel A (copy of trigger
event)
  PIOB->PIO_PDR = PIO_PB25B_TIOA0 ;     // disable PIO control
  PIOB->PIO_IDR = PIO_PB25B_TIOA0 ;     // disable PIO interrupts
  PIOB->PIO_ABSR |= PIO_PB25B_TIOA0 ;   // switch to B peripheral
}

void timer_setup (){
  pmc_enable_periph_clk(TC_INTERFACE_ID + 0 *3 + 0); // clock the TC0 channel 0
  TcChannel * t = &(TC0->TC_CHANNEL)[0] ;             // pointer to TC0 registers for its
                                                      // channel 0
  t->TC_CCR = TC_CCR_CLKDIS ;                         // disable internal clocking while
                                                      // setup regs
  t->TC_IDR = 0xFFFFFFFF ;                            // disable interrupts
  t->TC_SR ;                                          // read int status reg to clear pending
  t->TC_CMR = TC_CMR_TCCLKS_TIMER_CLOCK1 |            // use TCLK1 (prescale by 2, = 42MHz)
              TC_CMR_WAVE |                           // waveform mode
              TC_CMR_WAVSEL_UP_RC |                   // count-up PWM using RC as threshold
              TC_CMR_EEVT_XC0 |       // Set external events from XC0 (this setup TIOB as
                                      // output)
              TC_CMR_ACPA_CLEAR | TC_CMR_ACPC_CLEAR |
              TC_CMR_BCPB_CLEAR | TC_CMR_BCPC_CLEAR ;

  t->TC_RC = TMR_CNTR;               // counter resets on RC, so sets period in terms of
                                     // 42MHz clock
  t->TC_RA = TMR_CNTR /2;            // roughly square wave
  t->TC_CMR = (t->TC_CMR & 0xFFF0FFFF) | TC_CMR_ACPA_CLEAR | TC_CMR_ACPC_SET ;  // set clear
  and set from RA and RC compares
  t->TC_CCR = TC_CCR_CLKEN | TC_CCR_SWTRG ;  // re-enable local clocking and switch to
                                             // hardware trigger source.
}
void adc_setup (){
  pmc_enable_periph_clk(ID_ADC);
  adc_init(ADC, SystemCoreClock, ADC_FREQ_MAX, ADC_STARTUP_FAST);
  NVIC_EnableIRQ (ADC_IRQn);                 // enable ADC interrupt vector
  adc_disable_all_channel(ADC);
  adc_enable_interrupt(ADC, ADC_IER_RXBUFF);
  ADC->ADC_RPR  = (uint32_t)  inp[0];        // DMA buffer
  ADC->ADC_RCR  = INP_BUFF;
  ADC->ADC_RNPR = (uint32_t)  inp[1];        // next DMA buffer
  ADC->ADC_RNCR = INP_BUFF;
  ADC->ADC_PTCR = 1;
  adc_set_bias_current(ADC, 0x01);
```

```
    adc_enable_channel(ADC, ADC_CHANNEL_7);   // AN0
    adc_configure_trigger(ADC, ADC_TRIG_TIO_CH_0, 0);
    adc_start(ADC);
}

void ADC_Handler (void){
  if((adc_get_status(ADC) & ADC_ISR_RXBUFF) ==  ADC_ISR_RXBUFF){
      flag = ++sptr;
      sptr &=  0x01; // alternate buffer to use
      ADC->ADC_RNPR  =  (uint32_t)  inp[sptr];
      ADC->ADC_RNCR  =  INP_BUFF;
      }
}

void setup(){
  Serial.begin (250000); // fast baud
  pixels.begin(); // This initialises the NeoPixel library
  wipe();
  pixels.show();
  adc_setup ();
  timer_setup ();
  pinMode( 2, INPUT); //
 }

inline int mult_shft12( int a, int b){
  return (( a  *  b )  >> 12);
}
void loop(){
  if (flag){
    uint16_t indx_a = flag -1;
    uint16_t indx_b = 0;
    for ( uint16_t i = 0, k = (NWAVE / FFT_SIZE); i < FFT_SIZE; i++ ){
        uint16_t windw = Hamming[i * k];
        f_r[i] = mult_shft12((inp[indx_a][indx_b++] - dc_offset), windw);
    }
    radix.rev_bin( f_r, FFT_SIZE);
    radix.fft_split_radix_real( f_r, LOG2_FFT);
    radix.gain_Reset( f_r, LOG2_FFT -1);
    radix.get_Magnit1( f_r, out1);
    radix.get_Magnit2( f_r, out2);
     // Magnitudes:-
    bufferToBinTotal();
    //showBins(); // show in plot window
    binsToLEDs();
    // delay(200);
    flag = 0;
    }
}
```

```
void bufferToBinTotal(){
  int number = 0;
    for(int i=0; i< 20; i++){
      number = 0;
       binTotal[i] = 0;
    for(int k = binSplit[i]; k < binSplit[i+1]; k++){
      binTotal[i] += out1[k];
      number++;
    }
    binTotal[i] = binTotal[i] / number;
  }
}

void showBins(){ // to plot window
  int bin = 0;
  for(int i=0; i< 20; i++){
    for(int k=0; k < 15; k++){
      Serial.println(binTotal[i]);
    }
    for(int k=0; k < 10; k++){
      Serial.println(0);
    }
  }
}
void binsToLEDs(){
  wipe();
  for(int i=0; i< 20; i++){
   setStrip(i, binTotal[i] /scale[i]);
 }
   pixels.show();
}

void setStrip(int strip, int height){
  int stripColour;
  int angle = angleInc * strip;
  if(height > yMax) height = yMax;
  for(int y=0; y < height; y++){
      stripColour = colorH(angle + (y * partAngleInc) );
      pixels.setPixelColor(getPixPos(strip,y) , stripColour);
  }
}

int getPixPos(int x, int y){ // for a serpentine raster
  int pos;
  if(x &0x1) {
     pos = x * yMax + (yMax -1 - y) ;
  } else {
  pos = x * yMax + y;
  }
  return pos;
}
```

```
inline int colour( int a, int b, int c){
  return ((a << 16) | (b << 8) | c);
}

int colorH(int angle){ //# color returned H=angle, S=1, V=1
    // # get angle in range 0 to 255
    while (angle <0 ) angle += 256;
    while (angle > 255) angle -=256;
    if (angle < 85) return colour(255 - angle*3, angle*3, 0);
    if (angle < 170){
        angle -= 85;
        return colour(0, 255 - angle * 3, angle * 3);
    }
    angle -= 170;
    return colour(angle * 3, 0, 255 - angle * 3);
}

void wipe(){
    for(int i=0;i<NUMPIXELS;i++){
        pixels.setPixelColor(i, pixels.Color(0,0,0));
        }
}
```

The first part of the code deals with setting up the timers and the handler for the DMA for the input sample. By convention, anything in all capital letters is a defined constant and should appear in a file somewhere being defined. Most of these in the timer setup function and the handler functions are addresses and bit numbers that have been defined in the processor specific files of the Arduino IDE. Others are part of the FFT library.

The loop function checks the value of the flag variable indicating if a buffer full of data has been read. When it has a Hamming window, it is applied to the buffer. Don't confuse this with the Hann window function used in the last chapter. Then the various functions are called to complete the FFT. Next, it is time to do something with the data in the way of translating it into data for the LEDs. With 1024 bins of real data and a sample rate of 48KHz, and requiring two samples per cycle, each bin represents (48000/2) / 1024 = 23.4375Hz. To make this look more like it sounds, these bins should be gathered into the 20 available display columns in a logarithmic way. This is defined by the binSplit array. This contains bin numbers to average for each display column. These are averaged in the bufferToBinTotal function. Next, it is a matter of taking these totals and translating the numbers into LED colors with the binsToLEDs function. This takes each bin total and applies a scale divisor. This can be a different number for each display column but initially these are all set to 1. If your music peaks at a specific range of frequencies you can bring down the response by a scale factor for that bin total value. It is largely cosmetic, so experiment with it so that full columns are not displayed most of the time.

The way I arranged the colors is that each column has its own basic color and, as the LEDs progress up the column, they change by a very small amount. You could make the intensity change as it progresses if you like. The basis of the color generation is the HSV color space model and this is handled by the colorH function. It converts an angle from 0 to 360 into an RGB set of numbers to fill the Neopixel buffer with.

The setStrip function fills one column with lit LEDs controlled by the numbers in the binTotal array. Here is where the serpentine raster position converter is used, to find the right LED to target.

The result is that the display is very responsive to the music and when there is no sound, like in between tracks, or during pauses in the music, there are no lights lit. This is how you want it to be, but it is seldom like that. I was very pleased with the final result.

Summary

The Due offers a magnitude increase in processing capability and memory storage and it shows with these projects. You have seen that projects that depend on processing samples benefit greatly from better resolution A/D and D/A converters. The projects in this book are just a beginning to exploring the vast range of possibilities that digital computers and audio offer those with interest in the subject.

There are many other libraries to help with projects in this field, and maybe one of the most comprehensive is the web-based graphic input for DSP processes produced by Paul Stoffregen for his Teensy board. Check it out at `http://www.pjrc.com/teensy/td_libs_Audio.html`.

Index

■ X, Y, Z

Printed in the United States
By Bookmasters